Prairie Imperialists

AMERICA IN THE NINETEENTH CENTURY

Series editors: Brian DeLay, Steven Hahn, Amy Dru Stanley

America in the Nineteenth Century proposes a rigorous rethinking of this most formative period in U.S. history. Books in the series will be wide-ranging and eclectic, with an interest in politics at all levels, culture and capitalism, race and slavery, law, gender, and the environment, and regional and transnational history. The series aims to expand the scope of nineteenth-century historiography by bringing classic questions into dialogue with innovative perspectives, approaches, and methodologies.

Prairie Imperialists

The Indian Country Origins
of American Empire

Katharine Bjork

PENN

University of Pennsylvania Press
Philadelphia

Published by
University of Pennsylvania Press
Philadelphia, Pennsylvania 19104-4112
www.upenn.edu/pennpress

Printed in the United States of America on acid-free paper
10 9 8 7 6 5 4 3 2 1

Library of Congress Cataloging-in-Publication Data
Names: Bjork, Katharine, author.
Title: Prairie imperialists : the Indian Country origins of American
    empire / Katharine Bjork.
Other titles: America in the nineteenth century.
Description: 1st edition. | Philadelphia : University of Pennsylvania
    Press, [2019] | Series: America in the nineteenth century |
    Includes bibliographical references and index.
Identifiers: LCCN 2018023678 | ISBN 9780812251005
    (hardcover)
Subjects: LCSH: United States—Territorial expansion. | Scott,
    Hugh Lenox, 1853–1934. | Bullard, Robert Lee, 1861–1947. |
    Pershing, John J. (John Joseph), 1860–1948. | Indians of North
    America—Wars—1866–1895. | Indians, Treatment of—United
    States—History—19th century. | United States—Foreign
    relations—1865–1921. | Imperialism.
Classification: LCC E713 .B64 2019 | DDC 973.2—dc23
LC record available at https://lccn.loc.gov/2018023678

To Arjun,
for all the reasons

Contents

Introduction

Gray Wolves for Guánica

Nothing can be more preposterous than the proposition that
these men were entitled to receive from us sovereignty over the
entire country which we were invading. As well the friendly
Indians, who have helped us in our Indian wars, might have
claimed sovereignty of the West.

—"The United States and the Philippines,"
Address of Secretary of War Elihu Root,
Canton, Ohio, October 24, 1900

On the afternoon of July 21, 1898, a flotilla of thirteen American ships set
off from Guantánamo Bay in Cuba, "majestically plowing the waters of
the deep in the direction of Puerto Rico," as the commander of the expedition
later wrote.[1] For the troops traveling belowdecks, conditions were far from ma-
jestic. In spite of the intense heat and close atmosphere on board, the transports
steamed toward the island with lights extinguished and portholes closed so as
to avoid detection.[2] A hundred of the 3,554 men who had embarked for the
mission were sick; some would die of typhoid. The high incidence of disease
and death due to loosely diagnosed tropical fevers had already proved more
deadly to American troops fighting in Cuba than the Spanish enemy.[3]

Three days earlier, Santiago's central plaza had been the site of military
pageantry as Spain's General José Torál formally ceded control of eastern Cuba
to the Americans. As the Sixth Cavalry band played "Hail Columbia" and the
Ninth Infantry presented arms, Spain's flag, which had flown over the island for
almost four centuries, was hauled down and the Stars and Stripes hoisted above
the provincial palace. From these rituals solemnizing Spanish surrender, the

Cuban Army of Liberation, America's erstwhile ally, was conspicuously absent, deliberately excluded from participation in the ceremonies by the American occupying force. In authorizing its Declaration of War against Spain in the interest of liberating Cuba from Spain's colonial grasp, the U.S. Congress had disavowed any intention to exert its own claim of sovereignty over the island, but this did not mean that the United States meant to allow the Cubans un-mediated self-rule. Exclusion of the Cuban military leadership from Santiago foreshadowed the ways the Americans would circumscribe Cuba's hard-won freedom well into the next century.[4]

With Spanish surrender of all of Cuba seemingly imminent, the command-ing general of the army, Nelson A. Miles, who had arrived in Cuba only the week before, was personally leading the hurried assault on Puerto Rico. "It was important to seize Puerto Rico and make secure some of the substantial fruits of victory, before the enemy, seeing the hopelessness of the struggle, sued for peace," explained Captain Henry H. Whitney.[5] Disguised as a British sailor, Whitney had traveled to Puerto Rico two months earlier under the direction of the Military Intelligence Division. He had spent ten days reconnoitering in the southern part of the island, gathering information on Spanish troop strength and likely landing places. With information gleaned from Whitney's mission, Miles opted to land his forces at Guánica, which was the deepest harbor on the south coast for which the United States possessed a chart.[6]

For the fifty-nine-year-old Miles, the naval assault on Puerto Rico pre-sented a very different prospect from the kind of campaigning that had pro-pelled his rise to the top rank of the Army. Like the rest of the frontier army following the Civil War, Nelson Miles had spent most of his career pursuing Indians who defied the government's policy of confining them to reservations. In the aftermath of the Battle of Little Bighorn, Miles was one of the officers who had carried out General Philip Sheridan's call for total war against the Plains Indians most implacably. During the fierce Montana winter of 1876–77, Miles determined he would follow "the Indians . . . where they think we can not go," as he wrote to his wife. "It is only in that way that we can convince them of our power to subjugate them finally."[7] Miles outfitted his troops in spe-cial winter gear: buffalo robe coats, leggings, mittens, and face masks cut from woolen blankets as well as pants, overcoats, and caps fashioned from robes by Cheyenne women they had captured. Thus fortified against the subzero cold and blizzard conditions, Miles's men had relentlessly pursued the Cheyenne and Lakota (Sioux) hunting bands who searched for game and camped with

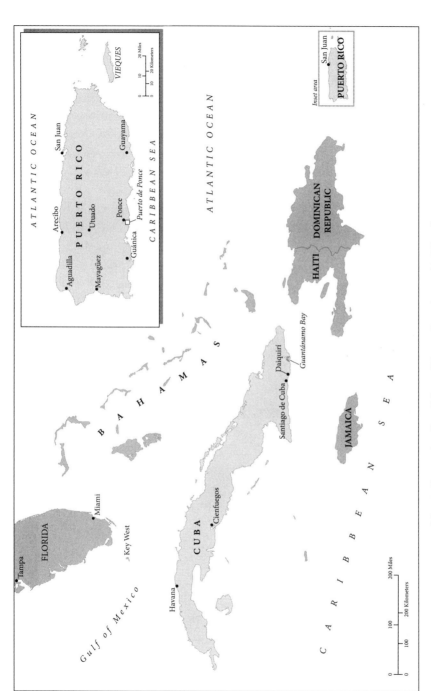

Map 1. Greater Antilles: Cuba and Puerto Rico during the War of 1898.

their families along the river bottoms of the remote Yellowstone country. The Lakota named him Bear Coat for the long overcoat trimmed in bear fur he wore under his military cape when he met the Indians in council to demand that they disarm and give up their ponies.[8]

The following year, Miles had intercepted Chief Joseph and about four hundred Nez Percé in their epic 1,700-mile flight from Eastern Oregon to seek refuge in Canada, compelling their surrender just forty miles south of the border. Nine years after that, he commanded the forces that brought in Geronimo on the Mexican border and sent the Chiricahua Apache into exile in the East. Miles had also marshaled the massive force that converged on the South Dakota Badlands, leading to the massacre on Wounded Knee Creek in 1890.

Now Bear Coat Miles stood poised to lead an invasion of Puerto Rico. Even transported to the Caribbean in summer, Miles's perceptions reflected the indelible frontier imagery inscribed by his years spent in Indian Country. Describing the ships' stealthy approach along Puerto Rico's south coast he wrote: "One familiar with the western plains of a quarter of a century ago might well have been reminded of a pack of large gray wolves cautiously and noiselessly moving in the shades of night, or the dim light that ushers in the dawn, upon their prey."[9]

Indian Country—doctrinal and discursive—has been at the center of American imperial expansion and nation building for two and a half centuries. In this book, I examine how the historical experience of domestic Indian Country shaped efforts to bring new areas where sovereignty was contested under American control following the war with Spain. The book traces the trajectory and dynamics of U.S. expansion by following and contextualizing the colonial careers of a cohort of army officers from the frontier to overseas posts. More broadly, it examines how the army's conquests in the North American West generated a repertoire of actions and understandings that structured encounters with the racial others of America's overseas empire during and after the Spanish-American War. In the vanguard of that movement overseas, soldiers served as diplomats and colonial administrators with a range of portfolios, from economic development to education. They also performed the role of interpreters of primitive culture and arbiters of the capacity for self-government of the alien peoples who were incorporated into the expanded empire. The men profiled in this book also mirrored the ideas of the nation that sent them to implement its policies—and reflect its prejudices—overseas.

The book focuses on the role of the military in an ongoing colonial project, closely analyzing the actions and attitudes of a handful of officers in particular, while situating them in the larger frameworks that structured the practice of empire. In tracing the colonial careers of the men on whom my analysis centers, I have therefore paid close attention not only to the influence of their careers in the army but also to how class, regional, and family backgrounds contributed to the actions they took in their roles as colonial administrators. Most important for my analysis is an examination of how the army's patterns of interaction with Indians at home played directly into the actions and habits of mind its officers directed toward the resistant subjects of the new overseas empire.

The American state project of consolidating territorial control over the continent entailed more than purely military conquest. And the same is true of the next phase of its expansion overseas at the turn of the twentieth century. Thus it was that General Miles, once established on Puerto Rican soil, addressed the island's residents in a register familiar to him from his days of conciliating and coercing Indians in the West. Following an uneventful landing at Guánica, Miles's forces moved on to take control of Ponce, the principal town on Puerto Rico's south coast.[10] On the morning of July 28, General Miles raised the American flag over his headquarters in the customs house and issued a proclamation "to the inhabitants of Puerto Rico" in Spanish and English,

> In the prosecution of the war against the kingdom of Spain by the people of the United States, in the cause of liberty, justice, and humanity, its military forces have come to occupy the island of Puerto Rico. . . . We have not come to make war upon the people of a country that for centuries has been oppressed, but, on the contrary, to bring you protection, not only to yourselves, but to your property; to promote your prosperity, and bestow upon you the immunities and blessings of the liberal institutions of our government. It is not our purpose to interfere with any existing laws and customs that are wholesome and beneficial to your people so long as they conform to the rules of military administration of order and justice. This is not a war of devastation, but one to give all within the control of its military and naval forces the advantages and blessings of enlightened civilization.[11]

Three weeks later in the far-off Philippines, another veteran Indian fighter named General Wesley Merritt issued a similar proclamation. Although the Spanish had capitulated to the United States, ten thousand American troops occupied Manila in a tense standoff with the forces of the recently declared Republic of the Philippines on its outskirts. Merritt's proclamation likewise alternated assurances of "beneficent purpose" with assertions of the absolute power of the United States to act as a "government of military occupation." By these ritual acts of proclamation and flag raising, U.S. commanders signaled America's claim over the Spanish colonies. As an occupying power, the United States promised protection and the "blessings of enlightened civilization" in exchange for recognition of its sovereignty and as a "reward" for "honest submission" to American authority.[12]

At first it might seem that Generals Miles and Merritt, as the advance guard for American overseas occupations of uncertain duration, were called on to improvise new words for the subject peoples their nation saw itself as liberating from the rule of a decadent empire. And yet there is something familiar about the messages each devised for the occasion, and in the attitude these frontier campaigners assumed in addressing their island audiences. Although delivered abroad, the generals' proclamations fell into well-established patterns developed over two centuries of talking to Indians across the expanding empire

Figure 1. Raising the flag over Ponce Customs House. Prints and Photographs Division, Library of Congress.

back home. In rhetoric and tone, there is little to distinguish the overtures of the newly arrived invaders of Puerto Rico, Cuba, and the Philippines from hundreds of pronouncements made to the native nations of North America by military ambassadors from the Great Father dating back to colonial times. They are also consistent with the messages delivered by American commanders who proclaimed the end of Mexican sovereignty over the lands and people the United States conquered in its war with Mexico.[13] Implicit in the language directed at Puerto Ricans, Cubans, and Filipinos was the presumption that American sovereignty derived not only from its military defeat of Spain, but equally from the manifest superiority of the enlightened civilization it proffered. Such professions of beneficent intent rested on familiar assumptions of racial and cultural superiority.

Eight years before he raised the Stars and Stripes over the customs house at Ponce, Nelson Miles had sounded similar themes when he addressed Oglala Lakota chiefs Red Cloud and Little Wound on the subject of the Ghost Dance movement at the Pine Ridge Agency in South Dakota. Miles had spoken then as the commander of the Division of the Missouri, with military jurisdiction over Indian Country. As in Puerto Rico, he claimed the mantle of upholding "order and justice." On that late October day in 1890, Miles had appealed to the Lakota leaders to suppress the "excitement" of the Ghost Dance "craze." As he would in his proclamation in Puerto Rico, Miles had stressed the sovereign power of American government and touted the benefits of submission to its authority. He began in a conciliatory vein, emphasizing the progress Indians had achieved toward becoming civilized: "It is not long since the Indians commenced to learn how to live and make themselves comfortable, and are getting horses and wagons and cattle, and they have made a very good beginning. . . . When we go back, we shall report to the Great Father that the Indians are well disposed, and are doing well."[14] Such gains in civilization were precarious, however; they would be jeopardized by Indians "becoming foolish and crazy and carried away by excitement," Miles admonished. The general pointedly reminded the chiefs that "All men in this country—, red, white and black men, live under one government, and that government is sufficiently powerful to punish all evil doers who commit acts of lawlessness under pretence of religion or any other influence or excuse."[15] Sovereignty and the authority to punish went hand in hand, but in Indian Country—and in American insular territories under military government—punitive violence was also deployed as a preemptive strategy for asserting sovereignty in places where the legitimacy of U.S. rule was rejected by the native inhabitants. As a colonizing power, the United States used punitive measures not just militarily, but also rhetorically. Violence underwrote sovereignty in situations where not only military control was in question, but also, more fundamentally, the moral or cultural claims on which sovereignty is premised were at issue.

The proclamation Miles disseminated among the Puerto Ricans might have served just as well to make the other point he had tried to impart to the Lakota chiefs in 1890: it was not his intention, nor that of his government, to interfere with "existing laws and customs" as long as they were "wholesome and beneficial," which, of course, the Ghost Dance was *not*, in the government's view. American legal doctrine recognized Indian nations as "distinct, independent political communities," yet the United States acted in myriad ways that contradicted those principles of autonomy and self-rule.[16] This was one of the anomalies that defined Indian Country as a colonial space within the American nation-state, one that would be replicated in the insular territories abroad where sovereignty was equally constrained and the limitations the United States placed on the peoples it incorporated into its empire were justified by familiar arguments about their unfitness for self-government.[17]

Two weeks after his conference with Red Cloud and Little Wound, General Miles summoned nearly a third of the army to the Dakota Badlands. Five thousand troops converged on the Pine Ridge and Standing Rock Reservations in a massive show of force intended to intimidate those Indians who just months before had been coerced into forfeiting nine million acres as their Great Sioux Reservation was broken up and land that had been promised them in perpetuity was made available for white settlement.

Said to be the largest army concentrated in one place since the Civil War, soldiers arrived by train from as far away as California, Colorado, and Texas. On December 29, an inept attempt to disarm Big Foot's band of Miniconjous led to the tragedy of the Wounded Knee massacre: more than two hundred people were killed, including women and babes in arms; many others were wounded.[18]

Eight years after the massacre at Wounded Knee, Bear Coat Miles became the first of four veterans of the Indian Wars who served in succession as military governor of Puerto Rico. In the Philippines, all four of the commanding generals who led the campaign to put down Filipino resistance to U.S. rule from 1898 to 1902 were also veteran frontier Indian fighters. Meanwhile, in Cuba, Leonard Wood, whose rough-riding career had its origins in the Apache Wars, transitioned from being governor of Santiago to serving as military governor of all of Cuba during the crucial years 1899–1902, during which time he superintended the process of demobilizing the Cuban Army of Liberation and installing a framework for circumscribing Cuba's sovereignty for the next three decades.

Popular accounts of the War of 1898 and its aftermath in the Philippines, Cuba, and the other colonies of Spain that became American protectorates or outright possessions in 1898 tend to stress the novelty of the moment when the United States landed troops overseas and installed its first colonial regimes abroad. According to the textbook view, the Spanish-American War represents the moment the United States emerged on the world stage and began to grapple with the challenges and contradictions of having an empire. In contrast to this view of U.S. colonies as an aberration or afterthought in the nation's course of development, there is another well-developed strain in the history of U.S. empire that focuses on continuity, rather than disjuncture, in American territorial expansion at the end of the nineteenth century. It is this tradition of examining the legacies and transformations of ongoing practices of American empire that I follow in this book.[19]

Of particular significance for my analysis of how colonial relations abroad were patterned on domestic Indian policy is an oft-cited but little heeded article published by Walter L. Williams in 1980. Williams's article, "United States Indian Policy and the Debate over Philippine Annexation: Implications for the Origins of American Imperialism," which appeared in the *Journal of American History*, made a compelling case for considering U.S. relations with Indians as a form of domestic colonialism. He demonstrated that turn-of-the-century politicians on both sides of the annexation question, as well as leaders in the fields of religion, philanthropy, and the military, all invoked the precedent of U.S. relations with Indian wards as a model for overseas colonial relations. Nineteenth-century Indian policy, wrote Williams, "served as a precedent for imperialist domination over the Philippines and other islands occupied during the Spanish-American War."[20]

Among the institutions surveyed in Williams's article—Congress, the Supreme Court, religious denominations, and philanthropic Friends of the Indians—the frontier army receives some attention. Williams spends a few pages analyzing continuities between the army's most recent experience of Indian Wars in the West and the idea that American soldiers abroad viewed—and fought—the 1899–1902 insurrection in the Philippines as more of the same.[21]

Although Williams focused his analysis on the Philippines, his observations on the continuity of personnel and the saliency of their recent Indian fighting for subsequent colonial policy making applies equally to the U.S. military enterprise in Cuba and Puerto Rico. In one sense, none of this is remarkable. In the three decades following the Civil War, the army's main function was to support the westward course of territorial expansion, a task that involved policing Indians and enforcing Grant's Peace Policy of confining them to reservations and defining as hostile those who resisted. In a calculation of the cost of the nation's Indian Wars, the U.S. Census Office reported in 1894 that the government had spent $800 million on military actions against indigenous people since independence. Excepting the War of 1812, the U.S.-Mexican War, and the Civil War, "at least three-fourths of the total expense of the army is chargeable, directly or indirectly, to the Indians," the report found.[22]

The army sent overseas in 1898 was preeminently an Indian-fighting army, in other words. Military historians have certainly taken note of this fact. In his book about the U.S. War in the Philippines, David Silbey makes this connection explicitly. Brian McAllister Linn's definitive histories of the Philippine-American War acknowledge the Indian fighting backgrounds of individual commanders as they trace institutional continuities between the frontier army and the adaptation of that army to the requirements of colonial service abroad.[23]

Senior military leaders—men like Miles, Merritt, and Wood—who led invasions and commanded the initial occupation of Spain's former colonies, are important to our story of the domestic Indian Country roots of overseas colonial rule. These generals all have their place in the chapters that follow. To describe the arc of imperial expansion, however, the book focuses in greatest detail on the experiences of three junior army officers.

The men profiled in these pages, Hugh Lenox Scott, Robert Lee Bullard, and John J. Pershing, were all shaped as soldiers and as future colonial officials by their formative experiences in what each of them referred to as "Indian Country." Like others in the military enterprise of which they were a part, each internalized ways of behaving in Indian Country that shaped his actions in later colonial appointments in Cuba and in the Philippines. In 1916 all three played prominent roles directing the massive force of roving occupation known as the Punitive Expedition dispatched across the border by President Woodrow Wilson, in which northern Mexico figured as the new Indian Country.

Upon graduating from the United States Military Academy at West Point in 1876, 1885, and 1886 respectively, each of the officers whose career is traced here received a commission on the frontier which involved him in the final skirmishes, punitive expeditions, and policing actions that were hallmarks of Indian fighting on the Great Plains and in the borderlands in the last quarter of the nineteenth century.

During the time he was stationed at Fort Sill in Oklahoma, Hugh Lenox Scott served as Geronimo's jailer, and also commanded a troop of Indian scouts in which he served. Mustered out of service in 1897, the Kiowa, Apache, and Comanche scouts of Fort Sill's Troop L constituted the last of such units of indigenous auxiliaries created by Congress in 1866 for service in the Territories and Indian Country. In his later career as a colonial official in Cuba and the Philippines, and as special emissary to Pancho Villa, Scott drew heavily on his experience of frontier warfare and diplomacy and especially on methods he had developed for interacting with those he called wild men.

Born on a cotton plantation in Alabama in 1861, William Bullard changed his name to Robert Lee in honor of the Confederate general and claimed to be the first southerner to carry that name back to West Point after the Civil War. Following his graduation in 1885, Bullard took part in the last campaign against Geronimo on the Arizona-Sonora border. At the start of the Spanish-American War, Bullard leveraged his home-state connections to get command of a black volunteer regiment.

Like Bullard, John J. Pershing began his army service chasing Apaches in the borderlands. When Nelson Miles summoned troops from all over the West to form a cordon around the Sioux reservations during the Ghost Dance scare, Second Lieutenant Pershing was part of an eight-company contingent of the Sixth Cavalry that made the train trip from New Mexico to South Dakota, along with all their horses and mules. In the aftermath of the Wounded Knee massacre, Pershing remained on the Pine Ridge Reservation until the company of Oglala scouts he commanded was disbanded the following summer. From policing Indians on both the Mexican and Canadian borders in the 1880s and 1890s, Pershing's career followed the trajectory of American expansion to Cuba and the Philippines. Twenty-three years later, in the final year of his governorship of Moro Province in the Philippines, Pershing's efforts to disarm Tausug warriors on the island of Joló would again lead to fear and resistance and a desperate last stand by Tausug men, women, and children inside the fortified mountain crater of Bud Bagsak in June 1913. In the military assault on that stronghold, Pershing deployed two specially organized companies of Moro Scouts as well as Philippine Scouts.[24] Key to the army's ability to track, engage, and treat with Indians in the West, indigenous auxiliaries (scouts, interpreters, and constabulary) became an integral part of pacification in the Philippines and Cuba as well.[25] In 1916 the Punitive Expedition led by Pershing crossed the border in pursuit of Francisco "Pancho" Villa just seventy miles south of Fort Bayard where Pershing had begun his career in Indian Country thirty years earlier.

The origins of Indian Country can be traced to the commitment of Anglo-American colonists to racial exclusion. In contrast to the French and Spanish who regarded native populations as "intrinsic to their imperial projects," the British sought to distance and exclude natives, both politically and geographically. By 1700 English maps of America began to include discrete areas of Indian Country as a spatial representation of the separateness of native politics and nations, depicted beyond boundaries drawn to demarcate the "frontier or wilderness."[26]

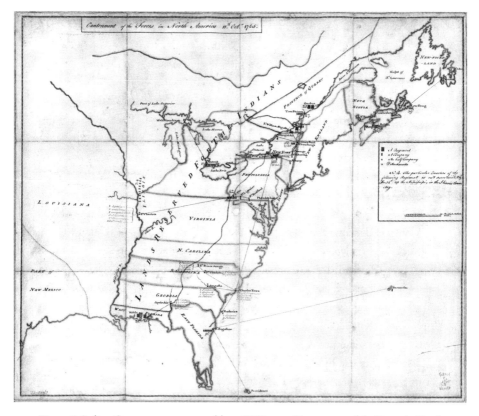

Figure 2. Indian Country as represented by a 1765 map. *Cantonment of the Forces in North America 11th Octr, 1765.* Geography and Map Division, Library of Congress.

Following its victory over France in the Seven Years' War, Britain's Proclamation of 1763 articulated the concept of Lands and Territories beyond the reach of European settlement that were to be reserved "for the use of the said Indians."[27] This commitment to racial separatism was inscribed in the far-reaching Indian Trade and Intercourse Acts of the 1830s, in which the geographical limits of Indian Country were pushed further west and the content of native sovereignty was further circumscribed. Nineteenth-century Indian Country fulfilled the role envisioned on the early maps; it was the place to which America's unwanted Indians could be removed.[28] Federal legislation for Indian Country both recognized it as a place where Indian law and custom held sway, but also regarded the people living there as in need of civilizing. As William Unrau put it, "The Indian country of 1834 was as much a place for controlling human behavior and modifying culture as it was a physical space simply to be occupied by a displaced people in need of security and the means of survival."[29] Throughout the nineteenth century, a succession of Anglo-American institutions were put in charge of civilizing and pacifying—and expropriating—the native peoples of the continent: the Bureau of Indian Affairs, denominational churches, and the army. The Indian Bureau, as Brian DeLay has pointed out, was a colonial office focused on the domestic sphere long before the War Department created the Bureau of Insular Affairs to coordinate policy making for the new island possessions.[30]

Just as it had in federal relations with Indians, a commitment to mediated and circumscribed sovereignty also went along with colonial assessments of the backwardness and the lack of capacity for self-government of the peoples of America's new possessions after the war with Spain. At the same time, Indian Country has also always referred to the places, and to the people acting in them, where the expansive sovereignty claims of the United States have been challenged and checked. In other words, limits on effective sovereignty in Indian Country cut both ways. The United States acted to curtail self-determination by natives, but just as the Lakota and Apaches had, Cubans, Filipinos, and other colonized peoples contested and evaded many of the forms of control the United States sought to impose on them.

Between its use by the British Crown as a way of designating Indian territories west of the Appalachian Divide that should remain beyond the reach of land-hungry American colonists to its invocation by soldiers in twenty-first-century wars of counterinsurgency, the concept of Indian Country has undergone changes both in meaning and in the contexts in which it is used. However, the original sense of being considered a place "apart from the lands of the whites," has endured, even as the practical meaning of Indian autonomy within those lands continued to be subject to constraints imposed by the United States.[31] In the 1830s, the limits on Native sovereignty were elaborated in several consequential Supreme Court cases. In 1831 the Supreme Court found that, in spite of their recognition in treaties with the United States, Indians were not "foreign nations" but "domestic dependent nations," subject to the authority of the United States. In outlining a "protected nation status" for Indian tribes, Chief Justice John Marshall wrote: "[Indians] occupy a territory to which we assert a title independent of their will. . . . Meanwhile they are in a state of pupilage. Their relation to the United States resembles that of a ward to his guardian."[32] The status of the Cherokee Nation, whose appeal of the Indian Removal Act led to Justice Marshall's decision, became a precedent for the relationship of the United States to its insular territories and their inhabitants that was taken up by the court in the early years of the century.[33] Like the Cherokee Nation, Cuba was recognized by the United States as a nation able to conduct its own affairs while simultaneously remaining under the "pupilage" of the United States. Cuba was recognized as a foreign country and yet remained "subject to control and even legislation from the United States."[34] Passed by Congress in 1901, the Platt Amendment placed limits on the sovereignty of the new government of independent Cuba even before it was formed. The amendment prohibited Cuba from entering into treaties with a "foreign power or powers," placed limits on the new nation's ability to contract a public debt, and obliged Cuba to provide the United States with a permanent naval station at Guantánamo Bay. Finally, the measure included a provision establishing the right of the United States to intervene for the "maintenance of a government adequate for the protection of life, property and individual liberty."[35] When the U.S. Military Government withdrew from the island in 1902, it left Cuba a protectorate. Puerto Rico, which the United States claimed outright, was defined as "a territory appurtenant and belonging to the United States, but not a part of the United States."[36] Cuba and Puerto Rico were recognized as separate nations, but were subject to the sovereignty of the United States in varying degrees.[37] The Philippines, too, remained under American rule, direct or indirect, for more than three decades.

Finally, no survey of the meanings of Indian Country is complete without noting that, for millions of Native Americans, the phrase connotes both home and homeland. Indian Country refers to geographical as well as cultural spaces within the United States that remain separate and distinct. Indian Country "may comprise ancestral territories and reservations, refer to sacred spaces, be framed by wins and losses in federal acknowledgement battles, and crosscut rural and urban environments," according to anthropologist Stephen Silliman. "It is a metaphor for what it means . . . to be Native American in the contemporary United States."[38]

Although each of them emphasized a different aspect of its practice and lore, by the end of their time in Indian Country, Hugh Lenox Scott, John J. Pershing, and Robert Lee Bullard all expressed veneration for a combination of skills and traditions collectively referred to as "scouting." Long a distinctive part of American frontier warfare, the use of scouts—both native and white— became central to the army's prosecution of wars of Indian dispossession and pacification as the country expanded westward after the Civil War. Drawing on the role that the Indian scouts played in the West, in its next phase of imperial expansion, the U.S. Army looked for ways to organize native auxiliaries to support the occupation of the Philippines, Cuba, and Puerto Rico.

The word scout comes from the Latin *auscultare*: to listen. In the military sense, scouting means reconnoitering, "searching out the land."[39] By the time Colonel Bullard's white volunteer regiment in the Philippines adopted the name "Bullard's American Indians," however, the resonances of scouting far exceeded its narrow military definition. As Americans contemplated a diminishing frontier, the scout emerged as a nostalgic emblem of a heroic past. Bullard conveyed some of the mystique associated with the figure of the scout in an unpublished story he wrote about the Philippines: "No amount of learning or philosophy or civilization ever quite takes a man beyond a secret willingness, even longing to be trapper, ranger, hunter, woodcraftsman or fighter of savages or outlaws, all in one word, scout. In this the high and the low, civilized and savage, the general and the private soldier, differ not. Emperors and kings, princes, leaders, teachers, the greatest that the world has held, have aspired to the qualities, the name and reputation of scout."[40] In Bullard's rhapsodic account, the appeal of scouting is primordial and universal; it is democratic in the sense that it has the power to overcome differences among men regardless of their station in life. Scouting, he suggests, transcends social class. All these attributes help explain the late nineteenth-century enthusiasm for forms of recreation and hobbyism loosely based on scouting and romanticized ideas of frontier manhood.

The late nineteenth and early twentieth centuries were a time when the appeal and significance of scouting transcended its roots and function in military practice. As other historians have noted, it was no accident that the popularization of scouting in civil society occurred as the last Indian Wars were playing out in the American West and at the height of racialized colonial expansion by European powers in Africa and Asia. Such civilian and hobby scouting reflected ideals of manhood in an industrializing America as well as the politics of race and empire. The real key to the appeal of scouting, however, lay in its ability to furnish models for bridging that other gap alluded to in the story, the gap between civilized and savage, the very gap that preoccupied so many of the scientists, moralists, and colonial administrators of the day. In particular, organizations that emerged to promote Indian scouting for boys were interested in harnessing the inborn natural longing for the salutary primitive pursuits, identified by Bullard, to channel them for the good of the young scouts as well as in the service of empire. Less recognized is the way native scouting developed as an embodiment of colonial policy and racial relations within the military itself. Finally, army officers in command of Indian Scouts, including Hugh Lenox Scott, served as frontline ethnologists. In this way, military scouting reinforced and informed late nineteenth-century theories about the very nature of the categories civilization and savagery themselves.[41]

In another sense, the logic of empire rendered all colonized people scouts. After the first American troops landed on Cuban shores in June 1898, U.S. General William Shafter offended some Cubans, who had been fighting for their independence from Spain for thirty years, by suggesting that their role should now be to serve as scouts for the newly arrived American troops, who were unfamiliar with the country and in need of orientation.[42] In the context of their most recent experience of pacifying the West, the arrangement made sense to the Americans. According to this view, the role of the invading force was to take over command and apply superior force of arms to impose order. The expected role for the natives in this scenario was to provide local knowledge and act in a supporting role.

As the theater of resistance to U.S. expansion shifted from the Great Plains and the desert Southwest to a new island empire in the Philippines, Cuba, and Puerto Rico, the ethnographic knowledge and experience of dealing with primitives imputed to military men like Scott became valorized as an asset for colonial service. Similarly, officers like Bullard and Pershing who had commanded African American troops, were regarded as particularly suited for roles in the pacification and administration of colonial peoples overseas. That experience of "commanding men of other than [his] own race and color," as Pershing put it, was variously acquired by white officers in the Ninth and Tenth Cavalry

Regiments (the famed Buffalo Soldiers) or through association with one of the immune regiments, like the Third Alabama Colored Volunteers organized by Bullard, who were specifically recruited for war in the tropics because of their supposed innate resistance to diseases such as yellow fever and malaria.

Our analysis begins by revisiting some key events that have played a significant role in the national epic of westward expansion. Throughout these episodes in which American sovereignty claims were contested on the ground—from the northern Great Plains, to the Sierra Madre, to southern Luzon—a focus on the thoughts, actions, and reactions of three army officers, Scott, Pershing, and Bullard, allows us to trace continuities in the process of extending territorial and overseas empire. Contextualization of the lives and careers of these frontier soldiers, including an examination of their family, regional, and political affiliations also sheds light on the deep interconnections between overseas colonialism and the racial dimensions of political and social life at home—in peace and war.

Part I

———

Indian Country

I began then an intensive study of every phase of the Indian and his customs, particularly as to how he might best be approached and influenced, a knowledge that has stood me in good stead many times, has doubtless saved my life again and again, and has also been used to the national benefit by different Presidents of the United States, by secretaries of war and of the interior.

—Hugh Lenox Scott, *Some Memories of a Soldier*

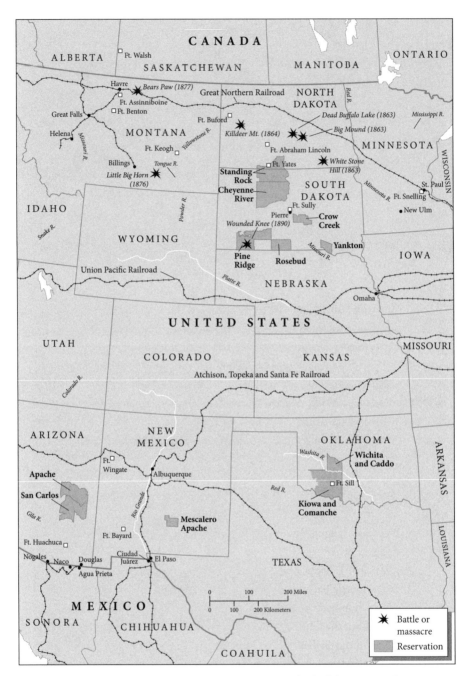

Map 2. Great Plains and borderlands. During the last third of the nineteenth century, American state efforts to consolidate control over the trans-Mississippi West were met with resistance. The map shows the areas of conflict that defined Indian Country for the post–Civil War generation of U.S. army officers like John J. Pershing, Robert Lee Bullard, and Hugh Lenox Scott.

Chapter 1

Coming to Indian Country

When the United States declared war on Spain in April 1898, Captain Hugh Lenox Scott had just moved to Washington and was settling his family into a new life far from the western plains he had grown to love. After two decades in Indian Country, Scott had reluctantly decided that he should return east so that his children would have educational opportunities not available to them at Fort Sill, where Scott had been posted for the last nine years. From 1891 until its disbandment in 1897, Scott had commanded Troop L, an all-Indian unit of the Seventh Cavalry made up of Kiowa, Comanche, and Apache enlisted men. It was the last such Indian Scout troop to be mustered out of service. At Fort Sill, Scott continued the study of Indian life and customs he had begun on the northern plains in the 1870s. As he had throughout his career in the West, Scott had also used his time at Fort Sill to further his studies of Indian languages and to collect a wide range of artifacts along with folk stories and other ethnographic information. By the time he was assigned to Fort Sill in 1891, Scott was recognized as an expert in the Sign Language of the Plains, an intertribal language used for communication from Saskatchewan to Chihuahua. He had used it as a tool during his first year there for gaining information about the Ghost Dance, which was alarming white settlers and certain elements in the civilian Indian Service. Besides its military and diplomatic utility, Scott was deeply interested in the potential for gathering ethnographic information through the medium of sign language. Working with a Kiowa soldier named Iseeo, Scott used it to record linguistic information, such as myths, stories, and his informants' accounts and explanations of the language itself.[1]

Just months before the USS *Maine* was blown apart in Havana's harbor,

Scott had obtained an appointment to the Bureau of Ethnology to work under the direction of John Wesley Powell. When the war came, he had just begun his research in the Library of Congress and Geological Survey for a book on the sign language of the Plains Indians. The war put an end to the book project. Scott abandoned his research to join the scrum of ambitious officers vying for command in the first foreign war to have come their way in more than a generation. He was never to return to the plains he loved so well. However, in the eyes of his army superiors, many of whom shared frontier experience, Scott's work with Indian scouts, his experience dealing with several hundred Apache prisoners sent to Fort Sill after the surrender and exile of Geronimo, as well as his reputation for understanding so-called primitives, all suited him for duty on the new frontiers of empire broached by the war, in Cuba and the Philippines. Following colonial service in the Philippines and Cuba, Scott was appointed superintendent of West Point from 1906 to 1910. He also served as army chief of staff under Woodrow Wilson, an old family friend to whom Scott once sent, from Cuba, a set of Spanish stocks used for punishing slaves.[2]

Like Wilson, Scott was the son of a Presbyterian minister who also happened to share the president's strong ties to Princeton University. Scott's grandfather was Dr. Charles Hodge, a prominent theologian and long-time head of the Theological Seminary at Princeton, where he taught for over half a century. It was as a student at the seminary that Scott's father, William McKendry Scott, had met and married Dr. Hodge's eldest daughter, Mary. The second of their three sons, Hugh Lenox Scott was born in 1853 in Danville, Kentucky, where his father served as a Presbyterian pastor and English professor at Centre College until his early death from tuberculosis in 1861. As a widow, Mary Hodge Scott brought her three young sons back home to join the lively household of her father and stepmother in Princeton.

At any given time, Dr. Hodge's gracious home near the Princeton campus provided a hospitable haven for friends and relatives, whether they were visiting or studying at Princeton. Some members of the extended family had rooms in the seminary or college, but took their meals at the house. Graduation and other ceremonial occasions brought throngs of students, alumni, and friends to the house to renew acquaintances and pay their respects to "the Presbyterian Pope," as Scott's grandfather was called—sometimes in admiration and sometimes in derision—for his unwavering defense of Calvinism.[3]

Young Hugh, who was known to his family as Len, had been named for his great-uncle, Dr. Hugh Lenox Scott, a physician and professor at the University of Pennsylvania. Besides connections to Presbyterian Church circles, family ties such as these provided the young Scott with a number of advantageous connections to people of influence in government, academia, and the military, and generally equipped him with an entrée into good society that was to serve him well throughout his life. Len's grandmother Sarah Bache was the great-granddaughter of Benjamin Franklin. She was also a niece of Caspar Wistar, an anatomist and paleontologist who served for many years as president of the American Philosophical Society. His grandfather's second wife came from one of New Jersey's leading families, the Stocktons, and was a cousin of Commodore Robert F. Stockton. The Stockton family home, known since colonial times as Morven, was one of the area's most distinguished old houses. When Lord Cornwallis's troops occupied Princeton, the general took it as his headquarters.[4]

Most significant for Scott's career, however, was the patronage of his step-grandmother's brother, Major General David Hunter, a friend of both Abraham Lincoln and Ulysses S. Grant. It was at his grandmother's instigation that Uncle David secured an appointment for Hugh Lenox Scott to West Point from President Grant.[5]

Uncle David accompanied Len Scott when he went up to West Point in the spring of 1871, introducing him to the superintendent and commandant of cadets as well as his many other acquaintances at the academy from which he himself had graduated a half-century earlier. Finally, he entrusted the young man to two sons of old army friends, one of whom was President Grant's son Fred.[6]

Hugh Lenox Scott's army career—both in the West in the 1880s and 1890s and later in Cuba and the Philippines—was notable for the ethnographic work he carried out among the various peoples the U.S. Army sent him to police and superintend, to pacify and subjugate, and to recruit to aid the army in its work: Indians, Moros, and Cubans. The work had a clear military purpose and application, but it was also furthered by a dogged scholarly inclination. On the strength of his interest and proficiency in native languages and seeming affinity for "Indian ways," seasoned frontier campaigners, including Generals Sheridan, Miles, Merritt, and Ruger, sought his advice and allowed him a degree of autonomy he relished—all while he was still a lieutenant of cavalry. When he was seconded to the Bureau of Ethnology to write a book on sign language, even Colonel John Wesley Powell deferred to his expertise in the subject. The work in military ethnography he undertook as a commander of Kiowa, Apache, and Comanche scouts in the 1880s and 1890s also provided the basis for the kind of diplomacy he pursued with other farther-flung "primitive peoples" on behalf of the United States.

As a student at West Point in the early 1870s, however, Scott showed few signs of the scholar he would become. Perhaps it was more the case that the curriculum offered a limited scope for the development of his particular scholarly potential. In Scott's day, the West Point curriculum concentrated on engineering, law, ordnance, and gunnery. To this was added some instruction in drawing, mathematics, chemistry, and language studies (Spanish, French, and German). The predominant method of instruction was recitation. After their first year, cadets were ranked in classes according to their performance on the previous year's exams, and attended recitations in the various subjects throughout the week.[7] In the winter, after recitations were over, the cadets practiced boxing, fencing, and dancing with one another to improve their technique; in the summers they spent the time in outdoor drill and swimming in the river at night. Scott was a strong swimmer who once saved a classmate from drowning on a return swim across the Hudson.[8]

In his second year, Scott was caught hazing a first-year plebe and was suspended for it and ordered to join the next lower class. Although forbidden at West Point, the practice of hazing was a time-honored and well-entrenched tradition. Scott was sanctioned for ordering a new man to walk with his palms facing forward with pinky fingers on the crease of his pantaloons in compliance with the drill regulations, and then catching his wrist to enforce his oral orders in the matter. Although such hazing (and worse) was common at the academy, Scott became the only member of his class to be "sent down" for it.[9]

In late January of his fifth and final year, Scott wrote to his mother apologizing for having missed his customary weekly letter, noting that he had been "more pressed for time" than he had expected as a result of his examinations. The rest of the letter gave a run-down on exams and resulting rankings in various subjects. He reported poor performance in his law exam in which he had been confronted with a question on "General Orders No. 100," which he had neglected to study, as he told his mother, because he had understood it would not be included on the exam. "Consequently, I didn't do very well," he wrote. The letter went on to detail his class standing in other exams: in Ordnance he had come thirty-seventh and had "lost about 9 files in Engineering."[10]

One implication of his exam results, as Scott saw it, was that he was unlikely to attain a commission in a white regiment. Scott preferred a white regiment over a black, but above all he had his heart set on the cavalry. There were thirty-five vacancies in white regiments, as he explained to his mother when she wrote to him in May expressing her concerns about his hopes for joining the Tenth Cavalry, one of the four African American regiments (two cavalry, two infantry) that had been organized following the Civil War. In apparent response to some strategies she had suggested—probably involving Uncle David—for securing a desirable place in a white regiment, he wrote, "The rest of your letter was just so much energy wasted. I shall come out 39 or 40 (of 48). So I must either take Nigger horse or Nig. foot & I infinitely prefer the horse."[11] While echoing the prejudice that prevailed among his classmates against serving with a black regiment, Scott tried to reassure his mother by telling her that he had spoken with several officers including Colonel Beaumont and Lieutenant Morton Stretch, one of his tactical officers, both of whom had served at posts with the black cavalry units, and that both had told him that "they [were] as good as any in the service."[12]

When they were small boys growing up in Kentucky, Mary Hodge Scott had told her sons frightening stories of the slave uprisings of the previous century in Haiti and Santo Domingo. These cautionary tales communicated a widespread fear among whites that they were vulnerable to the same fate at the hands of their slaves unless they kept them in check. Mrs. Scott retained this antipathy toward blacks and was opposed to the idea of her son's association with a colored regiment. Scott responded to her concerns by pointing out that he would not "have near as much to do with them personally as you would with a black cook."[13] In fact, the Hodge family's servants tended to be mostly Irish, black servants in Princeton being "not quite the thing" among their social set.[14]

In his determination to have nothing to do personally with black troops, Scott was typical of his generation of white army officers. This attitude was reinforced by army policy and traditions at the academy. The post–Civil War army was thoroughly racially segregated and remained so until 1948. Men of African descent—both enslaved and free—had fought in all the nation's wars, of course, but they had been accepted by the white officer corps and the country's leaders only reluctantly and never fully integrated into the overall structure of the army. When the Civil War broke out in 1861, blacks responded to the call for volunteers in large numbers, rushing to recruiting stations. Initially, the idea of black troops was rejected by both the civilian and military leadership. It took two years of petitioning Congress, the president, and municipal governments as well as—and perhaps more significantly—the government's realization of its need for more manpower, to reverse the idea, even in the North, that the war should be prosecuted by whites only. The change in policy was motivated not by idealism, "but rather by the dictates of a grueling war," according to one historian.[15] In the absence of black soldiers, many more white Union soldiers would die. "Since the Confederates were going to kill a great many more Union soldiers before the war was over, a good many white men would escape death if a considerable percentage of those soldiers were colored."[16]

Even when the decision to incorporate black troops into the war effort was reached, special permission was required from the War Department or Congress for those states that wished to organize volunteer Negro regiments. Instead of being inducted through established channels, a special Bureau for Colored Troops was set up to organize separate United States Colored Troops. In contrast to the Revolutionary War, when blacks had been scattered throughout the ranks, very few African Americans served in mixed units in the Union army. Instead, 178,985 men—mostly infantry—served in separate regiments, and they were paid less than white soldiers.[17]

In spite of their marginalization, the contributions of black soldiers in the Civil War were important in furthering claims for fuller civil and political rights. In the reorganization of the army that followed the war, Negro regiments were established by Congress for the first time in the nation's history. Initially, there were six all-black units—the Ninth and Tenth Cavalry and the Thirty-Eighth, Thirty-Ninth, Fortieth, and Forty-First Infantry. These were consolidated a year or so later into two infantry and two cavalry regiments.[18] Confined to the West and segregated in the regiments in which they served following the Civil War, black soldiers whose remains were sent back east were also buried in segregated sections on the fringes of Arlington National Cemetery.[19]

During the 1870s, several young African Americans won appointments to West Point. Scott's time at the military academy overlapped with three of them: James Smith, Johnson Whittacker, and Henry O. Flipper. Henry Flipper graduated the year after Scott, becoming the first African American to graduate. Upon graduation he was commissioned as a second lieutenant in the Tenth Cavalry "Buffalo Soldiers," the same regiment Scott had written to his mother about joining during his final year.

The presence of black cadets at the country's foremost military academy challenged the "fortified embattlement of officer and color caste" that West Point represented.[20] One of the more sensitive issues posed by the training of black officers at West Point was the likelihood it created for their possible command of and promotion over white officers. According to army doctrine of the time, which remained in force for another half century, blacks should not command white troops. Even the opportunities for blacks to command all-black regiments were limited and controversial. The orthodoxy was that Negroes had neither the initiative nor the savvy to make effective commanders and that they would perform well as soldiers only if commanded by whites. While conceding that "the colored race are a valuable military asset," James Parker, a white officer who fought in various Indian campaigns on the U.S.-Mexico border and was often garrisoned with black troops, expressed the common opinion that such "regiments must be officered by whites else they are of no account."[21]

Whites resented the very idea of submitting to the authority of blacks, whom they considered their racial inferiors. The wife of a white lieutenant expressed a common prejudice when she wrote letters to relatives from Camp Supply in 1873 in which she decried the spectacle of black sergeants at the post with authority over white privates. In her opinion, such an inversion of the natural order constituted a "good cause for desertion."[22] Unwritten policy thus imposed a ceiling on the promotion of African American officers above the rank of captain.[23] When the rare officer of color attained a higher rank, as in the case of Charles Young—who graduated from West Point in 1889 and achieved the rank of colonel during the Pershing Punitive Expedition in Mexico—an assignment was found that might evade such potentially awkward situations. In Young's case, he was assigned first to develop the military science program at Wilberforce University, and later appointed military attaché to Haiti and Liberia.

The professional implications for command and promotion of black officers at West Point was one thing. The thought of social fraternization across racial lines was quite another. If there were black officers, they would reasonably be expected to socialize with others of their rank at the places they were stationed. "The presence of Black officers also raised the possibility of an integrated officers' mess." Especially at the frontier posts where officers and their wives were already hard-pressed to uphold the social conventions appropriate to their status as officers and gentlemen (and ladies), the idea of living and socializing together was opposed by the white officer corps.[24]

Major General John Schofield, superintendent of West Point during the time Scott and Flipper were there, expressed his doubts about the ability of Negroes to succeed at the academy, basing his views on the widespread notion that they were backward and not fit to compete with whites. He acknowledged that qualified black nominees could not be denied admission to the national school, but he was doubtful about their prospects for success and did not see it as part of the institution's mission to work for that success. In his report for 1870, the superintendent wrote: "To send to West Point for four years competition a young man who was born in slavery is to assume that half a generation has been sufficient to raise a colored man to the social, moral, and intellectual level which the average white man has reached in several hundred years. As well might the common farm horse be entered in a four mile race against the best blood inherited from a line of English racers."[25] Schofield's racism was consistent with the prevailing ethnological thinking of the day, which held that the world's peoples passed through stages of evolution, from savagery to barbarism, and finally, civilization, before attaining the highest stage of development, epitomized by the Anglo-Saxons (the "English racers"), who were naturally assumed to occupy the top echelon.[26]

There is no record of any interaction between Hugh Lenox Scott and any of the black cadets who attended West Point with him. Nor did Scott mention any of his black classmates in his letters home, although he did refer derisively in one letter to his mother to the "moke fever" in Congress, by which he meant the supposed political preference for establishing and preserving black army units even as others might be reduced in an expected peace-time reduction of troops. While he was critical of legislative support for the all-black regiments, Scott was attuned—as were Robert Lee Bullard and John J. Pershing after him—to the politics of race in the military and to the possible advantages he might work from it. Part of his calculation about getting a commission in a black regiment, unpopular as it was among his fellow West Pointers, was his belief that it could provide a better chance of promotion and professional advancement for him than joining a white regiment. He made the same calculation about service with Indian scouts soon after arriving in Dakota Territory. In his closing words of justification for his decision to pursue a commission in a Buffalo Soldier regiment such as the Tenth, Scott confided to his mother, "most of the men here will hoot me [for it], but I don't care so long as I see it is to my advantage."[27] John J. Pershing—whose nickname Black Jack derived from his service with the Tenth Cavalry—shared a similar analysis with his Nebraska friend Assistant Secretary of War George D. Meiklejohn in 1898. Contemplating the best avenues for advancement from the vantage point of eastern Cuba following the war with Spain, Pershing concluded that they lay with command of one of the immune regiments he believed would be organized as an "imperial guard" for America's new tropical colonies following the war.[28]

Besides its presumed better prospects for promotion, the Tenth Cavalry had another attraction in its favor, as far as Scott was concerned. Its regimental headquarters were in Texas, and Texas, he had heard, was a "sportsman's paradise." There, he could "shoot all year around instead of being cooped up all winter in a little log hut snowed under in Wyoming Territory or else out on a scout 150 miles from home thermometer 15 degrees below zero—I hear accounts of it now and then that sets my teeth on edge."[29] Scott was an avid hunter. From an early age—rather to the consternation of his bookish family—he had spent all his available time outdoors, in the woods, chasing foxes or squirrels or other quarry. Since his mother would not allow him to use a gun until his fifteenth birthday, he hunted with a bow and arrow he had made for himself, with which he accounted himself "extremely skilful." Besides handling a gun, his passion for hunting helped him develop other "arts of the field" such as swimming, handling a boat, and riding a horse.[30]

Like the rest of his class, Scott admitted to being "mad for the cavalry." Capping off his arguments in favor of his preference for a commission in the Tenth Cavalry Buffalo Soldiers, Scott noted that cavalry officers were paid a hundred dollars more a year than infantry. They also got keep for two horses.[31] His greatest regret about leaving West Point was having to bid farewell to "his" horse. Cadets drew lots to determine an order for picking a mount for riding drill. Two weeks before graduation, Scott wrote regretfully to his mother that he had only two more rides left with his West Point horse. "I'm going to miss my horse very much—& he will me I guess. Whenever I come out he is looking for me & rubs his nose on my cheek & it is soft as velvet too. If I don't get out his sugar right away he pushes me till I do. I'm awfully sorry to leave him."[32] By all accounts, Scott was an excellent horseman. He was more sentimental about horses than he was about most people. He could remember and relate details of the appearance and temperament of horses he had owned or ridden half a century earlier. In the frontier army, Scott also became adept at handling mule teams, which were essential for transport, communication, and the provisioning of troops in the field.

Scott graduated from West Point on June 14, 1876. General William Tecumseh Sherman presented the diplomas to his class. At graduation Scott stood thirty-sixth in a class of forty-eight. He was assigned to the Ninth Cavalry, the other Buffalo Soldier regiment. He paid little attention to the commencement orations of the day, little suspecting that he would return many times to take part in commencement exercises in later years as a speaker himself, including during his tenure as superintendent of the academy from 1906 to 1910. Instead, newly commissioned Second Lieutenant Scott was intent on getting home to Princeton to make the most of the leave granted to him before reporting to the Arizona border when his orders came.[33]

Besides visiting friends and family in Princeton, Scott had been looking forward to attending the Centennial Exposition in Philadelphia. With his brother William, then a student at Princeton, Scott traveled to the nation's first capital to witness the celebration of its first hundred years of independence. Out of a population of some forty-two million, an estimated eight million attended the Exposition between May and October of 1876.

The exposition covered 285 acres of Philadelphia's Fairmount Park. It boasted five massive exhibition buildings as well as a number of state and foreign buildings, many restaurants, beer gardens, cigar pavilions, and a thirty-six-foot-tall ice water fountain erected by the Grand Division of Sons of Temperance of the State of Pennsylvania, which dispensed free ice water from twenty-seven self-acting spigots. The predominating theme of the exposition was Progress and the leading role of the United States in driving the innovations and achievements of the age. The president of the Centennial Exposition voiced the hope that people would come to the exposition "to study the evidence of our resources, to measure the progress of a hundred years, and to examine to our profit the wonderful products of other lands."[34] A visit to Machinery Hall, bragged one contemporary account, "must convince all that the world contains no fingers more cunning, no minds more inventive, nor tastes more refined, than are found on our shores.[35]

In the Government Building, exhibitions were intended to "illustrate the functions and administrative facilities of the Government in times of peace and its resources as a war power." Accordingly, the War Department awed fairgoers with a dynamic display of some of its most powerful and modern weaponry. All the machinery and skilled operatives needed to demonstrate the manufacture of the Springfield breech-loading rifle were assembled in the Government Building; fascinated fairgoers watched as "handsome weapons of death" were fashioned out of round bars of steel and blocks of black walnut before their eyes. The process of grinding a bayonet on a steam-powered grindstone as well as the manufacture of bullets and cartridges were also on view, as well as an array of cannons, Gatling guns, and mountain howitzers with carriages and ammunition, positioned realistically on pack saddles, just as they would be carried into battle on the backs of mules.[36]

Weapons also made up a significant portion of the American Indian artifacts exhibited in the same building, but these were presented in an entirely
different way. Stone axes, clubs, spears, bows and arrows, and knives were piled
together in museum cases or "huddled under tables." Without interpretation,
these "savage weapons" were displayed as relics, thus supporting the prevalent
idea about the backwardness of the men who had made them. As the author of
an article describing the weapons concluded: "The Centennial Exhibition was
mainly of the means and results of modern industry and art, and the primitive
objects were comparatively but strays and occasionals."[37]

The principal organizer of the Indian exhibit, Spencer F. Baird, assistant
secretary of the Smithsonian, intended the display of Indian objects to educate
Americans on the way of life of American Indians as well as to illustrate "the
change from a savage state to one of comparative civilization," but the overall impression created by the jumble of artifacts tended instead to reinforce common
stereotypes of Indians as primitives, whose culture and way of life represented
the antithesis of progress.[38]

Baird had also wanted to include living Indians in the Centennial Exposition. Working with the Indian Office, which shared responsibility for representing Indians at the exposition, plans to bring thirty to forty Indian families
to the exhibition were well developed, but ultimately abandoned due to lack of
congressional support. The idea was to install members of selected tribes (those
already subdued by the government) in a five-acre reservation on the exposition
grounds where they could demonstrate their skills at crafts such as weaving
blankets, making pottery, and dressing buffalo skins. Unfortunately for Baird,
Congress refused to fund the proposal, even when it was pointed out that such
an excursion would have the added benefit of providing an object lesson in the
power of the United States.[39] Instead of living Indians, visitors to the Indian
exhibit in the Government Building encountered life-sized effigies, made of
papier-mâché modeled on notable Indians who had been photographed on
diplomatic visits to Washington. One of the men whose image was rendered
in effigy was the Oglala chief Red Cloud, who had led his people's resistance to
incursions into Lakota and Shoshone territories along the Bozeman Trail; by
the time of the centennial, Red Cloud had long since accommodated himself
to the inevitable and acceded to the government's insistence that he settle near
an agency on the Great Sioux Reservation. Although Red Cloud had been at
peace with the United States since 1868, the manikin representing him was
dressed to appear warlike, presenting a "repulsive looking image with raised

tomahawk and a belt of human scalps."[40] Two years after touring the Indian exhibit under Red Cloud's scowling likeness, Scott would spend several days as an interpreter and guest in Red Cloud's lodge, where he found him to be "the picture of hospitality."

Ethnographic limitations notwithstanding, for the recent West Point graduate the exposition was enjoyable for the spectacle it provided and also for the chance to meet friends. Scott spent some of his time at the exposition in the encampment of West Point cadets. He also enjoyed the hospitality of the Seventh New York Regiment, also camped out within the fairgrounds. "Any soldier who got into one of the company streets of the Seventh Regiment was in for a strenuous time," Scott recalled years later. "Each tent floor had a small cellar under it, filled with ice, champagne, roast chicken, and other delicacies, and a passer-by would be hauled into those tents, one after another, and, with the cellar door opened wide, he would not be allowed to leave until some duty called his hospitable hosts elsewhere."

Scott was still in Philadelphia for the gala events to mark Independence Day 1876. These began with a torchlight parade to Independence Hall on the evening of July 3. At the stroke of midnight, Philadelphia's new Liberty Bell pealed thirteen times to thunderous applause. An orchestra was on hand to play "The Star Spangled Banner," with all the bells and steam whistles in the city joining in. The city's celebrations continued until two in the morning. The Fourth dawned hot. To avoid the worst heat of the day, the planned military parade of ten thousand troops was scheduled for early in the day. Taking part in the parade were two dozen regiments and national guard companies as well as a Centennial Legion composed of detachments from the thirteen original states of the Union. All were under the command of the governor of Pennsylvania; they marched through Philadelphia's streets and were reviewed by General William Tecumseh Sherman in front of Independence Hall. The parade was followed by the "Hallelujah Chorus" from Handel's *Messiah* as well as odes, orations, and songs composed in honor of the anniversary of American independence. At night the city was illuminated again and a fireworks display over the exposition grounds brought the festivities to a close.[41]

The following day, unsettling news began to spread through the exposition. Far to the west, in Montana Territory, troops of the Seventh Cavalry, led precipitously into battle by Lieutenant Colonel George A. Custer, had been routed by a larger force of Lakotas and Cheyennes. Scott heard the news from a friend he encountered on the street. At first he did not believe it. A newspaper soon convinced him of the truth of his friend's report. Among the dead were two of Scott's friends who had graduated the previous year, John Crittenden and James Sturgis.[42]

Shocking though the news was, the death of Custer's entire command also opened up certain opportunities for the recent graduate. Scott hurried back to Princeton to consult his uncle Sam Stockton about how to proceed.[43] Stockton, who had been a captain in the Fourth Cavalry, brushed aside Scott's scruples about "jumping for the shoes of those killed in the Little Big Horn before they were cold." Stockton counseled him to write immediately to his uncle David Hunter "who knew everybody in the War Department." Uncle David received Scott's application for the Seventh Cavalry at breakfast the next day and carried it to the War Department where they were making the transfers to the regiment, and made sure that Scott's name was added to the list. Scott's new commission as second lieutenant in the Seventh Cavalry was dated June 26, 1876, the day after the Little Bighorn battle, an event Scott referred to for the rest of his life as "the Custer disaster."[44]

It had taken ten days for the alarming news of Custer's defeat on the Little Bighorn River to travel from Indian Country to the fairgoing crowds in Philadelphia. The few details and rumors transmitted by telegram to newspaper offices in the East from remote places like Salt Lake City and Helena in time for the July 5 papers were supplemented the following day by a fuller account and the first official confirmation of the fight by the commander of the Yellowstone campaign, General Alfred Terry. Terry sent his official report on the events of June 25 from his field camp on the Lone Horn River on June 28 by way of a scout who arrived with the dispatch at Fort Ellis near Bozeman on July 3. From Bozeman the news was telegraphed through General Sheridan's headquarters of the Department of the Missouri in Chicago; from there it was transmitted to Philadelphia. Both General Sheridan and General Sherman were away from their headquarters, both having traveled to Philadelphia for the centennial events.[45] Other reports reached the press as eyewitnesses to the battle straggled into Salt Lake City and Bismarck.[46] The time required for the news to travel from the battlefield to the nation's hubs of political and military power testified to the vast distance, both spatial and psychological, separating Indian Country from the eastern centers of population and political power in the 1870s. The reality of the nation's relations with its Indian wards was very different from those suggested by the assortment of relics arrayed for visitors to the Centennial Exposition.

By the time Scott received his orders to join the remnants of Custer's regiment at Fort Abraham Lincoln in Dakota Territory, the initial frenzy of rumor, purported eyewitness accounts, and attributions of blame that followed the rout on the Little Bighorn had mostly subsided—only to be stirred up again later that year by the publication of Frederick Whittacker's provocative book *The Complete Life of George A. Custer*.[47]

Scott's journey to take up his commission in Dakota Territory traced in reverse the route the news of the disaster had traveled. It also traversed several earlier frontiers of the expanding empire, each of which, by 1876, had been successively incorporated into the republic of progress and Anglo-American civilization celebrated by the ongoing exposition in the City of Brotherly Love he had left behind.

Scott traveled by rail, taking with him a saber, two shotguns and a Henry rifle, a trunk, a roll of bedding, and two hunting dogs—a pointer and a setter given to him by friends. His first stop on his journey west was Pittsburgh where he visited his older brother Charles and his new wife. A century earlier, Pittsburgh had stood in the same relation to the Indian Country of the Ohio valley as Bismarck and Fort Abraham Lincoln on the Missouri to which he was bound now occupied in relation to the disputed Indian Country of the plains. During the period of rivalry between the French and British empires over control of territory and influence with the Indians of the Great Lakes and interior of the continent, the strategic location on the forks of the Allegheny and Monongahela, which later gave rise to Pittsburgh, had been the site of a contested outpost. A succession of forts at "the forks" changed hands four times within two decades of intense frontier imperial rivalries and shifting alliances with native groups. The object of several unsuccessful attempts by British forces to capture it during the French and Indian War—twice involving a young George Washington—Fort Duquesne was finally blown up by its erstwhile defenders as they fled in the face of an imminent attack by British colonial forces in November of 1758.

European struggles over strategic frontier locations such as Fort Duquesne/ Fort Pitt unfolded in the context of complex political, economic, and cultural relations with the Indians of the interior of the continent. The French referred to the vast lands beyond the skeletal outposts of European settlement in the Great Lakes region as the Pays d'en Haut. What developed in these areas of contested sovereignty was a complex and dynamic relationship among civilizations that Richard White has productively analyzed as a "Middle Ground" between European and Native peoples, a shifting zone in which an array of nations, tribes, villages, and empires not only encountered one another, but became "cocreators of a world in the making."[48] Contested sovereignty was the sine qua non of the Middle Ground, which was maintained by both diplomacy and accommodation among a shifting set of factional alliances.

But while the Old World empires adapted to the evolving give-and-take required by the Middle Ground, the colonists themselves chafed at being restricted to the eastern side of the crest of the Appalachian mountains, the 1763 "Line of Proclamation," decreed by a victorious Britain at the end of the war with her longtime rival France. Divergence over Indian policy for the Ohio valley between colonial officials and the backcountry settlers of western Pennsylvania and Virginia contributed significantly to the ruptures that became more pronounced following the French and Indian War. One expression of indigenous attempts to drive settlers out of the Ohio valley and to reclaim the earlier terms of relations with the European powers was the widespread Indian war known as Pontiac's Rebellion, in which the Ottawa chief united Shawnee, Delaware, and Ojibwe tribes in attacking British installations such as Fort Pitt.

Independence from Britain worsened Indian-white relations since no centralized authority remained to continue the Crown's interest in preserving its commitments to the Indians of the Ohio valley. On the contrary, removal of the royal interest in policing the volatile line between Euro-American settlement and Indian Country launched an expansion into the Ohio valley of settlers, squatters, land speculators, and veterans of the French and Indian War and the American Revolution who had been promised land in the West. The response of the Native nations to this betrayal of promises made by the former imperial powers was a determined defense of their sovereignty claims.

Scott's next stop on his journey west was Chicago, the largest metropolis in the continent's interior, and gateway to the Great West beyond.[49] Chicago was also the command center for the headquarters of the Department of the Missouri, commanded by Lieutenant General Philip Sheridan. From here, since the previous winter, Sheridan had plotted "total war" against the hunting bands who resisted the government's insistence that they "come in" to the Indian agencies and submit to military authority on the reservations.[50]

With a population that had recently surpassed 350,000, Chicago was a very different place from the small collection of huts around Fort Dearborn at the mouth of the Chicago River where Scott's uncle David Hunter had been stationed with the Fifth Infantry in 1828. There, Uncle David had once borrowed a Potawatomi Indian canoe to paddle across the Chicago River to bring back Jefferson Davis, who had been lost while on an expedition from Fort Winnebago to search for deserters. The canoe was built for one man, so to ferry Davis across, Hunter directed him to lie down on the bottom and then sat on him in order to keep the center of gravity low enough to avoid capsizing the canoe. Hunter and Davis also served together in the first regiment of Dragoons organized to police and intervene in settler-Indian relations in the trans-Mississippi West. They had remained friends until the outbreak of the Civil War.[51]

Besides the frontier experiences related by his uncle David Hunter, Chicago summoned up more personal memories from Scott's own past; the city had been his family's home from the age of six to eight, when his father had been a professor at the Theological Seminary of the Northwest (now McCormick Theological Seminary). It was from here that the young family accompanied him back to Princeton where he died in 1861.

From Chicago Scott continued on to St. Paul, the rough-hewn river capital of Minnesota, where he began to get "the feeling of the proximity of the frontier." Here, he encountered "blanket" or unassimilated, Indians for the first time: "tall, straight Chippewa [Ojibwe] Indians, wrapped in their blue and scarlet [trade] blankets, striding about in a very dignified way."[52] Shortly before Scott's arrival, the outlaw Jesse James and the Younger brothers had attempted to rob a bank in Northfield, Minnesota, some forty miles to the south of the capital. Several of the gang had been killed after they shot the cashier and were attempting to flee out of town. The body of one of the dead gang members was exhibited in the window of a store on Third Street close to the hotel where Scott was staying, adding to his sense that he had arrived at civilization's edge.

Like Pittsburgh, St. Paul had grown up under the aegis of a frontier fort established in Indian Country at the strategic confluence of two rivers. Scott's Uncle David had preceded his protégé here, too, and the young man's expectations of what he would find on the Mississippi were shaped in part by the stories he had heard about his uncle's five years at the frontier post. Half a century earlier, David Hunter had likewise graduated from West Point and made the trek from his home in New Jersey to what was then the most remote and skeletal outpost of American authority in the Northwest, the newly constructed fort at the strategic confluence of the St. Peter (Minnesota) and Mississippi Rivers. Fort Snelling was built into a bluff overlooking the place where two conduits of the still-dominant fur trade connected a vast northern interior with downstream markets. There had been no railroad in 1822 to convey Uncle David to his first army post, nor any roads. It had taken him six months to reach Fort Snelling to take up his commission in the Fifth Infantry; the last two hundred miles from Prairie du Chien he walked on the ice of the frozen Mississippi River.[53]

The construction and garrisoning of Fort Snelling in 1820 had been intended to bolster a tenuous American presence in the region. The young republic had done its utmost to assert sovereignty over the Great Lakes region in the War of 1812, but in the remote northern interior of the land that would become Minnesota, the Union Jack continued to wave over the trading posts of the well-established North West Company. While the owners and managers of the company were mostly Scotsmen, their employees who were actively engaged in the fur trade were French-Canadians and men of mixed French and indigenous ancestry. Almost all of them were connected by ties of kinship to the natives who trapped and hunted for furs and traded with the company for guns and ammunition, woolen blankets, iron pots, and other manufactured goods. President Monroe's 1817 ban on non-Americans trading on U.S. soil was toothless without a military presence to enforce it. Fort Snelling's purpose had thus been to counteract the still-powerful British influence in the region and to control access to the fur trade interior by regulating the Mississippi route.[54]

When David Hunter arrived at Fort Snelling in 1823, there was hardly a white person in the region who was not related to the Dakotas or Ojibwes—or sometimes both—either through birth or through marriage. By the 1830s, six generations of intermarriage "had produced an intricate web of relationships, with people of mixed ancestry acting as an essential bridge between their white and Indian kin."[55] On the Upper Mississippi such intimate and material relationships mattered more than national allegiances. French remained the lingua franca of the region; English was hardly spoken. Like that of the French and British empires before it, the military power that the Americans were able to project in the region was feeble, insufficient to enforce a sovereignty whose assertion on maps was belied by a more complicated reality on the ground. Garrisoned with a few hundred troops, American might was no match for a population of tens of thousands of Indians. Largely though, it was the monopolistic fur trade—not the army—that both kept the peace and provoked conflict.[56]

Well into the middle of the nineteenth century, Minnesota remained aloof from the general east-to-west pressure of white settler expansion to secure Indian "removal." White settlement was in fact antithetical to the interests of the fur trade companies. For the first half of the nineteenth century, it was the fur-trading monopolies, especially the North West Company, that had proved hostile—more than the region's native inhabitants—to the few pockets of intrepid (and usually uninformed) white settlers who attempted to establish agricultural colonies in the remote and inhospitable river valleys of the North Country.[57]

At mid-century, even as the new states hewn out of the Northwest Territory to the east and south sought to remove Indians from within their borders, Minnesota fur-traders-turned-politicians sought to relocate *more* Indians in Minnesota, not to remove them from the territory. Anglo-Minnesotans lobbied Congress to receive the Winnebago (Ho-Chunk) from Iowa and Wisconsin and also to have the government purchase a million acres of land from the Objibwes on which to resettle Menominees from Wisconsin. Such territorial maneuvering was motivated not by love of Indians, but rather by the desire to capture the economic benefits of the annuity payments settled on the tribes by the federal government in return for forfeiture of their claims to their ancestral lands.[58] The Ojibwe, meanwhile, had their own reasons for supporting the resettlement of other tribes in Minnesota. They saw the arrival of other tribes from the east as helpful in creating a buffer zone between themselves and the Dakota.[59]

With the disappearance of the fur trade by mid-century and the advent of the railroad, Fort Snelling's military focus shifted from the North to the West. Instead of controlling commerce and Indian relations along Minnesota's waterways, the fort now functioned as a remote command center in the continuing contest over lands further west where plains tribes continued to challenge the claims of the United States to exclusive sovereignty.

Minnesota's distinctive borderland society, so long in the making and seemingly so enduring, was quickly and violently unmade. As the fur trade entered a period of both local and global decline, Minnesota offered new rich prospects for resource extraction and agricultural development in which Indian presence on the land was seen by speculators and settlers as an obstacle to progress—and to profit—as it had been further east. Wisconsin Winnebagos who had been settled on timberland in the central part of the territory were divested of that lucrative land and relocated to the prairie in the southwestern part of the territory from where, against their will, they would later be removed again to Dakota Territory, and from there to Nebraska.[60]

When Congress recognized the last remaining unorganized part of the Old Northwest as the territory of Minnesota in 1849, pressures intensified on native tribes to cede most of their remaining lands to the federal government in return for payments representing a fraction of their market value. The annuity payments the Indians actually received were further diminished by the liens traders had written into the cession treaties, which guaranteed that the credit they had extended to the tribes would be paid first.

By the time Scott arrived in St. Paul and noted the stately bearing of the Ojibwes he encountered there, Ojibwe claims to land, which in his uncle's day had encompassed fully half the northern part of the state, had been reluctantly ceded to whites. The remaining six thousand or so tribal members in the state had "relinquished the meadows, forests and wild rice beds of the lake country for the harsh climate, poor soil, and 'immense swamps' of new reservations located hundreds of miles from population centers."[61] In the southern part of the state, the Dakotas, who had actively facilitated the establishment of an American presence at Mendota, the site of Fort Snelling, and along the valleys of the Mississippi's tributaries, had fared even worse. Their lands and subsistence had been squeezed and encroached on by an influx of land-hungry settlers and speculators and they had been extorted and strong-armed by traders and Indian agents.

By the outbreak of the Civil War, the once-dominant Dakota had seen their domain reduced to an untenable ribbon of land along the Minnesota River. When the exigencies of war being waged in the East further delayed annuity payments throughout the summer of 1862, frustrated and deeply angry young men launched an attack on white settlers in the Minnesota River valley with tragic consequences. The Dakota attacks on white communities in southern Minnesota left between four hundred and a thousand men, women, and children dead. The killings inflamed the white population of Minnesota against all Indians—not just the fraction of Dakota men who took part in the killing, but also against the majority of the bands who had rebuffed the incitements to war and provided protection for and even taken the side of whites in the conflict.

The Dakota War reshaped ethnic identity in the four-year-old state. The conflict destroyed the vestiges of the mixed-race border culture and sense of shared kinship between whites and natives. It also marked the beginning of a new phase of conflict between indigenous people west of Minnesota and an encroaching white civilization that would last another two decades. It led, in other words, to the war Scott was hastening to join.

For the Dakota, the war was devastating. They lost all but a tiny remnant of their once-extensive lands; Congress passed a bill authorizing the exile of Dakota people from the state, annulling all treaties the United States had made with any of the bands and diverting the remaining Dakota annuities to pay reparations to the white victims of the violence.[62] In the aftermath of the conflict on the Minnesota, thirty-eight Dakota men were hanged in a gruesome ritual of state-sanctioned retribution the day after Christmas 1862. Hundreds of others were imprisoned for three years at Camp McClellan in Davenport, Iowa. Some sixteen hundred women, children, and old men, those explicitly *not* guilty of involvement in the attacks except by virtue of tribal association, were force-marched from their communities on the Minnesota to a prison camp set up below the walls of Fort Snelling, where close to three hundred died during the winter of 1862–63 as the authorities waited for the ice on the Mississippi to melt enough to permit their deportation out of the state. Those who surrendered, including many Sissetunwan and Wahpetunwan who had not fought against the United States, were deported to Crow Creek, Dakota Territory, or imprisoned. Exiled from Minnesota, hundreds, especially children, died of disease and starvation. Others fled onto the western plains and north into Canada.[63] The Minnesota state legislature instituted a bounty on Dakota scalps.[64]

The Dakota had been defeated, but the war for control of Dakota Territory and eastern Montana was just beginning. In the aftermath of the attacks on Minnesota River settlements, the state's leaders joined with federal forces to mount massive punitive expeditions to chase the renegades who had fled onto the western plains. There, the exiles from Minnesota joined with bands of the Teton Sioux (Hunkpapa and Blackfeet) who were engaged in the crucial summer activity of hunting and drying meat to secure a food supply for the coming winter.

The Dakota (or Santee Sioux) of Minnesota represented the easternmost tribe in a loosely confederated and widely dispersed people who recognized common descent from seven ancestral political units called council fires.[65] The Lakota in turn were one of seven tribes of the Teton Sioux: the Lakota, Hunkpapa, Brule, Miniconjou, Sans Arcs, Two Kettles, and Sihaspas. In the course of making war on the Dakota who had sought refuge in the lands of their kinsmen, the Lakota, the United States attacked the Lakota indiscriminately as well. Just as significantly, the punitive campaigns into the Dakotas were intrusions into a country where the soldiers had no right to be, according to the Lakota view of the proper relations between their people and the *wasichu* (whites) who had recently begun encroaching on areas they had long viewed—and fought to defend—as their own.

Like other punitive wars fought for control over territory inhabited by people deemed to be savages by expansive colonial powers, the expeditions to punish the Dakota launched from Minnesota in 1863 and 1864 combined a rhetoric of righteous retribution with the strategic goal of extending sovereignty claims over contested territory. They were also intended to intimidate and serve as a warning to Indians further west, like the Lakota, and discourage their active resistance to white-settler expansion.

While punitive actions are associated with volatile and primal emotions, such as anger and the desire for vengeance, the military rationale for such wars stresses their role in disciplining the adversary; punitive actions are launched not just to punish but also to "teach a lesson." Not surprisingly, the military literature on the history and theory of punitive wars often discusses them in the context of colonial warfare. The theory behind punitive wars is that "primitive, less organized enemies" cannot be dissuaded from unwanted behaviors by the mere knowledge that their actions may elicit the wrath of a more powerful adversary.[66]

The concept of a military action whose primary objective is to punish implies the arrogation of the moral authority to mete out justice to the other side. Similarly, expeditions are one-sided actions in which the initiative to invade and pursue is claimed by the punitive authority, the one in *pursuit*. Such inherently asymmetrical language reveals the presumption that the great power possesses a monopoly on moral authority to act in a way that is intended to teach a lesson. Moral right is assumed to lie with the greater power that is in pursuit. This is an unquestioned premise of punitive actions. Indeed, one might say that the rhetorical force of acting with punitive intent is in itself an act that asserts the moral high ground and overwhelms contesting claims of justice and moral authority.

The punitive expeditions of 1863 and 1864 represented the largest forces yet assembled against western Indians as they pursued the remnants of the Dakota fleeing as far as the Missouri River. Led by Henry Hastings Sibley, a fur trader who had become Minnesota's first governor, and by Alfred Sully, a general redirected from the Civil War to lead the effort, the punitive raids penetrated deep into the Coteau du Missouri country, a land of elevated rolling plains stretching from close to the Canadian border generally east of the Missouri River and south into what is today north-central South Dakota. This was a hot, dry, and inhospitable region, which Sully famously described as "Hell with the fires put out."[67]

The massive expeditions that set forth into the Dakota Territory each in-cluded thousands of soldiers and hundreds of Indian scouts drawn from the Winnebagos and also from among the Dakotas. Sully and Sibley ranged up the Missouri River and across the hot arid grasslands in search of Indian en-campments to chastise. The brigades were supported by hundreds of wagons and mule teams, as well as herds of cattle brought along to furnish meat for the soldiers.[68] During the summers of 1863 and 1864, the forces of Sully and Sibley attacked Indian villages camped at Big Mound (northeast of present-day Bismarck) as well as at Whitestone Hill to the south and Killdeer Mountain further west. Made up of different Sioux bands who had come together to hunt, the number of lodges ranged from hundreds to an estimated fifteen hundred at Killdeer. In each of these major engagements, the Indians fought first to cover the retreat of women and children from their encampments. Estimates of the number of casualties in each battle vary widely, but run into the hundreds. At Whitestone alone, it is thought that 150 to 300 Santee, Yanktonai, and Teton Sioux were killed, including women and children. The number of soldiers killed is better known; in the same battle, Sully's forces lost twenty-two men killed and fifty injured. At Killdeer Mountain, about forty U.S. soldiers died.[69]

The punishment the forces applied to the Indian villages they encountered was intended both to demonstrate the army's ability and determination to in-flict damage and to make life and even survival difficult not just by killing them but also by destroying their shelter and especially the meat they were gathering for the winter. Lodges, meat, robes, utensils: the soldiers methodically burned it all. After the battle of Whitestone Hill (September 3, 1863), it took a hundred men two days to gather up and destroy all the provisions and possessions left behind by the Santee, Yanktonai, and Teton Sioux as they fled. This included plunder the Dakota had brought from their attacks on settlements in the Min-nesota valley along with three hundred lodges and 400,000–500,000 pounds of buffalo meat (roughly 1,000 butchered buffalo). All of it was burned. Captain Mason, a wagon master for the expedition, remarked that "fat ran in streams from the burning mass of meat."[70]

Following the Killdeer fight, Sully's troops systematically destroyed every-thing the fleeing Indians had left behind (which they had intended to return to recover). It took a thousand men a whole day to burn forty tons of pemmican (dried buffalo meat packed in buffalo skins), dried berries, tanned buffalo, elk, and antelope hides, brass and copper kettles and mess pans, saddles, travois, and lodge poles. "Even the surrounding woods were set afire." Soldiers also shot the three thousand dogs left tied to pickets in the village. Two toddlers discovered in one of the abandoned lodges were also killed, their skulls bashed with tomahawks by Winnebago scouts.

The Indians had been severely punished, while their property loss had reduced them to a state of destitution. "Not the least of their losses was the exhaustion very largely of their supply of ammunition," commented one observer, "for upon this they must depend principally for their subsistence."[71] In a war intended to strike a blow at the Indians' will to resist and ability to survive through the region's notoriously hard winters, Sully was quoted as saying: "I would rather destroy their supplies than to kill fifty of their warriors."[72]

In the fights at Big Mound, Whiteside Hill, Dead Buffalo Lake, and Killdeer Mountain as well as in smaller engagements and skirmishes, the superior weapons of the U.S. forces were decisive. Even when some of Sibley and Sully's forces were confronted by superior numbers, the punitive forces used artillery to kill and disperse the enemy. Forerunners of the howitzers on display in Philadelphia a decade later were decisive in winning engagements. The hunting villages the punitive forces tracked and attacked also had to fight covering actions to protect the retreat of their women and children.

Following the Killdeer Battle, as Sully's forces pursued the fleeing Sioux across the Missouri and onto the western edge of the Badlands, the two sides again engaged in battle. After several days of skirmishes in the choking dust of the grassless buttes, a thirty-year-old Hunkpapa warrior called Sitting Bull engaged some of the Indian scouts serving with Sully in shouted conversation. Why were they fighting with the whites, Sitting Bull wanted to know. "You have no business with the soldiers," he told them. "The Indians here have no fight with the whites," he shouted to them. "Why is it the whites come to fight with the Indians?" In Sitting Bull's estimation, sovereignty over the country into which the punitive forces had penetrated lay entirely with its native owners. The soldiers were interlopers. If the whites would only recognize this simple truth, there need be no grounds for war. If they would not recognize it, Sitting Bull would resist all their efforts to encroach on the Lakota homeland.[73] Sitting Bull had articulated his people's sovereignty claims over Dakota territory. It was a view of sovereignty that was inimical to the westward pressure of American expansion, but one under which Sitting Bull and others would unite in unyielding and often resourceful resistance to incursions by miners, settlers, and the army itself.

Two summers of campaigning had exacted a high cost in Indian lives. And the forces of Sully and Sibley had inflicted another blow as well. When their columns of blue-clad soldiers withdrew, kicking up the dust of the dry prairies, they left in place companies of soldiers at established forts like Berthold and Union. More ominous yet, from the Lakota perspective, they began building new forts: Forts Sully, Rice, and most hateful of all, Fort Buford, which would become the focus of attacks by Hunkpapas led by Sitting Bull for four years after its construction on the Missouri River opposite the mouth of the Yellowstone in 1866.[74] Through punitive war and the establishment of offensive outposts, the frontier had been extended almost to Montana Territory. This was the frontier that Fort Abraham Lincoln—where Scott's new regiment, the Seventh Cavalry, was headquartered—was intended to secure and defend. The Sully and Sibley punitive campaigns fit into a well-established pattern for empires aiming to project sovereignty claims onto contested territory; they combined the rhetoric of punishment and retribution with the strategic objective of establishing control over territories that had previously been recognized as part of the Sioux domain.

From the Dakota Badlands in 1864 to the Yellowstone country a decade later, Sitting Bull's position did not waver: the incursion of white civilization with its farmers and railroads destroyed forests and drove away the wild game. It threatened the very existence of his people and it would be resisted, along with the government's insistence that they cede their lands, live within the reservations established for them, and take up farming in the white fashion. It would take Scott another four decades—and military and diplomatic experiences throughout the continent and on the other side of the world—to gain some perspective on the transformative historical forces at work in the activation of the frontier army in the Great Sioux War he was about to join. For now, Second Lieutenant Scott was attuned to the challenge of his first commission and the thrill of being on the threshold of the wild country that had captivated his imagination for so long.

Chapter 2

Scouting

From St. Paul it took Scott three days to make the trip across Minnesota to Dakota Territory, since the train traveled only during the day. In Fargo he borrowed a boat and spent a couple of days hunting ducks and prairie chickens. From Fargo to Bismarck, where the Great Northern Railroad came to an end, was another day's journey. Scott found Bismarck, mainly board shanties, to be very crude. He was struck there by the thought that "one might go a thousand miles west or travel north to the Arctic Circle with the probability of not seeing a human being."[1] This was pure fancy on Scott's part, of course. However remote it might have felt to a young man coming from the East, the region he was entering was not an empty land devoid of people. Quite the contrary, as he was about to discover.

No doubt Scott received some kind of advice and orientation from those he met at each of his stops on his journey west, though there is no record of what this might have been. Perhaps as important as any counsel he received as he journeyed to take up his first army assignment was the influence of a guide who had accompanied him through West Point, and who, even earlier, had interpreted for him the mysteries and majesties of Indian Country. As he would throughout his life, Scott carried with him a favorite work by the man he called "the great historian of the North," Francis Parkman. For ten thousand miles, wherever he went on the plains he took with him Parkman's *Conspiracy of Pontiac* in his pack basket. Even in the Philippines and Cuba, he reread Parkman's works "with perennial pleasure." Before he saw the "wild Missouri" with his own eyes, Parkman's prose had fired his imagination with an image of that mythic river. "Nowhere," Scott thought, had it been described so fitly and so beautifully as by Francis Parkman."[2] The historian's descriptions added interest—and meaning—to everything Scott was encountering in the country he had dreamed of since boyhood.

In fact, though born a generation apart, Scott and Parkman had much in common. Both came from genteel East Coast families in which clergymen figured prominently. Boyhood enthusiasm for the strenuous life out of doors led to unusually ambitious hunting expeditions in the remote West. While still young men, both moved in the social circles of leading scholars and scientists of their day. A generation earlier, also in his early twenties, Parkman's first foray west had taken him through the frontier posts of New York and Pennsylvania where he sought the historical detail, but above all, the authentic atmosphere of wild America with which to color his early works, such as *Conspiracy of Pontiac*.[3]

As he waited on the banks of the Missouri for the ferry to carry him across the river so that he could take up his post at Fort Abraham Lincoln, Parkman's prose had predisposed Scott to see in the landscape before him the primitive America he sought. With Parkman as his literary guide, he had in fact been prepared to arrive at the threshold of wild America with "a spirit attuned to understand it and to rejoice in becoming a part of its life."[4] For Parkman, and no less for Scott, the destinies of this "savage scenery" and the "savage men" who lived there were intertwined, one and the same. And both were doomed. "The Indian is a true child of the forest and the desert," wrote Parkman, "The wastes and solitude of Nature are his congenial home, his haughty mind is imbued with the spirit of the wilderness, and civilization sits upon him with a blighting power. His unruly mind and untamed spirit are in harmony with the lonely mountains and cataracts, among which he dwells, and primitive America, with her savage men and savage scenery, present to the imagination a boundless world, unmatched in wild sublimity."[5] Besides equipping the younger man with a romantic reading of Indian Country and an epic historical context in which to frame his own experience for the part he would play in its conquest, Parkman served as a kind of guide for Scott in two other important respects as well. His work served as an example of ethnological writing as a way of making sense of the world that mattered to literate men of the East. In addition to conducting his research among the documents he found in French and British archives and even traveling to defeated Richmond in 1865 to take possession of Confederate documents for the Boston Athenaeum, Parkman wrote in a way that conflated the natural historical writing of explorers like Henry Schoolcraft with the literary appeal of writers like Henry Wadsworth Longfellow and James Fenimore

Cooper. At the same time, Parkman was perceptive enough to recognize that politics, not just savage nature, played a role in Indian actions, something that was overlooked in most contemporary accounts of Indian life and warfare.

More importantly than the impact of Parkman's prose on the young man's imagination, Parkman suggested the rudiments of an ethnographic method that the young Scott admired and could emulate. In his preface to *Conspiracy of Pontiac*, Parkman explained his methodology (and personal predilection) for obtaining knowledge of "primitive life" through what would later come to be regularized by various ethnographically oriented sciences as participant-observation, in which "knowledge of a more practical kind has been supplied by the indulgence of a strong natural taste, which at various intervals, led me to the wild regions of the north and west. Here, by the camp-fire, or in the canoe, I gained acquaintance with the men and scenery of the wilderness. In 1846 I visited various primitive tribes of the Rocky Mountains, and was, for a time, domesticated in a village of the western Dhcotahh, on the high plains between Mount Laramie and the range of the Medicine Bow."[6] Entering the region whose scenery had been so romantically rendered by Parkman thirty years earlier, Scott, too, sought out opportunities to visit and "domesticate" himself in Indian villages and scout camps as a way of pursuing an interest in the language and customs of the various tribes among whom he lived and campaigned for the next quarter century. The habits of observation he developed on the plains he later employed as military governor of Sulu and also in Cuba and on the border with Mexico. His own observations of native Americans led him to modify Parkman's essentialist constructions of primitive men to a degree. Scott's intimacy with Native Americans complicated the proposition that Indians were fundamentally different from white men. From his close contact and dependence on scouts in the field, as well as from his interest in the language and culture of the people of the plains, Scott gradually learned to relate to the Arikaras, Crows, Cheyennes, and others with whom he worked and fought as men, not merely as Indians. With at least one of them, Kiowa Indian Scout Sergeant Iseeo at Fort Sill, Scott formed a friendship as deep, mutual, and enduring as any he made with a white man.[7] Throughout a lifetime of interaction with Indians and involvement in Indian affairs, first in the army and later as a member of the Board of Indian Commissioners, however, Scott never changed his belief that Indian cultures represented an earlier stage of civilization and that progress and the Indians' own best interests required that they change and adopt white ways. Scott applied such an evolutionary schema to assessing stages of development in Cuba and the Philippines as well.[8]

Crossing the Missouri River downriver from Bismarck, Scott reported to Fort Abraham Lincoln, the headquarters for the Seventh Cavalry, in September 1876. He found his new regiment in the midst of a major reorganization. Survivors of the Bighorn battle had only recently returned to the post. When he reached Fort Lincoln, Second Lieutenant Scott, along with eight other newly arrived junior officers, bedded down on the drawing-room floor of the house that had just been vacated by Elizabeth Custer. Within a short time, five hundred enlisted men and five hundred horses arrived at the post. Many of the new recruits turned out to be "Custer Avengers," men from the cities who were motivated to sign up by what Scott called the "stress of excitement of the Custer fight." As a young officer, he struggled with the indiscipline of this "rough lot," many of whom ended up deserting or being court-martialed.[9]

Besides preparing for a renewed campaign against the Lakota (Sioux) and Cheyenne in Montana, the soldiers also policed the Great Sioux Reservation on which the Seventh Cavalry was located, sixty miles upriver from the Standing Rock Agency. Their role was to chase and discipline Indians who "broke out" and to prevent them from joining the forces of open resistance to U.S. authority over the country. This work employed the same strategies that became central to the army's work of pacification in the Philippines and Cuba: concentration and surveillance of populations, strategic alliances to obtain intelligence and allies in war, and an emphasis on disarming those under their jurisdiction and taking away their horses. Some of Scott's first assignments away from the post were to enforce efforts by the army to confiscate weapons from Indians on the reservation. Fort Abraham Lincoln continued as the base for campaigns after hostile Indians in the West. The army defined as hostile Indians who defied the government's directive to report to an agency, renounce resistance, and adopt white ways, like farming, on the reservations.

Soon after arriving at Fort Lincoln, Scott determined that his best chance for advancement in the frontier army lay in becoming a commander of Indian scouts. Indian auxiliaries were just as important to the current campaign to contain and disarm Indian resistance to the encroachment of white civilization onto the prairies and mountainous West as they had been in earlier wars of imperial expansion in North America. As in George Washington's day, the success of American soldiers depended on maintaining strategic alliances with tribes with shared or complementary objectives. Indian scouts provided crucial information that was essential to the success of any campaign in the West: deep cultural knowledge, geographical knowledge, and highly developed observation skills.

The role of scouts in the military changed and gained new prominence following the Civil War, as the army shouldered the mission of policing areas of the trans-Mississippi West and the formerly Mexican domains of the Southwest, where incursions of white settlers threatened not just the vestiges of native self-determination, but Indian survival as well. As the army tried to negotiate the unfamiliar and forbidding terrain and climate of the plains and desert Southwest, as well as the complicated military and diplomatic challenges posed by their frontier missions, they turned for assistance to earlier arrivals in the West, men familiar with the physical and cultural landscape in which they now had to operate. As historian Louis Warren put it, the army needed indigenous scouts because "the soldiers who came to fight the Plains Indians so easily got lost in the strange grasslands."[10]

Army officers also needed scouts to serve as intermediaries between the military and Indians—both adversaries and allies. Not surprisingly, some of the most valuable scouts were "half-breeds," men whose joint European and Indian kinship gave them an advantage in moving between different cultures. Then there were the "squaw men," white men who had come to the plains as fur traders and hunters and who had married native women. Men such as Will Comstock, Abner "Sharp" Grover, John Y. Nelson, and Ben Clark all spoke one or more indigenous languages.[11] Clark, who was married to a Cheyenne woman, had been working as a scout and interpreter for the army for more than a decade when Scott met him in the late 1870s. Scott developed great respect for Clark, who he thought was unequaled among white scouts for his mastery of Plains Sign Language.[12] Such scouts also possessed knowledge of Indian social organization and customs that was of strategic value. At the same time, their role as intermediaries between cultures sometimes made them suspect to whites in the army and larger society, who found their transgressions of racial boundaries unsettling and even threatening.[13] "Scouts' intimacy with Indians and the frontier was thus a double-edged sword. It provided the army with keys to white conquest of the savage wilderness, but simultaneously, it implied the danger of race decline, in which the savagery of the frontier essentially conquered the race, turning white men against civilization."[14] A few white men, untainted by mixed-race marriage or ancestry, also served as scouts for the plains army in the 1860s, notably Frank North of Nebraska, who had become fluent in Pawnee while working as a clerk on the reservation and who organized three battalions of Pawnee scouts to fight alongside the army against the Cheyennes and Sioux.[15] In the Southwest, Charles B. Gatewood and John Bourke also fit this mold. Without question, the most famous white scout of this period was "Buffalo Bill" Cody. William F. Cody was a Civil War veteran who worked as a civilian scout for the army before launching his successful career as a showman. Cody's Wild West show presented an epic drama of the conquest of Indian country for audiences in the East—and even in Europe—who were eager consumers of mythic depictions of conquering Indians and settling the frontier.

Legendary figures such as Buffalo Bill notwithstanding, a majority of the scouts who fought with the army in its Indian Wars were other Indians. For the first two hundred years of their involvement in the wars and frontier skirmishes of the Anglo-Americans, native auxiliaries had remained outside the army's formal organization. By the 1850s a number of men in the army were advocating a more systematic organization of Indian auxiliaries. In 1852 Captain Randolph B. Marcy recommended attaching Delaware scouts and guides to each company of troops on the frontier. Captain George B. McClellan of the First Cavalry went a step further. Sent to Europe in 1855 to report on the Crimean War, he was so impressed by the Cossacks that he endorsed the potential use of "tribes of frontier Indians," who would serve as "partisan troops fully equal to the Cossacks in both Indian and 'civilized' warfare."[16] In 1866 Congress authorized the formal enlistment of scouts. Though it limited Indian service to "the Territories and Indian country," the Army Reorganization Act incorporated Indians into the structure of the army for the first time. Scouts could enlist for periods ranging from three months to one year. They received the pay and allowance of cavalry soldiers and their duties were determined by the military district commander. The highest rank available to Indians was that of sergeant.[17] The same legislation also organized six all-black regiments for deployment in the West, including the Ninth and Tenth Cavalry, more famously known as "Buffalo Soldiers." Both African American and Indian troops were to be commanded by white officers.[18]

Indians rendered service to the military as scouts for a number of reasons. Some sought alliances with the expanding power. In return for acting as guides and interpreters and sometimes for fighting, scouts obtained guns and other goods. Their relationship to the army offered opportunities for taking booty from enemies they helped the Americans fight. Horses and other livestock provided a particularly desirable form of compensation for Plains Indians who accompanied the bluecoats into battle. No less importantly, Native people were motivated to join forces with the Americans for diplomatic reasons, in an attempt to stave off destructive wars or otherwise influence the destinies of their people and the other tribes around them. Until the Civil War, however, scouts were attached to, but did not form an integral part of the army. This was generally true of white scouts also, such as William Cody, who always scouted for the army as a civilian.

Besides the possibilities for professional advancement, Scott also relished the autonomy and scope for personal initiative that working with Indians in the army afforded a junior officer. He later compared being a commander of Indian Scouts in the frontier army to being an aviator in the Twenties and Thirties; "one could always be ahead of the command, away from the routine that was irksome, and sure to have a part in all the excitement," he wrote.[19]

In his early days with the Seventh Cavalry, Scott chafed at any assignment that threatened to tie him down in camp or involved responsibility for the transportation of heavy equipment or supplies. As he saw it, he had not "undergone five years of toil at West Point to come out to the Plains to be a wagon soldier." He had "come west to be a flying cavalryman . . . [not to] travel at a walk behind the column."[20]

In the beginning, Scott applied himself to learning the language of the Lakota Sioux, on whose reservation Fort Lincoln was located. He reasoned that since the Lakota were the dominant group on the northern plains, their language would function as a kind of "court language," like Latin or French. This assumption was reinforced by the fact that the Arikara scouts attached to the regiment all spoke it. He thus began to study the language under their tutelage. He quickly discovered that while the Lakota's language did not function in this way and was of limited use to him in communicating with other groups, there did exist a lingua franca on the plains: sign language. Scott continued his study of sign language throughout his time on the plains. By the time of his assignment to the Bureau of Ethnology in 1897, he was acknowledged as the white man—in or out of the army—with the most knowledge and expertise in signing.[21]

On his first expedition away from the fort, Scott was given an assignment to form a battery out of some muzzle-loading guns and some cavalry horses that were no longer fit to ride. His task was to train the horses and men in his troop to move and handle the battery. Scott chafed at this onerous assignment and instead arranged with his friend Lieutenant Luther Hare to take command of the battery along with his own troop while Scott took every opportunity to travel with the Arikira scouts, who broke camp before daylight and rode out in advance of the soldiers, "covering the country far in front as carefully as pointer-dogs in search of quail."[22] Scouting also gave him the opportunity to hunt, which he loved. He attributed his commanders' continued acquiescence in his absence from the column in part to their appreciation of the loads of prairie chicken, snipe, and ducks he brought back to camp. "The procurement of game made [the Colonel] more willing to let me go ahead with the scouts . . . and it soon became a matter of course for me to leave the battery with Hare, my superior, in command, and go off with the scouts before daylight every day."[23] He spent as much time as he could in the company of scouts, either riding with them and learning from observation how they operated or pursuing his study of language in their villages and scout camps.

In the spring of 1877, two battalions of the Seventh Cavalry were sent west to join the army's renewed campaigns against the Sioux and Cheyenne in Yellowstone Country. Miles's Fifth Infantry had been campaigning in this remote country all winter. Following the rout of the Seventh Cavalry that June, General Philip Sheridan had planned "total war" against the Sioux from his headquarters in Chicago. Colonel Miles, in particular, did not intend to "hibernate" for the winter by holing up in a fort or cantonment. Instead, he believed that "a winter campaign could be successfully made against those Northern Indians, even in that extreme cold climate."[24] With troops augmented by civilian "Custer Avengers" and the full support of a Congress and nation prepared to pay any price "to end Sioux troubles for all time," Miles led the Fifth Infantry in pursuit of hunting bands into the winter hunting grounds of Montana's forbidding terrain.[25] Following the hostilities of the summer, the matter uppermost in the minds of tribes as they dispersed along rivers to the east of the battleground was hunting to secure food and buffalo hides for the winter.[26] They viewed the return of soldiers to the region with alarm and some puzzlement. It was not the accustomed season for war. In October, Sitting Bull left a note in the path of a wagon train carrying supplies intended for Miles's winter garrison on the Tongue River that read:

> I want to know what you are doing traveling on this road. You scare all the buffalos away. I want to hunt in this place. I want you to turn back from here. If you don't I will fight you again. I want you to leave what you have got here and turn back from here.

I am your friend,

Sitting Bull

I mean all the rations you have got and some powder. Wish you would write as soon as you can.[27]

About a week later, Colonel Miles with the entire Fifth Infantry overtook Sitting Bull near Cedar Creek, Montana, north of the Yellowstone River. Over the course of two days, Miles met in council with Sitting Bull and other Lakota leaders: Pretty Bear, Bull Eagle, Standing Bear, Gall, and White Bear. Bent on provisioning their people for the winter and alarmed by the incursion of soldiers into their hunting country, the chiefs sought a truce for the winter. Sitting Bull made clear to Miles that their objective in the territory was to hunt buffalo and trade for ammunition. He did not want rations or annuities, but rather to live free and hunt in the open country. In return he offered that their side would not fire on the soldiers if they were left to hunt unmolested. Miles later reported that the Hunkpapa chief had asked him "why the soldiers did not go to winter quarters." Miles rejected what he termed "an old-fashioned peace for the winter."[28] He informed Sitting Bull and the other principal men who had met in council with him that this offer was not acceptable to the government. Nothing short of his surrender at an agency and submission of his people to U.S. authority could stave off a war through the winter. Miles later expressed his view that "it was amusement for them to raid and make war during summer, but when constant relentless war was made upon them in the severest of winter campaigns it became serious and most destructive."[29]

Determined to follow the Indians wherever they went, Miles fitted his men out with improvised winter gear, including leggings and mittens as well as face masks cut from woolen blankets.[30] As the winter and the relentless raiding of Indian camps by the soldiers wore on, additional warm clothing was fashioned out of some of the hundreds of buffalo robes that were looted from the sacked encampments of the Lakota. A raid on Sitting Bull's camp led by Frank D. Baldwin near the Milk River in December captured several hundred buffalo robes, which were fashioned into pants, overcoats, and caps by Cheyenne women who had capitulated. These were worn by Miles's troops as they launched a January offensive up the Tongue River, where the Lakotas had gone in pursuit of the buffalo. This was the winter they gave Miles the name "Man-with-the-bear-coat." Since the soldiers had looted or destroyed their lodges, utensils, tons of dried meat, and many horses and mules, they were both in need of fresh supplies and demoralized by the constant harrying presence of the soldiers.[31]

In November Colonel Ranald S. Mackenzie had also dealt a devastating blow to the Cheyennes, raiding the village of Dull Knife (Morning Star) and Little Wolf, which consisted of about two hundred lodges in a canyon on the Red Fork of the Powder River. Thirty Cheyennes were killed in the raid. Those who survived were left with only what they could carry away. The soldiers burned the village and everything in it: meat, clothing, and all the tribe's finery and art work. Seven hundred ponies were confiscated by the army. As the survivors fled north to seek refuge with Crazy Horse on the Tongue River, temperatures fell to thirty below zero. Eleven babies froze to death.[32]

Throughout the winter, the army's campaigners pursued their quarry through the snow, across the frozen Missouri River. Facing starvation, killing cold, and the perpetual threat of the "long knives" of the U.S. Army wreaking havoc on their villages and threatening their families, many leaders made the decision to surrender to their agencies, where they were forced to give up their guns and thousands of horses. Red Horse explained the pressures that led him to surrender at the Cheyenne River Agency in February 1877. "I am tired of being always on the watch for troops. My desire is to get my family where they can sleep without being continually in the expectation of an attack."[33]

By March only about fifteen lodges remained with Sitting Bull. Others had already crossed into Canada and Sitting Bull was considering this as an alternative to surrender or to continued harassment by the bluecoats. In May, around the time Scott was heading west with the Seventh Cavalry, Sitting Bull crossed the border with 135 Lakota lodges, totaling about a thousand people.

The anniversary of Custer's defeat the previous year found Scott on the Big Horn battlefield, where his troop was assigned the task of recovering the bones of Custer and the other officers who had died there for reburial elsewhere as well as reburying the best they could the remains of others, which had been exposed by erosion in the intervening year. Following this detail, Scott and the rest of his troop reunited with their regiment near Fort Keogh on the Yellowstone. "The whole of the Northwest seemed very peaceable and the talk of the Seventh was that we should soon go back to Fort Lincoln. Everybody built sunshades over their tents and generally made themselves comfortable," Scott recalled.[34]

Soon, however, word of hostilities erupting between the army and several Nez Percé tribal groups, who were being forced from their lands in Eastern Oregon, reached the command on the Yellowstone. As a Nez Percé group of some 250 warriors and 500 women and children along with thousands of horses and other livestock began an arduous trek through some of the wildest and most challenging terrain in the country, the Seventh Cavalry was split up and sent in various directions in an attempt to stop Chief Joseph and his dispossessed people from reaching sanctuary, like Sitting Bull, with the Canadian "Grandmother" across the border.

During the summer of 1877, Scott deepened his experience of working with scouts. He also developed an abiding interest in the way of life and customs of the indigenous nations with which the army brought him in contact. In July Miles sent him out to search for a Sioux war party on the Musselshell rumored to have come down from Canada. Scott accompanied some Northern Cheyenne scouts who had fought against Custer the previous summer and had only recently surrendered. The party included Two Moons, Little Chief, Hump, Black Wolf, Ice (or White Bull), Brave Wolf, and White Bear. Scott's friends warned him against accompanying them, saying they would kill him and escape across the border to Canada, but Scott did not share these fears. Instead, he admired and learned from the Cheyenne warriors: "They were all keen, athletic young men, tall and lean and brave, and I admired them as real specimens of manhood more than any body of men I have ever seen before or since. They were perfectly adapted to their environment and knew just what to do in every emergency and when to do it, without any confusion or lost motion. Their poise and dignity were superb; no royal person ever had more assured manners. I watched their every movement and learned lessons from them that later saved my life many times on the prairie."[35]

Scott also spent a lot of time with Crow scouts and observing life in the large Crow villages. On one occasion, exposure to the heat and insects of a Montana summer, against which his army issue tent provided insufficient protection, led him to seek hospitality in the lodge of Iron Bull. Seeking respite from sun, dust, and flies, Scott presented himself at the entrance of the huge buffalo-hide lodge of the Crow chief. The hide lodge cover, which was made in two pieces from the hides of twenty-five buffalo, was well smoked from the fire, so that the sun did not penetrate. Scott estimated the poles supporting the covering to be twenty-five feet long and five inches in diameter. It took six horses to transport them. Entering the lodge, Scott wrote, was like "passing at once into a new world." Inside, it was cool and there were no flies. "Beds of buffalo robes were all around the wall, and the floor was swept clean as the palm of one's hand." Addressing Iron Bull, who was lying on his back in bed wearing only a breechclout, Scott said, "Brother, I want to come and stay in here with you until we leave." Accordingly, Scott abandoned the porous white canvas of his "bit of a tent," and instead was made "most welcome" in the lodge of the Crow chief and his wife.[36]

On this and other occasions, Scott paid close attention to the village life taking place around him. Besides providing ethnographic information and military intelligence, Indian village life on the prairie was a source of intense interest and often delight. During the summer of 1877, he traveled with a large village of Crow Indians near the Big Bend of the Musselshell. Encompassing about three thousand people from various mountain and river bands of Crows, the camp moved often to find grass for their large herd of horses. They hunted buffalo about once a week to provide meat for such a large group. Scott was fascinated by the great village and the life he observed there:

> The camp had meat drying everywhere. Everybody was care-free and joyous in a way we do not comprehend in this civilized day. All the life of a nation was going on there before our eyes. Here the head chiefs were receiving ambassadors from another tribe. Following the sound of drums, one would come upon a great gathering for a war-dance, heralding an expedition to fight the Sioux. Or one came to a lodge where a medicine-man was doctoring a patient to the sound of a drum and rattle. Elsewhere a large crowd surrounded a game of ring and spear, on which members of the tribe were betting everything they owned: the loser lost without dispute or quiver of an eyelid. In another place a crowd was witnessing a horse race with twenty-five horses starting off at the first trial. . . . All day and far into the night there was something happening of intense interest to me.[37]

After the army, led by Nelson Miles, finally caught up with Chief Joseph and the exhausted bands of Nez Percé in the foothills of the Bears Paw mountains and fought them to defeat, Scott spent time in the Big Open country of Montana searching for Nez Percé who had escaped capture. From Fort Buford to Bismarck—225 miles along the Missouri River—Scott's Troop I served as an escort for Chief Joseph and the Nez Percé prisoners who were being transported to the end of the railroad to be shipped to prison from Bismarck by rail. In spite of Miles's promise to Chief Joseph that he and his people would spend the winter at the Tongue River Cantonment and then return to the Pacific Northwest in the spring, they were not allowed back to their homeland.

Instead, they were forced to go to Fort Leavenworth. After a terrible winter at Fort Leavenworth, they were sent first to the Quapaw Reservation in Indian Territory (present-day northern Oklahoma), which they called "Eikish Pah" or hot place. Chief Joseph remained in exile until his death in 1904.[38]

From a Nez Percé called Tippit, Scott was able to learn some Chinook, an intertribal language used on the Columbia River and up the Pacific Coast. As they rode along the Musselshell River toward its confluence with the Missouri, where the Seventh Cavalry was camped, Scott induced Tippit to pose questions in Chinook followed by answers aimed at conveying their English translations.[39] On the same trip, he spent time in the wagons with Sioux and Cheyenne scouts, working on improving both spoken and sign language. Another part of each day he spent in Chief Joseph's wagon, along with a Nez Percé translator from Idaho named Arthur Chapman. During a stop at Fort Berthold, members of the Hidatsa, Mandan, and Gros Ventre tribes gathered in a large council to learn of the tribulations of Chief Joseph, who spoke in sign language to some fifteen hundred people representing eight different languages (Nez Percé, Cheyenne, Sioux, Crow, Mandan, Arikara, Gros Ventre of the Village, and English). Scott wrote that Chief Joseph was "completely understood by all that vast concourse."[40]

A couple of months after returning to Fort Lincoln for the winter, Scott resumed his study of the sign language under the tutelage of White Bear and other members of the Cheyenne band captured by Miles the previous year, who had been brought as prisoners to spend the winter at the post. Scott visited the Cheyenne prisoners' village regularly. There, in exchange for his language lessons, he subsidized White Bear with coffee, sugar, and other rations. During one visit to the Indian camp, White Bear told Scott that the group was planning to run away that night to go back to the buffalo country leaving all their lodges standing. He complained that the rations their families were issued for ten days were not sufficient to feed them even for three. Therefore, they had packed their belongings and were prepared to make a break. Not entirely believing what he was hearing, Scott moved as casually as he could among other lodges of the village and confirmed that, indeed, the Cheyennes had packed up their movable property and were preparing to leave. Scott quickly returned to the post and reported the plans for escape to his commanding officer. A squadron of cavalry were then dispatched to guard the camp and prevent them from leaving as planned. Scott received formal commendation for his discovery of the planned escape and for his "knowledge of the Indian's character, his human nature, his method and thought of action, and of the Indian Sign Language."[41]

Scott's growing reputation as an interpreter and as a man who knew Indian character led to an assignment the following year as an interpreter for the army in its dealings with the Oglala chief Red Cloud, who had broken away without permission from his agency, taking the agency beef herd along with him. In reality, Scott's assignment was to keep Red Cloud under observation and discover what had upset him and what his intentions were. Under these strained circumstances, Scott spent three days in Red Cloud's lodge, essentially as a spy. Even though he was at best an imposed guest, Scott found Red Cloud to be "the picture of hospitality." The two men passed the time conversing in sign language. Scott wrote about the incident in his memoirs: "Red Cloud was an excellent sign talker, but he made his gestures differently from any one I had ever seen before or since. While each was perfectly distinct, they were all made within the compass of a circle a foot in diameter, whereas they are usually made in the compass of a circle two and a half feet in diameter. We talked about everything under the sun, but he would not give me any clue to what made him so ill-humored, and to what was actuating his young men."[42] Scott learned much later that Red Cloud's flight from the reservation had been triggered by the mobilization of army troops from Fort Laramie and several other points to rendezvous near Pine Ridge. Fearing that the troops were coming to arrest him, Red Cloud had fled with around five thousand of his community and they remained suspicious of and angry with the whites for the harassment and aggression they experienced.

In the parlance of modern anthropology, Scott gained his knowledge of Indian language and culture through participant-observation. He was not alone in valuing the kind of knowledge to be gained by such methods, nor in pursuing it, but the science of ethnology, as it was called at the time, was in its infancy. It was more concerned with the study of kinship and theorizing the stages of human progress, such as those on display at the Centennial Exposition, and not so developed as it would become with respect to what we now recognize as the ethnographic method. Yet Scott and a handful of other officers were practicing it in the context of the army's work with Indians on the frontier.[43]

Scott's ethnographic techniques were not limited to the study of sign language; he extended his close and critical observation to the landscape and culture of Native North America more generally. Observations and analysis of the behaviors of animals, including other humans, were part of the repertoire of the scout, providing valuable tactical knowledge of the surroundings in which the complex strategies of assessing, anticipating, and pursuing the enemy were carried out. By learning to recognize the differences in the grazing habits and differing behaviors among herd animals such as horses, cattle, and buffaloes, for example, Scott was able to gain clues about the proximity and actions of other groups of people associated with the animals, such as the Crows. Scott felt that the cultivation of such techniques of reading the landscape separated him from soldiers on the frontier who never learned to read such signs. "Many were first-rate garrison soldiers, who knew their drill, took good care of their men, and who never made a mistake in their muster-rolls," he wrote. "But [they] were blind on the prairie."[44]

Scott proceeded on the idea that every action had a motive that could be discerned. As a hunter he had long studied the laws governing the actions of various animals. Scott believed that all animals were governed by "laws of their nature that compel each kind to do the same thing under the same circumstances." Some of these he prided himself on learning through his own observation, for example, those governing the behavior of rabbits and ducks. The laws governing the movement of black bears, mountain sheep, and black-tailed deer he learned from watching the movements of Crows, Caddos, Sioux, and Cheyenne while hunting. He also believed there was a motive for human actions, which could be discerned. Indians, however, according to Scott, could not themselves articulate the reasons they hunted these animals in certain ways. The only way of learning these secrets lay in Scott's close observation and analysis. "They cannot give one their reasons for doing certain things," he wrote. "The only means of learning lies in close observation." He expounded on this theory in his book. Indians were not always able to recognize the motives for their own actions, but he believed that he could ascertain them by posing questions and by observing and analyzing their behavior.[45] An example of this method at work is in Scott's account of how he went about finding out what made a good buffalo-hunting horse in the Crows' estimation. Scott's inquiry into this topic, which was of existential importance to people who depended on the buffalo, began by close observation of the methods of hunting. Scott also asked questions, and in at least one case, provoked discussion among his informants so that he could learn from their exchange of ideas. In 1877, while traveling with the Crows, he instigated a debate among the chiefs in council as to who had the best buffalo horse. "After a week it was determined that Iron Bull Chief of the Montana Crows had him, and on the next run I borrowed him to find out what a really fine buffalo horse was like," Scott wrote. After riding the best buffalo horse, Scott went on to borrow the second best and so on "until I had ridden twenty-five out of the cream of over 12,000 head—the great majority of which were pack horses and mares and colts." From this experience, Scott noted some significant points about what made a good buffalo horse: "He did not have to be fought with like our [cavalry] horses. All he needed was to be pointed at the animal selected; then he would take one so close that one could put his hand on the buffalo's back if one wished."[46] In his memoirs, Scott reflected wryly that he must have been a "sore trial" to the native informants whom he badgered over the years, "boring away at a subject they were unable to elucidate" until he had found the motive, which Scott thought they were often unable to formulate themselves.[47]

In the beginning, Scott's interest in ethnographic knowledge was instrumentalist. In particular, he applied himself to acquiring a mastery of sign lan-

Figure 3. Hunting party on the Washita River in the Kiowa-Comanche-Apache Reservation. The group includes Hugh Lenox Scott (standing, third from left), Mary Scott (seated in front of him), Lieutenant Oscar Charles (seated on the ground next to Mary). Also pictured are General Nelson Miles and Frank Baldwin, who was then the Indian agent at Anadarko. Prints and Photographs Division, Library of Congress.

guage and other languages as a means of furthering his career in the army and securing more satisfying work for himself as well as winning respect and stature. However, Scott quickly became interested in learning all that he could about Indians. What began as a strategy to achieve advancement and autonomy developed into a profound lifelong interest in indigenous languages and customs.

In 1889 Scott was assigned to Troop M of the Seventh Cavalry at Fort Sill in what was then Indian Territory. Scott's tenure at Fort Sill coincided with a transformation of the role of Indians in the army. Although still referred to as scouts, after 1891 Native men were enlisted directly in the army. In each of the twenty-six regiments of Infantry and Cavalry serving west of the Mississippi *except for the black units*, one company or troop was reorganized as an all-Indian unit. Thus, Troop L of the Seventh Cavalry, a unit ironically wiped out at the Battle of Little Big Horn, was reconstituted at Fort Sill in 1891 as an Indian Scout troop. Initially, all officers were white, although later Indians served as noncommissioned officers. From June 1891 to May 1897, Troop L was composed of a majority of Kiowas, Comanches, and Apaches. After 1894, some of the Apache prisoners who had been resettled from Florida and Alabama to Fort Sill also served in Troop L under Scott's command.[48]

By the time he made the move to Oklahoma, Scott was widely recognized as an expert on sign language both within and outside the army. Scott was one of a number of frontier officers who kept up a correspondence with the Bureau of Ethnology after its founding in 1879 under the direction of John Wesley Powell. He also wrote to missionaries and corresponded with foreign experts on sign language, such as Ernest Thompson Seton, the British artist and author who founded the Woodland Indians to promote woodcraft and scouting among white boys. When Seton wrote his book *Sign Language for Scouting*, he sent a copy to Scott for his comments. "I hope you will scribble as freely as you feel disposed on the [manuscript]," Seton wrote to him. "Of course you know I attach the greatest importance to everything you say about sign language. You are admitted to be the greatest living authority on the sign language of the Indians."[49] Perhaps the Englishman was engaging in some strategic flattery, but in fact, there were few nonnative signers who shared Scott's interest, experience, and facility with the language. In addition to Scott's study of vocabulary, he also wrote thoughtfully on the structure of the sign language and analyzed how its properties were analogous to those of spoken language. He recognized sign language as a living, evolving language, with its own rules and grammar, although he persisted in fitting it into a hierarchy of languages in which some (like the sign language) were primitive and some were more advanced. Scott's thinking about the evolution of increasingly complex language was consistent with prevailing racial ideas, such as those informing the exhibitions at the Centennial Exposition.[50]

Soon after arriving at Fort Sill, Scott was detailed by the post commander to study the religious movement known as the Ghost Dance among the Indians of western Indian Country. In December 1890 the War Department commissioned him to investigate the meaning and causes of the movement and assess whether it constituted a danger to white settlers, who had become alarmed by the rumors of possible uprisings linked to the new craze. From 1890 through February 1891, Scott visited camps in the vicinity of Fort Sill, observed dances, and interviewed practitioners about the meaning and power of the religion and its rituals.[51]

To carry out these inquiries among eight tribes in the western part of Indian Territory, Scott recruited several Indian soldiers from Troop L, including Sergeant Iseeo, who became one of Scott's closest associates and collaborators in his ethnographic work. In addition to Iseeo, the investigating party included several enlisted Indian soldiers who served as orderly, scout, cook, and driver. So as not to alarm the Ghost Dancers they visited, the group traveled under the guise of being a hunting party, obscuring the true interests of their expedition.[52] Of course, at the same time Scott was leading his ethnographic fact-finding tour through Oklahoma, preoccupation with the Ghost Dance was reaching a crisis point among whites on and near the Sioux Reservation to the north. In fact, as Scott's undercover ethnographers gathered information and formed an impression of the movement on the southern plains, the largest army assembled since the Civil War was converging on the Sioux agencies from around the country. By the end of December, overreaction to the religious movement had led to the tragic killing of more than 250 Lakota as well as a number of soldiers of the Seventh Cavalry when they attempted to disarm Big Foot's Minnecounjous on Wounded Knee Creek.

In contrast to the semi-hysterical view of some in the civil Indian service and many anxious settlers around the reservations, who worried that the vision of a world in which whites had been replaced by resurgent buffalo would be sought through violence against them, Scott's conclusion was that the dance was purely religious and posed no threat. "These songs and the dance itself are of a purely religious character," he wrote. "Being a prayer to and worship of the same Jesus the white man worships and who has come down in the North." As far as threatening violence to whites in order to bring about the prophecy of a restoration of buffalo and the return of dead relatives, Scott wrote: "The doctrine of the separation of races, the red man from the white called for no action on the part of the former, it was to be accomplished by supernatural means alone Jesus was to do it all that the red man had to do was to push this dance and stand by see it done and reap the benefits."[53] Scott counseled that the dance be allowed to run its course without interference, "that the whole structure would fall from nonfulfilment of the prophesies."[54]

Scott wrote up the findings of his ethnographic hunting trip in a paper for the Fort Sill Lyceum the following winter. Several things emerge from this report. One is Scott's wry and ironic sense of humor. Commenting on the wide appeal of the Ghost Dance prophecy of the resurrection of dead relatives and their return to earth, Scott noted an exception to the general happiness at the prospect of being reunited with lost dear ones. "These tidings brought great joy to all who heard them," he wrote. "Except to Tabananaca the Comanche Chief who did not relish the idea of furnishing all his departed relatives with horses from his large herd."[55]

Scott's report is also notable for the level of detail and nuanced and contextualized ethnographic description it provides. Take, for example, his description of the ritual at the center of the controversy over the movement, the dance itself. First, he provided a precise description, revealing both attentive observation and his ability to convey the details of unfamiliar practice in understandable terms.

> Our first view of the dance was at a small Kiowa Camp in the northern foot hills of the Wichita Mountains; there nicely sheltered from the cold winds from the north in a timbered bend of Sulphur Creek was found the village, the lodges arranged in the shape of a horse_shoe. When we arrived there were gathered together in a ring in the open space in the centre of the horse_shoe about fifty people having hold of each others hands the fingers interlocked dancing with a peculiar side step. the mechanism of which seems to be : first the weight of the body being on the right leg the right knee is bent lowering the body slightly then a short step is made to the left with the left foot, the weight is then transferred to the left leg which is immediately straightened,the right foot brought to the side of the left and the weight again placed upon the right leg,this is repeated continuously all keeping time to the singing.[56]

To this he added his own analysis and commentary on the dance.

> The music of these songs is unique and distinctive; none of us had
> ever heard anything precisely like it. The Messiah songs could be
> distinguished at once from the war songs or those used at the "wo-
> kowie" feasts or sun dances by the character of the music even if
> the words and air were unknown. There was a great variety to the
> songs, some owing to the minor key in which they were sung were
> very weird some were low rich and beautiful but all had a certain
> monotony owing to the fact that each line was repeated and the
> song itself sung over and over again in making each round of the
> circle: yet all were pleasing one especially delighting us, it gave all
> the impressions of a noble chant and when sung by a large con-
> course of people in the moonlight with the wild surroundings the
> peculiar accompaniment of the crying and the solemn dance, its
> effect was most striking and will never be forgotten by those who
> heard it.[57]

Scott made sense of the landscape and the work before him by recourse to
another nineteenth-century heuristic for knowing and classifying the natural
world: collecting. The nineteenth century gave rise to all kinds of colonial collecting. From geology to folklore, amateurs with natural curiosity and a scientific bent searched places both familiar and remote for everything from fossils
to birds' nests.

As would be the case later in the Philippines and Cuba, Scott's early attempts to know his surroundings and to make sense of them relied heavily on
classifying and articulating the similarities and differences among classes of
things, creating a typology and then elaborating and refining it. Thus, an early
letter home to his mother from Fort Lincoln bragged that in his first year in
the Northwest he had seen "nearly all" the Indians with whom the army had
dealings. He proceeded to provide a typology for his mother, clearly informed
by his own cultural categories and values and also attuned—one suspects—
to his knowledge of his mother's prejudices. "The Cheyennes are the Indians
I like. The braves—cleaner and more manly in every way than any I've seen
in the Northwest and I've seen nearly all of them—the Nez Perces are too
much like the Crows and of all horrible cowardly wretches the Crows are the
worst—the Nez Perces are not cowardly, but in stature, appearance dress hair

& filth they are very much alike—the Yanktonais Siouxs don't pan out well or the Assiniboines or the Rees Mandans or Gros Ventres—the Cheyennes beat them all."[58] Confident of his young man's ability to judge types of men, although he had as yet little knowledge of them, his early assessments reflected most of all the prejudices of the East and of the civilization from which Scott came. To a great extent, Scott's close and interested association with Native peoples over the next two decades of service in Indian Country led him to move away from such crude typologies. With more experience with Indian scouts and more time spent actively seeking ethnographic knowledge for strategic military purposes in Indian villages, Scott's knowledge progressed increasingly beyond such superficial and impressionistic typologies. What started out as little more than a cataloging of tribes in a way that reinscribed the stereotypes and prejudices available to him through the dominant Indian-hating culture, developed over time into a more finely tuned ethnographic sensibility. Interestingly, he later wrote not just with sensitivity but with admiration of the village life of the Crows in particular, the group that seems to have provoked the disdainful assessment he expressed in his letter to his mother during his first winter in Indian Country.

Scott's penchant for classifying and collecting, on the other hand, increased over time. Like many soldiers, Scott had a taste for exotic memorabilia and trophies collected in the field. He collected artifacts for their intrinsic curiosity value as well as with awareness of their more practical exchange value in his own society. Half a century after the event, he ruefully recounted the loss of six fine Crow buffalo robes lost in the course of trading duties with another officer during the Nez Percé campaign.[59] The most significant collecting Scott did was carried out during the nine years he spent at Fort Sill in Oklahoma (1889–97). His home at Fort Sill became a veritable museum of artifacts of all kinds, from feather work to pottery to hides and weapons.

Several years after Scott's return from Oklahoma to the East, a collection of 124 artifacts he had collected during his time in the Southwest was acquired by Phoebe Hearst (mother of William Randolph Hearst) and became the foundation for the collection of the Phoebe A. Hearst Museum of Anthropology at the University of California, Berkeley. The objects sold to Mrs. Hearst were all things he had collected from the Kiowa and Apaches, including clothing, cooking and household objects, ceremonial calendars, and baskets, as well as shields, clubs, bows, and arrows.[60]

Scott carried his enthusiasm for collecting to Cuba and the Philippines.

Figure 4. Artifacts on display in Scott's Fort Sill home. Prints and Photographs Division, Library of Congress.

Like other soldiers abroad, he collected and sent home trophies. In a nod to his guru Parkman, he described some medals and military decorations he sent his wife from Cuba as "spoil of the Spaniard" (and cautioned her not to wear them anywhere she was likely to encounter any Europeans). In addition to a set of Cuban stocks he sent to Woodrow Wilson at Princeton, he also collected weapons in the Philippines.

Without question, the most significant collecting Scott did was his work to record legends, history, and linguistic information from the people of the southern plains during his nine years at Fort Sill, detailing several of the scouts in his troop to travel to villages in a large region around the fort tracking down words, signs, and stories. The ledgers he compiled at Fort Sill have survived as a unique source of ethnographic information collected through the medium of sign language about the life and history of the Kiowa, Comanche, and other peoples interviewed in the vicinity of the Fort.[61] He also used the tours of inspection of Indian reservations on which the Board of Indian Commissioners sent him to continue his studies of culture and language in the 1920s.

In the research he began at the Bureau of Ethnology after leaving Fort Sill in 1897, Scott tracked down a few scanty observations on sign language in the records of European explorers dating back to the expeditions of Álvar Núñez Cabeza de Vaca and Francisco Vásquez de Coronado in the mid-sixteenth century. He also studied the journals of the Lewis and Clark expedition looking for evidence of the Corps of Discovery's awareness of the use of this lingua franca among many of the Native nations they encountered on their trek up the Missouri. Scott was struck by how little notice earlier colonizers had taken of sign language. In an early draft for the book he never completed, he wrote: "I have always been amazed at the little attention the Singlangue has received in the past especially soldiers and explorers—for it is certainly a wonderful language and most useful to the above classes—for 200 years—but instead of perfecting themselves in its use they have merely left a reference apparently to show that they knew of its existence—this is the more remarkable in the case of Lewis & Clark 1804–6 whose was directed by President Jefferson to investigate every thing they found that was new and interesting."[62] Besides the history of sign language, its spread throughout the central plains region, and its military and diplomatic utility, Scott was also interested in it as a linguistic phenomenon. He faulted others who had written on the subject with failing to recognize it as a natural language "subject to all the general laws of linguistic science, save those of sound ... [having] its own place in the hierarchy of all human speech, akin to all through our common humanity."[63]

Even though Scott had an appreciation for the adaptability and expressiveness of sign language, he nonetheless theorized it as representing a simple root stage of language, analogous to the primitive germ out of which more advanced languages, such as Indo-European speech "with all its fullness and inflective suppleness," had descended over generations. In this he seems to have been influenced by the views of the evolution of complex language put forward in the work of Yale University philologist William Whitney.[64]

Scott's research for his book on sign language was cut short by the start of the Spanish-American War. By his own account, he then became "engaged for years in matters more important to [his] career than writing any book."[65] There is evidence that he continued to think about the project, however, even when he was in the Philippines. In a letter to his wife written when he was governor of Sulu in 1905, Scott asked Mary to send him some books on linguistics. Specifically, he asked her to buy a book on "deaf & mute language showing its structure etc—not of the artificial alphabetic language but the natural language of the deaf." He wrote that Dr. Gallaudet of Washington could help identify the kind of thing he was interested in. He also asked her to send him several other books that he had used to prepare a talk General Nelson Miles had asked him to give on sign language at the Columbian Exposition in Chicago in 1893. These included works on linguistics by Max Müller, F. W. Farrar, and A. H. Sayce. "I seem to want to know something about the real essence of spoken language," Scott explained to his wife, "but the thing has become dim & I am in the mood for it now if I had the books—as it all bears on sign language more or less."[66] Several letters requesting materials from libraries in Texas suggest he had renewed efforts on his research again during the time he was stationed in San Antonio in 1911 and 1912 with the Third Cavalry.[67]

Scott's interest in sign language had its origin in his passion for scouting and his ambition to make himself useful to commanding officers and to the frontier army, which he did. As that same army faced the challenges of an expanding overseas empire, Scott would continue to be called on to put his scouting skills to work—on the new frontiers of that empire in Cuba and the Philippines, and eventually back on the border with Mexico.

Chapter 3

The Right Kind of White Men

" It was your handkerchief that saved you," the leader of the Mexican Rural Guards told him. Second Lieutenant Robert Lee Bullard stood frozen with fear inside the rim of a mountain crater in Sonora as three *Rurales* kept their rifles trained on him. While the Yaqui Indians attached to the Fourth Cavalry's expedition south of the border were away from camp searching for signs of Geronimo and his band of Chiricahua Apaches, Lieutenant Bullard had taken the opportunity to go hunting. He was dressed "in Indian style—hat-less, coatless, pantless; in shirt, drawers and moccasins only."[1] Absorbed in the pursuit of a pronghorn antelope among the rocks and crevices of the Sierra Madre mountains, Bullard had been unaware that he was in turn being tracked by the Mexicans, who mistook him for an Apache. When he finally noticed them, Bullard's first thought was similarly that the crouching figures who had him in their sights were Apaches.

In August of 1886 all the Mexican borderlands were attuned to the move-ments of the Apache leader and the followers who had joined him in fleeing intolerable conditions at the San Carlos Reservation in Arizona, where the army sought to confine the Chiracahaus. In arduous campaigning, sometimes involv-ing up to a quarter of its forces, the army had spent the previous four years in fruitless pursuit of three dozen hostiles, only seventeen of whom were fighting men.[2] Penetration by American troops into Mexican territory also created ten-sions between the two countries. The urgency of Geronimo's capture or death was one of the few things on which Mexicans and Americans agreed.

In words calculated to belittle the American soldier, the leader of the Rural

Guard made it clear that Bullard owed his life to his own ineptitude—and to the Mexicans' superior scouting skills and knowledge of the terrain. "Two hours or more we have followed you and three times have we rested our guns as just now to kill you for an Apache," he told the chagrined Bullard. "But you were so careless, unsuspecting, so easy to get," the Mexican concluded scornfully, "that each time luckily we waited to have you better, though each time we could have killed you."[3]

In that tense moment in the mountain crater, as "the desert . . . and the solitude of nature filled the spot," Bullard wrote later, the rookie army officer had expected death. "My life stopped; I stood nailed to the spot. I did not move or cry or think but waited in dumbness and numbness for the end."

Aside from the personal drama of his situation, Bullard's tableau captures the uneasy alliance between U.S. and Mexican forces in Sonora and Chihuahua less than forty years after the United States had forcibly wrested the northern frontier territories from Mexico, thereby acquiring the present-day states of California, Nevada, Utah, Arizona, New Mexico, Texas, most of Colorado, and parts of Wyoming, Kansas, and Oklahoma.[4] The scene also illustrates the prominence of indigenous techniques of warfare, including knowledge of the country, tracking, and ambush. All parties to the Apache conflict relied on such methods, but Mexico was suspicious of the U.S. Army's employment of Apache and other native scouts in Mexican territory. Dependence on Apache scouts was also a source of deep racial anxieties within the leadership of the U.S. military as it struggled to reconcile axiomatic Anglo-Saxon superiority with the manifest failure of well-equipped white troops to subdue, contain, or even keep up with an opponent described by one contemporary historian as "the most savage and intractable Indians in the country."[5]

Finally, our attention, like that of the Mexican Rural Guards, is drawn to the incongruity between Bullard's handkerchief, that vestige of civilized attire, and the rest of his self-described "Indian togs." As the Yaqui scouts of Troop H ranged over the desert below, matching their skills as trackers against the U.S. Army's most elusive quarry, the young lieutenant assigned to the expedition as quartermaster and commissary had been caught playing Indian.[6] Bullard's inept efforts to embody cultural knowledge by dressing up and chasing antelope after a romantic ideal of Indian hunting had attracted the attention of other actors in the contested landscape of the Sierra Madre. However, as the Mexicans pointed out to him in insulting terms, there was something in Bullard's obvious inability to embody Indianness convincingly that stayed their hands from killing him, until they could get close enough for the telltale handkerchief to confirm their sense that they had the wrong target.[7]

By his own account, Robert Lee Bullard made a *bad* Indian. What is more, he was proud of how poorly he played the role. Bullard was not interested in truly transforming himself, either physically or culturally. He was not one to "go native," to take on the identity, even provisionally, of an Apache or any one of the other so-called primitive peoples he encountered during the successive wars of colonial pacification in which he took part. He was, however, deeply interested in the tactical knowledge he believed could be acquired through inhabiting such roles. In this, his outlook and actions were in keeping with a long line of frontier soldiers.

Like other military men and civilian elites of his generation who found virtue in "the strenuous life" and saw in it an industrializing nation's salvation from effete overcivilization, Bullard advocated activities that brought white men into contact with the elemental forces of nature. The relationship between civilization and primitiveness, for Bullard, like others of his generation who grappled with the question, was complex and contradictory. Wildness promised renewal and empowerment for the civilized man who embraced it; it also threatened to corrupt him.[8]

Bullard's explanation of the behavior that led to the standoff in the Sierra Madre is telling: "I was new," he wrote of the incident, "and in those days these Indian togs caught all new men's fancy. On the least lead the most civilized of us quickly reverts to the primitive." Bullard's account speaks to his embrace of different mores and the general freedom for new men such as himself to shed some of the constraints of civilized comportment in the frontier posts to which they were assigned. It also underscores Bullard's belief in the tenuousness of the white man's claim to be civilized and the inevitable tendency to "revert to the primitive." For Bullard, the tension between the civilized and the primitive was one he felt he had contended with all his life. For him, the distinction was racial.

Born in 1861 on a cotton plantation in eastern Alabama, Bullard was socialized early into the power and immutability of racial hierarchy. He remained acutely aware of racial difference throughout his life. His diaries and autobiographical writings constitute a ledger in which he weighed the costs and advantages of his association with those he regarded as his racial inferiors. His writings also include frequent observations and hypotheses about the relationship between race and the capacity to attain civilization among the peoples he encountered and read about during a military career that encompassed the

Indian Wars in the Southwest, spy missions in Cuba and Mexico, and a stint as military governor in the Philippines.

Bullard's childhood was shaped by intimate but racially circumscribed relations with his family's former slaves and other freedmen and women on and around the family's farm in Lee County, Alabama. Bullard blamed his early childhood "association with Negroes big and little" for having "marked" him in negative and enduring ways. "I grew up with them, both short on morals, purpose, manners and education. It told on me. Skipping the morals, I was fifteen before I felt the moving of any ambition; twenty before I began to correct my plantation manners to which reversions are still not uncommon; thirty before my African methods of speech began to yield to grammar; forty before 'aint' gave way to 'is not' and 'are not', and to this day 'r's' and 'ings' are a difficulty."[9] Bullard feared that racial inferiority was inscribed in his speech as well as in his character. Its effects were expressed through his behavior; it was part of his very way of being. His embodiment of such defects was something he struggled against for much of his life, always fearing a "reversion" to "plantation manners." Bullard's association of inferiority with ways of speaking also reflects his awareness of the stigma attached to southern culture—white as well as black—in the aftermath of the Confederacy's defeat, which was construed by the victorious North as proof of the inherent backwardness and decadence of southern society. As the first cadet to "carry the name of Robert E. Lee back to West Point," Bullard was sensitive to the claim of the regnant Yankee culture to define the norms of civilized behavior to the detriment of an Alabama-bred boy like him, whose childhood heroes had been two sisters' husbands who served on the staffs of Robert E. Lee and Jefferson Davis.[10] At the same time, Bullard believed that the humiliation his family had felt after the war provided him with insights into the psychology of resistance to the American occupation of the Philippines and Cuba.

Later in life, when he had achieved success in his army career, and the bitter memories he associated with growing up under Reconstruction had faded, Bullard was able to reflect with amusement on the ironies of his elevation through the ranks of the "Grand Army of the Republic," or GAR, as the Union army became known. Bullard's humor on the subject, like the reabsorption of the white southerners into the federal army and the attenuation of Reconstruction, was accomplished at the expense of African Americans.

Three decades after he became the first southerner with the name Robert Lee to matriculate at West Point since the Civil War, Bullard paid a visit to Lee

County (which, like Bullard, had changed its name following the war). There, a chance encounter with one of his father's former slaves provided the material for a story that served as a commentary on the ironies of history and on the complexities of Bullard's loyalties as both soldier and southerner.

As Bullard later recounted the tale, he was visiting his family in Opelika when he met a former slave of his family named Frank Bullard. The two Bullards—one white and one black—encountered one another "within two miles of where both he and I were born." When Robert Bullard told Frank who he was, the older man looked puzzled, as "he evidently struggled with old memory to locate himself and me together," Bullard remembered. At a GAR meeting years later, Bullard slipped into dialect to tell the rest of the joke:

> Then, after a moment or two, [Frank] said, "Oh, yes, yes, I remember. You's 'Babe'. Dey tol' me you went away long time ago into the yankee army what come down thr'ough heah when freedom come fer de niggers. Are you with de yankee Army now?" I told him I was and that they treated me very well. I could see that Frank, still kinky but white-haired, old and worn, was still struggling with his memory about the time 'the yankee army came down thr'ough heah' and the how of my being with that army. "Well, 'Babe,'" he said, "when dey come down thru' heah, dey met me on de 'big road' drivin yo' Pa's fo'-mule team an' they onhitched my lead mule that I had trained to lead the team on a 'jerk line', the best lead mule I ever see'd. Dey told dey was goin' to bring him back. They didn't; they never did bring back that mule. I wish you would 'quire 'round 'mong them yankee soldiers fo' dat mule."[11]

For Bullard—and for the white audiences he regaled with this story in later years—the humor lay in the portrait of the former slave seemingly locked in an antebellum past—the loyal retainer indignant over the confiscation of his master's mule. "For Frank," Bullard told appreciative northern audiences, "the passage of time did not count in his memory." The punch line of Bullard's joke was that "Frank's heart and mind were set on getting that mule back."

Bullard told this story to a national meeting of the GAR, where he claimed it was received with "much laughter among the old fellows." When Bullard joked that he was doing what Frank had asked, inquiring after the mule, "some two dozen hands went up in acknowledgement that they had carried off Frank's mule." This was followed, Bullard wrote, "with a sort of honorary membership for me (and almost for Frank) and my decoration with the badge of the GAR." Bullard described himself as "rebel born and rebel bred." Yet he eventually found success—and even acclaim—as an officer in the "Yankee Army." In the younger man's telling, Frank Bullard, the devoted black retainer, was depicted as stuck in the past, unable to fathom or adapt to the changes wrought by the Civil War.

As he began his army service in the Southwest, Bullard fit his perceptions of Indians into familiar and axiomatic ideas about race and the hierarchies of civilization. His fears about the danger of "reverting to the primitive" in Indian Country had their roots in the stigma of racial taint he felt from his upbringing in Alabama. For Bullard, only two things offset the disadvantages he felt he had suffered as a result of his childhood association with blacks on and around his family's plantation. The first was the understanding he felt he had gained of racial difference itself, to which he credited his first significant career advance, which came as the commander of a black volunteer regiment in the Spanish American War. He expressed this belief in his autobiography: "My compensation for these, their stamp and marks upon me, has been an appreciation of the difference between negros and white men, just, I believe; for, guided by it, I was at thirty-seven to make my first military reputation commanding negroes."[12]

Besides the specific expertise that Bullard claimed in "commanding negroes," he also claimed analogous knowledge and insight into the character of Filipinos, Cubans, and later Mexicans, again all based on an analysis of the ways they supposedly differed from Anglo-Saxons. As his career took him from the border region of the United States and Mexico to the southern Philippines and then to Cuba and finally sent him on a spy mission into Mexico following the outbreak of the revolution in 1910, Bullard continued to work out his theorems on the relationship between race and the capacity for self-government. Successive colonial postings led him to claim increasing authority on how to pacify and govern the empire's lesser races. His observations on recalcitrant Moros and deceitful and ungrateful Cubans under U.S. occupation frequently led him to comparisons with the South of his boyhood.[13]

A second redeeming feature of his childhood association with blacks, which Bullard recognized, was the influence of Peter Christian, a freedman whom the young Bullard admired for his woodcraft and storytelling. Years later, Bullard recalled the impact Pete had had on him in a speech in which he reflected on the early influences on his life, particularly those that had inclined him toward a military career. "You know a small boy usually wants at various times in his life to be all sorts of things. I remember a fine young negro man, Pete Christian, that had married my nurse Sally. Pete could make more kinds of traps and snares to catch birds and rabbits and squirrels and he knew how to place them with skill and he knew all the trees of the forest and he knew before they were ever written at least half of Joel Chandler Harris' Uncle Remus' stories and had told them to me," Bullard said. "There was a period in my life when I thought I would like very much to be a fine negro man like Pete."[14] Bullard's youthful identification with Pete Christian is clear. So, too, is the way the older man became associated in Bullard's memory with two significant enthusiasms of his life: scouting and storytelling. These central themes appear again in Bullard's unpublished autobiography, in which he wrote at length of his admiration for Pete and of his appreciation for the things he had learned from the former slave. Again, Bullard stressed the tutelage Pete offered him in woodcraft, which Bullard would later extol as one of the foundations of scouting. He also valued the appreciation Pete awoke in him for the Uncle Remus stories:

> Strong, kind, good humored, a boy in way but a man in fact, he was a fellow indeed for boys. He knew and could do so many things! From watching him I learned to be something of a cobbler, carpenter and basket-maker; from being with him, the names and habits of birds and animals; the names and something of trees; something of woodcraft, trapping, fishing and what-not; and from listening to him, an appreciation of those sweetest and most delightful of all stories, the "Uncle Remus" child's stories of Brer Rabbit, Brer Fox, Brer B'ar and the others that Joel Chandler Harris has later lovingly put among the classics. For all of these, their pleasures and their helps, I owe something to Pete Christian, Negro.[15]

Even obscured by the lyricism of nostalgia and boyish admiration, Bullard's attempts to recall and explain the nature of the relationship between Pete and the white boys of his family opens a window on race relations in the era of Reconstruction. By what it omits as well as by what Bullard attempts to explain, his depiction of postemancipation social relations inadvertently reveals enduring patterns of race and power. By way of explaining Pete's special role in the family, Bullard writes, "Pete was never really a slave. He had grown up in the house and almost as a member of the family of his master."[16] The probable explanation for Pete's presence in the house of his master and the ambiguity about his former slave status is that Pete was the son of a white man. Bullard never mentions Pete's parents, nor calls him "mulatto," as biographer Allan Millett does.[17] However, he notes that Pete was distinguished by "a freedom and non-servility of manner found among no negroes about him." To explain why a grown man would keep the company of white boys such as Bullard and his brother, he continues, "Cut off by racial and social conditions from association with white men and desiring often other company than that of negroes, he turned to the white boys of our family, my brothers and me." Then, as if to forestall any further reflection on the matter, he concludes, "Custom allowed it."[18]

In later life, Bullard expressed revulsion toward interracial sexual relations, so it is perhaps unsurprising that he left out the detail of Pete's paternity, while suggesting it by the inclusion of other details, such as his allusion to Pete's "freedom and non-servility of manner" and his curious status as "almost . . . a member of the family of his master."[19] Bullard's assumption that "the company of white boys" would appeal to Pete more than the society of adults of his own community is consistent with an unquestioning sense of white superiority and a disdain for African Americans to which Bullard subscribed until the end of his life.[20]

Appreciative though it is in tone, his description of Pete deploys a dominant stereotype that cast blacks (as well as Indians and other colonial peoples) as childlike, not fully adult in capacity or behavior. In a seemingly benign—even admiring—way, he depicts Pete as a "boy in way but a man in fact." Here, Bullard unselfconsciously articulated one of the emasculating and dehumanizing tenets of white racist ideology. Reinforced by violence and lack of opportunity, such constructions stripped men such as Pete of their manhood and adult social stature and instead attempted to consign them to a lifelong status of "boy."

The Uncle Remus tales, which delighted the youthful Bullard and inspired his later attempts at writing about the folkways of colonial peoples, appealed to whites because they reflected a view of black culture that was childish and unthreatening—less developed than the supposedly more evolved Anglo-Saxon culture—and because they denied manhood to African American men, infantilizing them. According to David Murray, "a great part of the appeal and power of Harris's writings lay in the indefinite suspension of any recognition of power relations or historical change." Instead, Murray suggests that "keeping the focus on the close relation between the boy and Remus made it possible to provide a sentimental image of rapport as well as to deny the African American any mature manhood."[21] This was not new. An earlier book, Edward E. Pollard's

Black Diamonds Gathered in the Darkey Homes of the South, quotes an approving review from the *New Orleans Delta* claiming that the author knows the Negro nature "not by intellection merely, but also by heart; knows it, not through the cold light of ethnological science only, but most of all through the warm, enkindling recollections of boyhood and youth. The negro, who in his true nature is always a boy, let him be ever so old, is better understood by a boy than a whole academy of philosophers."[22] For white men, childhood was an individual developmental stage through which they progressed. Primitive people, on the other hand, were perpetually childlike. The developmental childhood of entire races of people made them apt playmates and also, oddly, the sources of folk wisdom and elemental skills derived from being close to nature, which might be adapted and fashioned to suit the purposes of more "grown-up" civilizations.

Robert Lee Bullard's ideas about race were typical of his time and upbringing. What is interesting is the connections he made between common racist tropes of black backwardness and childishness and his celebration of the "pleasures and helps" of scouting, which he associated with African American folk knowledge and later with Indian fighting techniques.

Bullard thought that white civilization was antithetical to the values of scouting, which he extolled in many of his writings. He remained equally insistent on the redemptive power of such a connection with the primitive precisely for "super-civilized" (presumptively Anglo-Saxon) men. One example of the relationship he saw between the two is apparent in a short story he wrote about the Philippines which was never published. "No amount of learning or philosophy or civilization ever quite takes a man beyond a secret willingness, even longing to be trapper, ranger, hunter, woodcraftsman or fighter of savages or outlaws, all in one word, scout," he wrote. Scouting, for Bullard, was transformative, not because it allowed white men to become Indians, but because it put them in touch with an essential part of their own nature, from which civilization had alienated them. "In this the high and the low, civilized and savage, the general and the private soldier, differ not," he wrote. "Emperors and kings, princes, leaders, teachers, the greatest that the world has held, have aspired to the qualities, the name and reputation of scout. Is it, as some supercivilized these days would have us believe, the call-back of the wild, the echo of savagery? Ah, no, but something better than they with all their reason can offer us—touch with nature."[23] According to this view, reason contrasted with nature; savage people were closer to nature, but the supercivilized were even more in need of the benefits of scouting precisely because they had lost touch with it.

During the four years Bullard spent at forts in the Southwest, he made his first observations and wrote his first notes on a project that lasted throughout his military career and into retirement. Bullard was obsessed with articulating a hierarchical schema of civilizations and races. Unlike Hugh Lenox Scott, who took an ethnographic approach to the living cultures of the native peoples who so fascinated him, Bullard's intellectual project was characterized by a historical abstraction of civilizations past and present. The project was teleological of course. Anglo-Saxon civilization, epitomized by its political and industrial achievements, represented the pinnacle of human development. The question was how long it would take other races to attain the same level of advancement. Bullard's study was an ideological project with immediate and real applications. Part of the colonial authority he increasingly assumed, as his career led to positions of command over men of races he viewed as inferior to his own, derived precisely from the claim he made to possess privileged knowledge about the character of primitive people. Like other army officers whose careers encompassed the trajectory of American expansion, his early impressions of Indian Country inculcated categories of perception and behavior, and especially ways of relating to subject peoples that informed his approaches to the colonial situations he later encountered in the Philippines and Cuba. For these men, the core of their later relationships to projections of Indian Country abroad was based on their formative experience of Indian Country on the plains and in the desert Southwest. For Bullard, dressing in "Indian togs" and going hunting was a way of assimilating the meaning of Indian Country. So was reading the landscape and romanticizing its past.

Bullard was less steeped than Scott in the poetry of Indian Country, less inclined to embrace "the land of romance, adventure, and mystery" that Scott anticipated as he rode the Great Northern Railroad to the end of the line in Bismarck in 1876.[24] Whereas Scott depended on Francis Parkman to orient him to the landscape and people of the North, the book that Bullard had chosen to bring with him when he reported for duty to Fort Union was *Don Quixote*. Their choice of books says a great deal about the inclinations and temperament of each of these West Point graduates as they embarked on their frontier army careers. Each had his own dreams and romantic notions. Significantly, though, Scott, like Parkman, focused his imagination on the land before him and on relations among the peoples vying for control over it. He was especially fascinated by all the ways Indians had adapted themselves to survive on the northern plains. His descriptions of native peoples extol their oneness with the natural landscape. On the southern border, with only Miguel de Cervantes as guide, Bullard encountered a landscape that seemed to him alienating and uncivilized. "Mighty nature ruled here," he wrote. "For the hand of man had barely touched her face."[25] Where Scott registered the sublime, Bullard read into the landscape grandeur, but also menace. He found the Sierra Madre wild and dark. He wrote that "the mountains were sometimes frightful in their grandeur, their black repulsiveness and loneliness."[26] Bullard's descriptions of human settlement in the region emphasize its timelessness and remoteness from the world of movement and consequence, the modern world, the world of men who mattered.

Bullard showed none of the interest in contemporary Indian cultures that so absorbed Scott. His imagination was instead captured by "the occupation of the region in ages gone by a civilized people."[27] Bullard's racially determined ideas about the advancement of civilizations throughout history allowed him to admire the pottery and earthen mounds of vanished civilizations while disparaging the culture and character of the contemporary inhabitants of the region.

Considering how much Bullard later referred to his experience of commanding Indians, it is striking how little attention he paid to the real Indians he encountered in the borderlands, either inhabitants, auxiliaries, or adversaries. Although they later formed a significant point of reference both for his reflections on military pacification and the development of his schema of civilization and barbarity, at the time Bullard seems to have written and reflected little on the Indian scouts, even those attached to his unit. Since he assumed that the contemporary Indians descended from the earlier civilizations whose achievements he found praiseworthy, Bullard viewed the contemporary Indians of the Southwest as the degenerate "half-civilized" descendants of the civilizations that had created the earth mounds and pottery that spoke to him of higher achievements in the past.

Aside from his imaginative affinity for the exploits of empire, Bullard also pinned his career hopes on mastering the languages of empire, even defunct empire; and, like his study of men and civilizations, Bullard's choice of language was expedient, too. Aided by his copy of *Don Quixote* and a Spanish dictionary, Bullard began a study of Spanish which he kept up as long as American imperial engagement with areas of the old Spanish empire made it seem worthwhile. He continued this study throughout his time in the Southwest and during training in Alabama in anticipation of going to Cuba in 1898. The beginning of Bullard's study of the Spanish empire and Hispanic civilization in the Americas and the Philippines also dates from his time on the border. In the margin of the diary in which he noted his interest in the "curiosities of Old New Mexico, the Pueblo Indians, their history and traditions," Bullard mused that, as he was being introduced to one chapter of the history of the expansion of the Spanish empire, he was at the same time contemplating going on to Manila "to renew the impressions on the other side of the world of the Spaniard and his ways— Santa Fe on the great Plains of the west, America, and Manila, over the great seas in the far, far East."[28]

Bullard reported to Fort Union in the fall of 1885. His first assignment was to guard a border supply base for pack trains that carried supplies for the use of scouts in the Sierra Madre. The following July, Bullard became quartermaster and commissary for a mule train as it moved supplies a hundred miles south across the border into the Mexican state of Sonora. He recorded some of his first impressions in a diary he kept on the journey: "We passed through beautiful park-like mountain villages; dry parched lowlands, brown, crumbling adobe Mexican villages with their great old Catholic churches far, far out of the great busy and inhabited world; through old towns and fields whose people had long long ago been killed or driven off by the fierce apaches. It was most interesting, new and strange to me."[29]

The arid mountainous country through which Bullard's company drove its mules had a long history as Indian Country, a place where successive colonial governments had been unable to exert effective control over native peoples. It was also the context in which Bullard had his first opportunity to observe the role of the Apache scouts who were attached to the army. He was not impressed: "From time to time detachments of troops came into our camp in passing or to obtain supplies and I gradually learned how troops worked in Indian warfare. We used Indian scouts after the hostiles but from what I saw of them I concluded that the scouts were almost as hostile and uncertain as the hostiles themselves. I saw a whole company of them get drunk and almost break away to go on the war path right under the eye of their commanders and at the muzzles of the rifles of our two companies of U.S. troops. That was a great object lesson in control and discipline or rather in the lack of these."[30]

Bullard was contemptuous of contemporary Indians. The cursory observations he later committed to his diary rehearse common prejudices of the time; he found the Apaches lazy, prone to drunkenness, deceitful, brutal. In short, he constructed racial difference between Indians and whites along the lines of familiar stereotypes widely available in popular culture. At the same time, he had a wistful reverence for what he regarded as the more accomplished civilizations of the remote past. Ever susceptible to a romantic reading of the landscape, Bullard imagined the crater in which he encountered the Mexican *Rurales* as a remnant of one of the ancient volcanoes that had "vomited their fires upon these lands before Aztec, Toltec or white men ever came."[31] This was pure fancy on Bullard's part; neither the Aztecs nor any of the other settled agriculturalists who had made the valley of Mexico the center of expansive civilization for a millennium before the coming of the Europeans, had exercised any influence over the north. The land did not favor the intensive cultivation which nourished the concentration of population in the valley of Mexico. More importantly, the inhabitants of the region were not amenable to conquest and subjugation to an empire based on tribute and trade. The Mexica people, known to history as the Aztecs, regarded the seminomadic tribes of the north as barbarians. Their collective name for them was *chichimecas*, the sons of dogs.[32]

The Spanish, who overtook the Aztec empire in 1521, initially found little to hold their interest in the mountainous desert regions beyond Mexico's central plateau. While Spain putatively claimed territory reaching far into the North American plains and contested the rival claims of Britain and Russia in the Pacific Northwest, in fact, the Viceroyalty of New Spain, as Spain's richest and most populous colony was called, remained anchored in the central and southern parts of Mesoamerica, where the new rulers were able to command the labor and tribute of people who were conditioned to the demands of empire and had fewer viable means of long-term resistance.[33]

Discovery of silver deposits in 1548 in areas of what is today Zacatecas provided the initial impetus for Spaniards to explore and settle the frontier. They founded cities near the mining centers and developed haciendas to produce food for the mines and associated settlements. The Spanish also enslaved native people to provide labor in the mines and other Spanish enterprises. These initiatives were met with strong resistance from the region's original inhabitants, who attacked their mule trains and raided the isolated outposts of the Spanish empire.[34]

Paralleling the mining frontier that developed northward from Zacatecas and Durango to Chihuahua and Sonora, the Spanish established a system of missions and presidios. Franciscans began their missionary work near the mines of Parral in the 1560s and by the early seventeenth century had established several missions. Over the next two centuries, they founded many more missions throughout New Spain and as far distant as Taos, New Mexico. After 1769 they were charged with missionizing Alta California, where they established a line of missions from San Diego to San Francisco. The Jesuits, meanwhile, administered missions in northwestern New Spain and Baja California from 1591 until the expulsion of the order from the viceroyalty in 1767. In addition to the goals of religious and cultural indoctrination, the missions sought to consolidate disparate indigenous communities through the process of *reducción*, or concentrating Indians into settlements under the jurisdiction of the mission. These *reducciones* also served as sites for the recruitment and organization of Indian labor. To protect the missions the Spanish maintained presidios, or fortified outposts, garrisoned by the military. The Spanish also sent colonists among the people of the north. By the end of the sixteenth century, some four hundred families from Tlaxcala had been recruited to resettle in several colonies around Saltillo, Coahuila. In return for privileges not usually accorded the Crown's Indian subjects, the Christianized Tlaxcalans were meant to demonstrate to other indigenous peoples the advantages of accepting Hispanic ways.[35] Over time, the colonization efforts took on an increasingly defensive and explicitly military function.[36]

None of the Spanish colonial institutions—the presidio, mission, forced *reducciones* of Indians, or military colonies—had the desired effect of pacifying Mexican Indian Country. Instead, by the end of the eighteenth century, autonomous Indian tribes, the *indios bárbaros*, who had not been incorporated into patterns of Hispanic life, dominated the north. In 1768 a Spanish official who had spent two years traveling 7,600 miles throughout Spain's frontier territories reported to the king that much of present-day Texas, New Mexico, and Arizona were in reality nothing more than "imaginary dominions," under the control of hostile Indians. Apaches, reported the Marques de Rubí, controlled the lands from southwestern Texas to California. Comanches, Kiowas, Wichitas, and Pawnees harassed Spanish settlements and missions in Texas and New Mexico, stealing horses and cattle and killing other Indians who had joined the missions. Even tribes like the Utes, who sought to remain at peace with the Europeans, behaved as though settlers' animals "were there for the taking," complained the marquis.[37]

Recent scholarship has sought to look beyond the often alarmist rhetoric of frontier residents and officials to examine cross-cultural interaction and accommodation between Mexicans and the indigenous people of the north, and the state-level diplomatic initiatives they undertook to minimize and contain conflict. However, peace was elusive and racial enmity, once ignited, produced a conflagration that engulfed the north. As Brian DeLay has written, "once

Mexicans and the 'cruel and indomitable Apaches' started killing, enslaving, and stealing from each other, hatreds, reprisals, and calls for revenge acquired a fierce and ultimately irresistible momentum."[38]

Faced with increased Apache raids and large-scale depopulation of Sonora and Chihuahua, the Spaniards decided to try something new. In 1776, the same year that the Franciscan mission was established in San Francisco, New Spain created a new military organization for the frontier provinces called the Commandancy General of the Interior Provinces. The commander general was charged with waging a war of extermination against the Apaches all along the frontier. To support this mission they also created the *compañía volante* or flying company, essentially a highly mobile cavalry unit. It was the forerunner of the efforts mounted by the U.S. Army a century later. This period also saw the regularization of the use of Apache auxiliaries recruited from one band to join with the Spanish effort against another.[39] This was another technique the United States would later adopt.

Though the primary policy was one of extermination, Viceroy Bernardo de Gálvez also offered Apaches the opportunity to settle near the presidios in camps called *establicimientos de paz* where they would be provisioned with food, aguardiente, and even firearms, as a way of securing their dependence on the colonial government. Significantly, the Chiricahua and other bands accepted these terms and settled provisionally near the Sonora and Chihuahau presidios.

Independence from Spain in 1821 brought with it a host of challenges for the new nation, constrained by fiscal woes and a weak and unstable central government that was unable to devote the military or administrative resources necessary to preserve a fragile peace that had allowed areas of endemic conflict such as Chihuahua and New Mexico to experience an encouraging period of tranquility and blossoming prosperity during the first three decades of the nineteenth century. After 1830, an escalation in raiding, attacks on Mexican ranches and settlements, murder, kidnapping, and theft of animals and property turned the northern third of Mexico "into a vast theater of hatred, terror, and staggering loss for independent Indians and Mexicans alike."[40]

The first chaotic decades of Mexican national independence and increased conflict with Comanches, Kiowas, Apaches and Navajos also coincided with intensifying pressures on the border region from Anglo-Americans to the north. Even before President James Polk launched the opportunistic war that cost Mexico half its territory, restless expansionism to the north upset the balance of power in the borderlands. Westward migration in the United States had two main effects on frontier dynamics south of the border. First, it created new demographic pressures that heightened tensions between Indians and Mexicans. In 1826 a prominent citizen of Santa Fe, Juan Bautista Pino, complained that a growing population of North Americans was forcing the Kiowas toward the west. In time, he predicted, "we will probably have them on top of us." He compared the Indian nations to "balls in a row" through which a "strong impulse . . . is passed along until it reaches the last." He had no doubt that the source of the strong impulse sending a chain of reactions through the Indians of the west was the Indian policy of the U.S. government. With the election of Andrew Jackson in 1828 and the pursuit of Indian removal, that policy was intensified.[41]

Another way in which American expansion increased Indian-Mexican conflict was through the market. U.S.-based traders sold Indians weapons and provided a market for the animals and other goods the guns helped them steal. Besides disrupting the ties of dependence with which the Spanish colonial state had attempted to bind the Indians, American traders provided both the means and the motives for Indian raiding in Mexico.[42] Mexicans were especially bitter about the role of the United States in arming them and providing an incentive—and a refuge—for Indians to raid and steal across the border.

In the decade following independence, Mexico's northern states began offering bounties for captured and killed Indians. In 1846 the state of Chihuahua paid 50 pesos for each dead Indian. In 1849 a warrior's scalp fetched 200 pesos. In reality, bounties were paid for any scalp—man, woman, or child. As one historian commented, "Long black hair was an invitation to disaster."[43] An adult male prisoner was worth 250 pesos to his captor. Dead women and children brought 100 pesos each. From the 1840s to the 1870s Chihuahua and Sonora paid out thousands of pesos in bounties.[44]

Although it contributed to the gruesome violence of the frontier, the scalp policy was not effective in discouraging Apache raiding. On the eve of the Mexican-American War in the mid-1840s, one Chihuahua state legislator lamented the situation in which the Mexican inhabitants of the region found themselves: "Subjected effectually to the domination of a few barbarians, we travel along the roads until this hour at their whim; we cultivate the land where they wish and in amount that they wish, we use sparingly things that they have left to us until the moment that it strikes their appetite to take them for themselves, and we occupy the land while the savages permit us."[45]

The loss of half its territory as a result of the revolt of Texas and the Mexican-American War was a humiliating blow to the young Mexican republic. However, there was one provision of the peace treaty with the Americans that was welcomed by Mexicans, especially by those in the north. Article 11 of the Treaty of Guadalupe Hidalgo made the United States responsible for the Indians on its side of the new border. With an arrogance born of racism, the United States agreed to restrain the Indians from committing incursions into Mexico and assumed responsibility for punishing those who did and for compensating Mexico for such incursions when they could not be prevented. But the Americans soon learned that they were no more effective than the Mexicans had been in controlling cross-border raids. Accused of bad faith by the Mexican government and anxious to escape the impossible task of policing the border, in 1853 the United States negotiated a new treaty with Mexico. Known as the Gadsden Purchase, the treaty paid Mexico $10 million for the cession of the Mesilla valley; more significantly, perhaps, from the U.S. perspective, the treaty relieved the United States of responsibility for Indian actions against Mexico.[46] At issue were the activities of the Apaches.

The Apaches were not signatories to either agreement. From their perspective, the new international border laid down an arbitrary line through the middle of *Gran Apacheria*, which they did not accept as binding on them. As they were quick to point out, they had never been defeated by either Mexico or the United States. They did not accept that they could be restricted in moving across what was to them a fictitious line in whose creation they had no part. At the same time, they recognized that the border did offer tactical opportunities to them. In this they were not alone.

Lieutenant Bullard's early impressions of the frontier society he encountered in the 1880s include his observation that it was not just Indians who used the border as an aid to conducting autonomous (and illegal) activities outside the control of the law. Bullard described the border as a place "without touch with ordinary life and people . . . because the country was infested by outlaws and hostile Indians, 'rustlers,' smugglers and cattle thieves, ready on either side on a moment's notice to jump for safety to the other side of the international border."[47] Even fortified by dozens of forts and thousands of federal troops, the border remained a zone of autonomous actors, struggling for advantage against one another and confounding the efforts of the states on either side to impose a comprehensive regime of control; in other words, the border was Indian Country.

Bullard's assignment to the border came at a key moment in the campaign to catch Geronimo. For the previous four years up to five thousand troops—

nearly a fourth of the Regular Army—had chased the small band of renegades. In command of the effort for most of that time was the veteran Indian fighter (or as he preferred to describe his role, "Indian-thinker"), General George Crook. General Crook favored a strategy that privileged the use of Indian scouts to track Geronimo's band. Shortly before Bullard was detailed to accompany the mule train, Crook had been replaced in command by General Nelson Miles. Miles was highly critical of Crook's reliance on scouts.

Following the Army Reorganization Act of 1866, Crook had become one of the first Indian fighters to incorporate Indian scouts into his troops in 1867 for campaigns against the Snake Indians in Oregon and later in Idaho, California, and Nevada.[48] In 1882 Crook was placed in command of the Military Department of Arizona. At first Crook experimented with Mexicans and Pimas to aid the regular troops because they "knew the country and the Apache."[49] He quickly concluded however, "that only an Apache could even find an Apache, much less engage him in battle."[50]

To compel the capitulation of several renegade bands of Apaches, the U.S. Army relied on Indian scouts to an unprecedented degree. To explain and justify why Apache scouts were needed to do things that regular troops seemingly could not accomplish, Crook and other advocates of the use of Indian scouts elaborated on already existing images of Apache barbarity and alterity. Indeed, the Apaches had already been thoroughly demonized and dehumanized by a succession of civilized cultures that began enslaving them in 1600, stole their children, placed bounties on their heads, and hunted them like animals.[51] As Americans added their voices to the centuries-old discourse of Apache barbarism, Apaches were constructed as animal-like savages who lacked both the needs and the sensibilities of other human beings. By this logic, Apaches made superior fighters because they were inferior humans. Accordingly, Crook claimed that the "wilder" the Indians were, the better soldiers they made. "The nearer an Indian approaches to the savage state the more likely he will prove valuable as a soldier," Crook wrote about his recruitment of Apache scouts. "I therefore selected, preferably, the wildest that I could get."[52] In a similar vein, he compared the Apaches to horses: "I saw that the key-note of the problem lay in my success or failure to win to my side the boldest, most daring, most savage of all the young chiefs. These men are the high-mettled horses of the herd, the born leaders who, if once curbed and broken, help in the management of the negative spirits in all communities."[53] Among the white officers commanding the Indian scouts, it was common to refer to Apaches as "broncos," with the connotations suggested by Crook. Even more common was the term "buck." Crook also famously called the Apache "the tiger of the human species."[54] He frequently compared the Apaches to dogs, wolves, and coyotes. In contrasting them with other Indians, he said, "The Apache warrior resembles as little the well-fed Indian of the eastern reservations, as does the hungry wolf the sleek house-dog." Crook's aide-de-camp John Bourke compared the White Mountain Apache scout William Alchesay (also known as Alchisay), whom he both liked and admired, to a "faithful Irish hound."[55] While Bourke's analogy was tempered by familiarity and affection, a writer for the *Tombstone Daily Epitaph* of the same period declared that Apaches were as untamable as hyenas, and said that they were classed as human beings only "because of [their] erect position and articulation approaching language."[56]

Crook insisted that the warrior's nature "differs but little from the wolf or coyote, and from his earliest infancy he has been accustomed to defend himself against enemies as cruel and revengeful as his own nature."[57] Like the coyote, the Apache was "perfectly at home, anywhere in the immense country over which he roams and which affords him all the sustenance he requires. Even in his rapid flights he gets a rabbit here or a rat there, and this, with the wild roots and the mescal, gives him all the food he needs." In further elaboration of this analogy, Crook concluded: "The Apache can be compared most aptly to the wild animal he fittingly calls his cousin—the coyote. The civilized settlements are his sheep-folds, and even supposing that a toilsome campaign results in destroying forty out of a band of fifty, the survivors are as much to be dreaded as ever, until the very last one can be run down, killed, or got under control, and taught to labor for his bread."[58] The comparison with coyotes was especially insulting to Apaches, who looked on the coyote, not as a cousin, but as a scheming and treacherous character.[59]

Crook is usually portrayed as being sympathetic to the Apaches, even as he commanded the troops who chased and harried and killed them in an effort to compel those who broke out from the reservations to return to the supervision of the army and the Interior Department. To support the idea of Crook's sympathy with Apaches, historians cite his self-proclaimed policy of honesty and fair dealing. Certainly, he seems to have been more respected than the reviled Nelson A. Miles, whom the Apaches (and some whites) accused of deceit and extreme injustice for deporting noncombatants, as well as scouts loyal to the United States, along with the hostiles in Geronimo's band. All were shipped off on trains to imprisonment in Florida for twenty-seven years. They were treated "like cattle," according to Eustace Fatty, grandson of the Warm Springs scout Gordo.[60]

While Crook recognized the military utility and superiority of Apaches as scouts, he described them in terms that emphasized their barbaric nature and often drew close analogies between Apaches and animals. Perhaps more eloquent than anything Crook said or wrote, was the message he conveyed by riding a mule he called Apache.[61] However, by the time Lieutenant Bullard arrived on the border in late 1885, General Crook, unsuccessful in his attempts to catch Geronimo, was on his way out. In April 1886, Crook was replaced by General Nelson A. Miles.

When he took over command of the Department of Arizona and the effort to capture Geronimo, General Miles was a newcomer to the Southwest, but he was a veteran Indian-fighter, and a critic of what he saw as Crook's excessive reliance on Indian scouts. General Miles's opposition to the use of native scouts went well beyond strategic considerations. Miles was unwilling to acknowledge that there was any area in which whites were not superior to any Indian, including Apaches. Since it was a mark of their primitiveness, the preternatural possession of superior scouting abilities was something that most white men were willing to concede to Indians or other "natives." Variously ascribed to the influence of their environment, their savage nature, or their evolutionary backwardness, Apache prowess in tracking and ambush might be feared and even admired, but it was not something of which most white men were jealous, since its price was thought to be civilization itself. However, there were some in the army who were reluctant to concede Indian advantage in any comparison with white troops. This was the case with Nelson Miles. He regarded Indians off the reservation more as criminals than as military adversaries, and certainly not as members of independent nations. Miles was especially suspicious of Crook's reliance on Apache scouts, believing that the Apaches could not be trusted to deliver their own people to the Americans. A firm believer in Anglo-Saxon racial superiority and a man of great personal strength and fitness, which he maintained through a vigorous regime of exercise, Miles was determined to show that regular (white) troops could succeed against the Apaches where other Apaches (and Crook) had failed. In this he had the support of a young army contract surgeon named Leonard Wood. Both Miles and Wood were known for their athleticism. Wood was something of a fanatic about his physical fitness. Twelve years later, Wood emerged into the national spotlight as commander of the most famous volunteer regiment organized for service in the war in Cuba, the Rough Riders, with Theodore Roosevelt as his second-in-command. Following the war, Wood and Miles were appointed to serve as military governors of Cuba and Puerto Rico, respectively. Wood also played a leading role in the military pacification of the southern Philippines, which he approached in ways that drew on his formative experiences of Indian Country.

Wood was of the opinion that "the right sort of white man" could beat the Apaches at their own game. Miles charged the young doctor with carrying out a field test aimed at finding out which was superior. To lead the expedition after Geronimo, Miles chose Henry Lawton, a captain with the Fourth Cavalry stationed at Fort Huachuca. Miles assigned Wood to accompany Lawton's troops as their medical officer. Lawton's orders were to ride after the Apaches until they "died or surrendered." It was to be a test of Miles's theory of white superiority. Miles counted on the basic physical superiority of Wood and Lawton and their white soldiers to accomplish the defeat of the enemy. "We have heard a good deal about the strength and endurance of the Apaches," Miles told Wood. "You are probably in as good physical condition as anyone to endure what they endure. I want you to go with Lawton and to take every opportunity that is given you to study the Indians. If they are better men physically than the white men, I want you to find out what makes them better."[62] Wood wrote in his diary for May 4, 1886, "I told him I believed the right sort of white men could eventually break these Indians up and compel them to surrender."[63]

Although he claimed victory, Nelson Miles's test of white superiority in the deserts and mountains of Sonora was not a success. What ensued was one of the most grueling campaigns of the Indian Wars. After the hardships of their first month in the field, of the original twenty-five infantrymen, only fourteen were capable of further duty.[64] Even after nearly dying himself from an infected tarantula bite, Wood was not willing to concede much. He merely concluded "that the Indian Scouts were physically equal, if not actually superior, to the best of the white troops; at least none of them were broken down from the service."[65] More important, although Wood's "right sort of white men" had failed to outperform Indians, the field test did nothing to negate the presumption of white superiority. The episode merely reinscribed tropes of Apache otherness.

Warm Spring Band member James Kaywaykla's assessment of the scouts' performance was rather different. He concluded that Lawton's troops could not keep up with their Indian scouts. "They could not stand the rains and other hardships of the pursuit over mountains and through canyons." Significantly, he thought physical endurance was less important as an advantage from the

Apache point of view than was cultural knowledge. Kaywaykla recalls that for this reason Geronimo and his band regarded Lieutenant Charles Gatewood, who was in charge of the scouts attached to Lawton's mission as "a real menace." Gatewood had been brought from Fort Stanton because of his knowledge of and experience with Apaches. With him were Martine and Kayitah, two men who were familiar with the terrain and who had close family ties to people in Geronimo's group. In the end, it proved to be their influence with Geronimo that created the opening for negotiating a surrender.[66]

In compliance with Miles's preference for the use of non-Apaches as scouts, the Indians detailed to Lieutenant Parker's expedition of the Fourth Cavalry, with whom Bullard served, were not Apaches but Yaqui Indians. They were not enlisted scouts; rather, they were working for an American from Calabases, Hank Frost, who had formerly employed them to make adobe bricks. Parker was dismissive of both Hank Frost, whom he describes as a "loudmouthed, boastful ruffian" and of the Yaquis, who he thought "differed little from the ordinary sedentary Mexican Peon." Rather than "knowing the country, they were continually getting lost," according to Parker, "and so far as following a hostile trail, not only were they incapable of doing so, but if they found one they were probably not anxious to follow it or even to report it.[67]

Bullard managed a grudging admiration for the legendary endurance of the Apaches, whose adaptability to the difficult terrain had enabled them to withstand three centuries of concerted effort on the part of the Spanish empire, the Republic of Mexico, and now the expanding U.S. empire to eradicate or contain them. He wrote: "Over these mountains and plains went the swiftest moving Indians of all history, afoot or on horseback indifferently, 60 to 90 miles a day! The Indians could stand it; the horses were killed. That made no difference to the Indians; they would anyway in the end kill and eat those horses, robbing and killing for others."[68] The Apaches' very ability to thrive in the region was, for Bullard, evidence of their fundamental otherness, their primitiveness. Furthermore, he had ultimate faith in the superior abilities of "their blue clad pursuers, our soldiers" to subdue them eventually. He put his faith in "the tale of the hare and tortoise. How often it is repeated!"[69]

Bullard wrote little about the Indian scouts, even when he was in command, dismissing them at one point as all savages. His thinking on this developed over time but did not fundamentally change. Scouting was something worthwhile and deeply interesting for white men; he recognized the origins of valuable martial techniques in the practices of indigenous allies. In retirement he developed a complex and romanticized reverence for Indian warriors and an interest in the methods and even culture of scouting, which were completely absent during his first deployment in the Southwest.

Although his own role in the surrender of Geronimo was peripheral, Bullard was among the troops on hand to witness the shameful aftermath of Geromino's surrender, as 434 Chiricahua and Warm Springs Apaches were rounded up and shipped into exile in the East, first imprisonment in Florida, then Alabama. Far from home, the Apaches suffered ill health and high death rates. In 1894, surviving members of the two tribes were resettled at Fort Sill in Oklahoma, under the supervision of Hugh Lenox Scott.[70]

Bullard's career was built on the privileged knowledge he claimed about subject peoples from the southwestern United States and northern Mexico to the Philippines and Cuba. On the thinnest basis of firsthand observation, but with a great deal of imaginative projection and elaboration augmented by selective appropriation—both of elements of cultural practice and of symbolic power—he became recognized as an expert on the Cuban character by President Theodore Roosevelt and Secretary of War William H. Taft. Later, he was influential in opposing greater integration of black troops in the army during World War I. Even before his Apache experiences emboldened him to channel the symbolic power proclaimed by the name "Bullard's American Indians" and to glory in its application to his (white) volunteer regiment in the Philippines, Bullard was experienced in strategic cultural appropriation. He learned it in childhood, along with an appreciation for African stories and scouting.

Just as for Scott, Bullard's initial experience of Indian Country continued to inform his military practice and colonial policy making long after he left the borderlands. The same would be true for John J. Pershing too. Like other Indian fighters turned colonial governors, these three men carried the core racial notions ingrained in them on domestic frontiers with them to the colonial situations they encountered in America's far-flung insular territories. It is equally important to note, however, that the lessons each drew also varied, shaped as they were both by the preconceptions that each brought with him to his overseas assignments and by the distinctive tenor of each man's experience of Indian Country.

Chapter 4

Prairie Imperialists

"Nigger Jack" was the nickname given to John J. Pershing by the cadets who chafed under his exacting discipline at West Point when he returned there as a tactical officer in 1897. Intended as an insult, the nickname was a sneering reference to his command of black troopers of the Tenth Cavalry, the Buffalo Soldiers with whom he'd served on the border in Montana. It reflected the continuing disdain for African Americans still rife at the academy and throughout the white office corps two decades after Henry O. Flipper had become West Point's first black graduate. It was meant to disparage Pershing with exactly the racial association Scott's mother had sought to avoid for her son. That Lieutenant Pershing would berate his white officers-in-training by comparing them unfavorably to black enlisted men in his frontier regiment they found insulting. It offended both their racial and class pride. Euphemized to "Black Jack," this was the name that stuck to Pershing during his meteoric rise from policing Indians in the borderlands to his command of the American Expeditionary Forces in Europe during the First World War and Congress's subsequent conferring on him the title general of the Armies of the United States, a title held before him only by George Washington.[1]

Like the roots of his enduring nickname, the Indian Country origins of Pershing's extraordinary military career have been obscured by the later fame of his command of the Punitive Expedition against Pancho Villa and then his supreme command of American forces in World War I.[2] Perhaps more prominently than any other field commander, Pershing's life and career exemplify the long-lived resonances of Indian Country experiences on the trajectory of American imperial expansion and the far-reaching effects of a template of Indian

Country formed on the domestic frontier, which he carried with him overseas to Cuba and the Philippines and back again to the border and Mexico's northern territories during the Mexican Revolution. In Mexico, as in the Philippines, he relied on the maneuvers, tactics, ways of reading the land and calculations about racialized others that he had learned as a new trooper at his first post. Moros and Mexicans replaced Indians in the punitive wars abroad.

Long before President Wilson tapped him to lead a twelve-thousand-man mission to pursue and punish the errant General Francisco "Pancho" Villa for his attack on Columbus, New Mexico, Pershing became an avid student of the tactics of punitive warfare against those who challenged American control over its borderlands.[3] Villa's raid on Columbus in 1916 occurred just seventy miles south of Fort Bayard, where Pershing had been posted as a new second lieutenant of cavalry two decades earlier. While his quarry in the Mexican War would be different, and the army's pursuit of the bandit general would be augmented by automobiles, rudimentary armored vehicles, and even a small squadron of airplanes, the strategies of asymmetrical punitive warfare drew on those Pershing had practiced on horseback in the alkali deserts and rugged mountains of the borderlands against the dwindling resistance of the Apaches, who were now consigned to reservations or exiled to prison camps in the East. Pershing's preemptive and punitive suppression of resistance to U.S. rule in the southern Philippines, which prompted President Theodore Roosevelt to propose his promotion over the heads of 862 senior officers, similarly had its roots in Indian Country.[4]

John Joseph Pershing, six-star general of the Armies of the United States and preeminent military figure of his generation, was in fact an incidental soldier. Unlike Scott and Bullard, for whom admired uncles and brothers-in-law in uniform provided martial models to emulate, and who could be counted on for advice and useful connections that furthered their protégés' ambitions along a chosen military path, Pershing sought a place at West Point because it offered a college education his family could not afford for him.[5]

Pershing was paying his own way at the Normal School in Kirksville, Missouri, some fifty miles from the family home in LaClede, when he learned of a competitive exam for entrance to the military academy and decided to try. Slightly over the age limit, Pershing altered his birth date and took the exam, besting seventeen other aspirants to win a place. At the time, his ambition was not to join the army or become a teacher, but to become a lawyer. He reassured his mother, who was loath to see her eldest son embark on a career that would take him far away on uncomfortable and perhaps dangerous tours of duty, with the prospect that, following graduation, he would resign his commission and return home to study law.[6]

The law continued to beckon to Pershing up until and even after the Spanish-American War. A four-year appointment as commandant of cadets at the state university of Nebraska afforded an opportunity to earn a bachelor's degree in law and test the waters in that profession. The detached service in Lincoln also returned Pershing to his first vocation—teaching.

Pershing's talent for commanding men and the premium he placed on obedience, somewhat out of place in the classroom at the University of Nebraska, were apparent early on and won him coveted recognition as captain of cadets at West Point as well as election as president of his class. Robert Lee Bullard, who was a year senior to him at the academy and had the chance to observe him there and in the Philippines, as well as later when he served under his command on the Mexican border and in France, described the impact Pershing had on others, even as a cadet: "His manner carried to the minds of those under him the suggestion, nay, the conviction, of unquestioned right to obedience. There was no shadow of doubt about it."[7]

Pershing was a middling student, who especially struggled with languages. He graduated in 1886, thirtieth in his class out of seventy-seven. As captain of the Corps of Cadets, Pershing had his pick of service: artillery, cavalry, or infantry. He chose the cavalry and received a commission in his preferred regiment: the Sixth U.S. Cavalry, then headquartered at Fort Bayard, near the Mexican border. Like Bullard, who had graduated the year before, he began his frontier service in Apacheria. Following a furlough during which he took in the sights in New York, Washington, and Chicago and visited his family who had moved west from Missouri to Lincoln, Nebraska, Pershing boarded a train in Omaha bound for the southern reaches of New Mexico, close to the border of both Arizona and Mexico. He took the train as far as Deming, New Mexico Territory, then trekked westward to Silver City, and then eight miles further to Fort Bayard, where he reported for duty on September 30, 1886.[8] Thirty years later, Pershing's Punitive Expedition captured some of the men who had taken part in the Columbus raid about three hundred miles inside Mexico; they were sent first to Silver City and then to Deming for trial.

Part of Pershing's calculation in asking for the Sixth Cavalry was the promise of promotion through action in the campaign to catch Geronimo. But by the time Pershing arrived in Arizona Territory, Geronimo and over four hundred

other Chiricahua Apaches who were exiled with him had already been igno-
miniously dispatched eastward on a train headed for prison in Saint Augustine,
Florida. Many of those who survived their first few years of captivity in Florida
and Alabama would end up at Fort Sill under the watchful eye of Hugh Lenox
Scott.

Bear Coat Miles remained in charge of the Department of Arizona when
Pershing arrived. He had presided over the surrender of Geronimo and the
Apaches' deportation to the East. The unruly border had been brought under
a semblance of state control for the first time in three centuries; breakouts,
such as the one that had precipitated the epic pursuit of Geronimo, were rare
and short-lived, but pursuing renegade Apaches remained the raison d'être for
maintaining the army's archipelago of forts along the border.

Though its frontier days were over, the army continued to project punitive
force along the border. Asymmetrical use of power focused on a racially defined
other with an emphasis on pursuit and the use of overwhelming force, whose
purpose was both to punish and also to provide an object lesson in the futility
of resistance to the U.S. land and settlement policies.

The department was subdivided into districts of observation, each one
under a commander responsible for patrolling his domain. The main work of
the cavalry was pursuit and capture of Indians who had left the reservations.
The objective was to "hound the Indians until they were caught."[9]

Shortly after his arrival at Fort Bayard, Pershing took part in one of the last
pursuits of a Warm Springs Apache who was a fugitive from the army. Mangas,
who had been with Geronimo in Mexico, had escaped capture with the rest
of the band. In early October, he crossed the border from Mexico and was reported to be heading for the Black Range and Mogollon Mountains in New
Mexico. In command of a troop from Fort Bayard, and supported by a mule
train to carry additional ammunition and supplies, Pershing was in the field
for three weeks on a futile chase. Mangas eventually surrendered to Captain
Charles Cooper of the Tenth Cavalry, who pursued him over five mountain
ranges. Mangas and the rest of his group were sent east to imprisonment in
Florida. Mangas eventually ended up at Fort Sill along with Geronimo and the
other Apache prisoners.[10]

Although there were few opportunities to chase actual Indians, General
Miles prescribed exercises to keep the troopers in trim for the real thing. He
devised field maneuvers that reproduced the dynamics and tactics of punitive
warfare: pursuit and capture. At each post, troops took turns playing the roles

of raiders and pursuers. The raiders were given an eighteen-hour head start.
Their objective was to raid an army post by coming within a thousand yards of
its flagstaff in daylight without detection. The job of the pursuers was to catch
the raiders before they were able to accomplish this goal. Referred to as rabbit
hunts by the troopers, the exercises were designed to simulate Indian fighting.
They emphasized scouting skills such as tracking, sign reading, horsemanship,
and—for the raiders—moving without being detected.[11] In one episode in
September of 1887, Lieutenant Pershing, commanding Troop L out of Fort
Stanton, pursued a rival troop led by Captain W. M. Wallace 130 miles in forty
hours, which included seven hours rest in camp the first night and three the
second. This kind of maneuver was Pershing's métier and won him favorable
notice from General Miles.[12] Policing, pursuit, and punishment with the objective of demonstrating overawing control and force became his signature. It was
a template inscribed by his frontier service.

Another conflict far to the north would provide a more brutal demonstration of the army's preemptive and punitive approach to pacifying Indian Country. In early December 1890, the Sixth Cavalry received its orders to become
part of the massive force being deployed around the Sioux Reservation in South
Dakota. In response to fears generated by a religious movement, the U.S. military marshaled the largest army since the Civil War, with disastrous results.

The Ghost Dance or Messiah Dance movement had its origins in the
prophecies of a Northern Paiute named Tävibo, who shared his vision of a
utopian world in which dead relatives would return to life and white people
would disappear. The movement spread through Nevada and to parts of California and Oregon in the early 1870s, but waned when the prophecies did not
come about. In 1889 another Paiute named Wovoka (Jack Wilson) revived the
movement, which this time spread through Kansas, Oklahoma, Texas, and as
far as Nebraska and the Dakotas. In his study of the movement among eight
tribes in western Oklahoma in 1890, Hugh L. Scott concluded that many of its
teachings were beneficial from the government's point of view. Scott shared his
analysis in a report he wrote based on his investigations: "A great many of [Jack
Wilson's] teachings are most beneficial to the Indians; he told the Kiowas for
instance that they must throw away that old Indian road behind them where it
could not even be seen; that they must not steal, run away with another man's
wife or do any other wild or crazy thing 'because Jesus don't want it'; that they
must plant corn and live at peace with the white man for Jesus says all men are
brothers; that they must take up the white man's road and persevere on it to

the end 'because Jesus wants it.'"[13] Scott also noted in his report that military authorities had taken the "large view" of the situation and "refused to be guided by outside influence, for they recognized that this dance was entirely peaceful and religious in its character." Unfortunately, this judgment was largely wishful thinking on Scott's part, at least in terms of what had happened in South Dakota. In particular, a civilian Indian agent named Daniel F. Royer at Pine Ridge raised the alarm about the possibility that the excitement the religious movement had generated among the Lakota would lead to violence. On November 16, 1890, he sent a telegram to General John R. Brooke, who commanded the Military Department of the Platte, that said: "Indians are wild and crazy over the ghost dance. . . . We are at the mercy of these crazy demons. We need the military and need them at once."[14] Military commanders, including Brooke in Omaha, and Miles, who commanded the Division on the Missouri from his headquarters in Chicago, were inclined to watch and wait and were not convinced that the Ghost Dance posed the threat that civilian authorities saw in the activities. Nonetheless, warnings of an imminent outbreak at Pine Ridge had reached President Benjamin Harrison and he was concerned. On November 17, Miles ordered Brooke to Pine Ridge and began marshaling a massive force to converge on the reservations from all over the West.

The Sixth Cavalry was ordered to Fort Meade, South Dakota, on December 1. The troop train that carried them there had nineteen boxcars, twenty-eight stock cars, two Pullmans, and sixty-two cars containing forage for the horses for six days. Aboard the train, under Colonel Carr's command, Pershing was one of twenty-one officers, 450 men, and several hundred horses and mules.[15] Fort Abraham Lincoln, where Scott had begun his frontier service, had been expanded in 1873 to provide protection for the Northern Pacific Railroad, the first railroad to extend its reach into what was then Dakota Territory. Two decades later, railroads cut through and around Indian Country and had played a key role in its conquest. In the context of the imminent crisis in their encircled land, the Oglala scout and statesman American Horse cautioned others who thought to resist the government's power: "How long can you hold out?" he reportedly asked some of those who proposed armed resistance. "Your country is surrounded with a network of railroads: thousands of white soldiers will be here within three days."[16] Even as he spoke the prophetic warning, American Horse's prediction was coming true. Troops were being conducted by rail from as far away as California. By mid-December half the nation's infantry and cavalry troops (approximately 3,500 men) were assembled in and around the remnants of the Great Sioux Reservation, six reservations that together made up less than a fifth of the sixty million acres originally reserved to the Sioux in the 1868 Fort Laramie. To open up land for white settlement in the process of creating two new states out of Dakota Territory, federal commissioners and local politicians pressured tribal members at the agencies to approve the land cessions or face having the nine million acres seized by force.[17]

Pershing was with troops of the Sixth Cavalry assigned to form part of the cordon around the Bad Lands. In late November, Sitting Bull, who had fiercely criticized the most recent loss of land to whites, was again a focus of concern for Indian agents as well as the military. Both sought his arrest in connection with the Ghost Dance. On December 15, a botched attempt by agency police to arrest him resulted in Sitting Bull's death, along with eleven others who were killed in the resulting melee.

Thereafter, the army's focus on leaders they suspected of stirring up unrest through the Ghost Dance shifted to the Miniconjou chief Big Foot. Feeling threatened and encircled, and becoming increasingly ill from pneumonia, Big Foot defied the orders of Colonel E. V. Sumner to take his people to the agency at the mouth of the Cheyenne River. Instead, Big Foot headed south for the Pine Ridge Reservation. He sent three messengers on ahead to let the Pine Ridge chiefs know he was coming, and that he was sick. On December 20, a squadron of the Sixth Cavalry, which included Pershing, was directed to be on the lookout for Big Foot and his band on the White River. However, the Miniconjous eluded them and were intercepted instead on December 28 by troops of the Seventh Cavalry. By this time, Big Foot was very ill. He was traveling in a wagon, wrapped in blankets. Blood was coming from his nose, and froze where it dripped on the floor of the wagon. This was how he was when Major Whitside came to meet him and told the chief he must bring his people into the soldiers' camp on Wounded Knee Creek. Nelson Miles had given the order to disarm Big Foot's band and take their horses. They were to be escorted to the railroad as soon as possible to be shipped to Omaha and kept there until the Ghost Dance had subsided.

The Miniconjous with Big Foot allowed themselves to be escorted to the army camp on Wounded Knee Creek. There they spent an anxious night. Whitside ordered two Hotchkiss guns installed on a hill overlooking the ravine where the Indians had pitched their teepees. After dark, more troops continued to arrive. Colonel James W. Forsyth also showed up to assume command from Whitside. Forsyth's orders were to take away the Miniconjous' weapons.

The following morning, a council was held and Forsyth quickly proceeded with the business of confiscating guns, knives, and swords. This was bitter medicine for the Indians to swallow. As it would later in the Philippines, American military insistence on relinquishment of weapons led to violence. The Miniconjous were divided about whether they should surrender their weapons. The Americans were insistent that all must be collected. From his sickbed, Big Foot advised turning over only the old and broken weapons. Accordingly, all nonfunctional muskets were brought forward. Forsyth ordered a search for weapons, including body searches of some Miniconjou women who were sitting on weapons or hiding them under their skirts. Accounts differ as to what happened to start the fighting at Wounded Knee Creek. What is known is that, as the search for weapons continued, at least one rifle discharged by accident; shortly after that, four or five young Miniconjous fired into a line of soldiers. This set off a fusillade from the soldiers' carbines; there was hand-to-hand fighting with knives. Bullets tore through the teepees; women and children were killed as they tried to flee. Big Foot was shot as he lay on the ground. The

Figure 5. Mass burial of Wounded Knee dead. Prints and Photographs Division, Library of Congress.

Hotchkiss guns fired exploding shells at groups of men, women, and children. In a few hours 25 soldiers and over 150 Indians were dead. The probable dead among the Miniconjous was even higher. Some have estimated that as many as 300 died at Wounded Knee. Very few of Big Foot's band escaped without injury. And all had suffered a great trauma.[18]

Following the Wounded Knee massacre, Pershing remained on the Pine Ridge Reservation for another six months in command of an Oglala Scout troop. This assignment lent both personal conviction and professional credibility to his proposals later on for native scouts for the Philippines. Techniques and attitudes acquired in the West while "commanding men other than my own race and color," as Pershing put it, were an important part of frontier military experience and helped pattern his approach to colonial occupation and military government in the Philippines. Besides the experience of commanding native troops, Pershing also adapted techniques of counterinsurgency, of surveilling, tracking, rounding up, and disarming Indians, which became the centerpiece of his policy as military governor of Mindanao.

Pershing's Oglala scout troop was disbanded in August of 1891. With the capture of Geronimo and the massive concentration of deadly force in and around the Pine Ridge Reservation of the Lakota with such devastating effect the previous winter, the army judged its need for Indian scouts to be nearing its end. At Fort Sill, Hugh Lenox Scott's Indian troop lasted longer than any other in the army. Pershing would see some of the scouts he had commanded twenty-three years later, when he took his children to see Buffalo Bill Cody's "Wild West Show."[19]

Pershing was not in favor of breaking up the Indian troops. He thought them well suited to irregular warfare. Like Scott, he thought military service was good for discipline and morale among the men who enlisted, and also encouraged loyalty and inculcation of civilized ways. He wrote that it "would have been an excellent idea to have formed one or two permanent regiments of them, as we had with the Negroes."[20] Although the chapter was closing on the use of Indian scouts on the domestic frontier, the practice of recruiting natives—different ethnic groups to police and make war on one another—would be revived and expanded within the decade on the far-distant frontier of empire in the Philippines. Men like Pershing and Scott, as well as other veterans of cavalry service in the West, made immediate connections between their experiences commanding Native Americans and the potential usefulness of native auxiliaries in colonial warfare. In the meantime, Americans joining the Cuban cause would cast Cubans as scouts in their own war for independence.[21]

In the summer of 1891, the future of native auxiliaries in the U.S. Army was not of great concern to Pershing personally, however. For several years, he had been seeking the opportunity for detached service as an instructor in military science at the state university in Lincoln, where his family had relocated from Missouri several years before. Following the muster out of his scout troop that summer, Pershing followed his family to the capital city of the dynamic young state of Nebraska.

Pershing's assignment in Lincoln represented an opportunity to reassess his long-term prospects in the military and to explore other ways of living and making a living. The contrast between the remote posts of cavalry service and the seeming oasis of expanding prairie civility and culture could not have seemed greater to Pershing. The four blocks of the university were well integrated into the capital city of a new western state that was playing a growing role in national politics. And yet, although located some 350 miles southwest of the killing ground on Wounded Knee Creek, the two prairie realities in fact represented two aspects of the same process of the transformation of land ownership, occupation, and use.

Figure 6. Oglala Scouts with Lieutenant Pershing, Pine Ridge, 1891. Prints and Photographs Division, Library of Congress.

Land grant universities like the one in Lincoln were themselves institutions that served to develop U.S. interests on the newly consolidated frontier of the expanding westward empire. Passed by a Yankee Congress in the second year of the Civil War, the ambitious and farsighted Morrill Act provided land and federal funds for the establishment of western universities. Among their other functions, the universities established on land granted to the states for the purpose would include military science and a program for officer training for the national guard. Even as the North and South fought to determine the basis on which the new western territories would be incorporated into the expanding continental empire, the 1862 Morrill Act set down provisions that would profoundly shape the dynamics of that expansion on the ground. Besides the important emphasis given to agriculture and to engineering, two bulwarks of the expanding agricultural civilization, the university headed by Dr. James Canfield offered a classical liberal arts curriculum. In addition to the Academic College it comprised the Industrial College, the School of Fine Arts and Music, the School of Graduate Instruction, and a newly organized College of Law.[22]

As a thirty-one-year-old junior officer who had spent the five years since his graduation from West Point at remote forts and policing Indian agencies, Pershing would benefit both personally and professionally from the four years he spent at the University of Nebraska. Although impossible to foresee at the time of his arrival, connections formed in Lincoln would help launch him on his overseas colonial career. But it was equally true that the provision for military science as a component of training in institutions that otherwise hewed to a model of classical liberal arts education, and "sponsored student activities which were almost entirely intellectual," introduced a martial ethos to counterbalance the influence of the debating and literary societies that otherwise predominated. As the journalist (and later army censor in World War I) Frederick Palmer commented: "Second Lieutenant Pershing as he walked across the campus . . . was an example and an apostle of military training."[23]

The presence of a federally sponsored member of the armed forces on the faculty met varied responses from the civilian members of the community. In his initial meeting with Chancellor Canfield, the two men discussed the indifference and even hostility toward the military that characterized a considerable part of the student body and faculty. Pacifist sentiment was rife even among the cadet corps.[24] Part of Pershing's campus mission as an officer of the regular army on the faculty of a civilian, public state university was precisely to introduce military values and perspectives into the mainstream of university life. At this Pershing was very successful. In particular, the success of his cadet corps in winning top honors (and a $1,500 check for the university) in a national competition earned him a following—as well as an oyster supper provided for the victorious squad by the chancellor. Pacifism notwithstanding, the glory won for Nebraska by the Pershing Rifles "stirred the exuberant pride of the faculty and student body."[25]

The armory, Grant Memorial Hall, where Pershing conducted training exercises, represented the military purpose at the core of the university's mission. A decade later, celebrations of the university's Charter Day in 1903 included the formal presentation of a "Filipino cannon" (probably a brass *lantaca* from Mindanao) that Pershing had sent to his former company of the Pershing Rifles at the university. During the February 16 ceremony, Chancellor E. Benjamin Andrews accepted the cannon for the university and pledged to care for it.[26]

With Chancellor Canfield's support, Pershing sought to increase his teaching duties and professional presence on campus by applying to the state legislature for an appointment—and an increase in salary—to teach mathematics. In his request to be "appointed to Instructor in some branch of learning at the University, preferably Mathematics," Lieutenant Pershing noted that the federal government was "very liberal in its allowance of arms, ammunition and equipment, the Military Department being practically at no expense to the State." He suggested, therefore, that "the latter [could] well afford to be liberal to the Officer instructing her youth." He asked that his compensation be set at $750 a year. He expressed his opinion that such a salary would secure for the university in the future "a much better class of officers than if no pecuniary inducement were offered," adding: "This I am in a position to know."[27]

The Board of Regents responded to Pershing's request by appointing him to teach math in the Latin School, which was the preparatory department of the university, which at that time had almost as many students as the college proper. The "prep" was established to address the educational deficiencies of many students who wished to attend the university, but whose high school education—especially in Nebraska's small towns and rural areas—had not prepared them for the challenges of the university.[28]

Among Pershing's students in the "prep" were several who later made significant contributions to American intellectual life. The writer Willa Cather, whose family had a farm near Red Cloud, Nebraska, was one of his students. Already noted at college for the drama criticism she contributed to local newspapers and as a leading contributor to campus literary endeavors, Cather also commanded her classmates' attention with her "mannish styles" of dress, bobbed hair, and "daring" skirts that "were not sidewalk length."[29] Her literary achievements and promise notwithstanding, Willa Cather was not a good math student. It was the only course she failed, in her freshman year, and it almost prevented her from receiving her degree.[30] Along with the noted folklorist and pioneer in women's education Louise Pound, Cather drilled with a company of female cadets at the university; both held ranks as noncommissiond officers in the corps.[31]

The students Pershing taught at the University of Nebraska, both in the classroom and on the parade ground, remembered him as rigid, quintessentially military in his bearing, and exacting in his demands of his students. Dorothy Canfield, daughter of the university president, who was one of his students when she was fourteen, later related that he "taught a living subject like geometry as he would have taught a squad of raw recruits."[32] Alvin Johnson, one of the founders of the New School for Social Research in New York, remembered Pershing as the one of his teachers who had interested him most: "Lieutenant Pershing was tall, perfectly built, handsome. All his movements, all play of expression, were rigidly controlled to a military pattern. His pedagogy was military. His questions were short, sharp orders, and he expected quick, succinct answers. Woe to the student who put a problem on the board in loose or slovenly fashion! Pershing's soul appeared to have been formed on the pattern of 'Present—arms! Right shoulder—arms! Fours right! Forward march!'" Due to the harvest demands on his family's farm, Johnson arrived late for the start of his first semester at the university. He found many of his professors "were very considerate" and allowed him time to catch up. Not Pershing. When Pershing ordered him to the chalkboard to work an algebra problem in his first week on campus, Johnson asked to be excused on the grounds that he had not had time to catch up with the class. "You have been here a week," said Pershing grimly. "By next Monday be caught up."[33]

The students who trained with him as cadets found him similarly stiff and exacting. As Canfield had predicted, there was some resistance to the expectations Pershing had for the members of the cadet corps. Many of the students worked jobs around town to pay for their education. Cadet drill was an extra demand on their time that not all were inclined to treat seriously. Pershing soon made it clear that he considered such a view inimical to participation in his corps of cadets. An anonymous verse posted on the chancellor's bulletin board one day provided a glimpse of some of the dissenting views on the value of the martial education Pershing represented:

The Commandant
May rave and rant,
And utter military cant,
And say you shall and say you shant
And sing his military song
In accents loud and harsh and long,
Unto a servile gaping throng
Who to the butcher's gang belong.[34]

A martinet he seems to have been, but interestingly, there was none of the punitive or retributive character in Pershing's approach to teaching that would later surface in his harsh and sometimes bullying treatment of his West Point cadets when he returned there as a tactical officer in 1897, nor any evidence of the enthusiasm for hazing cadets as an upperclassman during his own time at the academy or that had manifested itself in the alacrity and preemptive approach to dealing with boys who challenged his authority in the LaClede schools where he taught before West Point. Perhaps he saw in the Nebraska farm-bred youth the boy he had been before school teaching and then a place at the military academy had offered him his own desperately sought escape from a life following the plow.

Most significantly for Pershing's future as a colonial policy maker, the time in Lincoln offered him the opportunity to earn a bachelor's degree in law. Law had been the career Pershing had had his sights set on when he entered West Point. Now the University of Nebraska gave him the opportunity to pursue that earlier ambition and test whether a life as an attorney might offer better prospects for him.

Local lawyers supported the enterprise of the nascent law school by making their own libraries available to would-be lawyers such as Pershing and others enrolled in the law program. With offices located close to the university and also easily accessible to and involved in the business of the state legislature, Lincoln's legal fraternity in the 1890s included several men destined for prominent political careers. One of them, William Jennings Bryan, was already well on his way to national renown. Others included Charles Gates Dawes, Roscoe Pound, who was the brother of former cadet Louise Pound, Charles Magoon, and George Meiklejohn.

As a bachelor, Pershing had both the time and inclination to spend time in the offices and dining out with many of Lincoln's up-and-coming young men.

Several of these friendships proved mutually beneficial to their later rise to power in ways unfathomable to them at the time. Among the many consequential associations that Pershing formed in Lincoln, the ones that had the most impact on his colonial career were his friendships with Charles Magoon and George Meiklejohn. However improbable it might have seemed in Lincoln in the early nineties, before any of them had reached his fortieth birthday, these three men would make up the nucleus of a de facto colonial office of the United States that developed under the direction of Meiklejohn as assistant secretary of war. Even more unlikely, it would be Pershing who became the chief of that office after returning from the war in Cuba. Meiklejohn brought Magoon on board as "legal officer" in 1898, and he supported Pershing's appointment to his first colonial administrative post.[35]

Pershing completed his bachelor's degree in law in 1893. He continued to ponder the idea of leaving the army to pursue law. Among the issues he considered and discussed with friends in Lincoln during this time were the unpromising conditions for promotion. A foreign war, the surest avenue for advancement for a young officer, seemed unlikely. Indeed, Pershing told a friend he doubted whether "there'd be another gun fired in a hundred years." Pershing wondered whether a legal career might offer better prospects than a military one in which he could optimistically expect to retire with a rank of major.[36]

Pershing's vacillation over his career course was brought to a head when he received his long-awaited promotion—but not in the "Galloping 6th" as he had hoped. Instead, he was offered a lieutenancy in the Tenth Cavalry where a position had become vacant. Pershing hesitated. He wanted the promotion, but was not eager to leave his accustomed regiment for command of a company in a black regiment. Pershing tried to hedge his bets. At the risk of alienating the adjutant general's office, he wrote to ask whether he might accept the promotion but remain in "the regiment whose officers and men I have been with during the past six years."[37] The reply was not as peremptory as it might have been, but the upshot was not encouraging; he could remain in the Sixth only if he could find an officer to trade places with him. Such a feat was impossible. No such officer was available, as Pershing well knew. His aversion to joining a black regiment was not unique; nor was it the result of merely personal preference. His wariness reflected a widespread prejudice in the army. His own commanding officer in the Sixth, Eugene Carr, had also turned down a higher rank with a black regiment because he believed that "black men would not make good soldiers." Carr had accepted a lower rank in a white regiment instead.[38] Army attitudes in turn reflected the general prejudice of the society at large. As Captain Matthew Steele wrote a decade later, "The prejudice against the negro and the negro regiment is national; it is as wide as our territory."[39] In the course of exploring alternatives, Pershing proposed a law partnership to his friend Charles Dawes, who turned him down. "Better lawyers than you or I can ever hope to be are starving in Nebraska," the future vice president told Pershing. "I'd try the Army for a while yet. Your pay may be small, but it comes in very regularly."[40] Charlie Magoon, too, counseled him to stick with the army. Finally, Pershing made his decision for the Tenth.

Pershing's new commission took him west again—further west and further north than he had ever been. A decade earlier, he had begun his frontier service on the U.S. border with Mexico. Fort Assinniboine, headquarters of the Tenth Cavalry, was also a border post, serving the same military functions on the Northern Great Plains that Forts Bayard and Wingate did in Apacheria.[41] Built in 1879, the fort was part of the army's post–Little Big Horn strategy for containing the Lakota within the limits of the Great Sioux Reservation. Besides checking their movement beyond the limits of their reservations, the army sought to deny them access to the rich hunting grounds of the Northern Great Plains. The high plains, short-grass prairie, mountains, and woodlands of northern Montana and present-day Saskatchewan sustained an abundance of game, including buffalo, which had provided the basis of the economy and lifeways of a number of native groups that hunted them: Crow, Assiniboine, Gros Ventre, and Blackfeet. Along with the Plains Cree, the Lakota were more recent arrivals in the territory; these two Eastern Woodland tribes had become powerful and moved westward over the plains in the eighteenth and early nineteenth centuries.[42]

Until Sitting Bull fled across it in 1877, the vast plains punctuated by the Bears Paw Mountains in the south and the Cyprus Hills in the north represented a stretch of an unobserved border that "was the last quiet eye in a storm of exploration and settlement, conquest and convergence," according to Beth LaDow. The construction of Fort Assinniboine was an attempt to close that eye, to secure the border against unauthorized movements of people, including those who had been moving across the land for centuries, to reorient the economy on an east-west rather than north-south axis in conformity with the new delineation of imperial power indicated by the cairns marking the border at three-mile intervals on the open prairie.[43]

At the time of its completion in 1880, Fort Assinniboine was one of thirty-

one permanent military installations established by the army to police the movement of Indians in and around the Great Plains. An imposing brick structure
built to accommodate thirteen companies (over two thousand officers and men),
the fort represented the determination of the army to throw a cordon around
even the most remote and unsettled of the hunting grounds in the north, to
impose itself on "the last buffalo stronghold in America," the lands of the Big
Open and eastern Montana. By the time Pershing reported for duty there in
1895, the number of garrisons in Indian Country had been reduced by two-
thirds, reflecting the waning ability of the Lakotas and Northern Cheyenne
to challenge American control over the last contested reaches of the Northern
Great Plains. The encroachment of white civilization in its various manifesta-
tions introduced additional stresses on the dwindling buffalo herds and on
the people and cultures depending on them.[44] Railroads reinforced the army's
pacification of the formerly remote country by bringing hunters who accelerated
the bison's demise. The railroad also moved troops, provisioned the forts, and
heralded an influx of hostile settlers without end. As a Canadian lands surveyor
working on the other side of the border in the 1880s put it: "Oh, the handwriting
is on the wall.... Where there is a railroad our work [of settlement] is done."[45]

Railway magnate James J. Hill controlled private syndicates supported by
government grants—over $100 million in loans and subsidies—to construct
two railroads, one on either side of the international boundary. His Canadian
Pacific Railway pushed through the Great Plains in 1883, reaching its terminus
in British Columbia in the winter of 1885. In 1887 the Great Northern Railroad reached Montana's Hi-Line country. The two railroads ran parallel, separated in some places by fewer than a hundred miles of flat windswept prairie.

Despite agreements among the colonial powers following the Louisiana Purchase, the War of 1812 and the Treaty of 1818 between the United States and
Great Britain, which ratified the forty-ninth parallel as the international boundary, native people continued to cross the border as they had done for generations.
"The Great Spirit makes no lines," an Oglala called The Hero said. "The meat
of the buffalo tastes the same on both sides of the border." The Cree and Assiniboine in particular made regular seasonal movements from the south to the
north, a practice, as historian Beth LaDow points out, that left them almost as
tribes without a country. For all the Native peoples inhabiting the borderlands,
the international boundary line—and the ephemeral posts and cairns erected to
demarcate it—"had all the authority of a loosely anchored buoy at sea."[46]

Under the intensifying pressure of the U.S. Army's campaigns against the

Sioux in 1877 and 1878, thousands of Lakotas sought refuge in Canada.[47] In spite of the way that historical writing about the aftermath of the Custer defeat has portrayed it, seeking refuge in Canada was not a new strategy for the Lakota nor for other Native nations. They were adept at pursuing advantage among a range of colonial usurpers of their domains, of which the Canadian "Grandmother" was merely the latest personification in a procession of imperial and territorial powers with whom they both sought alliances and fought for more than two centuries.[48]

The transborder movements of Native peoples led to periodic tensions between the Grandmother and Washington, especially during the late 1870s when the army was fixated on Sitting Bull's continued presence there. Unlike Mexico during the Apache Wars, Canada did not countenance cross-border raids by the bluecoats. Instead, the British Dominion territory provided a refuge, and more importantly, a source of guns and ammunition and even some sympathy for the Indians who fled north and availed themselves of the power of the "Medicine Line" to evade the reach of the U.S. Army. For the most part, it was Canada that served as a refuge for Indians fleeing the U.S. Army, but the geopolitical divide between the two continental nation-states also afforded protection to Indians fleeing the jurisdiction of Canadian law. In the case of the Métis, a quintessential borderlands people, it was the Montana side of the line that afforded refuge in the aftermath of an unsuccessful rebellion that challenged the same forces of Canadian expansion that the Sioux War had challenged on the American side.

The name Métis reflected the French word for mixed race. The people to whom this term was applied formed a distinct ethnic group that straddled the border throughout the lands of the fur trade that had given birth to them: Minnesota, Manitoba, and the Montana, Dakota, and North-West Territories. Culturally, the Métis were indeed a hybrid people. They were connected to and moved between European and indigenous worlds; they also developed their own distinctive culture, as well as carving out their own niche in the fur trade as it spread to the interior of the continent by the early nineteenth century. In this endeavor, so transformative of the continent's economy and social relations, they performed the roles of interpreters, guides, and canny and resourceful traders and middlemen. They had their own settled communities and claims to land, especially in the Red River valley. In addition to long-distance trade, they also participated in the buffalo hunts on the prairies—for as long as those hunts lasted.

The Métis who rose up against the Dominion Government in 1885 were led by a Métis man who had played a leading role in the establishment of the province of Manitoba and in championing the rights of mixed-race people. Like their Indian forebears, Louis Riel and his followers insisted that they, too, held aboriginal title to land in Canada. In spite of these claims, the Métis found themselves increasingly squeezed out and dispossessed. The decline of the fur trade and the buffalo herds both dealt harsh blows to the basis of their economy. Their communities were further threatened by European settlers' demand for land and the lack of respect (as they saw it) by the Ontario Government for their aboriginal rights to it. Such concerns had prompted the Red River Rebellion in 1869–70. Regarded by the Ontario Government as a criminal for the court-martial and execution of an opponent of Métis authority in the Red River country, Riel had gone into hiding and periodically crossed the border to seek refuge in Montana. Fourteen years after the Red River Rebellion, he made the decision to recross the Medicine Line with the goal of establishing an autonomous government territory for Native and Métis people in the Northwest Territories. In addition to the Métis, Riel's cause was joined by Salteaux, Cree, Sioux, and Canadian allies. The newly self-governing Dominion colony of Canada sent eight thousand troops to crush the uprising and forestall the formation of the short-lived Provisional Government of Saskatchewan. The war ended with Riel's arrest, trial, and execution for treason.[49]

Following the defeat of Riel's rebellion, Métis and Cree continued to cross back and forth over the Medicine Line as they had done for generations; some sought refuge in Montana Territory. It was Métis labor, in large part, that built Fort Assinniboine. Its unique brick design incorporated the work of five hundred Métis workmen who were recruited from nearby Lewistown to make the bricks that gave the garrison its distinctive appearance.[50]

Inside the brick fort raised with their labor, the Métis and particularly the Canadian Cree had become the focus of army policing of Indians during the time Pershing was stationed there. Since the early 1880s, troops from Fort Assinniboine had engaged in periodic efforts to intimidate Crees into crossing into Canada. If they were successful in capturing the Cree, the troops confiscated their belongings and escorted them to the border where they were left with four or five days' worth of rations.[51] The army's practical ability to control the border was limited. The Cree roundups continued, however. Settler tolerance for the presence of Indians decreased after Montana statehood in 1889, just as it had in Minnesota three decades earlier.[52]

In the summer of 1896, Lieutenant Pershing led an expedition to track and arrest several different groups of Crees throughout the northern part of the state. Their Cree captives totaled about two hundred, some captured near Great Falls and others at Camas Prairie and in the vicinity of Missoula. The soldiers then escorted their prisoners north to the Canadian border. In the process, they rode, walked, took the train, and forded several rivers, including the Flathead, which Pershing described in his memoirs: "The crossing of the Flathead [River] by that nondescript outfit made a wonderful picture—naked Indians swimming horses barebacked, yelling, handling broncos that had never been roped, the black troopers manning an old ramshackle ferry to carry the women, children, property and vehicles across the swollen river—all added rapidly and impressively to one's experience. We were a day and a half here at the crossing, but the task was accomplished with the loss of only a few Indian ponies."[53] Other than policing the Cree, there was little to occupy the troops at Fort Assinniboine. It was a remote post in a harsh climate. Daily drills with horses were "generally conducted with the men in buffalo overcoats and the animals protected by heavy blankets." During Pershing's time at the fort, the temperature once reached 60 degrees below zero.[54] However, the country around the fort did provide ample opportunity to pursue the activity that had played a role in the fort's strategic purpose: hunting. Hunting the wild game that had drawn people to the region had provided the primary basis for social organization—and for conflict—among groups on the northern prairie for centuries. The U.S. Army was no exception. Pershing and other officers at the post hunted antelope, deer, prairie chickens, ducks, and hill cranes. The post kept six large borzoi that they used for hunting wolves. Hunting for wild game was an integral part of life at Fort Assinniboine. It provided both sport as well as a way to supplement the menu at the remote post.

One hunting trip in particular would prove consequential for Pershing in ways that involved more than just sport or food, and also demonstrated the continuing political significance of hunting in the West. In the fall of 1886, it fell to Lieutenant Pershing to organize a hunt for Nelson Miles, by then the commanding general of the United States Army, during a visit he made to Fort Assinniboine. The prospects for a hunt in the Bears Paw Mountains had been broached in correspondence between the post commander Jacob Mizner and General Miles in advance of his visit. When General Miles showed up at the fort accompanied by an entourage including the artist and chronicler of army life Frederic Remington, it was Lieutenant Pershing who was designated to organize and lead a recreational outing that afforded the veteran Indian fighter the opportunity to reminisce and reacquaint himself with the landscape in which he had achieved several of his most celebrated victories as well as endured a good measure of frustration in standoffs against adversaries now defeated.[55]

Nineteen years earlier, Miles had tracked and intercepted the Nez Percé leader Chief Joseph and some four hundred of the Nez Percé Indians at the base of the Bears Paw Mountains. In an epic three-month trek across some of the most rugged terrain in the country, the Nez Percé had fled in response to efforts by the U.S. government to remove them from their homeland in the Wallowa valley in eastern Oregon. In their determined bid to reach sanctuary in Canada, they had traveled 1,700 miles across the Idaho and Montana Territories, eluding and outrunning the army forces marshaled to pursue them, fighting skirmishes along the way. From where the exhausted group rested at their camp on Snake Creek, the border was just 40 miles away. For his part, Miles had marched his troops rapidly over 300 miles to reach Chief Joseph's camp on that bitter September morning in 1877. The surrender of Chief Joseph six days later was heralded as a great victory for Miles and the army.[56]

The following year, 1878, Miles had been prepared to attack Sitting Bull when he led a hunting party south over the border. Miles had already sent out his supply train with escort when a telegram from Washington ordered him back.[57] Sitting Bull's hunting party quickly withdrew beyond the border. By the next year, Miles had received the approval he needed from his superiors to drive the renegade Sioux back into Canada when they strayed south of the line. In July 1879, with a force of about 700 troops and 143 Crow, Cheyenne, and Assiniboine auxiliaries, Miles attacked Sitting Bull's camp after a buffalo kill on the Big Bend of the Milk River. They killed five men and captured a woman.[58]

Over the next four years, Miles hoped to earn the glory of bringing the Hunkpapa leader in, so he policed the Big Open country, effectively discouraging Sitting Bull's refugees in Canada from hunting south of the Medicine Line.[59] In the winter of 1881, American forces had come close to getting Sitting Bull. When some of the Lakota ventured south of the border to hunt, Miles's troops killed three of the party, including a woman. In grief or outrage, another woman, Whirling Bear's sister, then tried to fire arrows against the American soldiers, but she was stopped by some in her party. Some of the group surrendered; the rest retreated into Canada. The Lakota's survival there was becoming untenable.[60]

A few months later, pressed by the hunger of his people and pressured by the Canadian Government, which had grown weary of providing sanctuary to Sitting Bull and his followers, the uncompromising Hunkpapa made the fateful decision to cross back over into American-controlled territory in 1881. In July of that year, at Fort Buford, three hundred miles southeast of Fort Assinniboine, he became the last Lakota leader to surrender his rifle to the Americans. Significantly, while clearly recognizing his captivity and his people's subjugation to the reservation system whose creation he had never countenanced, Sitting Bull yet expressed the wish "to be allowed to live this side of the line [border] or the other," as he saw fit. He added that he wanted to "continue my old life of hunting, but would like to be allowed to trade on both sides of the line."[61]

Thus, the hunting trip organized for Miles's return to the high-line country by Pershing had a larger symbolic significance that transcended its recreational aspects. At the time of its construction, one of Fort Assinniboine's chief purposes was to deny the Lakota the use of that part of the country for hunting. Besides affording the general of the army the personally gratifying opportunity to revisit the environs of his victories over the Nez Percé and Sitting Bulls' folk in the relaxed company of an appreciative retinue, the hunting trip organized by Pershing in the fall of 1896 embodied the Federal government's achievement of a monopoly over hunting in the Bears Paw Mountains. In this sense, the organization of a hunting expedition for the entertainment of the general of the army, who had had a personal role in thwarting Sitting Bull's efforts to engage in the same activity, conveyed a symbolic meaning as powerful as any punitive campaign. The campaign to starve Sitting Bull's people into surrender was in fact just as punitive as the army's relentless pursuit of the Nez Percé.

Writing about the hunting expedition into the Bears Paws, Pershing judged it a success. Their bag of two days "was sufficient to supply the General's party with all they would take and leave enough for a feast all around for the garrison."[62] It is, of course, impossible to know what reminiscences the hunting trip in the Bears Paws brought forth; neither Pershing nor Miles mention their thoughts on the occasion. Frederic Remington, who was also along for the hunt, wrote several times of similar hunting trips, but left no specific description of the conversations around the campfire or in the mess tent on this particular occasion. However, it seems clear that the excursion and the opportunity it afforded him to observe and interact with Lieutenant Pershing left a favorable impression on General Miles. When Pershing visited Washington on leave three months later, Miles directed that Pershing join his staff as his aide. However impressed the general might have been with Fort Assinniboine's black troopers, it seems likely that it was the hunting trip that assured him of the younger man's compatibility for duties of a more social nature in the capital.

Even transplanted to the East, the mantle of his western experiences continued to impact Pershing's career prospects and direction. Perhaps no meeting was more consequential for his later career than the one facilitated by his West Point classmate Avery D. Andrews. Andrews had resigned from the army and was serving as a New York police commissioner, along with Theodore Roosevelt. He invited both men to share his box at the old Madison Square Garden one evening in January 1897 when a military tournament was taking place there. Here, in America's most urbanized space, Pershing and Roosevelt bonded over stories and experiences in the West that were so crucial to each man's career and destiny. Observing the two men's enthusiastic exchange of views and stories of the West, Andrews wrote, "They were nearly of the same age, Roosevelt being 38 and Pershing 36. Both were enthusiastic and expert horsemen and both had seen much of the West. Both knew the Indians and the Indian country, and both spoke the language of the plains and mountains . . . and formed a friendship which lasted through life." For his part, Pershing wrote, "I had no idea then that his [Roosevelt's] estimate of me would play such a role in my future.[63] They would meet again in Cuba only a year later. By then, Roosevelt was second-in-command of the First United States Volunteer Cavalry, better known as the Rough Riders (a name the regiment had borrowed from Buffalo Bill performances, already mythologizing the Wild West). On the road from Siboney to Santiago, Pershing helped pull Colonel Roosevelt's wagon out the mud.[64]

While on Miles's staff, Pershing used a different kind of pull to help secure appointment as assistant secretary of war for his friend from Lincoln, George D. Meiklejohn. After discussing the idea with Miles, Pershing made the case for Meiklejohn with Nebraska Senator John M. Thurston, an early supporter of William McKinley's nomination for president. Senator Thurston took the matter up with President McKinley, who made the appointment. "Meiklejohn was very grateful for my interest in his appointment," Pershing later wrote.[65]

Pershing's duties—and his ambition—kept him in the East. Following his three-month stint as Miles's aide-de-camp, Pershing accepted an appointment as assistant instructor in tactics at West Point, which was where he was when the war with Spain was declared. Constrained by an order that no officer on duty at the military academy should be relieved in order to join his regiment,

Pershing sought a special dispensation that would enable him to go to Cuba. Taking leave to go to Washington, Pershing lobbied George Meiklejohn, whose position as assistant secretary of war he had helped secure, to arrange his appointment as quartermaster with the Tenth Cavalry. On a day Secretary of War Russell Alger was out of the office, Meiklejohn made the appointment. Pershing hastened to Tampa to join his regiment.[66]

.

Part II

Indian Country Abroad

The sovereignty of the United States is not confined within territorial boundaries. Broadly speaking, it is coextensive with the world.

—Charles Magoon, legal officer, Bureau of Insular
Affairs, War Department, *Report on the Legal
Status of the Territory and Inhabitants of the Islands,
Acquired by the United States During the
War with Spain*, 1902

And they call us Bullard's Indians
Down on the Southern Line
Though he wears no buckskin mantle
Or quills of porcupine
But we'll follow our gallant chieftain
Without a flinch or fear
As true as the reds of Sitting Bull
Red Cloud or Standing Bear.

—"Song, respectfully dedicated to
Colonel L. R. Bullard [sic]
of the 39th Infantry U.S.V."

PHILIPPINE
SEA

SOUTH
CHINA
SEA

LUZON

Luzon
U.S. Military District

Malolos
Manila
Manila
Bay
Cavite
Laguna de Bay
Santo
Tomas

PHILIPPINES

MINDORO

SAMAR

Balangiga

LEYTE

Visayas
U.S. Military District

NEGROS

SULU SEA

MINDANAO
Iligan
Marahui
Lake Lanao
Binadayan
Bayan

Zamboanga

Jolo

TAWI-
TAWI

Mindanao-Jolo
U.S. Military District

NORTH
BORNEO

SULU ARCHIPELAGO

CELEBES SEA

0   50   100   150   200 Miles
0   50   100   150   200 Kilometers

Map 3. The Philippines. With the creation of the Military Division of the Philippines in March 1900, the U.S. Army introduced an administrative structure adapted from its experience on the frontiers of domestic empire.

Chapter 5

Spoil of the Spaniard

The nineteenth century was the golden age of colonial collecting. As European powers vied with one another to extend their claims over new and existing colonies, far-off tropical lands supplied the field laboratories and proving grounds for scientific pursuits as well as new hobbies, all of which valorized and depended on the collection of specimens and data. At the beginning of the century, Lewis and Clark's expedition combined elements of the traditional colonizing mission of discovery with an Enlightenment penchant for observation, measurement, and the collection of specimens of plants, animals, and fish, which were sketched, described, and—where possible—dispatched back east to be studied further and to be preserved as evidence of the nation's accretion of knowledge as well as its expansion of domain.

At mid-century America pursued its manifest destiny westward to the Pacific and south into Mexico, acquiring over 550,000 square miles of territory through war with its southern neighbor. Beyond its expanded Pacific and Gulf Coast shores, American citizens were empowered by the 1856 Guano Islands Act to lay "claim to every island, rock, or key around the globe that might possibly possess fertilizing agents." In the second half of the nineteenth century, entrepreneurial Americans, supported by their government, laid claim to ninety-four such outcroppings of nitrate-rich deposits of bat and bird excrement, much in demand for domestic agriculture. The guano islands became the first—and some of the most enduring—overseas possessions of the United States.[1] To connect its Pacific and Atlantic ports, the emerging colossus contemplated ways of acquiring territory in Central America through which to build a transoceanic canal. In 1842 President John Tyler had extended the purview of the Monroe

Doctrine to encompass not just the independent republics of Latin America, but also Hawaii, a position reinforced by James G. Blaine, then secretary of state, who had reiterated that Hawaii, like countries in Spanish America, was "part of the American system."[2] Having accomplished the purchase of Alaska from Russia, Secretary of State William Seward made no secret of the fact that he viewed Mexico City as a logical site for the future capital of the North American Empire.[3]

When it came to Cuba, Seward embraced an American political maxim older than the Republic itself, namely, that the island would "gravitate back again to the parent continent from which it sprang."[4] Seward's use of the gravitational metaphor to express the inevitability of that island's incorporation into the United States evoked an earlier comparison made by John Quincy Adams between Cuba and "an apple, severed by a tempest from its native tree ... [which] can only gravitate towards the North American Union."[5] In arguing for the extension of U.S. sovereignty over Cuba, both statesmen used scientific metaphors to underscore the political inevitability of union with Cuba. However, it is notable that a generation after Adams made his allusion to Newtonian physics, Seward augmented the familiar Enlightenment rhetoric by overlaying it with the language of geology. Cuba, he suggested, should be brought under American control because "every rock and every grain of sand in that island [Cuba] were drifted and washed out from American soil by the floods of the Mississippi, and other estuaries of the Gulf of Mexico."[6] Seward's reasoning represented natural history as political destiny. His imagery also suggested that Cuba could only be properly reconstituted and redeemed from a state of degradation by being reabsorbed into the upstream empire.

Geology was one of a number of scientific pursuits that came into its own during the nineteenth century. Geology, ornithology, botany, entomology—all made advances in the context of colonialism. The discovery of new species of plants and animals as well as fossils and rock formations previously unexamined by western explorers spurred interest and advancement in the natural sciences. In the social sciences, the political dynamics of colonial relations became naturalized in the very categories of analysis used by anthropologists to frame their questions, such as the presumed dichotomy between primitive and civilized people and societies. At the same time, colonial dominions also became privileged sites for the collection of all manner of data and specimens, from cranial measurements to beetles and birds' nests.[7]

Both governments and individuals undertook ambitious programs to capture and maintain collections of exotic animals, exhibiting the curiosities of their colonial domains for the edification of the population of the metropoles. The period saw the founding or expansion of museums in all the colonial capitals. The British Museum of Natural History was established in the fashionable South Kensington District in 1887. Two years later, a museum of natural history opened in Berlin. In addition to the grand metropolitan museums, collections of all sorts proliferated at the local and regional levels.

In the case of mammals and birds, the act of collecting necessarily involved killing them. The most essential tool of the nineteenth century naturalist was the shotgun. To be preserved in a museum, even eggs had to have the life blown out of them. This was the tradition of natural history collection pursued by the young Theodore Roosevelt, who took up the hobby at the age of eight, after becoming fascinated by the sight of a dead seal exhibited outside a neighborhood market. By the time he was ten, young Teddy had collected over a hundred specimens for his own personal "Roosevelt Museum of Natural History."[8] In addition to the skull of the seal he had persuaded the shopkeeper to part with, the collection contained nests and eggs of birds, seashells, pressed plants, and other natural objects. Roosevelt's enthusiasm for collecting led him to convince his parents to pay for lessons in mounting his specimens from the famed New York taxidermist John G. Bell.[9] When Roosevelt matriculated at Harvard University in 1876, his ambition was to become a scientific man in the mold of John James Audubon and Spencer Fullerton Baird. Roosevelt changed his academic focus out of frustration with the way biology was pursued as "purely a science of the laboratory and the microscope." Roosevelt favored a broader, more muscular approach to natural history, the kind where collecting was done with a gun, which also turned out to be his chosen instrument in the pursuit of Cuba.[10]

In addition to the metaphorical similarities between colonialism and scientific acquisition of specimens, the practice and ethic of collecting developed in ways that were complementary to and informed by European possession of overseas territories and the cultivation of skills and attitudes conducive to their control. John Edward Gray, keeper of the zoological cabinet at the British Museum and author of an early manual for stamp collectors in 1862, described both the appeal and the intellectual virtues of the collector's engagement with the world. "The use and charm of collecting any kind of object is to educate the mind and the eye to careful observation, accurate comparison, and just reasoning on the differences and likenesses which they present, and to interest the collector in the design or art shown in the creation and manufacture, and the history of the country which produces or uses the objects collected."[11] Gray's appreciation of the virtues of collecting highlights the link between the organization of knowledge and the mastery and control over colonial possessions themselves. Such habits of observation and comparison underlay the approach of army men like Leonard Wood in Cuba. They were also notable in the orientation of more minor colonial officials on the island such as Scott and Bullard. Lieutenant Pershing's acquisitiveness in Cuba mirrored that of the nation that sent him there.

By the mid-nineteenth century, acquisition of Cuba had become "a fixed feature of U.S. policy."[12] At mid-century the Ostend Manifesto made clear the importance attached to the possession of Cuba for securing U.S. power in the region. "The Union can never enjoy repose nor possess reliable security as long as Cuba is not embraced within its boundaries," the 1854 document declared.[13] Presidents James K. Polk, Franklin Pierce, and Ulysses S. Grant all pursued initiatives aimed at purchasing the strategic island from Spain. Spain rejected these overtures, and while the United States decided it could live with Spanish sovereignty over Cuba, the northern republic remained adamant in its opposition to the exercise of that sovereignty by any other power, including, as it turned out, by Cuba itself. It was the consistent U.S. view that "Cuba was far too important to be turned over to the Cubans."[14] In the face of a likely Cuban victory during the summer campaign of 1898, President William McKinley pressed for an armistice, a proposition that was understandably rejected by the Cuban Army of Liberation, whose leaders felt they had the upper hand in the conflict, and anyway, had nothing to gain by laying down their weapons and allowing the beleaguered and disease-ridden Spanish forces to regroup.[15]

The United States intervened in Cuba's war of independence to ensure a dominant American role in mediating Cuban sovereignty. U.S. economic and security interests on the island made it impossible for the government to view with equanimity the prospect of an independent Cuba, unrestrained by the exercise of either Spanish or American imperial power. At the same time, popular sentiment in the United States, inflamed against well-publicized acts of Spanish cruelty and oppression, called for American intervention to liberate Cuba from the Spanish colonial yoke.

The "neutral intervention" proposed by President McKinley in the war message he sent to Congress on April 11 carefully avoided any recognition of Cuban sovereignty. Instead, the United States acted "to neutralize the two competing claims of sovereignty in order to establish a third by force of arms."[16]

McKinley was determined to avoid the possibility of a truly independent Cuba.

By the time the United States mounted an intervention, which was popularly conceived as a strike against Spanish tyranny in the cause of Cuban liberty, the United States had in any case supplanted Spain as the preeminent economic and strategic power on the island in all but name. The United States provided markets, which Spain could not, for Cuban exports. By the 1880s Cuba shipped almost 95 percent of its sugar to the United States. The United States also constituted the largest market for tobacco and other exports. The bulk of Cuba's imports also came from the United States and American capital was the driving force in Cuban industrial expansion. North American firms dominated shipping, banking, and mining. A growing number of Americans also took up residence on the island, buying up plantations, working as machinists for the American-built mills and railroads, and both intermarrying with Cubans as well as founding their own distinctively American settlements.[17]

As North Americans invested in and traveled to Cuba, cultural and political ties to Spain were also challenged by the significant phenomenon of Cuban migration to the United States. Tens of thousands of Cubans of all classes traveled to the United States for employment and education. Others sought exile there, like Tomás Estrada Palma, who taught school in New York and became a naturalized U.S. citizen before returning to Cuba in 1902, where he was elected president of the short-lived First Republic of Cuba. The experiences that Estrada Palma and others had in the United States "guaranteed that North American influences would penetrate Cuban society deeply and indelibly."[18] In particular, Cuba's elite, many of whom had been educated in the United States, looked to their northern neighbor as a model of modernity and dynamism in contrast to what seemed like the increasingly untenable and undesirable prospect of continued Spanish rule.

The explosion of the battleship USS *Maine* in the Havana harbor on February 15, 1898, was interpreted by the United States as evidence of Spain's inability to provide for the safety of American ships in waters ostensibly under her control. More nefarious interpretations were immediately attached to the explosion, which killed 266 men on board. The yellow press blamed Spain directly for the attacks. A naval court of inquiry, quickly convened by President McKinley, was definitive (though later proved wrong) in its conclusion that the explosion could only have been caused by the explosion of a mine under the ship.[19] For the first time since the Mexican-American War, the United States prepared to send troops abroad.

For the army, the "splendid little war," fought over the last remnants of the once-great Spanish Empire, promised two things. First, it offered the prospect of unifying southerners and northerners against a common foreign foe. As Amy Kaplan put it, the war provided "the final antidote to Reconstruction, healing the conflicts of the Civil War by bringing together blue and gray on distant shores."[20] Troops were drawn from all over the country, but an effort was made to give prominent leadership positions to southerners. As Booker T. Washington observed sardonically, "in the distribution of military honors, [President McKinley] was extremely generous to the whites of the South."[21] Three of the generals given command in Cuba were former Confederates: Fitzhugh Lee, Joseph Wheeler, and M. C. Butler. Thus, the Spanish-American War marked the definitive reabsorption of (white) southerners into the Grand Army of the Republic.

In spite of the racial segregation under which they served, the prominence of African American troops in the early battles of the war at first seemed to offer the prospect that the struggle for Cuban liberation might also unite American soldiers across the color line. More important than achieving fraternity on the battlefield, many African Americans saw the war as an opportunity to press claims for citizenship rights at home through the demonstration of black manhood and patriotic sacrifice abroad. Such an expectation was expressed in the African American press at the time and was an important factor in motivating black men to volunteer to fight in Cuba.[22]

However, hopes that an imperial war abroad might provide a balm for racial divisions at home were quickly dashed. As in civilian society, so too in combat: unity among whites was secured at the expense of blacks who fought in Cuba. The American army also introduced a more extreme color line to Cuba than had existed during the course of the foregoing independence struggle, when as many as 60 percent of Cuban soldiers and 40 percent of commissioned officers were men of color, which was unheard of in the segregated U.S. military at the time.[23] As an African Methodist Episcopal (A.M.E.) superintendent of missions, the Rev. H. C. C. Astwood, complained from Santiago in late August 1898, "The color line is being fastly drawn by [American] whites here, and the Cubans abused as Negroes. It has been found out at last, as I used to tell them in the United States, that the majority of Cubans were Negroes; now that this fact has dawned upon the white brother, there is no longer a desire to have Cuban independence, but they must be crushed out."[24]

The second chance that the Spanish-American War offered the army was merely that afforded by any foreign war: the opportunity for ambitious officers to distinguish themselves on the battlefield and win recognition and advancement. Such was the opportunity sought by Scott, Bullard, and Pershing at the outbreak of the war. Although only Pershing was successful in his bid to be among the forces that landed in Cuba in the summer of 1898, Scott and Bullard secured higher positions of colonial authority on the island during the two periods of U.S. occupation that followed Spain's surrender later that year. Each of the officers collected on his Cuban experience in ways that advanced his career and helped determine its colonial trajectory. In addition to promotion and enhanced status in military circles, each man used his experience in Cuba as the basis for claims of privileged knowledge about the day-to-day requirements for ruling an empire. In the best traditions of colonial collecting, Scott and Bullard, in particular, used their respective positions in the first and second occupations of the island to gather observations, artifacts, and stories that they would interpret for interested audiences back home. More fundamentally, the American invasion and occupation of Cuba furnished each man with the material out of which to fashion colonial expertise, a valuable commodity indeed at the dawn of the twentieth century. For each man, in different ways, Cuba was also the place where the significance of the years he had spent on the frontier was reevaluated and repurposed to suit a new imperial reality.

Lieutenant Pershing

> We call the Tenth Cavalry the "Imperial Guard" and are all very proud of our record. . . . This is a beautiful country and I should like to own a ranch near here.
>
> —Letter from J. J. Pershing to Assistant
> Secretary of War George Meiklejohn,
> Santiago de Cuba, July 16, 1898

When war with Spain came in April of 1898, Bullard, Scott, and Pershing all saw in it the potential makings of their careers. Each attempted to leverage his own particular connections to get a place in the action in Cuba. Only Pershing was successful in getting a commission that landed him on the island in time to participate in the battles of Las Guásimas and San Juan Hill. There was nothing mysterious about this. Among the three, it transpired that Pershing's acquaintance with the assistant secretary of war, George D. Meiklejohn, from their Nebraska days, provided him with the most effective "wire to pull." As Pershing had helped Meiklejohn gain the War Department post in the first place, the assistant secretary of war was in his debt.[25] Years later, when Pershing sat down to write his memoirs, the six-star general confessed—though only in a note scribbled in the margin of the unpublished manuscript—that his "action in going directly to Meiklejohn was not at all in keeping with accepted army procedure then, and would not be today."[26] However, he felt it had been "excusable" in the circumstances. At the time, Captain Pershing felt no such compunction about bringing pressure to bear on his friend to help him secure the position of quartermaster in the Tenth Cavalry. If anything, the effectiveness of the assistant secretary's patronage seems to have emboldened Pershing to ask for more. An excitedly jumbled letter, written in pencil shortly after the Spanish surrender of Santiago, is full of "importunities of one sort or another," from Pershing to his benefactor, including the pointed comment that he had never before "had a friend in power who could help me."[27]

Pershing's letter to Meiklejohn begins with an account of his "gallantry in the field." Although as quartermaster he explains that he "might have remained in the rear," he had instead pressed forward to obtain a position near the front. "I was here and there with the regiment during the whole three days fighting," he wrote. Pershing followed his account of the battle with a request for Meiklejohn's support in getting him a commission. "I hear that there is another call for volunteers. If so I should like to have . . . some sort of recognition: Preferably, I should like however to have a commission in any *immune* regiment or similar organization, anything, from majority-up- Would it be asking to much to ask you to put in a letter of recommendation so that it can be referred to. Then if you could have a talk with [Adjutant General] Corbin Or Secty Alger I think you could get it for me."[28]

Pershing's preference for command of an immune regiment, repeated several times in the letter, is interesting. It reflects his astute grasp of the way the logic of race was playing out in American's first colonial war overseas. Based on the Lamarckian notion that the descendants of enslaved Africans were more accustomed to the conditions of the tropics and possessed a hereditary immunity to diseases such as malaria and yellow fever, the War Department favored the use of black troops in an assumption that "the Negro is better able to withstand the Cuban climate than the white man." In March, even before the declaration of war, the Twenty-Fifth Infantry (Colored) was sent to the Department of the South in readiness for deployment to Cuba. They were joined the following month by the other black units of the regular army: the Twenty-Fourth Infantry and Ninth and Tenth Cavalry.[29] Congress also authorized the organization of ten volunteer regiments to be made up of men who possessed immunity from tropical diseases. After much debate over the make-up of such forces, the army announced that six of the ten immune regiments would be made up of white men from the southern part of the United States; only four would be organized as Negro units.[30] Colloquially, though, the term "immune" was used to refer to black soldiers recruited for service in Cuba, Puerto Rico, and the Philippines. In his letter to Meiklejohn, Pershing mentions the incidence of yellow fever at Siboney, and he was not alone in assuming that, in the face of such tropical diseases, immunes would be favored for the duties of occupation to follow the fighting. "Everything points to peace, but some troops must be kept here, I think, or at the Phillipines and immunes—so called—will probably be the ones selected. At any rate this seems to me to be the best opening if indeed there is an opening."[31] As quartermaster for the Tenth Cavalry, Pershing was returning to the same regiment of Buffalo Soldiers he had served with in the Dakotas and Montana. The Ninth U.S. Volunteer Infantry, the first of four black immune regiments to be filled, arrived in Cuba for occupation duty in the summer of 1898. Like other American soldiers of all races, they soon succumbed to the very diseases to which they were supposed to be resistant. Racial immunity was a lie. The soldiers some Cubans referred to as "Smoked Yankees" died from malaria and yellow fever at the same rates as their white counterparts.[32]

Like Bullard, Pershing prided himself on his facility with the command of black troops, which he attributed in part to having "grown up among Negroes" in Missouri. Unlike Bullard, and even Scott, there is no record of Pershing making disparaging comments about African American soldiers. Pershing also notably abstained, at least in writing, from the widespread racist dictum espoused by most white officers of his day that black troops required white leadership and were not capable of showing military initiative except under the direction of white officers. This contention played out in a political battle over whether black volunteer regiments would be officered by whites or blacks. For the four black immune regiments, the War Department appointed ninety-six black lieutenants; more senior officers were all white.[33]

The salient point about Pershing's request for a commission commanding black volunteers is not its demonstration of his relative lack of racial prejudice.

The point is that Pershing recognized the instrumentality of imputed racial characteristics like immunity and more generalized ideas about the adaptability of people of African descent to tropical conditions. While he was skeptical about the efficacy of that immunity, he had the foresight to anticipate the way race would be refigured to suit the ideology of imperial war in America's new tropical acquisitions. Following his experience with his so-called Imperial Guard on San Juan Hill, Pershing sought a commission in a black regiment based on his reading that it offered him the best chance for personal advancement. He explained the rationale behind this strategy in his letter to Meiklejohn: "As I understand it there is no limit to the number of officers who can be appointed to immune regiments—at least no limit which cannot be broken down with an earnest hope of receiving some appointment which will give me a chance at service as I believe appointment in immune regiment will."[34] Pershing's importuning letter continues for four pages, in the course of which he alternately boasts, begs, and cajoles his friend from Nebraska in an effort to secure a promotion. "I take it for granted that you are anxious to see me receive advancement," he confides at one point. "It may well be that the war is about to end but even so I no less desire to receive an appointment." In one sense there is nothing exceptional about either Pershing's ambition or his insistent entreaties to the assistant secretary of war to exert influence in his favor. As he notes at one point, "Every soldier serves with a hope of receiving something for it and desires to make a reputation for himself."[35] Indeed, Pershing was hardly the only one writing to seek Meiklejohn's help; the assistant secretary was inundated with such requests for commissions and other favors.

There is, however, one surprising deviation from the usual formula of such letters from ambitious soldiers to the War Department. Interspersed among the details of his role in the fighting and his strategies for obtaining a commission in an immune regiment, Pershing includes an observation in which he intimates a very different kind of ambition. From Santiago in eastern Cuba, Pershing wrote Meiklejohn: "This is a beautiful country and I should like to own a ranch near here." It is difficult to know what to make of Pershing's wistful aside in a letter otherwise devoted to the single-minded pursuit of his military career. Obtaining land through conquest is, of course, a time-honored practice in war. Many of Pershing's fellow soldiers found the prospect of owning land in Cuba equally attractive and joined the ranks of the approximately thirteen thousand North Americans who had acquired title to land in Cuba by 1905.[36] Within a decade, almost the whole north coast of the province from which Pershing had written would come under American ownership, and while Pershing never followed through on his notion of acquiring a ranch in Cuba, other Americans soon bought up three-quarters of the cattle ranches in the whole country.[37]

Pershing's passing fancy for the idea of owning land in Cuba must also be understood as another allusion to the Nebraska connections that formed the very basis of his bond with Meiklejohn. Like his not-so-casual invocation of University of Nebraska Chancellor James Canfield and a network of "other mutual friends," who Pershing implied in his letter would be pleased to learn of Meiklejohn's efforts on his behalf, a shared acquisitive interest in land was part of the basic outlook of their generation of frontier-bred professional men. In 1882 Meiklejohn, newly arrived in Nebraska from Wisconsin, had formed a legal partnership with the son of Nance County's founding rancher, Randall Fuller, who had exerted a preemptive claim on land that was at the time part of the Pawnee Reservation. His son, I. R. Fuller, acquired two thousand acres and four hundred head of cattle. Cuba, on the eve of the transfer of sovereignty from Spanish to American hands, represented a new frontier for exactly the kind of early settlement and speculation that Meiklejohn and his law partner had witnessed and from which they had profited in Nance County, Nebraska, in the 1880s. As Louis Pérez has pointed out, Cuba was promoted as a "new frontier" for American "pioneers" in 1898, just as Nebraska had been a generation earlier, and just as the Philippines would be promoted a decade later through advertisements that sought to draw white settlers from the Midwest to Mindanao.[38]

In contrast to Nebraska's pioneers, wrote an American resident of Havana named Irene Wright, American settlers in Cuba would have to struggle with "the rigors of a southern, not northern, climate; and the dangers of contact with decadent, not savage, contestants with them for control." Wright's comparison of Cuba to the frontier regions of the north, recently subdued and settled by the forerunners of the settlers now flocking to the island, represents one way the myth of the western frontier was reinscribed on the American colonial experiment in Cuba. As was the case in the American occupation of the Great Plains, the main obstacles to progress were conceived of as the "rigors of climate" and the "dangers of contact" with the natives, both perceived as challenges to American settlement.[39]

The most significant benefit that accrued to Pershing through participating in the Cuban campaign was not access to land in eastern Cuba, however, but the opportunity the war offered to cement his relationship with two of its most politically prominent commanders. Shared status as western men was crucial to his rapport and standing with both. In addition to the role it played in reuniting North and South, the war in Cuba also provided a new arena for highlighting and validating the supposed frontier virtues of rough riding and the other manly achievements of western cowboys and Indian fighters. Pershing was especially pleased by the recognition he won from Colonel Leonard Wood. At his request, Wood wrote a letter of commendation for Pershing that was instrumental in securing him an appointment as a major of volunteers the following month. Wood, of course, commanded the most famous and storied regiment of the war, the First U.S. Volunteer Regiment, more commonly known as the Rough Riders. Even more significant for Pershing's future career was the way that sharing hardtack and bacon and driving mules together along rough Cuban tracks threw him together with the Rough Riders' even more famous second-in-command, Lieutenant Colonel Theodore Roosevelt. According to a story President Roosevelt liked hearing recounted years later in the White House, the day following the armistice Pershing had come upon Colonel Roosevelt as both made their way along the road from Siboney to Santiago. Roosevelt, whose wagon had become mired in the mud, was "swearing a blue streak at the mules." Pershing came to his aid, hitching his own team of mules to Roosevelt's wagon and helping to extricate him. In the retelling of the story even Roosevelt's coarse language became a mark of their fortitude and frontier resourcefulness. When prompted by the president to remind him what he had said on the occasion, Pershing responded coyly that the president's words were not appropriate to "repeat in the presence of ladies."[40] Thus, in the mud of war, Pershing formed bonds that were both intimate and manly. They were to prove of political consequence as well.

Major Scott

You will have some of what Parkman calls the "spoil of the Spaniard" now yourself.

—Letter from Hugh Lenox Scott to
Mary Scott, July 1, 1899

When the battleship *Maine* exploded in the Havana harbor, Scott was just settling down to his study of Plains Sign Language under the supervision of

John Wesley Powell at the Smithsonian Institution. Determined to be part of the force that invaded Cuba, he set aside his historical linguistic studies and focused his considerable energy on pressuring General Nelson A. Miles to obtain for him any kind of command that would land him in Cuba. Scott begged to be sent in "any capacity," and told the general he "would even cook if I could not go otherwise." Unfortunately for Scott, Miles was viewed as a potential political rival by the administration and was opposed by powerful men in the War Department, including Secretary of War Russell Alger and Adjutant General H. C. Corbin. Much to his disappointment, Scott spent the war in training camps in Tennessee and Kentucky as adjutant general of the Second Division. His orders to go to Cuba arrived only after the peace treaty with Spain was signed in December of 1898.[41]

Scott may have missed the fighting, but he played a major role in the military occupation of Cuba that followed. During the three years he spent in Cuba, Scott held a succession of colonial offices that included two months as acting military governor of the island when Leonard Wood was incapacitated by typhoid in the summer of 1901. As chief of staff to Governor Wood, Scott was a trusted aide, troubleshooter, and liaison between the governor and the military as well as civilian bureaucracy. Scott's administrative duties in the Cuban capital marked a distinct break from the frontier regimen of his early career. Certainly, it would be hard to overstate the contrast in climate, landscape, and pace of life between the remote forts and Indian agencies, where he had begun the life of a cavalryman, and the imperial trappings and duties that occupied his attention in Havana, a vibrant port city with many reminders of its four-century history as a stronghold of the Spanish Empire.

Instead of swimming horses across flooded rivers and making camp in the snow, Scott dined in the recently vacated palace of the last governor general of Spain's empire in the Americas, eating off china emblazoned "with a big Spanish Crown," as he wrote to his wife, adding, "After dinner I sat in a chair which . . . had been the throne of Blanco, Weyler etc."[42]

The change in Scott's status and duties mirrored that of the U.S. military as a whole. The occupation of Cuba and Puerto Rico elevated Indian-fighters to vice-regal appointments. Leonard Wood, former Apache-chaser and commander of the Rough Rider regiment, became military governor of Cuba. Nelson Miles—who had superintended the ignominious removal of the Apaches from New Mexico to Florida, relentlessly pursued and fought the Nez Percé, Lakota, and Cheyenne, and had held command during the massacre at

Wounded Knee—became military governor of Puerto Rico. Perhaps more significantly, the ongoing occupation of the Philippines, Cuba, and Puerto Rico created a host of bureaucratic posts that placed junior officers like Pershing, Scott, and Bullard in long-term positions with explicitly colonial portfolios. Scott's first assignment was as chief of staff for the military Department of Havana, under the command of General William Ludlow. Like Scott, General Ludlow was a former officer in the Seventh Cavalry; he had been part of George Custer's expedition to the Black Hills in 1874. Their shared associations with Indian fighting in Dakota Territory provided a bond between the two men.

In spite of its four-hundred-year history as one of the bulwarks of Spain's empire in the Americas and its role as a crossroads of commerce and culture in the Atlantic, for the U.S. occupying force in 1898, Cuba still represented Indian Country. John R. Brooke, who had been the military commander of the Division of the Platte with responsibility for Pine Ridge during the Ghost Dance movement, became the first military governor of Cuba at the end of December 1898. Brooke divided the island into military departments corresponding to its provincial boundaries, each with a military governor, very much on the pattern of the structure of command over the military departments of the Trans-Mississippi West.

On the plains, Scott's principal form of entertainment had been hunting; in Havana, he swapped field glasses for opera glasses as he frequented the opera house where the Spanish tradition of reserving a box for the governor general was maintained. Scott became accustomed to occupying that box. For the time being at least, he had exchanged the study of Arapaho and Comanche for brushing up on his West Point Spanish. Yet the U.S. Army had not completely forsaken its frontier outlook and neither had Scott. Within months of arriving in Cuba, Scott wrote to his wife asking her to send him his copy of Parkman's *Conspiracy of Pontiac* as well as some Longfellow poems. Later, he wrote to her of his pleasure at receiving the books: "I have missed them very much and find that I am forgetting an immense amount of those things—losing the Indian cast of thought mode of expression etc."[43] His precious copy of *Pontiac* was, of course, the book he took with him in his pack basket wherever he went on the plains.

Far removed though they might feel from their cavalry days in the West, at the same time, service in Cuba actually concentrated self-conscious veterans of the frontier in a new and unfamiliar setting, where the most familiar point of reference was often their earlier service in the West (and the fact that they were now in Cuba). As did Pershing, Scott drew on a familiar frontier network to find his footing and to orient himself to his new responsibilities.

Scott's surroundings and his professional status had changed significantly, yet his perceptions and approach to understanding Cuba and Cubans were guided by the habits of ethnographic observation, amateur scientific collecting of artifacts, and recording of folkways that he had begun during his years among the Indians at the frontier posts where he had served.

In one sense, Scott's appointment as chief of staff first to Ludlow and then to Military Governor Leonard Wood seemed to mark an end to the freelancing ethnographic inquiries that had characterized his service on the plains, especially at Fort Sill. Scott had left behind forever his frontier service at remote western outposts. Instead, he was posted to one of the great port cities of the colonial Atlantic world. However, in his efforts to master Cuba, Scott applied the same methods of observation and categorization that characterized his early encounters with the unfamiliar landscape and Cheyenne and Lakota Indians who had so fascinated him when he first arrived at Fort Lincoln in 1876.

Scott's penchant for collecting and classifying was evident in his determination to master the names of Cuba's flora and fauna, which began soon after he arrived on the island. He proceeded to classify them in a scientific manner. His research method was to stop by Havana's open-air fruit stalls, where he purchased specimens of each kind of fruit unknown to him, obtained their names from the fruit-sellers, wrapped each fruit "in a separate paper labeled with its Spanish name [and] took them to the hotel for study." In this way, he "soon became acquainted with the appearance, name, and taste of all of them."[44] Attempts to involve his wife, who had remained at home in New Jersey, in his scientific observations were less successful. Mary reported that the specimens he shipped north to her arrived rather worse for the journey. Scott's enthusiasm for learning the names of Cuban flora did have its limits, however. In his memoirs, he related how his enthusiasm for botanical studies was checked: "Some months later I started to learn to differentiate between the various species of Cuban palms; I had conquered seventeen when some one told me that there were two hundred and fifty more, and my interest in Cuban palms suffered a severe check."[45] Military paraphernalia remained a particular focus of Scott's collecting. The Kiowa and Apache collection he sold to Phoebe Hearst for her museum was particularly strong in shields, clubs, bows, and arrows.[46] Like other officers in the Philippines, Scott collected knives and other weapons. In Havana he developed an interest in old Spanish military decorations. Several months after his arrival in the city, he wrote to his wife with some excitement about a "pin" he had arranged to have shipped to her by express. "You will have some of what Parkman calls the 'spoil of the Spaniard' now yourself," he wrote, drawing an analogy between the souvenir he had acquired in Havana and the "swords, candlesticks & the bull of the Pope dispensing the Spanish colonists of New Mexico from fasting during midsummer," whose discovery by La Salle among the Cenis Indians of Texas was recorded by Parkman in his book *La Salle and the Discovery of the Great West.* He further describes the decoration, which he says is the "best of its kind in Havana." Butchering the Spanish, he tells her the medal is called "La cruce rioja de Merito Militar," which he translates as the Red Cross of Military Merit. An analysis of the iconography of the pin follows: "The rampant Lion and the Castle represent the marriage of Ferdinand and Isabella and consequent federation of Leon and Castille the fleur de lis represents the Bourbon alliance and if I am not mistaken there is a pomegranate representing the province of Grenada." He adds a disclaimer that he is "by no means certain of any of this unverified knowledge." He further cautions his wife that the cross is a "decoration and you should not wear it at any place you will see a Spaniard or a full dress affair where there are foreigners."[47]

Perhaps the most curious example of the "spoil of the Spaniard" that Scott collected during his time in Cuba was a set of stocks used for punishing slaves, which he offered to Woodrow Wilson to add to Princeton University's growing collection of archaeological and anthropological artifacts. Princeton's president acknowledged the gift on behalf of the Board of Trustees, expressing the university's appreciation of his "thoughtful kindness" in sending it.[48]

In addition to his interest in relics of Spanish imperial pageantry and corporal discipline, Scott's ethnographic curiosity was excited by *danzón,* an African-derived dance style that had gained popularity in Cuban dance halls as well as on the streets. After first hearing its *cinquillo* rhythms during Carnival, Scott wrote enthusiastically to his wife of his fascination with the "barbaric" music. "I wish you could have been here yesterday you have never seen such a sight or imagined such a people all night long societies of men women and children of every shade & color were passing up & down with a lot of African music—that music is the wildest most barbaric I have ever heard—it is perfectly fascinating to me. . . . I love to hear it."[49] Scott's observation of the mixed-race character of danzón reflected one of the most controversial aspects of the dance form within Cuban society. Elite Cubans criticized the dance as dangerous both because of its African origins and for the racial mixing it supposedly encouraged. As a concerned newspaper columnist had warned earlier in the century: "The black race has introduced into our decent white families a malign influence, one to which we have become so accustomed as hardly to notice it. And the power that the black race has over us begins with dance."[50] Danzón had been generating controversy since the 1880s when it gained popularity as an expression of "cubanidad," in contravention of Spanish norms. In part, argues historian Marial Iglesias Utset, it embodied a rejection by the popular classes of the modernizing morality of the elite. The popularity of danzón also continued to grow under the U.S. occupation, although the military regime took published orders aimed at regulating Carnival in keeping with the sensibilities of the new rulers, who frowned on dancing in the streets.[51] Scott, however, must have missed the spectacle after his first taste, for he loved to hear danzón, which he claimed "takes you out into the mountains and free country right away." So enthusiastic was he about danzón that he sent his wife some sheet music in the hope that she could play it on the piano.

> I send you herewith some music called the "Danzón"—I have never heard it on the piano—but the Cuban bands play it with all kinds of wild instruments one a large gourd 2 ft long they strike in with a piece of steel—tom toms etc—it is the very wildest and most barbaric music I ever heard—more so than that of the N. Amer Indian—I believe that it came from Africa or rather had its origin there among the blacks & came over with the slaves & was adapted here or else copied I do not know which—the Cubans dance a peculiar dance to it something like our walz which among the lower classes is most immoral but it is danced in a better way at all assemblages of the chautvolée [sic] I would like you to see if you can reproduce it on the piano for I love to hear it—it takes you out into the mountains and free country right away—I suppose however the tom tom is left out.[52]

John Charles Chasteen has described danzón as "the close embrace under military occupation" and as a "transgressive national rhythm." Danzón was a dance in which partners clasped upper bodies tightly and executed close sinuous movements of the hips and legs. The danzón rhythm was based on the regular accentuation of off-beats. Danzón bands emphasized percussion. The two-foot-long gourd mentioned by Scott was most likely the *guiro*, which is scraped with a stick to produce a rasping sound. Scott's tom-toms were kettle drums.[53]

Though he usually exempted Cuba's Spanish citizens from such comparisons, Scott found many points of comparison between American Indians and Cuban natives, especially those of African or mixed ancestry. During his three years in Cuba, Scott also developed a template of the Latin American character, which he employed as a point of reference for his later diplomatic dealings with Pancho Villa, Álvaro Obregón, and other Mexicans with whom he negotiated as President Woodrow Wilson's special representative during the Mexican Revolution.

The United States had intervened in Cuba ostensibly on behalf of Cubans against Spanish rule, but from the beginning, the invading Americans often showed more sympathy and solidarity with Spaniards than with their erstwhile allies, the Cubans. They left Spanish officials in positions of authority in Santiago, for example, while barring Cuban troops from entering the city during the formal surrender. During the occupation, this prejudice in favor of the Spanish population of Cuba became more racialized and pronounced. As the Americans replaced Spanish rulers on the island, perhaps not surprisingly, they often aligned their perspective on Cuban society with that of the imperial government they had displaced. It is notable in Scott's collecting that he imbued Spanish articles with historical value and prestige. His interest in Cuba's native culture was different but familiar. In assuming their new colonial role in Cuba, the Americans did not merely take over the Spanish approach, they also had another frame of reference: the history of their interactions and observations of native American peoples as they encountered and struggled with them for control over the shifting frontiers of domestic empire.

As his enthusiasm for danzón suggests, Scott routinely compared Cubans, especially Afro-Cubans, with American Indians. Scott regarded both types as primitive peoples who were not yet prepared to govern themselves. Because of this basic similarity, he also believed that the experience he had gained in his diplomatic relations with Indians on the plains was transferable to settling disputes among Cubans. His self-described strategy in such situations was to let the adversaries "use up their power in talk."[54] In commenting on his role in adjudicating a labor dispute at the harbor of Cienfuegos, he wrote: "When negotiating with armed and angry Indians I am never anxious over the voluminous talker, but I watch the silent one over in the corner. His desire for action is not dissipated in talk, and he may act. When they talk out all their opposition there is no power of resistance left, and they must fall like ripe fruit into your hand. I have seen this happen times without number, not only in Cuba, but in Mexico, in the Philippines, on the Plains of the West. One only needs an unfailing and sympathetic courtesy and an unconquerable patience."[55] In particular, Scott was careful to extend this courtesy to black Cubans, as a way of managing them.[56]

Scott's condescension—and worse—toward Cubans of color was magnified throughout the government in which he served. Put simply, Governor Wood thought the majority of Cubans unfit for self-government. Race played a major role in this determination. "We are going ahead as fast as we can," Wood wrote, "but we are dealing with a race that has steadily been going down for a hundred years and into which we have to infuse new life, new principles and new methods of doing things."[57] The military government in Cuba thus faced a dilemma. Beyond pacifying the country and providing for its short-term security, its role was to prepare Cuba for elections and the establishment of a republican form of government. Self-rule had been the Cuban rallying cry for thirty years. In joining their struggle, the United States had seemed to endorse that independence when Congress passed the Teller Amendment disavowing American interest in the island. But the McKinley administration was not ready to countenance a truly independent Cuba. Wood's task, worked out over months in close communication with Secretary of War Elihu Root, was to pressure the elected Cuban members of the constitutional convention to accept provisions that would guarantee the United States a continued role in Cuban affairs even after the army withdrew. These provisions, which Root formulated with input from Wood, reserved to the United States the right to intervene to maintain "a government adequate to the protection of life, property, and individual liberty." The Platt Amendment also preserved a continued military presence on the island by establishing naval stations, such as the one at Guantánamo Bay. It further constrained Cuban independence by limiting its freedom to enter into foreign treaties or contract public debt. The proposed measures provoked protests and demonstrations throughout the country. Some Cubans called for a return to arms. The delegates to the constitutional convention resisted the proposal and suggested several countermeasures, but the United States was adamant in its insistence on a continued role in Cuban affairs. Wood pressured the constitutional delegates relentlessly, finally presenting them with a blunt ultimatum: the military occupation of Cuba would not end until they agreed to accept the hated measures. In June of 1901, the Platt Amendment provisions finally passed the convention by just one vote. Elections were organized for early the next year.[58]

Scott played a prominent role in the transition between the military government and establishment of the first Cuban republic. Wood deputized him
to carry a draft of the Platt Amendment to Washington during the ongoing
negotiations with the War Department. It was Scott, as Governor Wood's chief
of staff, who also represented the American government when the president-
elect of Cuba arrived back in Havana after a quarter of a century in exile. While
escorting the septuagenarian Tomás Estrada Palma to the palace, Scott performed the role of bodyguard, deflecting enthusiastic Cubans who attempted
to approach the hero of Cuba's long independence struggle by punching them
"with all my strength and knock[ing] them out of the way."[59] Before Scott departed Cuba, he also gave Estrada Palma a tour of his own capital city, "pointing out to him the monuments of antiquity," and "making him promise me to
do all in his power to protect them." Scott was particularly interested in the
preservation of the Castillo de la Real Fuerza, dating back to the sixteenth century. Scott claimed credit for having thwarted its destruction during the U.S.
occupation when it was proposed that a post office should be constructed on
the site. He also commended to the president's care a building that was built
as a watchtower after a pirate raid on Havana in 1598. He claimed to have
saved the watchtower from destruction by American engineers working for the
occupation who planned to site a street railway through the area. Finally, Scott
exhorted the new Cuban president to look after the Morro Castle and the Castillo San Salvador de la Punta. During his three years in Cuba, Scott had come
to value the historic significance and "rare medieval beauty" of many of Havana's
buildings. At the end of a life in which he had visited many cities of the world,
Scott wrote that he still considered Havana the most interesting of all, for its
"picturesqueness" and its sights of "surpassing beauty." By taking Estrada Palma
on his own version of a historic preservation tour of the city, Scott hoped to
ensure that Cuba's "magnificent heritage" would be "preserved forever." In his
memoirs, he noted with satisfaction that all the sites he had pointed out to the
president-elect were still standing in the 1920s, and reflected without irony that
it was "a curious thing that [Cuban heritage] should have been protected by the
Northern stranger from destruction by the native."[60] What the urbane Tomás
Estrada Palma thought of the soldier's proselytizing on behalf of Cuban architectural heritage is not known.

Scott's interest in historic preservation was selective, however. Keen as he
was to preserve Cuban architectural treasures, Scott seemed to have had no
such scruples about destroying the records of the same U.S. occupation whose

concern for preserving Cuban history he had supported and praised. Following the transfer of sovereignty and the lowering of the American flag from Morro Castle, Scott returned with the rest of Wood's staff to Washington, where he described his work as "mopping up" Cuban affairs. Scott was called on to do more mopping up several years later when he was asked by the chief of the Bureau of Insular Affairs to oversee the destruction of records of the occupation "that were no longer needed or useful." The task took him several months. The condemned records occupied 4,500 cubic feet of space and weighed 24,830 pounds. Sold for wastepaper, the records of the U.S. administration netted $202.61 for the treasury. Interestingly, the first page of Scott's report on the culling of the records was also destroyed. "Mopping up" seems an apt military euphemism for this activity. A quarter century earlier, as a second lieutenant, Scott had been detailed to rebury the fallen on the site of the Little Bighorn battle. Mopping up an archive, just like mopping up a battlefield, involves burying dead bodies and disposing of the distasteful evidence of war. "Mopping up" is the prerogative of the invader.[61]

Lieutenant Colonel Bullard

The island is pacified. Now we'll see how long Cuban character will let it remain peaceful.

—Robert Lee Bullard, diary entry,
Havana, January 22, 1909

Like Scott, Bullard had been disappointed in his ambition to be part of the force that invaded Cuba at the outset of the war in 1898. Through his successful pursuit of some home-state connections, Bullard obtained command of a volunteer regiment. "Foreseeing the probability of Negro troops," he noted in his diary, "I took pains to write to the governor of Ala[bama] that I had no objection to taking a commission with them."[62] Governor Joseph Johnston obliged and appointed Bullard to command the Third Alabama Colored Volunteers. This was an all-black unit. Except for its chaplain, all the Third's officers were white. Awaiting orders to embark for Cuba, the Third Alabama spent the better part of a year in training camps, without ever leaving the state. Following the quick surrender of Spain in August, Bullard still hoped that his regiment would be tapped for duty as part of what Pershing called "the imperial guard" during the phase of military occupation that followed. Bullard made several trips to Washington to personally lobby the War Department to send his troops to Cuba or the Philippines, all to no avail. The fact that the regiment never left its home state did not mean they did not experience conflict or loss, however. Throughout the year, the black troops of the Third Alabama were subjected to racial abuse and outright attack by white civilians and soldiers who feared and resented the presence of black fighting men in their midst.

Relations with the residents of Mobile during the regiment's period of mustering in and initial training were fairly good, apart from some altercations with white streetcar conductors who treated the black volunteers with abusive disrespect. However, when Bullard's men were ordered to Camp Shipp near Anniston in September, they immediately became the targets of unrelenting hostility, both from their white comrades in arms as well as from civilians in the area. Camp Shipp was located in the hill country of eastern Alabama, 350 miles by train from Mobile. There the Third Alabama joined several white regiments: the Second Arkansas, Fourth Kentucky, and Third Tennessee. These white soldiers were "greatly displeased" at the arrival of the black troops and they immediately made that displeasure felt. They subjected Bullard's men to verbal insults and also looked for opportunities to beat up off-duty soldiers. The white soldiers also encouraged Anniston civilians to cheat and abuse the blacks.[63] In late November, the violence directed against the black volunteers turned deadly. A group of some seventy-five men who had left the camp to go into Anniston were there surrounded by a "howling, frantic mob" of several hundred whites, some of whom had obtained weapons from the local militia armory. The provost guard of the Third Tennessee was involved in the melee and was responsible for killing Private James H. Caperton, a regimental clerk of the Third Alabama and a former Talladega College student. Two other men of the Third were also injured in the attack; all three were shot in the back. On several other occasions, the regiment's sentries were fired on; several times at night the black camp was fired on, causing, in Bullard's words, "much confusion, bitterness and uncertainty among the negroes." In another incident, two black soldiers ordered to deliver some papers to headquarters were stopped by a white sentry who raised a loaded rifle, aimed it at them, and announced his intention to shoot the "damned, mother-fucking black sons of bitches." Only the intervention of a white officer succeeded in averting violence.[64]

In his memoirs, Bullard wrote that he "wept in helplessness . . . could only weep, over the injustices" suffered by his men at the hands of the white troops who insulted and attacked them.[65] Perhaps he did weep. At the same time, Bullard both understood and generally subscribed to the racist tropes circulating among the white population of the South that promoted the fear and resentment of the enlistment of black troops and their mobilization for the Cuban war in Tampa, Mobile, Atlanta, and other camps throughout the South. His indignation on behalf of his men was largely self-serving. As his men endured attack, Major Bullard nursed his hope for deployment through the disastrous winter spent at Camp Anniston. But the orders to go to Cuba never came and the troops of the Third Alabama were mustered out in March 1899.

Although they never saw action in Cuba and in spite of the abuse from white soldiers and civilians his regiment had to endure, Bullard regarded command of the Third Alabama as a crucial turning point in his career, one that won him his "first military reputation." Like Pershing, Bullard had leveraged political connections as well as his supposed "understanding of the Negro" to

Figure 7. Third Alabama Volunteer Regiment, Camp Shipp, Anniston, Alabama, 1898: "In the Company Street of My Negro Regiment." Robert Lee Bullard Collection, Manuscript Division, Library of Congress.

obtain a commission. While omitting mention of the murder and assault on his men, Bullard wrote that the discipline and self-control of his troops "under great provocation had made a name for me in the army as a commander."[66] Bullard, who felt disadvantaged by his rural Alabama upbringing among blacks, found it "just" that he had at last had a chance to benefit from the "appreciation of the difference between negroes and white men," which was the one benefit he felt his plantation childhood had provided him.

In addition to its professional value, Bullard later wrote that the experience of working with the Third Alabama had proved to be "an engaging and profitable study in psychology, in negro character and ways" for him. Besides constituting a "great source of satisfaction and pleasure" in later life, Bullard wrote that his observations of the black volunteers had provided him with "the material . . . to write an account of Black customs and expressions." "At the end," he wrote, "I had the material if I had only had the genius to write a Joel Chandler Harris classic on the race."[67] Although he never achieved the literary fame of his model, and only published a fraction of the short pieces he wrote in this vein, the enthusiasm Bullard conceived for writing Joel Chandler Harris style depictions of racialized folkways blossomed during the tours of duty in the Philippines and Cuba that followed. Bullard's commission with the Third Alabama meanwhile informed more prosaic writings in which he offered his assessment of the fitness of black troops and shared his expertise on approaches to take in commanding them. In an article analyzing the "characteristics [of the] Negro volunteer," published in 1901, Bullard reflected on his experience commanding the Third and expressed his judgment that Negro volunteers could make a good emergency soldier in times of need for a rapidly raised volunteer force, provided that white officers understood the particular challenges of commanding black troops and how to adjust command to "differences so great they almost require the military commander to treat the negro as a different species."[68] Key to the methods Bullard recommended, based on his own experience and on his analysis of racial difference, was an appeal to the men's "race pride" as a way to motivate their best efforts. The commander's most powerful aid in securing good conduct, he wrote,

> [lay] in touching him at the most sensitive point in his nature, his color, and in appealing to him for the honor and advancement of his race. "Are you willing to be dirtier and more ragged, more unmilitary, to do less and know less than a white regiment? Your

government has given you all, your very freedom. Far more than the white soldier you owe honest and faithful service Will you allow the public to say "It's a negro regiment, nothing can be expected of it but poor drill, bad discipline and disorderly conduct"? Your service is a privilege, an opportunity to show the gratitude, manhood and worth of the negro, an opportunity to raise your race higher and faster in the world's estimation by a few acts in a few months than by all the agitating, talking and voting your whole race can do in ten years.[69]

As he advanced in years and rank, Bullard wrote with increasing authority and impact, though not with any more insight or empathy, on the character, contributions, and what he saw as the limitations of black troops in the U.S. Army. He also wrote extensively about the "Negro Problem" in American society—and in Cuba. "Poor Negroes! They are hopelessly inferior," he wrote of the Negro Ninety-Second Division in World War I.[70] The authority he claimed for addressing such issues was based on his childhood spent in the company of "Negroes, big and little," and the expertise he convinced himself and others he had developed for commanding blacks in the army.

Bullard did not make it to Cuba during the first intervention by U.S. troops at the end of the island's independence war, nor during the period of Wood's military government that followed. Bullard's first experience of the Spanish-American War—as detailed in the next chapter—was guerilla warfare in one of the areas of the most tenacious resistance to the U.S. occupation of the Philippines: southern Luzon.

Bullard arrived in Cuba in 1906 as part of the second U.S. intervention. The Platt Amendment required such an intervention when the political stability of the republic was threatened. Fraudulent elections at the end of Tomás Estrada Palma's four-year presidential term had provoked an incipient uprising by members of the opposition Liberal Party, who felt they had been illegitimately shut out of the electoral process. Both sides explicitly invoked the Platt Amendment to try to involve the United States in support of their own partisan political ends. Instead of guaranteeing stability, the Platt Amendment had introduced a perverse incentive for political actors who were dissatisfied with their standing in Cuba to involve the United States in settling internal disputes.

The six-thousand-man Army of Cuban Pacification, which landed in Cuba in October 1906, was led by J. Franklin Bell, another veteran of the Dakota

Indian Wars who had won subsequent fame in the Philippines through the unsparing campaign he had waged against the Filipino Liberation Army.[71] Bullard had fought in that effort and their shared experience of the guerilla war in Luzon created an opening for Bullard to approach General Bell to explore possibilities for an assignment in Cuba that involved more than garrison duty.

In the Philippines, the army's ability to overcome Filipino resistance in the provinces where Bullard and Bell had operated had depended on a system of intelligence gathering and dissemination. Under Bell's command, the Army of Cuban Pacification also set up a Military Information Division with twenty-six districts defined throughout the island for gathering information and forwarding it to headquarters in Havana. Based on Bullard's knowledge of Spanish and willingness to do more than the routine duty expected of a mission that was seen as more diplomatic and political than military, Bell assigned Bullard to intelligence work, briefly for the army, and then as a political officer reporting directly to the civilian governor installed by the Americans.[72]

That civilian governor was Nebraska lawyer Charles E. Magoon, one of Pershing's friends who Assistant Secretary of War George Meiklejohn had recruited from Lincoln to work as legal officer in the Bureau of Insular Affairs in the War Department. From the War Department, Magoon had been sent to Panama, first as legal counsel to the Isthmian Commission and later as governor of the Panama Canal Zone from 1905 to 1906.[73]

As a special political officer for Governor Magoon, Bullard traveled all over the island—by train, steamer, and by Cuban *guagua*, which Bullard compared to the "stage-coach of a hundred years ago." He worked as an investigator on behalf of the provisional government and reported directly to Governor Magoon. In particular, the American government of the island feared further uprisings by blacks and by the Liberals, whose refusal to recognize the recent Moderate victory at the polls had led to the U.S. intervention. Some of Bullard's investigations involved financial claims against the government. He also looked into alleged mismanagement and corruption of municipalities and customs houses. Many of his trips across Cuba were made in the interest of chasing down rumors of political unrest and agitation. He visited sugar plantations and mills to investigate "certain industrial and political questions affecting peace conditions." One trip to Camagüey involved observing a railroad strike "for political complications or conspiracy." Bullard also investigated an affray that resulted from an altercation between U.S. seamen from the steamship *Tacoma* and local Cuban police, which had heightened civil-military tensions in early 1907.[74] These investigations took him all over the island, from his base in Havana, where he usually returned to write up his reports, to Cienfuegos and Trinidad on the southwest coast, to Santa Clara in the center of the country, to Camagüey, Matanzas, Baracoa, and Santiago four hundred miles away at the far eastern end of the island. Most often, Bullard found the rumors that had excited the concerns of local American officials to be baseless or even ridiculous. His travels around the island brought him into contact with a cross-section of the Cuban population and Bullard fancied that he had acquired a knowledge of the common man in Cuba through this work.

Besides the confidential reports he provided to the governor, Bullard used his official assignments to collect material for articles he sought to publish in magazines in the United States. He relished the opportunity to come into contact with "la gente comun de Cuba" as he wrote in his diary after returning to Havana from an investigation into the alcalde (mayor) of San José de las Lajas in February 1907. Later that year, Bullard's observations on "the Cuban character" as well as on Cuba's "Negro question" began appearing in publications such as the *North American Review* and *Atlantic Monthly* as well as *Army and Navy Life*. The first article Bullard published, called "The Cuban Negro," comes the closest to indulging his ambitions to emulate his literary idol Joel Chandler Harris. The article begins with a description of Bullard's impressions of an "outlandish dance brought from dark Africa," performed by "grotesque[ly] costume[d] black men and women with faces barren of refinement, intelligence or thought, yet deep-set with fervor and intent." The rest of the article relates further observations on the customs and character of Cubans of color, with frequent comparisons of race relations in Cuba and the United States. Bullard comments on religious practice, the participation of black Cubans in the recent wars for independence, and their economic status and political aspirations. As with all his writings on race, Bullard assumes innate differences. His concern is with tracing the supposed reasons for the differences in attitude and outlook he observes between "the Cuban Negro" and American blacks.[75]

Observations on race relations in the South of his boyhood also contributed to Bullard's analysis of the counterinsurgency campaigns he took part in—and wrote about—in the Philippines and Cuba, in which he compared the secret Filipino independence society the Katipunan and political organization among Liberals and Negroes in Cuba after 1906 to the Ku Klux Klan and White Brotherhood in the post-Reconstruction South. Bullard's intelligence work took him all over the island to investigate rumors of black uprisings.[76]

The articles Bullard wrote won him something of a reputation as an expert on Cuban society and especially on matters of race in Cuba, as well as in the U.S. Army. When Bullard took leave and visited Washington in early 1908, he was gratified to find himself regarded as one of the army's noted authorities on Cuba by no lesser men than the president and General Bell, as well as by Brigadier General Clarence Edwards, the chief of the Bureau of Insular Affairs.[77] The reception of Bullard's literary efforts in Cuba and in particular the reaction of Bullard's superiors to what they judged to be his impolitic descriptions of the Cuban character was a different matter. Governor Magoon strongly disapproved of Bullard's journalism. When his first article about Cuba and Cubans came out, Magoon reproved Bullard personally. To his horror, Bullard realized that an even more critical article was about to be published. He immediately rushed to the Havana magazine distributor and spent $100 in an attempt to buy all seventy-five copies of the offending publication that had landed on the island. This was quite an outlay for a man with a salary of $400 a month, and of course it did nothing to assuage the governor's displeasure. On the whole, though, Bullard calculated that he had come out ahead. He weighed the wrath of his "chief" Magoon against the reputation the articles had won him back home.

American soldiers stationed in Cuba during the second intervention "watched, recorded, and condescended," in the words of historian Rebecca Scott.[78] This judgment serves as a fair summary of Bullard's three years of intelligence work in the country. He prided himself on his ability to talk to and move among ordinary Cubans, but in his writing he continued to classify and characterize those he observed according to race or type. Overall, they did not measure up. In particular, he was skeptical about the Cuban capacity for self-government. He enumerated the reasons for this in his diary as well as in the reports he made and articles he published. This kind of observation and report making constituted a kind of collecting of its own. Part of what Bullard, like Pershing and Scott before him, had collected in Cuba, were his experiences and judgments of the place and its people. Out of this, he fashioned his expertise on Cuban affairs.

As the second American occupation of Cuba in a decade drew to a close, Bullard accepted several invitations to go hunting in the Cuban countryside. His hosts on these occasions were Cuban Spaniards, and Bullard was uncharacteristically approving in his description of their hospitality: "I had the chance and the experience of being in a Cuban-Spanish family. I lived, ate, slept with them and came away with still further disappearing prejudice. I had little before. I have none now." The reader of Bullard's Cuban writings has difficulty accepting this assessment at face value. It does seem, though, that the activity of hunting, so conducive to camaraderie across the divisions of rank and class in the frontier West, also worked a certain rapprochement between this American officer and some prominent Cubans in the weeks before the army's withdrawal. It's also clear that Bullard prized the distinction of being "the sole Americano" on these trips, enjoying "the warmth of Cuban confidence."[79]

In 1908 a similar hunting trip had yielded a great prize for Bullard. He had shot a deer, which his Cuban hunting partners had asked him to carry directly to the White House as a tribute to President Theodore Roosevelt. Bullard wrote up the incident in an article he published in *Sports Afield*, a magazine devoted to hunting and other outdoor sports. From the southern coast of Cuba where the buck was killed, Bullard had it transported to Havana and then loaded into the refrigerator of the transport *Sumner* on which he had booked passage to go on leave to Washington. In Washington, Bullard tied a letter to the deer's antler and had it delivered to the White House. The message he brought from his Cuban hunting companions, according to the account Bullard provided in his article said: "To the Hunter, Theodore Roosevelt, President of the United States: Come share it with us." Bullard received a letter of thanks from the president and an invitation to come to lunch, which he did the following day.[80]

On one of Bullard's last hunting trips, he was the guest of José Miguel Gómez, leader of the Liberal Party and president-elect of Cuba, whose inauguration signified the restoration of some sovereignty to a Cuban government. Three years earlier, Gómez had led the Liberal revolt, which had triggered U.S. intervention under the Platt Amendment. Now, just a few weeks before taking office, he was hunting deer outside Havana with an intelligence officer of the American occupation. As an experience, this was an interesting one for Bullard to conclude his time in Cuba. Bullard shared a private assessment of the president-elect in his diary. He declared himself "favorably impressed. . . . He is simple, straight-forward and affable; also domineering."[81]

However impressed he might have been with Cuba's new president during the hunt, Bullard was not optimistic about Cuba's long-term prospects. As he prepared to leave the island immediately following José Miguel Gómez's inauguration, Bullard wrote, "The island is pacified. Now we'll see how long Cuban character will let it remain peaceful."

Chapter 6

The Buckskin Mantle

The time has come when it is necessary to conduct this warfare
with the utmost rigour. "With fire and sword" as it were. But
the numerous, so styled, humane societies, and poisonous
press, makes it difficult to follow this policy if reported to the
world, so what I write to you regarding these matters is not
to fall into the hands of newspaper men. At present we are
destroying, in this district, everything before us. I have three
columns out, and their course is easily traced from the church
tower by the smoke from burning houses. After cleaning out
the country toward the mountains, I shall march, with about
400 men, south as far as Manila; and there will be but little
mercy shown to those who are carrying on guerrilla warfare, or
giving them aid. Of course no official report will be made of
everything.

> —Matthew A. Batson, letter to his wife, San Miguel de
> Mayuno, Luzon, P.I., November 9, 1900,
> Matthew A. Batson Papers, Military History
> Institute, Carlisle, Pa.

The United States went to war with Spain over Cuba, but most of the
fighting—and dying—took place in the Philippines. Two months before
U.S. troops began their chaotic landing on Cuba's south coast, Commodore
George Dewey's Asiatic Squadron steamed in from Hong Kong to destroy the

Spanish fleet guarding Manila. Spain suffered 371 casualties in that devastating naval engagement, and the loss of all her ships. Nine Americans were wounded. The first battle of America's war in the Philippines was "little more than a massacre," in the words of one of its leading historians.[1] The surrender of Manila followed quickly and in December 1898 Spain formally ceded sovereignty over the archipelago she had claimed since the days of Magellan. No Filipinos—nor any Cubans—took part in the talks in far-off Paris that produced the treaty ending hostilities between the two imperial powers. Instead, Filipino resistance to American occupation coalesced around Emilio Aguinaldo's Constitutional Republic of the Philippines. In Manila a tentative and mostly illusory alliance between the U.S. military authorities and Aguinaldo's forces gave way to open hostilities even before the U.S. Senate had ratified the transfer of sovereignty by Spain in February 1899. In the guerilla war that followed, an estimated twenty-two thousand Filipino soldiers and half a million civilians were killed in Luzon and the Visayan Islands. Another hundred thousand people were killed in Mindanao. Destruction of crops and food stores carried out by the U.S. Army also led to famine and amplified the impact of diseases, which caused tens of thousands more deaths.[2]

In the Philippines, as in Cuba, the McKinley administration anticipated a quick transition from military to civilian rule once order had been imposed through military occupation. The difference was that, in Cuba, the United States had committed itself to the principle of self-rule for the Cubans. No such proviso was forthcoming for the Philippines. In the language of the treaty, Spain had *relinquished* her sovereignty over Cuba, but in the case of the Philippines, sovereignty had been *transferred* to the United States.[3]

In his instructions to the commander in charge of the expedition to occupy the Philippines following Dewey's capture of Manila Bay, President McKinley stressed his desire that "our occupation be as free from severity as possible." Waste no time upon arrival in the Philippines, the president instructed Major General Wesley Merritt, in publishing a proclamation "declaring that we come, not to make war upon the people of the Philippines nor upon any party or faction among them, but to protect them in their homes, in their employments, and in their personal and religious rights." The American occupation of the Philippines began in the naive faith that Filipino allegiance could be won through the manifest blessings of American good government. In the short term, a military government would oversee the establishment of institutions of civil government; army officers at the department and district levels would appoint local government officials and organize elections. McKinley's desire was to effect a complete transition from military to civil rule as soon as possible. All the United States required was that Filipinos accede to what seemed to the Americans to be their unimpeachable authority as the occupying power; in the American view of things, they would fulfill their duties as the War Department outlined them: recognition of the "absolute and supreme" governing authority of the "military occupant" and cooperation with its directives.[4]

The structure of that military occupation followed the one developed over the previous century for extending pacification over the shifting terrain of Indian Country on the domestic frontier. Cuba and the Philippines were organized into military districts, just as the American West had been. The army's department-division administrative structure, which had evolved as a means for pacifying and integrating western territories into the national polity, was extended to the Philippines with the creation of the Military Division of the Philippines in March 1900. As they had in the West, each department constituted a semiautonomous zone of command. The division was further divided into departments—as the Division of the Missouri or the Department of the Pacific had been during the Indian Wars. In the Philippines, these were the Departments of Northern Luzon, Southern Luzon, Visayas, and Mindanao-Joló, each further divided into districts and subdistricts.[5] At each level, civil as well as military affairs came under the direction of army officers. In the Philippines, the army was able to realize what men like Miles had called for at home—more military discretion over civil affairs in Indian Country. American initiatives in sanitation, education, commerce, road building, and civil policing were all introduced under military authority. In addition to establishing garrisons and fighting resistance to U.S. rule, the army presided over tax collection and also corveed laborers for work on constructing roads and marketplaces.[6]

By the time Pershing and Bullard arrived in the Philippines in late 1899, McKinley's desire for an occupation "free from severity," appeared increasingly utopian.[7] Rather than "cooperat[ing] with the United States in its efforts to give effect to [its] beneficent purpose," as President McKinley had hoped, Filipinos continued to reject the claims of U.S. sovereignty and the imposition of American rule.[8] Throughout the islands, the Americans were confronted by evidence that the objects of McKinley's "benevolent assimilation" did not accept the legitimacy of U.S. rule. Most infuriating to the officers charged with restoring civil government at the local level was the realization that the same Filipinos who took the oath of office under the American regime were often simultaneously serving in the structure of a shadow nationalist government. Bullard expressed the frustration of his fellow officers with the "successful double life [led] by practically an entire people who, accepting and living under a government established by the United States, at the same time managed to maintain everywhere another and insurgent government, the two being conducted often by the very same Filipino officials!"[9] To American soldiers like Bullard, this was proof of what he called "the subtle deception and treachery of the Asiatic."[10] Of his first encounters with the people the army was charged with subduing, Pershing wrote to George Meiklejohn, "They are really indians."[11]

At the end of August 1898, Major General Elwell S. Otis replaced Merritt. Like Merritt and the two commanding generals who followed him, Arthur MacArthur and Adna Chaffee, Otis was a veteran Indian fighter.[12] He was also the author of *The Indian Question*, in which he criticized the idea of sovereignty for Indian nations as impractical and undesirable. He called for the cancellation of Indian treaties and a recognition of Indians for what they were: "subject[s] of the U.S. to all intents and purposes, if not a citizen," and therefore entitled to protection, but not to independence, which he called a "fiction."[13]

Bullard and Pershing both got their introduction to the war in the Philippines in Luzon, including in Aguinaldo's home province of Cavite. By the end of 1899, Emilio Aguinaldo, president of the Philippine republic and commander in chief of its scattered revolutionary army, had retreated to the mountains of northern Luzon where he presided over a government in hiding, since American forces had captured and driven the government out of its capital of Malolos the previous March. After being forced to abandon his capital, Aguinaldo had issued a directive to his forces to give up fighting a conventional war and instead embrace the guerilla tactics of "ambush warfare."[14] As American forces continued the hunt for Aguinaldo in the north, Otis ordered two brigades (some eight thousand men) into the southern provinces of the island to engage the forces of the Army of Liberation and occupy the region. Both Bullard and Pershing served as part of the brigade commanded by General Theodore Schwan, Pershing as adjutant for an expedition in Cavite and Bullard as commander of a volunteer regiment.

Pershing's stint in Luzon was brief. From Cavite he was granted a requested transfer as adjutant general to the most southerly remote military department of Mindanao. Pershing made the six-hundred-mile trip from Cavite on an old Spanish steamer, arriving in the port of Zamboanga on the last day of 1899, in time to celebrate the turn of the century with the officers in this picturesque garrison town only recently vacated by Spanish troops. Meanwhile, back on Luzon, New Year's Eve found Bullard's (white) Volunteer Infantry regiment preparing for its first battle. Bullard's Thirty-Ninth was to remain in Luzon for another fourteen months before it was mustered out of service and Bullard, too, ended up in Mindanao.[15]

The first assignment for Colonel Bullard's regiment in the Luzon campaign was to relieve a regiment of regular infantry in the town of Calamba on the southwest shore of Laguna de Bay, an inland lake that empties into Manila Bay through the Pasig River. Here, the Twenty-First Infantry had been besieged by the forces of Filipino Brigadier General Miguel Malvar. Vowing not to allow his troops to get "shut up" by the enemy in this way, Bullard looked for his "military opportunity."[16] He found it on New Year's Day, 1900. Without waiting for orders from Manila, Bullard led a sortie of eight companies of "unseasoned recruits" against three thousand "well intrenched native soldiery," according to an account by one of the men who took part in it. In what Lieutenant Arthur Orton described as the "new regiment's first introduction to actual service," Bullard had two companies towed up the shore of the lake in *cascoes* (Filipino barges), so they could attack Malvar's left flank while the rest of the regiment drove through their lines to scatter them. "For three hours and fifty minutes the insurgents stubbornly fought, but had to fall back under the enfilading fire, their defeat becoming a rout, and eventually a panic."[17] From Calamba, Bullard's troops moved up the lakeshore, chasing the enemy and taking several other towns.

General Elwell Otis, commanding in Manila, was not entirely pleased by the initiative shown by Bullard. "You did right to attack the enemy," he wired Bullard, "but you should not have followed him so far."[18] The general's reproof failed to deter Bullard from launching another attack on Malvar's chief subordinate, Mariano Noriel. He then led two battalions south toward Malvar's hometown of Santo Tomas. Leaving one of his companies to garrison Santo Tomas after scattering the Filipino defenders there, Bullard headed for Lipa, one of the prominent cities of Batangas and another center of Tagalog resistance. "If the truth must be told, with a wink but no words, we slipped away from our commander, General Schwan, who was moving too slowly to suit us," Bullard later bragged in an unpublished account of the battle.[19] It was here that General Schwan was rumored to have attempted to send word to Colonel Bullard to tell him to "try to slow down those Wild Indians of his." From then on, the Thirty-Ninth became known as Bullard's Indians.[20]

Although intended as a disparagement of his troops' discipline, Bullard and his men embraced the name Indians. In a curious inversion of roles, a regiment commanded by a man who had witnessed the entrapment and exile of the Chiracahua Apaches acquired its nickname for "fighting like Indians . . . with dash and spirit." The Thirty-Ninth, Bullard wrote, won this reputation pursuing "a lot of bare-foot, shirt-tail, half-armed Filipinos."[21] To General Schwan, who reportedly applied the disparaging characterization as a rebuke, Bullard's men were Indians because they had "broken out" and were wild. They had defied the authority of the army's command structure. They had also demonstrated the agility and quickness of attack popularly associated with Indian tactics. In later boastful accounts of their military exploits, both Bullard and other officers used the same language of breaking out from command authority. Bullard was proud that he had refused to let his men get "shut up" by the enemy in Calamba; instead, like Indians who defied the army's attempts to control and constrain them, they had broken out. Individualistic leadership and breaking out from under authority were associated with the wild spirit and autonomy of Indians. Other attributes claimed by Bullard's *American* Indians, as the regiment styled itself, included fearlessness and loyalty to their "chieftain." These analogies were made explicit in a ballad memorializing the exploits of the Thirty-Ninth in Luzon, written by Private Thomas J. Breen:

> *And they call us Bullard's Indians*
> *Down on the Southern Line*
> *Though he wears no buckskin mantle*
> *Or quills of porcupine*
> *But we'll follow our gallant chieftain*
> *Without a flinch or fear*
> *As true as the reds of Sitting Bull*
> *Red Cloud or Standing Bear.*[22]

The logic by which a white volunteer regiment became heir to the spirit of American Indians in a war against other colonial peoples is deeply ironic. It depended in large part on the elaboration of scouting as a practice that allowed white men to access the atavistic power of the idealized Indian warrior. As a newly commissioned officer in pursuit of Apaches in Mexico, Bullard had adopted "Indian togs" to hunt according to an ideal of men attuned to their environment. In the Philippines, he continued to valorize the techniques he associated with Indian fighting in the West, especially scouting. Bullard attributed scouting skills to an instinctual connection to the natural world. "One may learn it a little," he wrote, "but to be really a scout, one must be born to it." In an account he wrote about one of his men who exemplified the "call-back of the wild" and the "instinct" of the scout, he wrote, "Captain Long of 'Bullard's Indians'. . . had it." As he explained to an officer of another regiment to whom he offered Long's scouting services, "he knows the country and the people." He compared Long's "nose" for Filipino "insurrectos" to that of a hunting dog: "The hound cannot tell how he knows it's a coon. No more can Long tell you how he knows that the Filipino he brings in is an *insurrecto*, but he is. You'll find him so, or, if you do not, it will be solely for lack of proof, not because he is not one. Long can smell 'em. He just knows 'em: that's all."[23]

For half a century after they left the Philippines, a military service organization formed by the veterans of the Thirty-Ninth continued to draw on the romantic resonances of Indian warfare to memorialize their martial achievements and to reinforce their fictive kinship in "the tribe of Bullard." They adopted mythic Indian symbols as motifs in their communications and rituals. The letterhead for the association's newsletter, the *Bulletin*, featured a sketch of a landscape that oddly melded elements of the plains with those of the Philippines: rice paddies and palm trees backed by volcanic peaks provide the backdrop to a scene depicting a figure armed with a bow and arrow and wearing a full feather war bonnet chasing two fleeing figures whose most defining characteristic is their flight—the fact that they are running away. Directly behind the masthead "Indian" with the bow and arrow is a stylized teepee. The newsletter opens with a salutation to the "Braves, Squaws and Papooses of the Tribe of Bullard."[24] The appropriation of imputed Indian martial qualities remained central to the identity and cohesiveness of the regiment even after their return home. Like the veteran associations of the Indian Wars, the Thirty-Ninth adopted a feather headdress as its costume in civic parades.[25]

Otis and his commanders in the field at first thought their campaign to establish control over southern Luzon had been successful. The enemy had been engaged and beaten, or had fled. In the view of the army, the January actions had achieved a military success. American troops now garrisoned provincial towns and the enemy was defeated and scattered. Bullard's troops were divided among four towns in the provinces of Laguna and northern Batangas.[26] Seemingly, all that remained for the army to do in order to prepare Luzon for the transfer of authority from the military to civilian government was to root out resistance

Figure 8. Robert Lee Bullard, photographed at 39th U.S. Volunteer Infantry Association veterans' gathering, date unknown. Robert Lee Bullard Collection, Manuscript Division, Library of Congress.

Figure 9. The tribe of Bullard: "Bullard's American Indians," 39th U.S. Volunteer Infantry Association veterans' gathering, date unknown. Robert Lee Bullard Collection, Manuscript Division, Library of Congress.

by the remaining fighters who, the Americans assumed, had taken refuge in the mountains and forests outside the settled areas. The work of the army was to find the bands, kill or capture members of the resistance, and destroy their supplies.

To win over the population, the military government also promoted civil initiatives. Besides going on raids, the Thirty-Ninth and the four other regiments stationed throughout Laguna, Cavite, and Batangas were charged with building schools and organizing elections. The four companies under Bullard's command built sixty-three schools, although they had difficulty obtaining books and other supplies for them. Bullard in any case was deeply skeptical about what he called "the fad of education," which he felt had no role in pacification. "Whenever for whatever cause a tribe or people has come under our care, we have prescribed them education—always book education," he wrote derisively. "We did it in succession with Indian, negro, Filipino and Cuban, with the same result in every case—the patient's stomach turned."[27]

In the tradition of the western frontier army, the volunteers of Bullard's Thirty-Ninth made long patrols in the hills. As commanders like Miles had done in the West, Bullard led his Indians on scouts. Besides engaging in skirmishes with small groups of fighters, they also looked for hidden caches of weapons and other supplies. They destroyed food so that it could not be used to sustain a fighting force outside the towns. Scouting parties to surprise suspected guerillas in villages deep in the mountains were common. In fourteen months, each of Bullard's companies reported marching two thousand miles.[28] Bullard's regiment carried out most of these scouting parties at night. After reaching their target village in the dark, they would cordon off the huts. When daylight came, part of the patrol would enter the village and demand the villagers' *cedulas* (identification papers). Villagers suspected of being guerillas had their huts burned. Suspected guerillas were taken to the district headquarters at Calamba for questioning and possible trial by military commission.[29]

However, it quickly dawned on the soldiers garrisoning provincial towns that resistance in southern Luzon had not been defeated by the army's sweep through the region and occupation of major towns. Instead, Bullard complained, "our officers and army were persistently beset, irritated, harassed by the petty and useless meanness, stealth and treachery of a people whose whole country, lives and last thing lay at our mercy."[30] Guerilla fighters ambushed patrols and targeted supply trains; unseen hands cut the telegraph wires that provided communication between the garrisons.[31] As the post commanders issued identification cards and carried out elections for municipal offices in February and March, Bullard also had them implement a system of spies and informers "to study the outwardly cooperative citizens of Calamba, Los Banos, Santo Tomas, Tanauan and San Pablo."[32]

The insurgent forces, meanwhile, had their own system of surveillance and intelligence gathering. "Under the blind eyes of the American troops," according to historian Allan Millett, "the Filipino guerrillas operated a spy system to check on the loyalty of civil officials, recruited men for the sub rosa militia, and collected and cached supplies."[33] General Miguel Malvar reportedly gathered intelligence on the occupying force in mid-January under the guise of attending a cockfight in his hometown of Santo Tomas, the regimental headquarters, which was under Bullard's immediate command.[34]

Pacification, Bullard reflected later, was "a more bitter dose" for a people to take than defeat in war. In notes he worked out in his notebooks and later published, Bullard interspersed analysis of campaigns in the Philippines and Cuba with his personal memories and understanding of Reconstruction in the postwar South of his childhood. "The pacifiers may therefore expect from those under pacification unwillingness and unsubmission running from passive aversion through dodging and evasion to vigorous hatred and obstruction," he wrote. This made "forceful measures," such as punitive expeditions, provost courts, military commissions, courts-martial and reconcentration necessary; "without them," he concluded, "there is no pacification."[35]

In May of 1900, Otis was succeeded by General Arthur MacArthur. MacArthur shared none of his predecessor's confidence in the power of beneficent American government to win over the Filipinos. As the insurgency continued in Luzon and elsewhere, MacArthur concluded, "every native, without any exception, residing within the limits of the Archipelago, owed active individual allegiance to the insurgent cause."[36] MacArthur's assessment was an obvious overstatement, but it reflected the military's frustration with its inability to achieve Filipino acquiescence to U.S. rule.

The experience and actions of Bullard's Thirty-Ninth Volunteers in the southern provinces of Luzon from the end of 1899 to March of 1901 reflected the changing character of the war in one of the core areas of resistance to the imposition of U.S. rule. What began as a conventional war for control of disputed territory transformed into a guerilla struggle as Filipino soldiers faded into the general population in the face of the superior firepower of the Americans. During the Thirty-Ninth's tour of duty in southern Luzon, in other words, the

Philippines took on the characteristics of Indian Country, or rather, the army began treating it as such. As the Philippine Revolutionary Army changed its tactics, the U.S. Army responded accordingly. Officers who had optimistically supposed at the beginning of the campaign that Filipinos would readily recognize the benefits of capitulating to U.S. rule were forced to reevaluate their assumptions about the kind of war they were fighting and the disposition of the people they were dealing with. Repeated guerilla attacks and mounting evidence of widespread sympathies for those resisting the United States made the troops suspicious of all Filipinos, whom they called by the racist epithet "gugu." The guile and deceit of Filipinos became a theme in accounts from this time by Bullard as well as others. "We are surrounded by traitors," wrote Major George Langhorne of the Thirty-Ninth in mid-August.[37]

Filipino treachery and especially the ways that the Americans were able to beat them at their own game emerge as central themes in several stories Bullard wrote about his interactions—and those of his troops—while they were stationed in Luzon. The stories, with titles like "The Tricksters Tricked," "Deafness Cured, Spanish Taught," and "A Scouting Party," were never published. Most relate and embellish incidents based on the experiences and lore of the Thirty-Ninth. These "Indian stories," as his children called them, celebrate the cunning, toughness, and especially the scouting prowess of Bullard's American Indians. They are written to be humorous, each with a punch line, which usually turns on the comeuppance of the "gugu" or "insurrecto" who has been outwitted or outgunned by the Americans.

In "The Tricksters Tricked" Bullard tells about "evening the score" with some of General Juan Cailles's men who had been ambushing "small bodies of Americans and then disappearing like snakes in the thick tropical growth of their country, not to be followed, never seen again." To deal with these depredations, two of Bullard's captains, referred to as Taylor and Kreger in the story, came up with a plan by which they would present themselves as targets and then arrange for two other parties of soldiers to move in on the Filipinos when they attacked. "Deliberate offering of a tempting target to the outlaws; that was the adventurer, the scout," wrote Bullard. Of course, the plan worked (otherwise there would have been no story):

> In a moment the Cailles men were gone in the woods on the other side, leaving behind their wounded. A let up for two minutes, then shots, and a hubub of outcries from the wood into which the

bandits had disappeared, quiet again and then a party of grinning Americans emerged on that side marching a goodly number of foolish looking bandit prisoners who had rushed right into their arms! And Taylor and his men? Two hit but not hurt enough to keep down a laugh at the sight of the outwitted sheepish-looking bandits that their comrades marched into the road. Good Scouting.[38]

The justification for the Americans' resort to trickery was provided by the characterization of the enemy as outlaws and bandits. Their revenge was in making the forces who had been eluding and provoking the Americans look foolish.

In "Deafness Cured, Spanish Taught," Bullard related a similar incident in which he sent out a small party, again with the intention of inviting an ambush on the garrison's lightly guarded frozen-beef delivery which had become the target of the insurgents. "In one particular spot, midway between ours and the next station occupied by American troops, the guerillas had been able especially to worry, elude and *laugh at us*. There they had managed repeatedly to shoot up our small escort parties and had once even succeeded in carrying off our supply of frozen beef coming to us that way," he wrote. "Here, as elsewhere, they watched for our outgoing and ambushed us when we returned. *Altogether the Gugus were having their inning*."[39]

It was bad enough that the guerillas were able to steal the army's beef, even once; but what especially invited retaliation was the idea that the Americans were being laughed at. Bullard decided to catch the would-be ambushers in the act and exact revenge. So the next time the frozen-beef escort passed through their station, Bullard and his orderly accompanied the detail, but deliberately hung back to trail two Filipinos on the road whom they suspected of being guerillas as they in turn observed the progress of the supply train. In this way they were able to catch them before the Filipinos could ambush the supply detail. "They had no firearms, only their sword bolos. Officers plainly, they were so intent on counting and sizing up my party that they never once looked back down the road in my direction."

Bullard and the orderly were successful in surprising and capturing the Filipinos, but one of them escaped. "The orderly and I were bursting with enjoyment of our smartness when suddenly the furthest fellow made a plunge and was gone in the bamboo thicket at the roadside before either of us could follow him with a revolver shot." In this account, Bullard immediately plunged into the thicket in pursuit of the man, yelling to his orderly to "kill the other fellow if he moves." After thrashing around blindly in the "thorny harsh bamboo brush," Bullard again apprehended the Filipino and related his triumph and mastery of both man and situation: "He was caught. He knew it, and the look on his face showed such dejected acceptance of his fate that, forgetting all about my recent fearful oath, I broke into a laugh again and marched him off to the road to rejoin my orderly and his prisoner. By the time we were out of the brush, my prisoner had recovered his composure and was primed again with oriental cunning and dissimulation." Bullard then related how the man affected deafness and pretended not to understand Spanish. Bullard "cures" his feigned deafness by delivering a beating.

> "You lying scoundrel," I cried, "You hear and understand every word I say," and, grabbing a bamboo brush near me, I "lit into" him. I didn't have to go far, a bamboo brush is a stinging thing. At the first "swish" his hand quit his ear: his deafness was gone: at the second, he broke into good Spanish, "Si, senor, hablo espanol" (Yes, sir, I speak Spanish): time, about one minute.
>
> Again I had a laugh at him, which he took very well. Then we had a chat in which he made due acknowledgement for the cure so quickly effected on his deafness and of the Spanish language so well taught him in so short a time![40]

Bullard's stories highlight a widespread ethic of the war that intensified in its guerilla phase. This was the imperative of punitive action, the desire to teach a lesson, to elicit better behavior through punishment. The story is a moral fable about the efficacy of punitive violence. The ultimate lesson is one Bullard later articulated in relation to the Moros, who became the next target of American pacification efforts: impressing on them that they "cannot hope to contend with white men."[41]

The sense that Filipino deceitfulness, treachery, and innate barbarism had provoked harsh measures such as reconcentration and the use of torture was widespread in the army. Bullard wrote dispassionately several years after leaving the Philippines that the incitement of the Filipinos' guerilla warfare "was great enough to provoke the trouble and scandals of the water cure."[42] As the guerilla war dragged on through the summer of 1900, some officers advocated the use of reconcentration of population and preemptive destruction of food and property as necessary and proper strategies to achieve pacification. Bullard shared the view "that ultimately we shall be driven to the Spanish method of dreadful general punishments on the whole community for the acts of its outlaws which the community systemically shields and hides, *always* [italics in the original]."[43] Others turned a blind eye when their men employed harsh methods such as the "water cure" to try to extract information or to intimidate Filipinos into compliance.

The water cure referred to a medieval form of torture in which simulated drowning was used to inflict the pain of imminent death and psychological trauma.[44] With modifications, it is the same form of torture the Bush administration adopted in its Global War on Terror after 9/11. Private Hines of the Seventeenth Infantry gave a contemporary account of how it was done in the Philippines: "The 'water cure' is a simple thing. The native is tied down flat on the ground and his mouth forced open with sticks or a string, which is tied behind his head. Then water is poured down his throat through a bamboo tube, which is nearly always handy. The native must drink the stuff and it is poured down him until he can hold no more. As much as a gallon can be forced into a man in that way. Then the water is pumped out of him by stamping on his stomach or rolling him over. When he comes to the native is always ready to talk."[45] Torture by drowning, then as now, evoked a horrified response among some segments of the American public. In both contexts, the practice also found its apologists, who attempted to minimize the suffering it inflicts or otherwise justify its use. President Roosevelt called it a "mild" form of torture. Governor William Howard Taft, when called to testify before the Senate, acknowledged the practice but tried to minimize its severity by claiming that Filipinos actually asked for this torture in order to provide cover for their confessions to the Americans and thereby avoid reprisals from insurrectionists.[46]

In November, the Thirty-Ninth was redeployed to the southwestern coast of Batangas province. Their work there was much the same: scouring local *barrios* for signs of insurgent activity, conducting intelligence work, and arresting Filipino officeholders in the newly established municipal government who were suspected of loyalty to the insurgents. The Thirty-Ninth was mustered out of service in March 1901, the same month Aguinaldo was surprised and captured by Frederick Funston and eighty-one Macabebe scouts who tracked him to a hideout in Palanan in the northeast of Luzon, then tricked and overpowered his guard.[47] Following his surrender, Aguinaldo issued a proclamation accepting the sovereignty of the United States and calling on the Revolutionary Army to lay down arms. In the provinces of southern Luzon where Bullard's regiment had spent the last fourteen months, however, resistance continued. Miguel Malvar exhorted his forces to keep fighting even if it took another ten years to win the independence for which so much blood had already been spilt.[48]

Frustrated with their inability to quash the continuing guerilla resistance in southern Luzon and especially to prevent the ability of the insurgents to extract support from the population, American district commanders expanded the kinds of measures Bullard and others had implemented to deprive the insurgents of support. Brig. Gen. Samuel S. Sumner, who took over command of Cavite, Batangas, Laguna, and Tayabas the month after Bullard's departure, advocated "harsh and stringent" methods to compel surrender. These included destroying crops and storehouses and closely monitoring and controlling the movement of food supplies in the region. Sumner also contemplated but stopped short of introducing the practice of reconcentratrion, which had elicited so much American outrage when the Spanish had employed it in Cuba.[49] "The world was twitting us," Bullard later wrote, "with doing in the Philippines what we had practically made war upon Spain for doing in Cuba; namely, allowing a trifling insurrection to run on indefinitely."[50]

This was the situation in early September when Bullard boarded the transport *Thomas* in Manila to return to the West Coast on sick leave. While he was making the north Pacific crossing, two events occurred that greatly shocked Americans and affected the prosecution of the war in the Philippines. The day after Bullard left Manila, President McKinley was shot by an out-of-work steelworker at the Pan-American Exposition in Buffalo; he died a week later. McKinley was succeeded by his vice president, Theodore Roosevelt, a man who believed that war and imperialism were salutary mechanisms for fulfilling the evolutionary prerogative of the strong dominating the weak. The news of McKinley's assassination had scarcely had time to reach some of the more remote army outposts in the Philippines when one of those stations, the garrison town of Balangiga on the southern coast of Samar, was attacked with devastating results, both for the troops stationed there and for the last vestiges of military restraint in targeting civilian populations in an all-out effort to defeat Filipino resistance to the U.S. presence on the island.

The attack on the garrison at Balangiga has been called "one of the most brilliant tactical operations of the war."[51] It was widely denounced in the American press as an act of treachery and barbarism. On September 28, Balangiga villagers and guerilla fighters under the command of Lieutenant Colonel Eugenio

Daza attacked the soldiers of the Ninth Infantry's C Company as they gathered for Sunday breakfast, thus catching the Americans off guard and without their weapons at hand. The attack, it later came out, had been carefully planned. Of the seventy-four men in Company C, forty-eight were killed during the attack or as they tried to escape by boat to the next garrison of Basey further up the coast. The attackers also captured a hundred rifles and a large amount of ammunition, medicine, food, and other equipment.[52]

The Balangiga attack was the most deadly attack on American troops by Filipinos of the war, a war that since Aguinaldo's capture the previous March, was widely assumed to be all but over. The army's retribution for the Balangiga Massacre, as the incident became known, was unhesitating, and it was not limited to Samar. In the aftermath of the attack on Balangiga, policies of reconcentration and destruction of crops, dwellings, and food stores were officially sanctioned and carried out in Samar as well as in the other area of entrenched resistance, southwestern Luzon.

The news of the attack on soldiers at Balangiga was received in the United States with the same kind of shock and outrage that had followed the Seventh Cavalry's defeat on the Little Bighorn a quarter-century earlier. Contemporary accounts as well as subsequent retellings of both disasters emphasized the cruelty and barbarity of the savages who attacked troops who were attempting to occupy and pacify their land. Part of the shock caused by both encounters was the scale of the casualties inflicted by an enemy over whom Americans believed—with good reason—they had a clear technological advantage. Like the Custer battle, events on Samar fueled popular outrage and calls for revenge; they also led to intensified initiatives by the military command in the Philippines to pacify and bring remaining areas of resistance to U.S. sovereignty under control. Just as it had after the Custer battle, the army responded in various ways to interfere with the Filipinos' ability to access the resources they needed to continue their resistance. On the plains, this had meant the construction and garrisoning of nine new forts and the institution of winter campaigning that targeted whole communities, forcing families to move camp and flee capture in harsh weather when food resources were scarce for people and horses.[53] On Samar, the strategy was the same: to wear down the ability of holdouts against American authority and target any resources that provided an alternative to surrender. In the Great Sioux War, the military had required Indians to register and go to agencies. The first action Major Littleton Waller took on Samar was to require all males in the area of Balangiga to report to his marines or be regarded as enemies.[54]

What followed was a punitive campaign aimed at the civilian population as much as at the Liberation Army. It is well remembered for the orders Waller received from Brigadier General Jacob Smith, who told him: "I want no prisoners. I wish you to kill and burn, the more you kill and burn the better it will please me. I want all persons killed who are capable of bearing arms in actual hostilities against the United States."

In addition to Samar, Chaffee was determined to put an end to continued resistance in southern Luzon. The officer he chose to carry the war to the civilian population there was Brigadier General J. Franklin Bell, who was appointed to lead the pacification campaign in late November. On both islands, Chaffee authorized a number of tactics aimed at intensifying pressure on the civilian population. Some of these he regarded as so controversial that he directed that the letter he sent to inform the secretary of war about them be destroyed.[55]

Almost every account of the aftermath of the Balangiga incident draws a stark contrast between the military response on Samar and the corresponding measures implemented on Luzon, particularly by General Bell in the province of Batangas. The leadership of General Smith is almost universally condemned; the actions of Major Waller are also generally deplored for their brutality and violation of the laws of civilized warfare, and, of course, both men were court-martialed. Apart from the specific acts that led to the charges against them, the scorched-earth polices they sanctioned have become legendary. In contrast, General Bell's "well-organized pacification campaign" was credited by contemporaries in the army with ending the war in Batangas and has been praised by military analysts and historians as "a masterpiece of counter-guerilla warfare."[56]

Whereas Waller and Smith ended their careers in ignominy, Bell won congratulations from President Roosevelt and Secretary of War Root, the respect of the army, and promotion. He returned to the United States to head the Command and General Staff school at Leavenworth. When the United States occupied Cuba in 1906, Bell was sent to the island as the commander of the Army of Cuban Pacification.

Although suppressed by the army as too controversial at the time they were written, Bell's written analysis of the war in Batangas and the series of carefully articulated orders that laid out his plans for pacifying the province were rediscovered during the Iraq War and invoked and praised again for their supposed relevance for America's wars of counterinsurgency a century after they were written.[57] Bell was no "Hell-Roaring Jake" Smith calling for wanton vengeance. In contrast to General Smith's infamous exhortation to make the interior of

Samar "a howling wilderness," J. Franklin Bell contemplated the eventuality of establishing "the peace of desolation" soberly and with great deliberation.[58] Although laid out in measured language that has won Bell praise for the control he exercised over operations in the areas under his command, Bell's rationale for the campaign he carried out in Batangas is in fact indistinguishable from those of colonial commanders from the Pequot War to the Punjab frontier who advocated punitive warfare "to make all suffer, and thereby, *for their own interests,* enlist the great majority on the side of peace and safety."[59] As always, justifications for the efficacy of punitive warfare depended heavily on arguments about the racial characteristics of the population to be pacified, which required demonstrative violence to secure capitulation.

One of the first things General Bell did after taking over command of operations in Batangas was to call a meeting of the thirty-eight officers of his brigade who would carry out his directives. Addressing the assembled officers as two stenographers took down his words, Bell said: "Gentlemen:—I presume, as is natural, you would like to know just why I have been sent here and what policy I expect to pursue and enforce. . . . I shall therefore take pains to explain my views to you at some length, in the hope that you may become convinced that they are sound and reasonable."[60] Bell proceeded to give his analysis of what had gone wrong with what he characterized as the army's "general policy . . . of great benevolence and forbearance, a policy of attraction and conciliation," which although "right in principle, had not proved as "successful or efficient" as hoped. The problem lay in the Filipino misapprehension of American intentions: "Unfortunately, from the very beginning, the natives entirely misunderstood this policy and attributed it to fear and weakness. They became very arrogant, conceited and aggressive."[61]

To convince the enemy "that they were trifling with a power far greater than they had any conception of," like every general waging war against primitives, Bell prescribed punitive measures: "It is not possible," Bell told his officers, "to convince these irreconcilable and unsophisticated people by kindness and benevolence alone that you are right and they are wrong." In the perennial complaint of colonial officials in the face of native intransigence, Bell lamented that the "only argument [they] can understand and appreciate is one of physical force."[62] Nothing else would achieve the respect and allegiance of the people of Batangas: "Without first whipping them and convincing them that we are able to accomplish our purposes by force if necessary, we can never gain their friendship, because otherwise we can never command their respect."[63] Bell ex-

pressed the same conviction in a long letter to his immediate superior, Major
General Loyd Wheaton: "These people need a thrashing to teach them some
good common sense, and they should have it for the good of all concerned."[64]

Unquestionably, Bell delivered the promised thrashing to the population of
Batangas. This was accomplished by causing the civilian population to resettle
in "protected zones" outside of which his troops relentlessly scouted for guerillas, and destroyed stores of food, crops, and anything else that might furnish
sustenance for continued resistance.

One historian who has resisted drawing a stark contrast between the final
months of fighting on Samar and Luzon is Glenn May. Most historians have
privileged the rhetoric of the respective commanders. May, to his credit, has
looked beyond Smith's inflammatory commands to "kill and burn" to assess
the actions taken in each place and their effects on the population. In Samar,
he found that General Smith presided over the destruction of "thousands
of homes, tons of food, hundreds of cattle, and much additional property."
American blockades further contributed to severe food shortages.[65] Bell's
rhetoric may have been more restrained, May found, but the deadly impact
of his well-implemented policies created even greater loss of life and suffering
among the population subject to his control in Batangas than the vindictive
but more haphazard campaign on Samar. Within a week of taking command,
Bell had issued the orders for creating protected zones, which he explained
in one of the first circulars he put out, on December 8, 1901. Bell ordered
station commanders to "establish plainly marked limits surrounding each
town bounding a zone within which it may be practicable, with an average
sized garrison, to exercise efficient supervision over and furnish protection
to inhabitants (who desire to be peaceful) against the depredations of armed
insurgents."[66] Enforcing the policy of protected zones meant that some towns
whose normal population was 3,000 swelled to over 30,000. Once the population was concentrated in these areas, Bell assigned almost 2,000 troops to
scour the countryside for "any signs of people, animals, shelter, and food supplies." In their first week out, American raids destroyed almost 1,500 tons of
rice and palay, hundreds of bushels of corn, hundreds of hogs and chickens,
200 carabaos, 800 head of cattle, 680 horses, and over 6,000 houses. The
troops caused "ecological destruction on a massive scale."[67] The combination
of congregating a large number of people with the predictable effect on sanitation, added to food shortages and compromised nutrition, created a situation conducive to the spread of disease, which became the major cause of

death during Bell's campaigns as well as afterward when people returned to homes, villages, and crop land that had been destroyed.

The number of casualties attributable to Bell's counterinsurgency campaign in Batangas is the subject of continuing debate. In the absence of much data, critics as well as apologists for Bell's policy then and later have minimized or exaggerated appraisals of the suffering caused by the reconcentration policy and other measures according to their ideological convictions.[68] Probably the most reliable analysis, and the only one based on contemporary local records, is again by Glenn May, who used parish records from 1902 to try to evaluate the human cost of the reconcentration policy. Based on the parish records, he concluded that "the zones were unhealthy places to live and that the number of deaths was extraordinarily high during the months of concentration."[69] How high? Acknowledging the challenges of arriving at definitive numbers, May estimated that "excess deaths" attributable to reconcentration were about seven thousand during 1902. He also noted that death rates from disease rose even higher in the months after people left the concentrated zones to disperse throughout a devastated countryside.[70]

By April, Bell's unsparing methods had achieved a devastating success; there was nowhere safe that guerilla fighters could hide and little left with which to carry forward their struggle. On April 16, Malvar surrendered, acknowledging that Bell's campaign had kept him constantly on the move and had led to the desertion of most of his officers. Another reason he gave for his surrender was his desire to avert the further humanitarian crisis of famine, which he expected to ensue if farmers restricted to the zones were prevented from planting rice the following month.[71]

As the army marshaled and deployed its forces in these two punitive campaigns against the vestiges of the Filipino Liberation Army, a parallel political drama was playing out eight thousand miles away in the halls of Congress and on the pages of the nation's newspapers. The shocking details of conditions on Samar as well as scattered reports by soldiers returning from the Philippines of torture and other atrocities prompted critics of the war to press for a Senate investigation. From January to June, the Senate Committee on the Philippines, which had been formed two years earlier to consider what should be done with the islands, heard testimony from military commanders and civil officials on the conduct of the war, the treatment of prisoners, and on the controversial subjects of torture and the targeting of civilians.

Meanwhile, some 500 miles further to the south of Luzon, the army was preparing for an assault on a new frontier of Indian Country. At the time of Malvar's surrender in Batangas, a force of some 2,200 officers and men, including 300 Magindanao scouts, was preparing for a punitive expedition into the interior of Mindanao, a region that had resisted Spanish attempts at pacification for over three hundred years. John J. Pershing, recently promoted to captain, was already in the thick of these plans; within the year, he would be joined in "Moroland" by R. L. Bullard and H. L. Scott and all three would be elevated from commanding troops to governing the new and reluctant subjects of America's far-flung empire.

Chapter 7

Sultan of Sulu

If you love yourselves and your country,
avoid coming to blows with the Americans,
because they are like a matchbox—
you strike one and they all go off.
> —Jamal-ul-Kiram II, Sultan of Sulu, 1899

We shoot at him to make him tame,
If he but understood.
> —Soldier chorus in George Ade, *The Sultan of*
> *Sulu: An Original Satire in Two Acts*

It is definitely settled now that I am to be the "Sultan of Sulu."
> —Hugh Lenox Scott to wife Mary,
> August 16, 1903

In March of 1902, the week before Waller's court-martial was convened in Manila, a musical comedy with a Philippine theme opened at the Studebaker Theatre in Chicago. Against a backdrop of continuing testimony about water torture and civilian reconcentration brought forth by the ongoing Senate hearings on the war, the operetta *The Sultan of Sulu* offered theatergoers a mildly satirical but generally benign view of American war aims in the Philippines.

The play presented military occupation as musical theater. The army, navy, and marines were well represented in the play, each with their own nattily costumed chorus. By the end of the first scene, the flag of Sulu, on which the curtain opened, had been taken down and replaced with the Stars and Stripes, thus establishing the central fact of the relationship between the United States and the Philippines: colonial sovereignty. The American civilizing mission was carried out on stage both by the military and by a complement of "School ma'ams from Boston (the Misses Roxbury, Dorchester, Cambridge, and Newton)," who constituted another chorus. The play also suggested additional motives for the American presence on the island, which were commercial. As a soldier chorus explained in an early musical number:

> *. . . though we come in warlike guise*
> *And battle-front arrayed,*
> *It's all a business enterprise;*
> *We're seeking foreign trade.*

The song's refrain emphasized the magnanimity of their mission even in the face of armed resistance by the Filipinos:

> *Our thoughts are set on human love*
> *When we hear the bullets humming,*
> *We teach the native population*
> *What the golden rule is like,*
> *And we scatter public education*
> *On ev'ry blasted hike!*

While gently lampooning the colonial project, the play reinforced popular understandings of American goals for the Philippines: to bring education and civilization to a backward people while also expanding markets for the benefit of Filipinos and Americans alike. The play poked fun at imperial pretensions, as when salesman Wakeful M. Jones was facetiously credited with having mastered the local language after only twenty-four hours on the island of Sulu. But it did not question the essentially beneficent intentions underlying the onslaught of commercial, martial, and civilizing initiatives on the island. Instead, the play reserved its most pointed satire for domestic politics. The staging of the play was in keeping with its light tone. Rather than setting the play in any of the islands recognizable to the news-reading public as theaters of an ugly guerilla war, playwright George Ade chose to set his comedy in the southernmost reaches of the Philippines, in the court of Ki-Ram, a caricature version of the real-life sultan Jamal-ul-Kiram, a choice that allowed the play to invoke all the tropes of Oriental splendor and decadence. Whereas four years of battling the insurgency of Christian Filipinos on Luzon and other islands in the north and central part of the Philippines might have tarnished their appeal as a setting for a comic opera, the Muslim south presented a fresh aspect for theatrical exploitation. Lush, mysterious, with "fanciful turrets and minarets," as imagined by the playwright, with "tropical vegetation" set against a "placid sea," the Sulu Archipelago, a near neighbor of Borneo, provided an exotic background as yet uncomplicated by active hostilities between the United States and the sultanate. Here, the U.S. role was presented as a peacekeeping measure intended to prevent internecine warfare among the sultan's own vassals, represented in the play by Datto Mandi, a menacing offstage presence who threatened violence against the sultan with a view to recapturing his six nieces who had been abducted by Ki-Ram to be added to his harem in accordance with barbarous Mohammedan custom, as explained in a prefatory program note.[1]

The Sultan of Sulu played on the aspect of the culture of the southern Philippines that was simultaneously most unfamiliar and also most titillating to Americans: the Muslim religion of its majority population, the Moros, and especially polygamy and slavery which, apart from their salaciousness, served primarily as foils for satirizing American social and political issues that were closer to the audience's own concerns, such as the temperance movement, changing roles for American women, and political corruption. The play's female judge-advocate character, Pamela Francis Jackson, who presides over the introduction of American law to Sulu, is described as a "sedate and rigid spinster," whose "attire indicates that she has made a partial compromise with the dress-reformers." She instructs Ki-Ram's eight wives in the advantages of divorce with alimony and also facilitates the emancipation of two of the sultan's slaves, Rastos and Didymus (who are described unaccountably as Nubian and played by white actors in blackface). Following their emancipation, Judge Pamela organizes them to run for political office in the newly created Republic of Sulu—one as a Democrat and the other as a Republican.[2]

At the time *The Sultan of Sulu* was written—and first performed—Mindanao and the archipelago of Sulu remained for most Americans, including those fighting in the Philippines, a remote and exotic realm. Its most salient characteristic, one sensationalized by the play, was the religion of the majority of its inhabitants: Islam. Although putatively part of the archipelago claimed by Spain in the name of King Philip II, in fact the islands of the south had deep cultural and commercial ties to nearby Borneo as well as to Malaysia and China. Their ties to the rest of the Philippine archipelago, by contrast, were tenuous and mostly antagonistic. Spain had never brought Mindanao under its control, something American politicians (including those negotiating the peace treaty) realized only dimly at the conclusion of the war and whose full implications began to dawn on the military only as they replaced departing Spanish troops garrisoning the dozen or so ports that represented the extent of the Spanish presence in the south. As Abinales and Amoroso put it succinctly: "The Muslim south represented a space inside the territory claimed by Spain that was *outside the control of the state*."[3] The people of the southern Philippines had effectively resisted integration into the Spanish colonial polity for centuries. For their faith and their antipathy to dominion by Catholic Spain, the Spanish called them Moros, the same term they used to refer to Muslims of North African (Mauretanian) origin in Iberia. The Reconquista, led by Ferdinand and Isabella, had finally wrested the last Moro stronghold from the emir of Granada in 1492. The Reconquista also contributed to the missionizing ethos of the conquistadors who took their conquering zeal to the New World after Spain had been unified and ridded of non-Christians. But in spite of three centuries of effort by soldiers and missionaries, including the intrepid Jesuits who embraced the thankless task of attempting to bring the inhabitants of the southern Philippines to Christ, the Moros of Mindanao and Sulu had steadfastly resisted conquest by Spain.

None of this, of course, was common knowledge among Americans, who presumed that their country's sovereignty over Mindanao and Sulu was absolute and continued to apply the Spanish misnomer, Moros, indiscriminately to the region's half dozen ethnolinguistic groups. Inverting American ignorance about the geography and history of the Philippines, the play had the sultan's adviser, Hadji, ask the newly arrived Lieutenant Hardy to help him locate "where on the map" the United States was. The soldier replies: "Just now it is spread all over the map. Perhaps you don't know it, but we are the owners of this island. We paid twenty millions of dollars for you."[4] In the play, the sultan's adviser—along with the audience, presumably—accepts this explanation for U.S. sovereignty over the sultanate unquestioningly. The American position was that Spain's military defeat and surrender led to cession of the Philippines to the United

States in its entirety. American title was further bolstered by a payment of the $20 million referred to by Lieutenant Hardy in the play. More significantly, the United States justified U.S. claims to sovereignty in terms of its superior moral authority, its claims to possess civilization, and its ability to implement good government, something the Spanish had failed to do, in the Americans' eyes.[5]

Not surprisingly, the historical Sulu sultan and his principal adviser Hadji Butu saw things differently. Much as the Apaches had contested the applicability of the 1848 Treaty of Guadalupe to them, on the grounds that they had never been defeated by either of its signatories, Sultan Jamal-ul-Kiram maintained that Spain had no right to cede territory that had never been under its control. Oscar Williams, who was serving as U.S. consul in Manila when the war broke out, and who accompanied the military delegation that visited the sultan in 1899 to negotiate a treaty with him, confirmed that there was "little doubt that Spain and other nations of Europe as well as nations and potentates of the Orient recognized [the sultan's] sovereign claims to the Sulu Archipaleago," adding that he had become aware while serving in Manila before the war that "Spain never claimed the Sulus or Palawan as she claimed Luzon."[6] Internal analysis of this issue within the Bureau of Insular Affairs produced a similar conclusion: "Spain never did have anything more than a nominal control over these islands. They recognized the Sultan and his powers. They paid him a bonus to keep order and to allow them the semblance of authority, but further than that, the Sultan was the ruler of that portion of the globe."[7] American negotiations at the peace conference also acknowledged their separateness. In addition to the $20 million the United States paid Spain in exchange for sovereignty over the Philippines as a whole, the Treaty of Paris stipulated a separate payment of $100,000 as a bonus for transferring the Sulu archipelago and the island of Mindanao, and internal documents acknowledged that "the boundaries fixed by the Commissioners representing the United States at Paris included the islands of Sulu and Mindanao, although they never had been considered part of the Philippines proper."[8]

In defending payments made to "the Sulu tribe or nation" to Congress, President McKinley stated that they were made "in conformity with the practice of this Government from the earliest times in its agreements with the various Indian nations occupying and governing portions of territory subject to the sovereignty of the United States."[9] This was the situation the United States inherited from Spain. Put another way, the Muslim south was Indian Country, a territory far from imperial centers of power where terms laid out in international compacts between colonial powers were contested on the ground by headmen with regional influence who had not been party to their creation.

This state of affairs was familiar to the generation of American soldiers whose government had sent them into the lands taken over from Mexico in the Southwest, where sovereign control was contested by Apaches, Comanches, and others. In the margins of the diary he had kept in his Apache-chasing days, Bullard reflected on this continuity, musing that after being introduced to one chapter of the history of the expansion of the Spanish empire, he was on his way "to renew the impressions on the other side of the world of the Spaniard and his ways. Santa Fe on the great Plains of the west, America," he wrote, "and Manila, over the great seas in the far, far East."[10] Notably, the role of native people did not enter into Bullard's characteristically broad-brush and romanticized view of the ebb and flow of empires. Beyond Manila his imagination did not extend, but in the drama of conquest that played out in the southern Philippines over the next decade, officers like Bullard, whose claims of knowledge of the ways of primitives found validation among the army hierarchy, used that expertise to leverage roles of authority and command in the military pacification of this new Indian Country. On that distant stage, American soldiers, like their counterparts in Ade's play, advanced American claims of sovereignty over Sulu and Mindanao through improvised performances of U.S. power adapted from an established frontier repertoire.

The challenge the U.S. Army faced in the South was different from the one dominating their attention and absorbing their manpower on Luzon and in other parts of the Philippines, where a struggle against nationalist resistance continued. With the exception of some early mobilization led by Christian Filipinos allied with Emilio Aguinaldo's cause in northern Mindanao and in Zamboanga, there was little support in the Muslim south for political movements organized by their traditional enemies, the Christianized Filipinos. Most of the region's tribal leaders (datus) saw no advantage in joining a nationalist independence struggle. They viewed a republic dominated by Tagalog elites as inimical to their interests. Some took steps to quash nationalist activities in the northern provinces even before the Americans sent troops into the area in late 1900.[11] A letter sent by Emilio Aguinaldo in January of 1899, broaching an alliance with "his great and powerful brother, the Sultan of Jolo," went unacknowledged by the sultan.[12]

Instead of an insurgency with a unifying republican vision, what the Americans faced in Sulu and Mindanao was widespread antipathy to their claims of sovereign power over disparate ethnic groups who were proud of their proven ability to withstand conquest by outsiders and deeply skeptical of resounding claims by the Americans that they brought a new and better form of centralized government. Initial reactions to the U.S. presence ran the gamut from disinterest to accommodation and alliance building to myriad forms of raiding and resistance.

Across the Sulu sea from Zamboanga, the 1899 Bates Agreement had shifted the sultan's acknowledgment of nominal sovereignty from the Spanish to the Americans. Mistakenly regarding him as the titular political and spiritual leader of all the Muslims of the south, the Americans had hoped this agreement would pave the way for recognition of the legitimacy of their rule in Mindanao as well as throughout the other islands of the Sulu archipelago. It did not prove so. When the sultan failed to conform to unrealistic American expectations that he could and would hold his people accountable for attacks and depredations, the Americans derided what they saw as his weakness and duplicity and moved to abrogate the Bates Agreement without ever pausing to reevaluate the faulty assumptions on which the compact had been based in the first place.

In the events surrounding the abrogation of the Bates Agreement in 1904, Hugh Lenox Scott played a role reminiscent of those he had performed so often in his earlier career on the plains when he was called on simultaneously to embody the force of the army and to deploy his empathic paternalism toward primitives. Shortly after arriving on the island of Joló in 1903, Scott wrote jokingly to his wife, "I am to be the 'Sultan of Sulu.'" Clearly aware of the play, he also urged his family to go to the theater to see it. "I hope you will see the play Sultan of Sulu in New York and tell me what it is like and I will tell you what he is like."[13] At his first meeting with the real-life Jamal-ul-Kiram II, he compared the sultan (unfavorably) to the Comanche leader Quanah Parker. In Scott's opinion, the sultan was "not so much of a sultan as Quanah Parker."[14]

For Scott, as for Bullard and Pershing, the work of governing the Muslims of the southern Philippines drew significantly on their experience with Indians at home. As commanders of outposts on the frontiers of the U.S. occupation of the Philippines and as district governors charged with pacifying Moros, all three men deployed similar techniques for asserting U.S. authority in the new Indian Country. Their assumptions about what techniques would be effective were informed by an axiomatic equivalence between Moros and Indians, which was an article of faith for many in the army. As the commander of the Department of Mindanao and Joló William Kobbé put it: "The Moros of Mindanao are very like the best of North American Indians—as the Nez Perce and Northern Cheyenne—in features and manners, in their love of independence, and in personal dignity and pride."[15] Such comparisons were commonplace as the army cast around for models for pressing its claims of control over people who rejected them. Pershing drew parallels between fighting the two peoples in letters he wrote to the War Department soon after his arrival in Zamboanga: "Military operations against the Lanao Moros differ from anything the American soldier has experienced previous to the occupation of that part of the Island of Mindanao known as the Lake Lanao District. It is probably more nearly akin to Indian warfare on the plains than anything else we know of."[16] Pershing went on to describe some differences in the way Moros fought, notably that, instead of choosing a strategic location and defending it as indigenous fighters in North America would, Moros retreated to their *cottas* (forts) instead of fighting in the open. Not surprisingly, to deal with the challenges posed by this new Indian Country, Pershing recommended the measures the army had employed against Indians at home. For Pershing, this meant more cavalry regiments would be needed. He also called for the organization of native troops. He outlined these proposals in several long letters dispatched to George Meiklejohn in 1900: "To those who have kept posted on the conditions of service among the indians as they have existed during the last thirty years the problem presented in the Philippines appears almost identical and will require for its solution constant vigilance by the same active, mobile, energetic arm—cavalry."[17] In addition to energetic cavalry units experienced in the business of chasing Indians, Pershing also advocated the organization of "irregular troops" made up of Moros. Pershing's inclination to return to familiar ways of thinking about Indians is apparent in his elaboration of the ethnographic observations that support his call for Moro auxiliaries:

> Down here in this District [Mindanao] the vast majority of the population are Moros and they are located, as you know, in separate tribes under Dattos or chiefs, whose power is almost unlimited. All Dattos in Mindanao are supposed to owe allegiance to one sultan, that of Mindanao, but the power of this man or of any of the sultans amounts to very little and the Datos have very little respect for him. So that the question resolves itself into dealing with the local Datto. They try to obtain the recognition of the local military commander, and thus, and in many other ways, arise jealousies and

feuds among them. Some of these are old and of long-standing and many frequently go at each other, tribe against tribe. Now these fellows would make splendid irregular troops and could be used against one another as we used the Indians in our own country. They are very warlike and fierce when aroused."[18]

In addition to aiding the army by fighting one another, Pershing suggested that "in case of necessity Moros could be pitted against Filipinos and vice versa, as they are born enemies."[19]

Pershing's call for the recruitment of native troops paralleled efforts by other officers, such as Lieutenant Matthew Arlington Batson. In September 1901, the army organized fifty Philippine or native scout companies (104 men each) based on tribe or language throughout the islands.[20] Filipinos were also re-cruited to serve in the Philippines Constabulary, a police force organized under the civil government that was deployed for pacification in the countryside. Both had white officers. About five thousand Filipinos of various ethnic groups were recruited as scouts in the first two years of the war, including Batson's Macabebe Scouts, who played a key role in the capture of Emilio Aguinaldo, as we saw in the previous chapter.[21] A decade later Pershing summed up their attributes in a letter to General J. Franklin Bell:

> It would be out of place here to discuss the merits of white troops as compared with Philippine Scouts or any other class of native troops. But the Philippine Scouts in this District have recently demonstrated that when led by white officers of experience they are especially valuable in operations against hostile Moros and Pagans. They fully understand the enemy's cunning and appreci-ate his sagacity, and know something of what to expect from him. The intuitive sense of self-preservation in the Philippine Scout is pronounced. They are always on the alert and seldom allow them-selves to be surprised. They are entirely reliable and trustworthy in the presence of an enemy. With little training they take advan-tage of natural cover and are able to accomplish their work with a minimum number of casualties. On the contrary, our white troops, under the influence of civilization, have to a large extent lost the natural instinct of self-preservation. They are generally careless both in attack and defense and unfortunately have more or less con-

tempt for the Moro as a foe. Whether on duty or off duty our white troops are easily taken unawares by the wily savage, as a long list of avoidable casualties fully demonstrate.[22]

Even before the organization of separate scout units, the people of Mindanao served the American troops as guides; they were recruited as spies and informants; they carried messages and also worked on clearing land and building roads. Bullard recruited some three thousand Malanaos to work on road construction from Iligan to Marahui in 1903. Moro Scouts formed part of the force Pershing commanded in what he called "the severest fighting I had seen in the Philippines," the capture of Bud Bagsak in 1911. During his time as governor of the province, Pershing also worked to have all-Moro scout units replace units of the Philippine Constabulary, but his enthusiasm for their martial fierceness was complemented by other racial stereotypes that came to the fore in that battle. In his account of the final frontal attack on the formidable mountain fortress, Pershing complained that "without white leadership the Scouts began to hang back."[23] Although savage, Moros lacked initiative and honor, according to their white officers; it was the same charge that had been leveled against African American troops in Cuba. Philippine Constabulary Chief Henry T. Allen likewise defended the fighting effectiveness of his native troops with faint praise: "I fully recognize the defects of the Filipino character, especially the absence of integrity," he wrote, "but over three hundred years of Christian rule, however bad it may have been, accrues enormously to our advantage."[24] Provided, of course, that they were commanded by white men who could counteract such defects.

Just as he had in his letters to Meiklejohn from Cuba two years earlier, Pershing interspersed his analysis of military affairs with a broader assessment of the country's potential, once pacified: "I think these islands are the richest in the world," he wrote to his friend in Washington. "Cocoanut palms grow without cultivation. Bananas, pine-apples and hemp grow wild and the mountains are covered with the finest of timber that includes all sorts of hard woods, capable of taking the finest polish, and there is no question but that sooner or later American prospectors will find the islands rich in minerals, especially the island of Mindanao." The letter went on to detail the other resources of the islands, such as gold, "splendid steam coal," copper, zinc, and pearl and shell fisheries, which he said the War Department should develop and about which he promised to write more at a later date.[25]

In describing conditions on this remote frontier for his well-placed friend, Pershing exaggerated both the number of Moros as well as the risk they posed to Americans and to him personally. "Think of it," he wrote, "600,000 barbarians each man with a knife ready as an individual if an opportunity presents itself to kill you for your pistol or a small piece of gold." Such an incident, Pershing continued with gusto, had been successfully dealt with a few weeks earlier by Captain Sydney Cloman, district commander at the former Spanish garrison town of Bongao. Pershing related to Meiklejohn what had taken place at this southernmost outpost of American occupation in March 1900:

> A party of four soldiers went hunting in the interior and one evening while playing a game of cards they were attacked by a gang of ten Moros. One man was killed outright; another had his head cut almost entirely off and a third died from his wounds. The Commanding Officer [Cloman] took forty-five men and went to the village [Bilimbing] and demanded the murderers. He marched the inhabitants of the village out on the beach near the town and held them all prisoners until the murderers were turned over to him. They all confessed and were executed without any further ceremony. The report of the Commander, which must be taken as official, asserts that the prisoners were sent for wood and water and in attempting to escape were killed.[26]

Pershing further noted that all the Moros had heard of the incident and from it had drawn the salutary lesson that the life of an American would cost them ten Moros. "It is fortunate that such ideas prevail among them," he concluded approvingly. Three decades later, when Pershing reworked this story for inclusion in his memoirs, he altered key details of the account he had sent to Meiklejohn. By then he was writing as the much-decorated commander of American forces in World War I and also as the last American military governor of Moro Province. Writing from such an exalted position of authority—and for posterity—it is easy to imagine why the general's later version glossed over the summary execution carried out by Captain Cloman, who was a friend of Pershing, and who—like him—had served in the army's campaign against the Ghost Dancers in South Dakota.[27] Also absent from the later account is Pershing's clear approbation of the way the Moros' behavior had been dealt with and his knowing wink at this American resort to the *ley fuga*, shooting prisoners as they purportedly attempted to escape.[28] Pershing also overstated the threat the people of Mindanao and Sulu posed to Americans—certainly, he faced little danger as adjutant general in the garrison town of Zamboanga. More to the point, in the first three years of the American occupation, there had been a total of only half a dozen American soldiers killed by Moros, Captain Cloman's unfortunate men constituting a large proportion of them.[29] Pershing's population figures, which seem to be based on records inherited from the Spanish, also exaggerated the number of Moros; rather than 600,000, the army's 1903 census estimated the population to be closer to 250,000.[30]

It is instructive, however, to return to the naive and self-aggrandizing letter Pershing wrote as a lieutenant, newly arrived in Mindanao and addressing the civilian assistant secretary of war, who also happened to be his friend and political ally. Unquestionably, Pershing wrote to impress his powerful friend, but his letter is not *merely* boastful. In this and other letters he sent to friends in the War Department, he wrote with a policy agenda in mind. Pershing included the account of the incident in Bilimbing to lend emotional force to his view that supreme control over Moros needed to be military, with as little interference by the civil authorities as possible. Military leaders, he wrote to Meiklejohn, should have the latitude and authority they needed to "handle . . . problems promptly and effectually as they arise," without interference from civil authorities or the necessity to obtain specific orders or permission before taking initiative. "The man on the ground is the one in whose judgment reliance should be placed," he wrote.[31] This was in fact the policy the United States adopted for Mindanao and Sulu, which remained under the control of the U.S. Army until 1913, with Pershing serving as the last military governor of Moro Province.

Pershing's correspondence with Meiklejohn provides insight into some of the assumptions then current among the army's leadership in its frontier outposts about what action was required to prevail over the Moros. First, the letter illustrates a strongly held belief in the efficacy of punitive action. General George Davis, who preceded William Kobbé as department commander, put it this way: "When these born pirates feel the weight of our power they will believe we are in earnest and respect us, but until then they will despise and hate us."[32] In its relations with Moros on Mindanao, General Chaffee wrote that the army "must not fail duty which demands application of the Mosaic Law, 'an eye for an eye,' when dealing with savages who know no other way of obtaining redress for wrong, and count all as cowards who fail to make the demand and execute it."[33] The greatest—and most disastrous—exponent of punitive lessons was Leonard Wood, former military governor of Cuba and the first to serve as the civil-military governor of Moro Province when it was organized and placed under military control in 1903.

Besides its emphasis on punitive force, Pershing's letter to Meiklejohn underscores two other key assumptions of the military about what was required to effectively occupy and pacify Moroland. The first is the necessity of empowering the army, which is what Pershing meant by "the man on the ground," to take decisive action. The second is a confidence in the instrumental value of understanding Moro customs and temperament. As Bullard put it, "Any fool can fight and kill Moros but it takes a man of some sense to manage them without killing them yet without loss of prestige and dignity."[34]

Bullard, Pershing, and Scott all exemplified the army's ideal of the "man on the ground." All three believed that an understanding of the Moro character was essential to managing the people and controlling the territory. And each was confident of his own ability to discern the natives' elusive essential nature and use it to advantage. Notably, this confidence was shared by their superiors. When Pershing was made intelligence officer for Moro Affairs in 1902, General George W. Davis outlined his mission as follows: "You seem to know how to handle these moros. I want you to make friends of them for us."[35] A year later, Davis again commended Pershing's "infinite patience in dealing with these fanatical, semi-savage [Moros]" and his "knowledge of the Moro character."[36] Bullard, and especially Scott, were both similarly credited with understanding Moro culture and ways.

In reaching their axioms on Moro behavior, these soldiers drew on the same methods of interaction and observation they had applied to ethnic others on the domestic frontier. At the end of a year of campaigning among the Malanaos of the Lake Lanao region, Pershing offered this authoritative-sounding assessment:

> The Moro is of a peculiar make-up as to character, though the reason is plain when it is considered first, that he is a savage, second that he is a Malay and third that he is a Mohammedan. The almost infinite combination of superstitions, prejudices and suspicions blended into his character make him a difficult person to handle until fully understood. In order to control him other than by brute force one must first win his implicit confidence, nor is this as dif-

ficult as it would seem, but once accomplished you can accordingly
guide and direct his thoughts and notions by patient and continuous effort.[37]

The extent to which Pershing, or any American soldier, understood Moros,
is of course questionable and, at the very least, seems at odds with the baffle-
ment they continued to express in the face of sustained resistance to the U.S occupation. Where such knowledge was regarded as valuable was within the army
itself. In terms of their reputations and the regard of their superiors, the point
was not the accuracy of these appraisals, but each man's own confidence in his
knowledge and his success in convincing others of it, which for Pershing, Scott,
and Bullard was prodigious. The appraisals of the Moro character such as the
one elaborated by these three men were aimed more at providing the rationale
for conquest (or, more rarely, for refraining from attack), in view of the manifest
inferiority of the Moro that such knowledge confirmed.

The soldiers' rehearsals of Moro traits fit perfectly with the popular ethnology of the day, which posited a hierarchy of races. As Bullard wrote in his notebook after reading Archibald Colquhoun's book *The Mastery of the Pacific*: "Of
the races of the Pacific the order of excellence is Polynesian, Indonesian, Malay,
[and] Ethiopic."[38] Before ever reaching the Philippines, Bullard diligently copied
out the "Malay special characteristics" that provided the template for his later
observations in the field: "lack of organizing ability, puerility, impracticality,
theoreticality, love of show and form."[39] Not surprisingly, he found that Moros
conformed to the image he had developed before encountering them.

Bullard commanded the Twenty-Eighth Infantry's Third Battalion, which
was put in charge of constructing a road from Iligan on the coast to Marahui on Lake Lanao's north shore. After several months of observing and interacting with Malanaos in the area, Bullard wrote: "I am gradually acquiring
much information and knowledge of the Moros as will, I think, enable me
later to manage them better."[40] Bullard later explained the role that "understanding of people" could play in carrying out military pacification: "Of first
importance is the study and understanding of the people upon whom we are
to work in pacification, their ideals, tendencies, history and characteristics, so
as to suit measures to men. . . . Further, there are surely to be found in every
people peculiarities, characteristics or customs that can be turned to valuable account by the pacifiers."[41] Bullard and Pershing were not interested in
knowing Moros in an abstract, merely ethnographic way. They sought useful

knowledge—instrumental knowledge—that could help in the effort to rule them.

Similarly, after a couple of months as military governor of Sulu District, Scott wrote to his wife that he was confident in his ability to extend American authority over the Sulu people, "for I feel that I am getting to understand these people already—and can work on them as I used to with the Kiowas and Comanches—the same ways seem to be successful with the Moros," he wrote.[42] The methods Scott regarded as most effective were patient listening, and acting in a way so as to convey justice and firmness. "Firmness is essential in dealing with all inferior races," Scott wrote. He also employed several ways of demonstrating his personal authority as well as the army's superior military force.

A week after expressing confidence in his knowledge of Moros, Scott was caught in an ambush and sustained serious injuries to both his hands while attempting to arrest a war leader (panglima) named Hassan who was leading the resistance to U.S. rule on Joló. Scott said he admired Hassan "as a savage" and liked him "as a man," feelings that did not prevent him from plunging the island into a punitive war with the objective of destroying the threat posed by the example of his resistance to Scott's authority.[43] In the war against Hassan and other dissidents, Scott's troops were reinforced by an additional 1,250 men (twelve Infantry companies, two troops of Cavalry, a battery of Field Artillery—and a packtrain), all transported under the command of General Wood to help put down the rebellion.[44] Bullard, who came over from Mindanao with Wood to take part in the punitive expedition, wrote: "There was considerable destruction of the country necessary to impress the natives. Many *cottas* were destroyed and many houses burned. Some women and children were unavoidably killed in battle as they mixed up with the men."[45] Some of the first people killed by Bullard's battalion were members of a wedding party, including the bridegroom, who were "killed like a flock of birds." Wood wrote in his diary: "Had with us a good deal of plunder, odds and ends picked up during the march, things captured in Moro camps, etc."[46] In the next few days, hundreds more were killed, wounded, and driven out of their homes. Support for the American effort to catch the renegade Hassan became a test of loyalty of the sultan and other datus to the American government. As Scott wrote to his wife from the field in February: "We have the head chiefs of the other provinces on the Island working for us, some unwillingly, like those of Look [Hassan's district], but they are out and the advices I hear from what they talk to each other, they want to get Hassan to get me out of the country as I evidently stay here

until Hassan is caught and there won't be peace and quiet until I have gotten
him. . . . The advance in less than three months has been greater than in the
previous four years, in extending the American authority here."[47]

When Moro allies helped the Americans destroy a cotta where Hassan was
thought to be hiding—he was elsewhere—with the loss of 226 Tausug lives
and several American casualties, Scott wrote: "I believe and hope that this will
be the last lesson of that kind that the Moros will require . . . and complete their
submission to the Government." In a handwritten postscript to a lengthy account of the campaign that he had dictated to a stenographer, Scott compared
the effect on Moros of Hassan's punishment to the breaking of two wild horses.
"Each thrown down, branded, one let go to run again in the range for a year
will be wilder than ever, but the other taken into the stable and handled well
[becomes] tame."[48] Scott, of course, regarded himself as a consummate horse
trainer. In this revealing postscript he expressed his faith in the efficacy of the
Americans' punitive measures to bring in and tame wild Moros, comparing the
techniques he used on horses with those used in subduing Moros.

A few days later, Captain Oscar Charles, who took over some of Scott's
correspondence when the major's hands were too mangled to write, echoed
Scott's confidence that the breaking of Hassan's resistance had had the desired
positive effect: "Fear and respect have taken root and placed them in a receptive
mood for changes essential to civilization and a continuation of the present firm
policy will keep them on the proper road of progress with the retention of their
respect, confidence and good feeling for us," Charles wrote.[49] Every confrontation that ended in a large number of Moro deaths was followed by similar statements on the necessity of "teaching Moros a lesson." The language of friendship,
peace, and "good feeling" masked the objective of "hitting these fellows a lick or
two by way of punishment," as Bullard put it.[50] The total number of deaths on
the island was estimated at between twelve and fifteen hundred. One American
soldier died and seventeen were injured.[51]

The punitive imperative prevailed even when officers admitted—at least
privately—that the killing they carried out was unnecessary. For example, Scott
had written to his wife with evident disgust about his initial introduction to
campaigning against "truculent" Moros on Joló when he first arrived on the
island with Wood before he had assumed command himself: "We are massing
troops at Joló—go there again tonight to march around all over the island with
sufficient force to show them our power and not to tempt them to resist as a
small force might. . . . We find a small hole well fortified to hold about 300 men

poorly armed & with no water for a siege—killed like rats in a hole—when an investment of a few days would compel their surrender without a shot for want of water and a lot of officers & soldiers killed & wounded for nothing to say nothing of a lot of moros exterminated."[52] The rationale for such actions was always punitive: to teach a lesson. Moros "had to be straightened out," as Wood wrote another officer in a letter justifying the killing of five hundred men, women, and children.[53] Force was the only intelligible message for such people. But perhaps it was Bullard, who was always talking about "teaching Mr. Moro a lesson," who best summed up the actual *point* of the lesson the army wanted Moros to learn when he claimed he had "taught some of the Moros *that they cannot hope to contend with white men*."[54]

The Moros, it must be said, did not draw the lessons the Americans intended, in spite of the confidence that all the American commanding officers involved in the hunt for Hassan expressed, that they had "given the Moros a very wholesome lesson," one that Captain Frank McCoy crowed "would last for all time." Instead, the indiscriminate killing, burning of houses, destruction of crops, and looting that were part of the punitive war against Hassan sowed the seeds for a later and even more deadly confrontation between Tausugs and the army, which culminated in the Battle of Bud Dajo in 1906, shortly after Scott's departure from the island.[55] This so-called Battle of the Clouds resulted in at least seven hundred deaths of Tausug men, women, and children, as well as seven killed and forty-five injured on the American side (with a disproportionate casualty rate among the Moro Constabulary who took part in the assault).[56] And even that was not the end of the resistance on Joló. The Americans returned to Bud Dajo yet again in 1911 when Pershing laid siege to the stronghold to force the capitulation of several hundred opponents resisting the disarmament decree he had instituted as governor.[57]

Punitive expeditions as well as the use of superior technology and overwhelming force against a primitive foe in order to instill the lesson of submission reproduced the dynamics of army interactions with native people on the frontier. The repertoire of familiar tactics deployed in the army's attempt to manage the Moros extended beyond outright acts of violence and the deployment of force to intimidate. There was a notable dramatic element to each officer's performance of his duties in Mindanao and Sulu. Proclamations, ritual greetings as well as raids, and mounted expeditions to inspire a "wholesome fear of a soldier mounted on a large American horse," were also part of a repertoire of actions aimed at disciplining Moros.[58] Carefully choreographed visits with influential datus and even fiestas and games hosted by the Americans on the Fourth of July and Christmas were all aimed at demonstrating prestige and hospitality; all played a role in the dramatization of power.

One feature of American diplomacy and the demonstration of power took the form of ritualized visits that district governors pressed upon sultans, datus, and other men of consequence in the areas where the army moved to extend its control after 1902. One of the first steps taken by both Pershing and Scott upon assuming the mantle of American civil-military authority in their posts in Mindanao and Joló was to require the datus of the region to "come in" for a meeting that would symbolize their submission to U.S. authority. The language of "coming in" was the same as that used in parallel rituals of submission when Lakota and Northern Cheyennes presented themselves at agencies during the Great Sioux War (1876–77).

As soon as Pershing had established his headquarters of operation at Camp Vicars on the south side of Lake Lanao, he began receiving visits and sending out invitations to local datus to come meet with him—or face the consequences. "The Americans desire to avoid further war and bloodshed of which there has already been too much," he wrote in one of the many diplomatic overtures he sent to the region's leaders, datus who were skeptical of American intentions. "I could explain all this much better if you would come here and visit us," he continued. "We could become personally acquainted," and thereby form a "lasting friendship." Refusal to submit to American authority, on the other hand, would be foolish, Pershing pointed out in the same letter: "You have only a few men and a few guns and a few horses, while we have millions of men and millions of guns and millions of horses. You ought to profit by the experience of the Moros of Bundaya and Bayan."[59] Binadayan and nearby Bayan had been targets of the first punitive expedition launched by the Americans in May 1902. Pershing's advice to the sultan that he should profit from the experience of the Moros of these two communities was a none-too-subtle threat of the violence that awaited those who crossed the Americans. Both communities had been largely destroyed; three to four hundred people had been killed, including the sultan of Bayan and his brother, and the sultan of nearby Pandapatan as well. The punitive expedition that resulted in such destruction was in retaliation for attacks on exploratory missions in March during which two American soldiers had been killed and another wounded and their rifles stolen. The first incident had involved a mounted detachment of seventeen men and native guides sent by Colonel Frank Baldwin from Parang to reconnoiter and open a trail into the Lake Lanao region. About thirty miles from camp, the detachment had come under attack. One soldier was killed. He, his rifle, and their horses had been left behind when the rest beat a retreat back to Parang. Later the same month, two privates of the Twenty-Seventh who were stationed at Malabang were attacked by six Maranaos with barongs. One soldier was killed, the other wounded, and again a rifle was stolen.[60] When the leaders of these two rancherias on the southern edge of the lake had resisted American demands that they surrender those who had killed the Americans, Commanding General Chaffee authorized a punitive force of 1,625, saying that it was "absolutely important that our authority be respected by these people, [and] that [the] sovereignty of the United States be fully acknowledged."[61] Only fifteen or twenty men survived among the people of Bayan. Four companies of the Twenty-Fifth Battery Light Artillery shelled the cottas with their mountain guns. The Moros fought back with *lantacas* (small muzzle-loading brass cannons), rifles, and spears. The Pandapatan community "had been almost obliterated."[62] Camp Vicars, named in honor of one of the officers killed in the battle, was established half a mile to the south the following month. It was from here that Pershing, and after him Bullard when he acceded to the office of governor of Lanao District, sought to extend American control over the Lake Lanao region.

Moros were the immediate target and audience for these demonstrations of power and prestige, but it is important to realize that these ambitious officers were performing for another audience, at least as important in shaping their actions—the military hierarchy and others with political pull.

Pershing set great store by such visits. He had initiated this form of diplomacy even before he took command of Camp Vicars. He noted in some detail an early visit made by Ahmai-Manibilang, former sultan of Madaya on the north side of Lake Lanao, who had traveled in state to visit him at Iligan, before he took over command at Camp Vicars:

> On the appointed day he came in great state, accompanied by a retinue of about thirty of his people. He was a tall, swarthy, well-built man, past middle age, clean shaven, as most of them were. His jacket was of many colors, his trousers tight-fitting, his turban smartly tied and set jauntily to the side of his head. Like all Moros, he was barefoot. He rode a fine-looking pony—a stallion—and for stirrups used a small rope knotted at the ends which he grasped between the first two toes. On each side of his horse a slave trot-

ted along on foot, one carrying his gold-mounted kris, the other his highly-polished brass box containing betel nut, buya leaves and lime—kept separate till the time for chewing, when, as was their custom, he mixed them in proportions to suit his taste. Leading the procession was a guard carrying a gun and behind this dignitary came another. Then came minor chiefs, relatives, and more slaves, all in their choicest finery.[63]

The datus who responded to his invitations to call at Camp Vicars were received with courtesy and ceremony. They also got the chance to be impressed by the size of the command and the weapons at its disposal. And they became sources of intelligence for Pershing and the army as they formed their plans to bring the whole region under American control. The questions Pershing asked visiting datus ranged from kinship relations and other forms of alliance (and feuds), to questions with more immediate military application. Although broached in the diplomatic language of friendship, Pershing kept transcripts of these meetings, which he filed as "interrogations." Besides ritualized avowals of friendship and support for American actions, including attacks on other datus and destruction of their cottas in punitive actions, the interrogations furnished important field intelligence for Pershing, ranging from the ethnographic to the tactical. The following transcript of Pershing's interrogation of the sultan of Pualas on June 4, 1902, about a month after the attack on Bayan and Binadayan, gives a sense of the range of topics covered and the nature of exchanges between the American officer and his visitors:

> JJP: Am Glad to see you and hope we will be friends
> Sultan: Am glad to know you and assure you of our friendship
> JJP: Where is Datto Limon of Barras, Your Brother? Is he not a relative of Ahmai-Manibilang?
> Sultan: Yes, he married a niece of Ahma-Manibilang
> JJP: Am glad to see friends of Ahmai-Manibilang
> Sultan: Yes, we are all friends of the Americans.

After a few more questions about the relations between Ahmai-Manibilang, whom Pershing considered a key ally and influential strong man in the Lake Lanao region, he turned to questions about the activities and inclinations of others who were opposed to the Americans. Continuing in this vein, Pershing asked the sultan of Pualas what news he had of the sultan of Bacolod, known to be hostile to the United States. The sultan confirmed that the sultan of Bacalod would resist the Americans; he had not been a friend of the Spaniards and did "not care to be friends with the Americans." Upon further questioning, the sultan of Pualas said he had heard that the people of Bacalod were cutting American telegraph wires. Further questions elicited information about the number of men at Bacalod's command (400); their weapons (50 guns and 40 lantakas) and the distance and state of the road to Bacalod (rocky). The conversation also went into great detail about Bacalod's defensive fortifications, including the main one, which the sultan said had walls made of earth about four yards wide and lined with stone inside and out and protected by a trench ten yards wide and ten yards long that could be filled with water. Pershing questioned him at some length about the means by which the Americans might broach these defenses.[64]

Figure 10. The Sultan of Bayan visits Captain Pershing at Camp Vicars, Mindanao, 1902. Photo by George O. Rice, chaplain, 27th Infantry. National Archives.

In a summary of the intelligence he had compiled some months later on forty-eight of the sultans and datus of the Lake Lanao region, Pershing summarized his impressions of the sultan of Pualas as follows: "Probably reliable; well to do; very good friend; uses influence for us."[65] The information gleaned about the sultan of Bacalod's fortifications was put to use less than a year later, when Pershing led an attack on the cotta that destroyed it and killed a hundred and twenty Moros.[66]

In an article published with the title "Military Taming of the Moro," Chaplain C. C. Bateman, who served in Mindanao with Bullard's Twenty-Eighth Infantry, wrote that interviews such as those conducted by Pershing, "serve[d] to acquaint the authorities with scandals, grievances, local hatreds, entertained by villagers or personal and family feuds of long standing."[67] Pershing was attuned to such cleavages and tried to use them to exploit personal enmities and recruit allies among the people around Lake Lanao. However, he found that fomenting intrigues presented some challenges: "It is the most difficult thing to get a Moro who has become friendly to us to use his influence with others, their independence of life and lack of mutual interest in each other make it so and it is only by finding out their family relationship with other *rancherias* that it is possible to bring about the influence desired."[68] Pershing maintained careful records of all his interactions with datus and constantly reevaluated their relations with the Americans, recording judgments such as "showed troops attention while in camp at his rancheria during expedition may 2–11, '03" (which he wrote about Datu Diumbla of Bantong); "Reliable; truthful in reports," he commented. "Has served well in efforts to influence hostile to be friends" (of Datu Adta of Paiguay); Sultan Marsao of Maul was "Friendly; of some importance; trustworthiness and honesty rather doubtful."[69]

Pershing's interrogations produced intelligence that he used in future military campaigns against datus who refused to come in, but their use as rituals that dramatized personalistic power and symbolized the datus' submission should not be underestimated. Chaplain Bateman thought that the Moros had a jealous obsession with receiving recognition from the American officers. "A cabinet seance with the commanding officer is made the basis of extraordinary tales which he narrates with gusto to his jealous rivals for recognition," wrote Bateman. While this perception from Bateman's point of view is understandable, he in fact seems to have inverted the relationship; it seems rather that it was the American officers who compelled influential datus to meet with them in order to demonstrate their own prestige.[70]

On Joló, newly appointed Governor Scott also demonstrated his authority by coercing visits from the most influential datus on the island, beginning with the sultan's brother and heir, known by the title raja muda, on his initial visit to the island with General Wood, who had been appointed governor of Moro Province. In later years, Scott liked to tell the story of how he had compelled the reluctant raja muda to pay his respects to Governor General Wood as their troops conducted their aggressive promenades across the island. Ruling in the absence of his brother the sultan, who was in Singapore, the raja muda pleaded ill health as the reason he could not pay a visit to Wood, who had landed a small force of infantry and artillery over from Mindanao in August 1903. In order to impress Joló's people—and especially its influential men—with visible power, Governor Wood refused to take no for an answer. The governor dispatched Scott, along with a translator, a doctor, and a hundred infantrymen to call on the suspected malingerer. Fixing on a boil as an illness that he thought could be disproved, Scott hatched a plan to mock the raja muda for dissimulating. When he arrived with the armed escort at the raja muda's house, Scott conveyed the governor's sympathy for his painful boil and inquired where on the raja muda's person he was afflicted. Scott related the encounter that followed in his memoirs:

> The Raja Muda was found wrapped up in bed and was informed of the sorrow of the governor-general at his sufferings from such a bad boil. He said yes, the boil was very painful; too painful for him to leave his bed. Inquiry disclosed that the boil was on his ankle, the most remote place under the covers from where I stood near the head of the bed; so I sat down at the foot and asked to see the boil, but it was far too painful to be shown. The request was repeated with a little tug at the covering which threatened to expose the ankle, whereupon the boil jumped to the knee and finally to the crotch. When the request to see it became more imperative, the Raja Muda said: "My friend, to tell you the truth I haven't any boil to show you. My real trouble is that I have not yet recovered from smallpox and cholera." I told him that if he had nothing worse than smallpox and cholera, he would have to get on the horse waiting outside and come with me, and he was forthwith delivered safely to General Wood, carried from the horse to General Wood's tent on the back of a slave, according to royal custom.[71]

Scott's humorous account of how he caught the raja muda in a lie and compelled him to meet with General Wood found an appreciative audience among the officer corps in the Philippines—if its inclusion in a number of contemporary accounts is any indication of its appeal. And no wonder. It represents a clear example of teaching Moros "that they cannot hope to contend with white men," as Bullard put it. Coercion is more muted than in Cloman's account of marching the villagers of Bilimbing onto the beach and then executing ten of them. Scott skips over the details of how his request to see the boil "became more imperative," but in the presence of the armed major and a company of infantry bent on carrying out the orders of the governor general, whose troops had been ranging over the island in a show of force, it is easy to conclude that the raja muda was left with little choice. He might as well have been taken "out of his bed and dragg[ed] off against his will to pay his respects to the infidel intruders," as Scott characterized the episode in the next paragraph.

When Scott sent the interpreter Charles Schück into Maibun to learn what effect the rough handling of the raja muda had had on political feeling

Figure 11. Governor Scott and Sultan Jamal-ul-Kiram II, Manila, 1904. Prints and Photographs Division, Library of Congress.

the next day, Schück reported back that the incident had produced "a vast ridicule directed at the Raja Muda for having been caught so neatly and completely in a lie."[72] Scott, Wood, and the entire military and civil government of the Philippines, up to and including President Roosevelt, found this incident gratifying, amusing, and worthy of repetition in half a dozen memoirs, but it is worth noting that neither the account, nor its reception among the raja muda's people—as reported by Schück— should be taken at face value. The interpreter was more beholden to U.S. military interests and subject to their whims than he was to the sultan and his brother. He seems to have told Scott what he wanted to hear. Whether it accurately captured the tenor of Tausug feelings about the raja muda's humiliation is another matter.

Another way of orchestrating and enacting submission was for the military commander to insist that a local datu receive him for a return visit. Scott and Pershing both insisted on such formalities. When Pandita Sajiduciaman professed friendship, but said that his people at Bayan did not want the Americans to visit (understandably, since the Americans had only recently wreaked destruction on them and killed their leaders), Pershing replied that "such friendship was of no value to us, and that I should therefore not consider him as a friend."[73] Once Pershing had wrought acquiescence, he would then visit the datu, either with a large and impressive military escort aimed at demonstrating the supremacy of American force, or without guard, in order to demonstrate a different kind of personalistic power and self-confidence. In either case, the object of the exercise was to prove that Americans could move around the territory at will.

Within months of establishing his command at Camp Vicars, Pershing led a number of punitive expeditions against the datus who refused to come in and were harrying them with opportunistic attacks and depredations, mostly in an attempt to capture weapons. In April the stronghold fort at Bacalod was destroyed. In May, one year after his arrival on Lake Lanao, Pershing led another expedition to circumnavigate the lake for the first time. He later gave a heroic account of this "March around the Lake": "floundering through swamps, cutting through jungles, carrying for miles its own cannon, enduring cholera in its ranks, destroying Moro fortresses and fighting its way step by step overcame all resistance and accomplished the complete circuit of the lake. Thus American troops entered the heart of the Moro country and stripped the malay lords of Mindanao of the prestige of hundreds of years."[74] Pershing's destruction of cottas regarded as impregnable, followed by the determined procession around

Lake Lanao, was a demonstration of the American will and ability to dominate and to make real their sovereignty over the territory they claimed.

The completion of Bullard's road from Iligan to Marahui the following August sent the same message: the Americans were here to stay. Like the march around the lake, the road Bullard was in charge of constructing from the coast to Lake Lanao also had the goal of opening up the country, thereby facilitating the movement of troops and supplies and establishing control.

Like Scott and Pershing, Bullard also sent letters inviting datus to come in, and fulfilled his duty to meet and talk with them. He invested energy in studying Maranao so that he could interact with them, in a limited way, without a translator. Bullard even collected genealogies and folk stories from some of the datus whose confidence he gained. He continued the writing he had begun in Luzon and, for the first time, had an article accepted for publication. It was here and in the context of his relations with Moros that Bullard seems to have articulated and claimed the generalized expertise of someone who understood primitives, no doubt because it was something valorized by the army.

Bullard accepted that this diplomatic work was part of the project of "civilizing our Moros." Whereas Pershing and Scott seem to have reveled in the ritual aspects of their governorships, however, Bullard regarded this part of his job with visceral distaste. He showed none of Scott's passion for ethnography nor Pershing's dogged devotion to amassing field intelligence. Instead, the prospect of meeting to talk with the people of the Lake Lanao region exasperated him and elicited the same disdain that dominated his attitude toward blacks and Indians. As work on the road neared completion and Bullard contemplated the governorship of Lanao, which he thought was likely to come to him, he wrote: "It almost sickens me to think of having to deal with Moros another year."[75] Once work on the road was complete, Bullard became more involved with punitive expeditions (which he relished) as well as diplomatic work (which he did not). At Camp Marahui, he received datus, whose mere presence tried his patience. In August he wrote: "It looks as if these Moros will never stop talking. From about 9 a.m. to 4 p.m. they talk, talk, talk, until one wonders what in thunder they can have in their heads."[76] Two weeks later he recorded more complaints: "A Sunday spent in wrangling with Moros until I am tired and disgusted." A few days later he wrote: "Past week has nearly worn out my patience. Have wrangled with Moros until I am ready to kill them." His exasperation with these interactions was somewhat ameliorated by the success he felt had resulted from his negotiations. He wrote that he recovered some arms and, more importantly, "taught some of the Moros that they cannot hope to contend with white men."[77]

The most notable verb that appears in connection with Moros in Bullard's diary is "punish." While superintending the road work and as governor of Lanao, Bullard sought the opportunity to "even the score" and to "teach a lesson—it will do good." In his diary, Bullard railed against what he saw as excessive restraint and "coddling" of "aggressive" and "sassy" Moros by General Davis. He heartily approved when General Wood became governor and "completely reversed Gen. Davis' policy of patient and mild treatment of Moros. We are going after Mr. Moro now with a rough hand, we are holding him up to all the high ideals of civilization," he wrote approvingly.[78]

A fervent believer in the efficacy of punitive force, there was yet another factor that contributed to Bullard's dissatisfaction with the policy of "maintaining peace according to the expressed wishes of our superiors, when fighting was not only justified but almost unavoidable." Bullard was ambitious, and he saw that the way to advancement in the army was through fighting. He was particularly sensitive to the contrast between the recognition and advancement Pershing had won through his attacks on Moro strongholds and a corresponding lack of attention to what he and his men had accomplished through hard work, but little fighting, on the road. "As I suspected," he wrote, "there seems to pan out but little glory for soldiers who civilize our Moros without fighting."[79] He also expressed the opinion that "it is not a soldier's business to make peace but to make war."[80] Though somewhat distorted by his ambition and by jealousy of Pershing, Bullard had nonetheless put his finger on an underlying contradiction in entrusting peacemaking to the army. Treating "Mr. Moro" with restraint was not what the army was trained to do. Moreover, ambitious officers like Bullard chafed against restrictions on their ability to "punish those who had been bad." Critical of what he saw as his superiors' misplaced leniency, Bullard did not always ask for permission to attack. As work on the road extended further into Lake Lanao country, he recorded in his diary that "the aggressive Moros will go unpunished, unless punished very slyly and quietly." Two months later he wrote: "Moros are becoming again more 'sassy.' They need a lesson about once a week."[81] As he had in Luzon when he had found his superiors' support for his initiates weak, Bullard again found ways to mete out his own justice "with a wink but no words."

In Mindanao and Sulu from 1899 to 1913, the army arguably achieved what its commanders had long advocated for Indian pacification at home: military authority to manage affairs in Indian Country without interference from civil authorities. Each of the offices they held in Moroland—from Bullard's district governorship of Lanao to Scott's governorship of the island of Joló and Pershing's administration of the whole Moro Province—represented a combination of civil and military authority with almost unchecked power to police and

Figure 12. Menu caricature from General Bullard's retirement dinner, April 21, 1925. Robert L. Bullard Collection, Manuscript Division, Library of Congress.

punish a colonial population that a far-distant government had charged them with pacifying. To do the job, these veterans of domestic Indian Wars drew on familiar measures in their efforts to realize the grandiose claims of sovereignty asserted over a territory and people the Americans understood little better than when they had signed the treaty to end the war with Spain in 1898. As in Cuba, it was not with Spaniards that the military struggled to impose its will, but with the inhabitants of the islands themselves, whose views of their own sovereignty in their native land could not be reconciled with those promulgated by the War Department.

In 1913 the army's exclusive responsibility for the southern Philippines came to an end and American civilian government was extended over the region. By this time the United States was preoccupied with threats to stability on its southern border and a significant part of the army had been sent there, Pershing, Scott, and Bullard among them. There, all three assumed significant leadership roles in preparing their forces for a new conflict on another frontier of empire, one in which Mexico would serve as the new Indian Country.

Part III

———

The Last Indian War

In the past, I had dealt mostly with the children of the world,
if I may so describe them. In more ways than one, the Sioux
and the Moros were of a temperament which demanded of
me a paternal forbearance—often a firm hand, to be sure,
but generally my assignment had been that of preceptor to
those whom, from the point of view of civilized mankind,
our government regarded as less advanced than we. Often I
found strains in them of chivalry, of ethical consciousness, of
spirituality, and philosophy, that I suspected were superior
sometimes to the equivalent qualities in us. But for all of that,
my rôle . . . had been that of instructor and administrator.
            —Hugh Lenox Scott, "Washington and the Border,"
                                    Some Memories of a Soldier

During the more than thirty years [Porfirio] Diaz had ruled
Mexico, he had maintained relatively peaceful conditions by
force and the people were given no voice in their government,
either municipal or national. That they continued to be held in
a state of servility was largely because they were ignorant, inex-
perienced, the Indian Strain being predominant, and incapable
of self-government as more enlightened people knew it.
            —John J. Pershing, *My Life Before the World War,*
                                                    1860–1917

'The big impression that I bring back from Mexico is that
Mexico is Indian, not Spanish.... They are so far, so different
in race and advancement from us that I do not see how friction,
conflict between us and them can help at sometime coming....
The U.S. will inevitably dominate Mexico.
                            —Robert Lee Bullard, diary entry, June 16, 1916

Punitive Wars on the Frontiers of Empire

From the Coteau du Missouri to Apacheria, Samar, and Bud Dajo, American
efforts to impose control over areas of contested sovereignty have been marked
by punitive actions—punitive wars, punitive strikes, and that curious frontier
maneuver, with its emphasis on the pursuit of an elusive and vilified enemy,
the punitive expedition. In 1916, five years into Mexico's revolution turned civil
war, the United States responded to a raid across the border that left eighteen
Americans dead by sending 5,000 U.S. soldiers into northern Mexico in pursuit of Francisco "Pancho" Villa. The invading force, which eventually swelled to
15,000 and penetrated over 300 miles into Mexican territory, was known as the
Punitive Expedition, and sometimes as Pershing's Punitive Expedition in view
of its leadership by Brigadier General John J. Pershing. Brigadier General Hugh
Lenox Scott, as army chief of staff, directed the mission. Lieutenant Colonel
Robert Lee Bullard, following a spy mission down the west coast of Mexico in
1911, spent the later part of the border mobilization policing the Rio Grande
valley.

Although the eleven-month occupation of parts of northern Mexico and
deployment of militia along the border in 1916 is often treated by U.S. historians as a mere prelude to World War I, the Punitive Expedition is better understood as the last Indian war fought by the U.S. Army on its domestic frontier:
a massive cross-border policing action dispatched to discipline an adversary
described in the same way as earlier barbarians, bandits, and renegades. Like
the Pope and Sibley punitive expeditions into Dakota Territory half a century
earlier, the mobilization of troops along the border and their penetration deep
into Mexican territory was retaliatory but also strategic. The administration of
President Woodrow Wilson asserted that the protection of its citizens from

frontier outrages required armed intervention to counteract the violence that had become rife in the borderlands. The Americans also attempted to use the occupation to leverage concessions from their southern neighbor.

In Mexico, as in other areas of disputed sovereignty at home and abroad, punitive actions and racialized language served the strategic purpose of advancing moral as well as military claims to contested territory and provided the rationale for armed intervention. As we have seen, punitive measures have recurred throughout the history of U.S. expansion into areas of weak state control. The northern Mexican borderlands were one such area of contested sovereignty in the context of the Mexican Revolution, just as the southern Philippines had been in the preceding decade when Pershing, Scott, and Bullard led punitive expeditions there.

Revolutionary unrest in Mexico's borderlands also heightened the tendency of American businessmen, military leaders, and diplomats to apply customary ways of talking about and dealing with Indians, not just to Villa and his followers, but more generally to other factions of revolutionary leadership as their fortunes rose and fell throughout the period of the revolution and the civil war that followed from 1910 to 1920. Once again, the borderlands figured as Indian Country, with diplomatic correspondence between the two countries explicitly invoking their relations during the Apache Wars of the preceding century.[1]

Pershing, Scott, and Bullard all played prominent roles on the border during the Mexican Revolution, both before and during the Punitive Expedition. Their responsibility for American initiatives ranged from command of the forces policing the border to espionage and high-stakes diplomacy as well as active military campaigning on Mexican soil. The armed intervention in Mexico also incorporated counterinsurgency techniques whose origins can be traced to the U.S. occupation of the Philippines. Meanwhile, Platt Amendment–like measures the Wilson administration tried to impose on Mexico as a condition for the withdrawal of troops closely echoed those the United States had left in place when its military withdrew from Cuba in 1902.

On both sides of the border during 1916, reciprocal charges of violation of national sovereignty animated a war of words that repeatedly threatened to escalate into actual hostilities. In terms that ranged from diplomatic to bellicose, high-ranking officials of the Wilson administration and their counterparts in the Constitutionalist Army headed by First Chief Venustiano Carranza aired grievances, justified the movements of their armies—when they admitted them at all—and issued ultimatums.

Both Mexico and the United States justified their antagonistic positions in terms of the defense of their national territory from foreign interference. It soon became clear, however, that the core notions of sovereignty over which each side seemed prepared to go to war, were in fact quite different and seemingly irreconcilable. In the end, it was the American interpretation of national sovereignty interests that proved unsustainable. Wilson commanded the larger army, but Carranza was unyieldingly consistent ("stubborn" said the Americans) in his insistence that Mexico would never countenance the presence of foreign troops. In this he had the almost universal support of a nation that remembered the catastrophic loss of territory it had experienced seventy years earlier in a disastrous war which had also begun in a border dispute.

The initial American impetus for sending troops into Mexico was to punish Villa for his deadly raid on U.S. territory and to destroy his "band." The immediate U.S. response to the attack on Columbus, New Mexico, was less concerned with insisting on the inviolability of U.S. territory per se. The raid on Columbus was neither the first nor the last such incursion and securing the border was an even more implausible goal a century ago than it is today. Rather, the objective of sending a robust force into Mexico was to deter future attacks on Americans and their property in the borderlands. Wilson also hoped to pressure Carranza to take the initiative against raiders from the Mexican side.

Not surprisingly, the politics of sovereignty seems to have played a key part in Villa's calculations and objectives in attacking an American border town in the first place. There are many theories about what motivated Villa to attack Columbus. Ultimately, his intentions are unknowable, but the most likely explanations for his actions involve some calculations on his part about the likely chain of events his actions would unleash. Besides exacting revenge against the United States for its recognition of Carranza's government five months earlier, many historians believe Villa intended to provoke intervention by the United States in order to embarrass Carranza and perhaps provide the opportunity for Villa to make a military comeback—as he had so many times before—rallying Mexicans to support him and abandon the traitor Carranza who had made the country vulnerable to the ultimate calamity: invasion from the north.[2]

Both Pershing and Scott became personally acquainted with Pancho Villa two years before the raid on Columbus, at a time when he was emerging as one of the strongest and seemingly most pro-American military leaders vying for supremacy in the revolutionary struggle. Scott, in particular, cultivated a relationship with Villa and acted for a time as a special envoy from President

Wilson to conduct negotiations with him. Scott viewed Villa as a "primitive" and a "wild man," but he also regarded him as a "natural leader." Throughout his colonial career, Scott had advocated the cultivation of just such men as Villa for leadership in areas where the United States sought to extend its influence. "I believe in putting natural leaders in control, even if you have to fight and capture them for the purpose," he had written of Panglima Hassan in the Philippines. Scott developed good relations with Villa, perhaps enjoying the highest level of trust Villa ever accorded any representative of the U.S. government. At the high point of Villa's power and favor by Wilson's government, Scott had suggested that all Villa needed was a little polish, which he might obtain from some officer training at Fort Leavenworth to teach him some morals.[3] The paternalism of Scott's treatment of Villa was similar to his indulgent tutelage of other "native" leaders over whom the U.S. Army had assigned him authority, such as Jamal-ul-Kiram II (Sultan of Sulu), Chief Joseph, and Geronimo.

As had been the case throughout their careers, formative experiences in Indian Country provided a template for the way now-senior army officers would respond to the new and complex challenges posed by the Mexican Revolution. In rhetoric as well as tactics, U.S. actions in the borderlands followed the pattern of struggles with indigenous adversaries for control over sovereignty in the domestic sphere. For Pershing and Bullard, Mexican missions returned them to the very landscape of their earliest Indian fighting. In his diplomatic negotiations with high-ranking Mexicans, Scott continued to deploy the same methods he had developed over decades of dealing with racial others on earlier frontiers of empire. Bullard, as usual, drew the most explicit and elaborate connections between the Indian Wars and the U.S. role in the current conflict. A special assignment during the first consequential battles of the revolution took Bullard deep into Mexico and brought him face-to-face with the powerful forces remaking the country. It is to that foray across the border that we turn first.

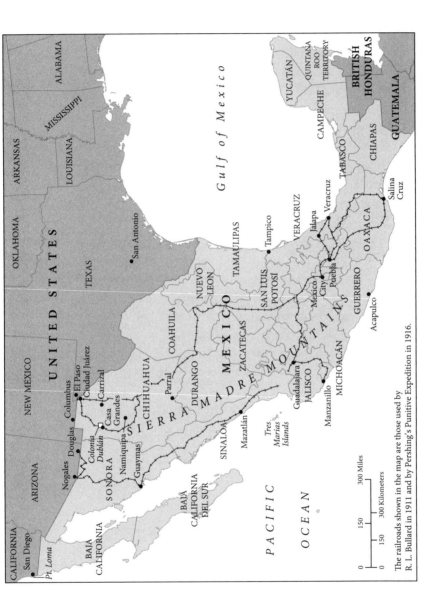

Map 4. Mexico. The map shows locations of consequence during the Mexican Revolution as well as places visited by R. L. Bullard on his spy mission.

Chapter 8

Spy Mission to Mexico: Lieutenant Colonel Robert Lee Bullard, 1911

General Villa never received the training at Leavenworth that Scott recommended for him, but in early 1911, Lieutenant Colonel Bullard did attend a course there for field-grade officers at the Army School of the Line. By this time, Bullard had come to regard what he called "Spanish American politics" as an area of special professional interest and his own particular bailiwick. Since his departure from Cuba two years earlier, he had taken the opportunity to study "everything that I could lay my hands on in the military library concerning Mexico and Central America . . . and everything I've been able to find outside."[1] He also kept up his study of Spanish. Bullard thought conflict between the United States and with Mexico (as well as points further south) was likely and saw competition for command in military operations south of the border as an area of comparative advantage for him:

> My study of Spanish at school, my service among the Mexican people of our Southwest, my service and experience among things and men of Spanish style, blood or tradition in the Philippine Islands and in California, all turn my mind at this time to Mexico and make me feel that if service should come in Mexico, I would not be unprepared for it. I believe I could do something worth a man's time. I have thoroughly studied up at least this west coast military situation and country in so far as Mexico is concerned. I believe if war were to come, I'd get a preference upon my preparations, that is, if I could have the latter known.[2]

After completing the Leavenworth course in late March 1911, Bullard resumed his duties as a regimental lieutenant colonel. His unit, the Eighth Infantry, had recently been mobilized for maneuvers on the border near San Diego, part of the army's heightened response to increased revolts in northern Mexico, and indeed throughout Mexico in the spring of 1911.[3] Back on the border, Bullard felt he was in his element. A visit to the Spanish mission at San Diego brought back memories of his earliest fascination with the history of "strange unique old Mexico."[4] His imagination was fired up with all the romantic notions that had captivated him when he had first reported for duty on the Arizona border twenty-six years earlier. Once again, he waxed rhapsodic in his diary. The arid landscape as well as the Mission Style architecture "brought up visions of the romance and adventure of the old unequaled Spain all over this new-old Western world," he wrote. He took the opportunity to practice his Spanish with "American Mexicans" he met near camp at Point Loma, including some sheep herders he engaged on the subject of the ongoing revolt against the Díaz government: they barely concealed their support for it. This kind of interaction further stoked his "longing to take some part again in Spanish-American affairs." In his diary, he expressed confidence that he knew "more about Mexico and the Mexican people, especially across the border near here, than the general [Tasker Bliss] or anyone at his headquarters here."[5] Bullard's Spanish may have been superior to that of his fellow anglophone officers, owing largely to his three years of intelligence and administrative work in Cuba, but his reading on Mexico was largely made up of travel literature and historical accounts that rehearsed a heroic version of Mexico's (Spanish) colonial history. Such reading was inadequate to the task of providing the background necessary to understand the momentous events unfolding in Mexico in 1911. In fairness to Bullard, it must be said that the events taking place in Mexico were unprecedented not just in that country's tumultuous history, but in the history of the world. As Bullard rode his horse along the border and hankered after renewed engagement in Spanish-American affairs, Mexico was on the brink of the first social revolution of the twentieth century.

Since independence in 1821, Mexico, which had been the wealthiest and most populous of Spain's American colonies, had endured a half century of political instability with frequent changes in government—most of them extra-constitutional—as well as half a dozen foreign interventions, two of which (the French occupation of would-be Emperor Maximilian and the American invasion of 1846) had led to wars that devastated the country. In contrast, under the presidency of Porfirio Díaz, the country had enjoyed an unprecedented three decades of relative peace and stability. Like many of his predecessors, don Porfirio had come to power through force of arms, but over the course of his (nominally elected) five terms in office, he had focused on restoring a sense of order and stability to Mexico and to promoting that image abroad. The image of Mexico abroad was key to Díaz's strategy for modernizing the country, which depended on attracting foreign capital to develop railroads, mines, a nascent oil industry, and light manufacturing. To an even greater degree than in Cuba during the same period, foreign investment also transformed agriculture. By 1910, 70 percent of Mexican landholdings were dedicated to the production of large-scale export-oriented crops. Smaller farms (ranchos) also shifted their production to export crops during the *Porfiriato*.[6]

Scott expressed the views of most of his peers in the American military when he approvingly described Díaz as "the grand old man of Mexico [who had] controlled Mexico for thirty years with great skill and efficiency for the first time in its history." He also credited Díaz with being "wise enough to perceive that without our [U.S.] friendship and support no administration can endure in Mexico."[7]

In an interview with the American journalist James Creelman in 1908, the eighty-year-old president stated that he would welcome an opposition party and intimated that he might not seek office again for himself at the next election. In the event, the old dictator did once again stand for election in 1910 (and was once again pronounced the winner). Prevented by house arrest from campaigning, Díaz's main rival in the election, Francisco I. Madero, took the momentous step of proclaiming a revolution against Díaz. The date set for the uprising was November 20, 1910. Madero escaped to San Antonio in July and established a revolutionary committee. In the borderlands the rebels, calling themselves "Anti-reelectionists," held clandestine meetings and raised money for arms on both sides of the border.

Francisco Madero was an unlikely revolutionary. The scion of a wealthy and prominent family from Coahuila, his vision for reform in Mexico emphasized political rather than structural change. But he was sincere in his opposition to Díaz and committed to the idea of democratic reforms. In 1910 and 1911, he became the focal point for proponents of change from disparate backgrounds. In the end, both his reform program and his leadership would prove inadequate in the face of demands for sweeping social and economic change he had neither the interest nor the ability to accommodate.[8]

The United States was never a passive observer of the revolution taking shape south of its border. For one thing, armed conflict in Mexico was fueled by resources flowing from the north, both money and weapons.[9] For another, American economic interests in Mexico were extensive. As he ordered thirty thousand troops to the border in March 1911, President Taft explained to U.S. Army Chief of Staff Leonard Wood that he was acting to safeguard the forty thousand or more Americans he estimated to be in Mexico along with "American investments of more than a billion dollars" that could be "injured or destroyed because of the Anti-American spirit of the insurrection" taking place.[10] As various factions in Mexico vied for supremacy, they sought to placate, accommodate, and occasionally, to provoke the colossus to the north. Villa was a master of accommodation as well as the author of the ultimate provocation—an attack on U.S. soil.

By March 1911, revolts were happening all over Mexico. By April, federal forces were struggling to maintain control over large cities while "revolutionaries controlled an ever-increasing part of the countryside."[11] Exhilarated by his return to the border and proximity to the developing revolution, Bullard sought permission to leave the camp at Point Loma to reconnoiter closer to the border. General Tasker Bliss, commander of the Department of California, granted his request to ride out on horseback to visit some of the camps set up to the south and east of San Diego to enforce U.S. neutrality laws. Bullard relished the trip, hoping it would "at least give me a taste of Spanish America.[12] Indeed it did. A three-day ride into San Diego's mountainous backcountry provided Bullard a vantage point on the tributary streams that had been diverted to slake the thirst of the coastal metropolis and also provided the scope for the same kind of romantic reveries he had indulged in as a second lieutenant in the Sierra Madre: "I thought of the pictures that my imagination had painted of Mexico from Prescott and others that I had lately been reading. In fact my mind is filled with the romance of the Spanish finding exploration and conquest of the land on which I am gazing, and I fall to dreaming about the wonderful ancient Indian civilization and chiefs that once held it, warriors, law-makers, rulers, patriots; and my dream is dispelled only by the vision, recalled, of some of the wretched descendants of these that I had today passed upon the road."[13] As usual, Bullard's fascination with the achievements he attributed to the ancient Mexicans was at odds with his disdain for their "wretched descendants," which was his dismissive assessment of contemporary Mexicans with whom he was once again brought into contact on the border.

> Judging from these we see today, their sons, is it possible that the
> Aztecs and other Mexicans whom the first Spaniards found knew
> and were all that Cortez and other Spanish conquerors . . . have
> said? Is it possible that exterior marking could change so little and
> the hidden intellect and moral of the subject have so utterly passed
> that we cannot call it a change but a disappearance? Looking at the
> average Mexican of today, idle, ambitionless, shiftless, ignorant,
> careless, is it possible to believe that so little while ago he repre-
> sented as much knowledge, civilization, progress and government
> as Spanish history alleges?[14]

In the two and a half decades since Bullard had first arrived on the border
with his copy of *Don Quixote* and the ambition to play a role in U.S. expansion
into the former Spanish dominions of the hemisphere, his estimation of their
inhabitants had barely changed. If anything, the self-directed study of the supposed character and racial hierarchy of civilizations he had outlined in a series
of notebooks compiled over the course of his colonial service abroad had merely
served to reaffirm his earliest ideas on these subjects. At the same time, a notion
of the Spanish empire in a mythic age of chivalry defined by acts of "knight-
errantry and romance," continued to dominate Bullard's imagination and color
his perceptions of "Old Mexico."[15]

Bullard returned from his three-day ride toward the border to find General Bliss contemplating a request from the War Department to send someone
into Mexico to investigate a particular concern about Japanese activities on
the Pacific coast. Aside from the military's preoccupation with revolutionary
activities inside Mexico, the War Department was also alert to other possible
foreign threats to U.S. interests in the Pacific and especially in the area of the
Panama Canal, which was still under construction. Japan's defeat of Russia in
1905 had signaled the emergence of another Pacific power. The Root-Takahira
Agreement of 1908 recognized spheres of influence for both nations in the Far
East while the United States kept a wary eye on Japanese overtures to Latin
American countries on the Pacific Rim, such as Chile and Mexico.[16] Now they
were looking into information they had received that the Japanese had entered
into a secret agreement with the Díaz government to establish coaling stations
for Japanese ships along Mexico's Pacific coast. "The Chief of Staff [Leonard
Wood] suggested that the general select and send an officer down into Mexico
to see if he could find out anything about this along the west coast. Would I like

to go?' 'Yes.' I said quick. I was literally tickled to death. I'd have some chance to put my Spanish-American study to use!"[17] In a reprise of the role he had played in Cuba, Bullard was to undertake an investigation of possible Japanese activity on the coast and see whether he could identify any stockpiles of coal. Bullard was delighted with this new assignment. "I went full of joy at the 'mission' to Mexico that was coming to me," he wrote in his diary after his initial meeting with Bliss. "It was important; it was confidential; it had danger enough to make a thrill. It appealed to me."[18]

Bullard immediately made arrangements to interview the source of Wood's intelligence, a businessman named Ernest Forbes with extensive political and commercial contacts in Central America and Mexico. Forbes believed he had reliable information that Japan and Mexico had entered into an agreement to give Japan use of a coaling station on the Tres Marias Islands off the coast of Sonora as part of an alliance against the United States. Such an arrangement, Forbes told Bullard when they met in San Francisco a few days later, was conceived as a way of challenging American control of the Panama Canal and generally as a way to "hurt the U.S. in the Pacific." Forbes claimed to have several sources for his information. One was a man who worked in the Mexican State Department who had told him of an unsigned agreement for Mexico to lease to Japan the use of the Tres Marias Islands for a coaling station. The agreement was to come into force once Díaz had resolved the Madero rebellion.[19]

Forbes also told Bullard that he had spoken with an agent of the Japanese Mitsui Company who had confirmed the coaling station pact in a separate conversation. Additionally, Forbes reported seeing a great quantity of coal at both Manzanillo and Acapulco. He estimated these Japanese stockpiles of coal at about a hundred thousand tons and told Bullard he "believed that it [coal] might be found anywhere along the west coast from Mazatlán to Panama."[20] Although Bullard and Forbes were unaware of it, rumors of a secret Japanese-Mexican alliance had been percolating through intelligence reports for several months. In March President Taft had told the Japanese he regarded rumors of Japanese-Mexican machinations as "well-intended fabrications," but others were not so sure. The following month the *New York Evening Sun* published an article claiming that a treaty did exist and that the U.S. ambassador to Mexico, Henry Lane Wilson, had seen it. The article further attributed the recent mobilization of U.S. troops to the border to concerns about an alliance between Mexico and Japan. It turned out that the information had been supplied to the paper by the German military attaché in the United States. Whether the Germans truly believed these rumors themselves or not, they continued to promote the idea of Japanese war aims against the United States.[21]

Bullard's assignment was part of a broader intelligence-gathering effort that had been going on in the Military Intelligence Division (MID) at the Army War College for about a year. Besides soliciting a range of information, including maps, and assessment of roads, bridges, and other infrastructure from the military attaché, consular officials and other contacts inside Mexico, the War Department had also dispatched a few other officers in disguise, like Bullard, to assess support for Díaz (weak) and the likelihood of unrest (high). In 1910 the MID's Committee on War Planning was working with a scenario that involved an invasion of northern Mexico requiring 30,000 to 60,000 U.S. troops and a separate "Vera Cruz project," which called for a force of 100,000 moving inland from the Gulf port to Mexico City.[22]

Having satisfied himself that his informant's concerns merited investigation and feeling increasingly excited at the prospect of his spy mission into Mexico, Bullard spent some time practicing his skills at estimating the size of coal piles around San Francisco as he waited for General Bliss to give him the go-ahead to cross the border. He also briefed his wife, Rose, who was living in regimental quarters at Monterey. He told her only the bare minimum about his confidential mission and cautioned her to let the neighbors "live in ignorance" about what he was doing. Rose did contribute to the cover story for his disguise, however. Bullard decided he would travel under the assumed name of L. Mizelle, a name adopted from his mother's side of the family in Alabama. As L. Mizelle, he would present himself as a commercial traveler representing a group of "eastern capitalists" interested in establishing a line of West Coast steamers in anticipation of the opening of the Panama Canal. Rose's brother in Chattanooga, whom Bullard esteemed as "an exceedingly discreet and able as well as close-mouthed fellow," would be apprised of his role as the supposed secretary and representative of the fictitious company. Besides his brother-in-law, the only other person outside the army Bullard admitted to his confidence was his old friend Judge Leon Armisen in Cuba. Bullard wrote to the judge requesting that he cable Rose immediately with the "substance of any communications" Bullard might send him that were signed "Brother."[23]

The rudiments of his cover story thus provided for, Bullard crossed the border at Nogales, Arizona, on May 8. He found Nogales full of people fleeing the fighting and upheaval in Mexico and almost all of those he spoke with expressed support for Madero. On the same day Bullard crossed into Sonora, Madero's forces, led by Pascual Orozco and Pancho Villa, launched an attack on the strategic city of Ciudad Juárez. Located next to El Paso, Texas, the border crossing was an economic center of the borderlands and a crucial nexus for the flow of people and goods, including weapons and other war supplies. After two days of street fighting, federal forces surrendered to the revolutionaries on May 11. It was the first of several significant victories by the rebels that led to President Díaz's resignation on May 21.[24]

Bullard entered Mexico with a pistol concealed under his money belt and twenty rounds of ammunition lodged painfully in his shoes. As the old regime was experiencing its first defeats on the battlefield, the main challenge facing L. Mizelle, commercial traveler, was how to conceal his true identity from two fellow Americans who—to Bullard's astonishment—turned out to be from eastern Alabama. One of these, a young man named McCalla, had attended Auburn University like Bullard and also knew his nephew and some of his in-laws. This made personal conversation challenging. "In talk I had to be very careful but this made it all the more attractive and it gave me a practice and a confidence in treading on delicate ground and playing my 'L. Mizelle'—commercial or steamer traveler role. I felt I came off well. My statements, all lies, seemed to hold water and appear plausible."[25]

McCalla was a paymaster with a contracting company involved in railroad construction. The other Alabaman on the train was working as a land agent in Sonora. The two men represented the large number of Americans whose investments in Mexican enterprises had been promoted and rewarded by the Díaz regime. Those enterprises now faced uncertainty. Playing the part of commercial traveler, Bullard continued his journey south to Guaymas. Everywhere he was reminded of the revolution that was taking place in the country. "Everywhere today but one thing is on every tongue, the insurrection. In shop, office, market, on street-corner, sidewalks in carriages and horse cars (for Guaymas has horse cars) every one is talking of Madero, and every one high and low is with him heart and soul."[26]

In Guaymas he hired a steam launch to search the area for possible coaling stations. He found none. To travel further down the coast, he and his fellow Alabaman boarded a Mexican steamer, the *Manuel Hererrias*, officered by Spaniards. At La Paz on the Baja California peninsula, Bullard identified a U.S. coaling station, but saw no evidence of any Japanese activity. At Mazatlán two American *enganchadores* (labor agents) for the Southern Pacific Railroad boarded the *Hererrias*. One of them told Bullard he had heard of a Japanese coaling station at Magdalena Bay. He even showed Bullard a souvenir flag, given to him by a Mexican girl, that was an amalgam of the Mexican and Japanese flags. He claimed a Mexican fleet had stopped at San Blas several months earlier, a claim Bullard later found to be untrue. With field glasses at the ready, Bullard continued to scan the coast and talk to his fellow passengers—Mexicans, Spaniards, and Americans—and wherever the steamer put ashore he conducted further inquiries. As the trip through Mexico continued, he became increasingly aware of the overwhelming support enjoyed by opponents of the regime. He also noted the behavior of insurgents, who he found much in evidence at almost every stop. Bullard was disparaging of what he saw as their lack of discipline and their martial pretensions.

When he went ashore at Manzanillo on May 17, Bullard learned of the agreement between President Díaz and Madero's forces signed on May 11. This agreement, the Treaty of Ciudad Juárez, stipulated that both Díaz and his vice president, Ramón Corral, would resign.[27] Bullard commented on the "general rejoicing and returning hope" engendered by this news. "This people does not want war; that's clear," he wrote.[28] Bullard had no way of anticipating that, only a week later, he would bear personal witness to the old dictator's journey into exile when Díaz's train came alongside the one on which he was traveling across the Isthmus of Tehauntepec.

Conversations with fellow passengers on the steamer and later with the vice consul in Manzanillo helped convince Bullard that the Japanese fleet Ernest Forbes and the Southern Pacific labor agent had reported was most likely made up of two or three war vessels which had visited Mexico in a ceremonial capacity during the celebration of the country's centenary of independence the previous year. Thus, Bullard wrote, "I cannot attach as much significance to its visit as Dr. Forbes seemed to." He could find no evidence that any other Japanese war vessels had been along the coast since then.[29]

Bullard's next stop was Salina Cruz, Oaxaca. From there, Bullard took what seems like a detour from the assignment to investigate possible coaling stations and Japanese connections. From Tehuantepec he boarded a train bound for Veracruz on the Gulf Coast. This side trip had no apparent relevance to his inquiries, other than, perhaps, the strategic value of the railway itself. It is hard to avoid the impression that Bullard undertook this side trip out of his personal interest in exploring the storied geography of some of the great exploits in the heroic history of the Spanish conquistadors he so admired. As the train passed the border of Chiapas in the night and descended "from the backbone of the continent . . . fast to the Gulf," Bullard—likely with his copy of T. Philip Terry's handbook for travelers to Mexico close at hand—wrote in a nostalgic vein about all of those who had traveled before him to Veracruz: Cortéz, the pirate Lorencillo, Maximilian, and General Winfield Scott, among others.

Veracruz itself left him unimpressed, however. All its romantic history as the entry point for would-be conquerors notwithstanding, Bullard found Veracruz itself to be disappointing. "It seems but a village," he wrote.[30] Still, in spite of his disappointment with the storied place, Bullard was thrilled with the train journey across the isthmus, both for its scenery and for the scope it provided for his historical reveries. "It was beautiful, surprisingly beautiful, indescribable," he wrote as the train ascended again toward Jalapa. "My mind is running on the history here made by the conquering Spaniards, what they did and the names they've left. I will not try to write my thoughts but sure it is I never felt greater inspiration in considering the things that men have done since the world began."[31] Bullard was no less thrilled by the unsettled conditions in the country through which he was traveling. As he began his return trip from Veracruz, he heard rumors of the "disturbed condition caused by the revolution" on the route ahead. Among the details he wrote in his diary, he reported hearing that foreigners were leaving the capital, including the American minister. He joked with the rail agent at Veracruz about the challenge of making it all the way to Mexico City by train. (The agent assured him he would reach the capital.) Commenting on the excitement he felt at the intimation of danger, Bullard wrote: "The thrills! Turn back? Not much. It's the first real running of the blood I've felt since Moro days seven years ago. I was scared, but I was grinning, joyful, jubilant. I cannot describe my feelings. I can only say that if I had seen sure death ahead, with that feeling of elation of elevation, ecstacy, I would have gone straight on to it. It was not bravery, nor moral courage; but a sort of drunken ecstacy; nothing else describes the feeling."[32] Whatever the real objective of this side trip, the journey through central Mexico brought Bullard face-to-face with the unfolding drama of Mexico's first tumultuous transfer of power in over three decades.

The most momentous episode occurred on the segment of the trip from Jalapa to Puebla. Bullard had been observing the demeanor of the train conductor, who looked "pale and strained and frightened." In despair the man announced that the telegraph line had been cut ahead. "We are sure to have trouble," was his prediction. At the small station of San Miguel, Bullard's train was switched onto a siding. Bullard described in detail the impression he had as another train carrying the former president of Mexico, Porfirio Díaz, who had resigned only days before, slid past on its way down to Veracruz and from there into exile. "A pilot engine filled with soldiers glides past us, a train with soldiers next doors and windows[,] flat cars, engine tenders, baggage cars all bristling with arms and swords & machine guns, all cocked and primed; a train of two or three special cars; another one of troops.'Porfirio Díaz' is the hushed whisper that runs through our train. The man who had ruled Mexico for 30 years was going into exile now: he who had made the whole world admire & wonder was gliding by unheralded save by the silent terror that seemed to go before him in the air."[33] Bullard glimpsed the man himself, seated in a sleeper car, which prompted Bullard to reflect: "For the first time in 80 years he is leaving his native land. . . . His will has been the law, his word the last command for thirty years. Now all is changed and he has been thrown down with violence. His life is threatened even after he has said 'I go.'"[34]

"What an end!!" exclaimed a German on the train. Bullard commented: "Never have I seen people so moved. . . . I shall never forget the sensation, the strength of feeling, the gasping state of all who saw. And on his train's every face of soldiers, officers, engineers and train crews was drawn & strained."[35]

Once Díaz's train had passed, Bullard's train resumed its journey inland to Puebla. The conductor was happy again, and generally the atmosphere of fear had lifted, "like the terror of a storm that passes by and leaves all unhurt," Bullard wrote.

Further up the line, the train was stopped again, this time by insurgents who were searching for arms or ammunition, according to Bullard. To Bullard's surprise, the revolutionaries "were absolutely welcomed by every passenger aboard. All sympathy was insurgent, plainly," he wrote, adding: "No one was molested in the least." Instead, Bullard described how all the passengers "came out and fraternized" with the men who had held up the train. Even Bullard seemed affected by the acclaim for the insurgents. Unaccountably, he gave away his pair of field glasses to one of the apparent leaders of the rebels, with a note with his address on it so the man could return the field glasses to him after the revolution. (In his unpublished autobiography, Bullard noted that he never got the binoculars back.)

Bullard arrived in Mexico City early the next morning. As with Veracruz, he found the city disappointing. He had expected more. "It is small," he wrote. The "Plains of Anahuac . . . are poor & bare looking, not what romantic history would leave the reader thinking. Yet there are the lagoons & the untranslateable Indians with their sombre looks and unsmiling faces. These two are the unchanged marks."[36] Bullard spent the day sightseeing. He marveled that the city seemed quiet after Díaz's departure the day before. "Hum-drum," he wrote, "as though great changes could never touch it." In the evening, he boarded another train for Guadalajara and from there to Colima.

Although undetected by Bullard, Mexico's capital was, of course, affected by the currents roiling the country and by the departure the day before of its erstwhile president and strongman, the center of gravity in Mexican politics for so long. The most immediate challenges to Díaz's power had come from the northern borderlands, it was true. Still, during the coming decade of internecine civil war, the ancient capital would see its share of bloodshed, perfidy, and suffering. Less than two years after Bullard passed through, Díaz's successor, the reformer Francisco I. Madero, would be overthrown and assassinated following ten days of deadly fighting in the heart of the capital, in which many civilians were killed. The fighting was brought to an end only when the American ambassador Henry Lane Wilson convened a meeting between the opposing commanders and supported the traitorous bid of Madero's chief of staff General Victoriano Huerta to become president.[37] Huerta's coup in February 1913 provoked renewed revolution by Madero supporters such as Pancho Villa, Álvaro Obregón, and Venustiano Carranza in the north, and Emiliano Zapata in the southern state of Morelos. It also marked a turning point in the political struggle in Mexico; after Madero's overthrow, the conflict increasingly took on the characteristics of a civil war, as multiple factions created and broke alliances and struggled for national supremacy.[38]

From Mexico City, Bullard again headed for the coast to resume his investigations in seaports as he headed north for the border. Taking a steamer again up the coast, Bullard carried out his inquiries conscientiously, and with elements of intrigue and deception, the details of which he recorded with evident satisfaction in his diary. One gets the sense, however, that he had already concluded that the rumors of Japanese coal were unfounded. He was also tiring of the spy game and was ready to head home. Bullard felt that his mission into the heart of Mexico had provided him with valuable insights, and a true sense, he wrote, of the political situation in the country. He had also become more acquainted with what he found to be Mexico's essential—and problematic—nature. In a word, it was *Indian*, which in Bullard's mind made conflict with the United States inevitable. "The big impression that I bring back from Mexico," he wrote in the concluding pages of his diary "is that Mexico is Indian, not Spanish." "They are so far, so different in race and advancement from us," he concluded, "that I do not see how friction, conflict between us and them can help at sometime coming." The United States, he predicted, "will inevitably dominate Mexico."[39]

Chapter 9

—————

Washington and the Border: Brigadier General Hugh Lenox Scott, 1911–1916

As Bullard scouted for Japanese coal in Mexico, Hugh Lenox Scott was concluding the work of culling the records of the military occupation of Cuba.[1] After the end of his term as governor of Sulu, Scott had served as superintendent of West Point from 1906 to 1910. In early 1911, along with an increasing proportion of the army, Scott had been assigned duties closer to the southern border. Initially he was sent to San Antonio, where he commanded the Third Cavalry. Upon his promotion to brigadier general in March 1913, Scott assumed command of the Second Cavalry Brigade and Patrol with responsibility for policing the border from Fabens, Texas, to California. Although Scott's letters home from Texas to his wife back in New Jersey during this period included frequent references to the situation in Mexico, Scott's reputation as a mediator of Indian troubles also meant he was frequently on detached service as the government sent him to settle disputes with and among tribes throughout the Southwest—including, at various times between 1908 and 1915, the Navajos, Mexican Kickapoos, Hopi, Apaches, and Paiutes. In the same spirit, the Wilson administration called on him to negotiate with several Mexican chieftains of the revolution, including Francisco "Pancho" Villa, Manuel Chao, José Maria Maytorena, Venustiano Carranza, and Álvaro Obregón (the last two became president of Mexico in 1917 and 1920, respectively).

There were many points of similarity between the approach the army took toward policing unrest on its border during the Mexican Revolution and its accustomed responses to outbreaks on the shifting frontiers of Indian Country over the previous century. Some of the responses and tactics were, of course,

those that any army of the time might have made in response to political instability in a neighboring country with a long and porous border and a history
of cross-border raiding, gunrunning, and filibustering. (The Americans had
historically supplied most of the guns and all of the filibusters.) However, continuities with earlier Indian Wars have not received the analysis they deserve.

First, it is significant to look at the language used to describe the conflict
taking place in the sister republic to the south. Although the fighting in Mexico
passed through several distinct phases, it is notable that the language used by
American military leaders remained remarkably consistent throughout the
period, regardless of whether they were describing the initial uprising phase
of the revolution or the later fighting after Victoriano Huerta's ouster in 1914,
when struggles among factions for national supremacy took on the characteristics of a civil war. Throughout the conflict, American military observers used
the word "Indian" in the course of describing events—and the threat they posed
to American interests and border security. The word was used to describe the
population as a whole; it was also used frequently either as an explicit or implied characteristic that came up in descriptions of Mexican military leaders,
or chieftains as they were often referred to. Americans used the word "chief,"
with its connotations of localized personalistic rule and its close association
with dismissive notions of the leadership among Indian tribes to refer to high-
ranking officers in the Mexican revolutionary forces. It was also how Americans
glossed the Spanish word *jefe*, meaning boss, leader, or head.

Americans applied the word "Indian" to participants in the Mexican Revolution in spite of the fact that the regions of Mexico where most of the fighting took place, and certainly the battles in which the United States was most
focused, were not areas where indigenous people predominated. In fact, the
northern states of Chihuahua, Sonora, and Coahuila were, in general, more
mestizo than the central and southern part of the country. Even more significantly, recent settlers in these states often defined their own identity in opposition to the mobile Athapascans—the Comanches, Apaches, Yaquis, and others
who had prevented extensive European settlement of the north until the late
nineteenth century. The borderlands had developed a culture distinct from that
of the central and southern part of Mexico.[2] These distinctions were lost on
the Americans, however. To them, Mexicans were Indians, and they referred to
them as such. For example, Major Frank Tompkins, who was in command of
the garrison at Columbus when it was attacked and who had pursued the raiders fifteen miles into Mexico, referred to the Villistas he chased in the Punitive

Expedition as Indians as matter-of-factly as he described his squadron's tactics.[3] Besides racial terms and the references to revolutionary leaders as chieftains, Scott also talked about Villa coming in (or, more precisely, *not* coming in), to parlay, much as army officers on the plains had measured Indians' compliance with Grant's Peace Policy by their willingness to present themselves to military authorities at agencies and to come in to reservations.[4]

American press depictions of Mexicans during the period of the revolution employed the same stereotypes used to describe Indians at home. These included "intemperance, sexual promiscuity, lust, lechery, venality, war-mongering . . . personal filth, cruelty to captives of war, laziness, cowardice, and deceit," according to Mark Anderson, who has analyzed depictions of Mexicans in the U.S. press and diplomatic record during this period. Significantly, he notes that the positive attributes of the "noble" American Indian are largely absent from these later representations of Mexican Indians.[5]

Beneath the racial language in which combatants were described lay a deeper and more significant similarity between the nineteenth-century theaters of the Indian Wars and the shifting terrain of conflict in Mexico. It is the one we have considered earlier as the sine qua non of Indian Country. In short, Americans regarded northern Mexico as Indian Country, not just because of the racial stereotypes they projected onto the people who lived there, but also because sovereignty over those territories was contested and Americans had an interest in who prevailed. Significantly, the sovereignty of Sonora, Chihuahua, and Coahuila was contested not just because, by 1915, different factions were waging their battles for control of the Mexican state there, but more importantly in terms of continuity with other phases of Indian Country, because Americans still entertained the idea of extending control over these territories, even incorporating them into the domestic territory of the United States. Northern Mexico's economy had become thoroughly integrated into the U.S. economy during the reign of Porfirio Díaz. Now, the chaos and destruction of fighting threatened significant American economic interests, particularly mines and ranches. In this sense, northern Mexico was Indian Country because Americans had an active interest in maintaining economic access—if not territorial control—in those regions.[6]

One revolutionary leader to whom the tropes of Indian fighting were often applied was Francisco "Pancho" Villa. Although much vilified on both sides of the border as a bandit and outlaw, Villa nonetheless enjoyed the support of a number of American military observers, including Scott, who played a prominent role as an intermediary between Woodrow Wilson's government and Pancho Villa from 1912 to 1915. Scott's promotion to brigadier general in 1911 and then his expanded portfolio for border affairs as chief of staff of the army coincided with Villa's rise to prominence as one of the key leaders in the Division del Norte (Division of the North). For a brief time, the Wilson administration flirted with the idea of throwing its support behind Villa in his struggle with the first chief of the Constitutionalist Army, Venustiano Carranza. When the United States abruptly recognized Carranza as de facto president of Mexico in October 1915, Scott regarded the action as a mistake—one he had counseled President Wilson against. Villa regarded it as an act of betrayal, although interestingly, not one that seems to have dimmed his regard for Scott.

The relationship between Scott and Villa was complex. It was necessarily instrumentalist, as each man attempted to use the other to further his side's political goals—and also to leverage his own power and prestige. In spite of this, the relationship that emerges from the record of their words and actions over the nearly three years of their intermittent interaction and communication

Figure 13. Pancho Villa (center) and Hugh Lenox Scott (right front) at the races, Ciudad Juárez, 1914. Prints and Photographs Division, Library of Congress.

is one of genuine regard and mutual respect, even admiration. Remarkably, the raid on Columbus did not entirely dim Scott's esteem for Villa, even though, as army chief of staff when it occurred, Scott was responsible for coordinating the military response of the Wilson administration. It was Scott who directly advised the secretary of war (who had taken office just days before the attack) on the formation of the punitive expedition that was dispatched to hunt down and destroy Villa's band. Still, Scott never completely gave up his belief that Villa was "too wise to make such an attack willingly."[7]

Villa, for his part, also seems to have held on to his faith in the friendship he felt he had forged with Scott, or perhaps his enduring confidence was in his own ability to continue to succeed in wooing the influential American general and statesman. Even after his raid across the New Mexico border, Villa sent two envoys to meet with Scott. Although Scott refused to receive them until Villa had been exonerated of the Columbus raid, his regard for Villa remained substantially unaltered. Less than a week after he had played a key role in launching the punitive expedition that would hunt Villa for half a year, Scott sent a message to George Carothers, U.S. consul in Torreón and sometime confidant and adviser to Villa, in which the American general's sympathies for Villa are still apparent just days after the Columbus attack: "I am sorry about that course that makes Villa an outlaw; nothing can be done for him, on either side of the border. I can not understand why he should have taken such an action. I thought he had better natural sense than to close out every avenue of escape for himself. He can never seek asylum in the United States now, for he would at once be arrested and tried for murder."[8] There are several reasons for this. First, Scott admired Villa's military prowess and especially his cavalry tactics. This began with what Scott called Villa's "brilliant stroke of genius" in November 1913, when Villa seized a train used for ferrying coal and other supplies between Ciudad Chihuahua and Ciudad Juárez and used it to transport two thousand of his men directly into Ciudad Juárez, where they took the federal forces by surprise and overcame all defenses within hours. The "stroke of genius" that so impressed Scott and greatly increased Villa's fame as a master campaigner, was that all the while Villa's troops were headed north toward the important border city, Villa was able to control telegraph communications (by having his soldiers hold guns to the heads of local telegraph operators) to make it *appear* that Villa's forces were headed in the other direction. Thus, the approach of Villa's army went undetected until it was too late for the federal garrison to mount an effective defense.[9]

Undeniably, there was also an element of self-interest in Scott's regard for Villa. Villa's confidence in Scott and his willingness to deal with him greatly increased Scott's prestige. Scott had also invested a lot of time in nurturing the relationship. As he wrote to his wife in 1914: "I have been struggling for fame ever since coming into the service nearly forty years and have at last arrived at the result that my title to consideration in Washington is that I am known as a friend of Villa's—that is my distinction. They all thought me crazy when I came up from the border a Villista last April but the Spanish [and] English ambassadors have both told me that they have come around to my view and have so informed their governments."[10] Scott was, of course, using a certain amount of irony in depicting his fortunes as dependent on Villa. When Scott wrote this letter he was assistant chief of staff of the army, soon to succeed to the top position. Both he and his wife knew that his influence far exceeded his relationship with Villa, whom he referred to in the same letter as "the idol of the Peon" in Mexico. But there was an element of truth, too, in Scott's tongue-in-cheek acknowledgment of the cachet that access to the revolutionary general had brought him.

Villa looked after Scott's interests in another significant way. Always assiduous—at least in the early days of his rise to power—to seek favor with Americans and to discourage intervention by their government, Villa provided protection for American property and businesses in territories under his control, which by 1914 included all of Chihuahua in addition to shifting control over parts of Durango and Sonora. This patronage from Villa struck close to home for Scott since his son Merrill was employed as an engineer at the Alvarado mine near Parral in Chihuahua. Villa personally provided assurance to Scott of his protection of the mine. After the United States occupied Veracruz in April 1914, for example, Scott wrote to reassure his wife about their son's safety in Mexico. "Things are looking bad at El Paso," he wrote to Mary on April 24, 1914, "but telegram from Villa not to bother about things," which Scott interpreted as an assurance of their son's safety.[11] On June 24, Scott again assured his wife of Villa's protection, adding by way of explanation that Villa was "anxious to accommodate" him.[12]

Scott admired Villa's prowess as a cavalryman and military strategist. He commended Villa's concern for his troops and the efforts he undertook on their behalf. Dislike for Carranza also helped burnish Villa's image in contrast with the civilian former governor of Coahuila and self-styled first chief of the Constitutionalist forces. "I will tell you the way I look on Villa," Scott wrote to his wife in September, 1914: "Carranza has climbed to what power he has on Villa's shoulders and is trying to kick him down—he has no real power of his own—Villa is the real force of Mexico and has caught Carranza by the neck each time he has broken his agreements and put him back on the track until now when it has arrived at such a stage in the game that his [Carranza's] falsity can be stood no longer."[13] Like many American officials involved with Mexican affairs, Scott disliked Carranza, whom he viewed as venal, corrupt, and irritatingly anti-American. In contrast to what he saw as Carranza's self-serving ambition, Scott applauded Villa's renunciation of personal ambition to secure the presidency for himself, telling him that he would be "the Washington" of Mexico. Instead, during the period when he possessed convincing power to make such a scenario plausible, Villa supported the idea that one of his close political allies, Felipe Ángeles, might fill that role. Ángeles was an educated man, who had served as director of the Chapultepec Military Academy. Villa felt his own lack of education disqualified him for high office. Scott shared Villa's esteem for Ángeles, calling him "the most cultivated and loyal gentleman I have known in the history of Mexico."[14]

Villa's fighting techniques rounded out Scott's sense of him as a wild man, a primitive, a throwback to the Cheyenne warriors he had followed and studied on the Musselshell River during the Great Sioux War in July 1877, almost four decades earlier (see Chapter 2). The veteran of the last of the Plains Indian Wars seemed particularly impressed by Villa's signature tactic of drawing the enemy on with an apparent retreat only to renew the attack on the pursuers once they gave chase. These were Indian fighting techniques. By 1915, however, such tactics were all but obsolete, and in fact would be rendered tragically ineffectual by the modern weaponry that Obregón and Carranza would throw up against Villa's forces in the battles of Agua Prieta and Celaya, where such cavalry prowess was no match for barbed wire and machine guns. Villa's characteristic nighttime cavalry charge, which he expected to weaken the Carrancista forces garrisoning the border town of Agua Prieta, was met with "withering fire from Carrancista machine guns, artillery, and rifles." Worse yet, the battlefield was illuminated by searchlights. Villa's forces were utterly routed.[15]

Scott seems to have viewed the acts of barbarity—the killing of prisoners and the wounded that led to denunciations of Villa in the United States and to what biographer Friedrich Katz has called the "black legend" of his barbaric cruelty—as an inherent part of Villa's primitive warrior nature. It was what intrigued Scott about him and also provided the contours of the civilizing mission that provided a role for Scott in the U.S. Government's assessment of its conundrum in dealing with him.

At their first meeting on the international bridge between El Paso and Ciudad Juárez in February 1914, Scott told Villa,

> "Civilized people look on you as a tiger or a wolf."
>
> "Me," he exclaimed in great surprise.
>
> "Yes," I told him, "you."
>
> "How is that?" he asked.
>
> "Why, from the way you kill wounded and unarmed prisoners. Didn't you kill a hundred and twenty-five unarmed prisoners the other day at Cases Grandes?"
>
> "Why, those were my enemies," he exclaimed, as if that was what enemies were meant for.
>
> "There it is," I said. "Civilized people don't do that. You will only bring down on your own head the execration of civilized people when you do that."
>
> He answered, "Well, I will do anything you tell me."

A careful reader of the memoirs in which the general provides his account of this exchange will notice that this is how Scott's negotiations with the intransigent Indians the government sent him to deal with always end! However difficult, however alienated, however angry, however long his negotiation with exasperated Indians takes, the outcome is always the same: they agree to do whatever Scott recommends. "I am going to do just what you tell me to do," said the old Navajo Bizoshe after several days of talking with Scott in New Mexico in 1913. The sultan of Sulu, likewise, in Scott's telling, had quickly learned to do what he was told.[16]

Whether General Villa in fact pronounced these deferential words (or their Spanish equivalent) during his first meeting with General Scott, it is clear that Villa had an interest in forging good relations with Scott. At the same time, he had little reason to do everything the American general advised or demanded that he do. On one level, Scott certainly realized this. At one point, the State Department was exploring a scheme to send him to live with Villa "with the idea that I would restrain him from these barbarous acts," as Scott explained to his wife. The plan is reminiscent of Scott's earlier assignments in which he "domesticated himself" in the lodges of Indians on the prairies, or when he was detailed to "keep an eye" on Red Cloud. Scott was realistic about his ability to exert influence over Villa. He wrote to his wife that while he "could do a great deal of good with him [Villa] in small matters like the taking of that cotton and the looting of foreigners I could not prevent and would be told when remonstrating against them that friendship ceases right there—only a large armed force can prevent that and I would be foredoomed to failure."[17] At other times, however, Scott wrote that he thought he was having a good influence on Villa. Others echoed this assessment, both in the press and in diplomatic reports to the State Department.

Scott regarded—and treated—Villa in the way his frontier experience had conditioned him to perceive and deal with racial others on the contested frontiers of empire: the Great Plains, the Philippines, Cuba. On the one hand, Scott respected Villa's intelligence and cunning. Detailing a negotiating session in January 1915, he wrote to his wife: "I watched him across a desk with the greatest interest—he is very intent on what he is doing—his intelligence is most apparent—he looks you right in the eye and you can see him catch an idea and you get an answer back in a flash."[18] At the same time, Scott also put Villa squarely in the category of the other primitive leaders with whom he had negotiated on behalf of his government in the past, referring to him as a wild man and a primitive and adjusting his approach accordingly. His attitude toward Villa was paternalistic and even indulgent, even as he recommended applying a strong hand in dealing with him. "There is nothing men like Villa respect," he wrote, "so much as truthful, direct, forceful statements, no matter how unpalatable. *Like a child or a dog these primitive people know well with whom they are dealing and are impressed accordingly* [italics added]."[19] Tiger, wolf, dog, child: the metaphors are familiar from the Apache Wars and from the Moro campaign.

How did Villa regard Scott? To answer this intriguing question, we have unfortunately fewer of Villa's words (mostly telegrams, and conversations filtered through the reports of others). Scott claimed, in his ironic way, that Villa seemed "to have taken a romantic regard" for him, and there may be some truth in this. According to Katz, Villa admired professional military men, "especially when they did not look down on him." Katz also speculates that the two men shared the same "code of honor."[20]

Although Villa left no descriptions of Scott nor accounts of their dealings, we do have some telling gestures on which to base interpretations of his views of Scott and they all point to a regard for Scott that went beyond the usual requirements of diplomatic protocol. In fact, Villa's overtures toward Scott hint intriguingly at a diplomatic technique Scott himself had described as part of his strategy of engaging a resistant interlocutor. In his memoirs, Scott says that the way he won the confidence and cooperation of the many "exasperated Indians" he was sent to pacify was to hunt out their weak spot, by which he meant a point of interest he could exploit to gain their sympathy, something that provided an opening for him to win their trust and eventually to be able to persuade them to comply with the government's demands. Scott credited his ability to search out and engage his interlocutors on their particular interests as the key to his ability to win them over.[21] In the Navajo Bizoshe's case, for example, it was the tribe's history that provided an entrée into a conversation with the old man. Villa seems to have quickly ascertained and appealed to several of Scott's deep-seated interests—his weak spots—and he used them to engage the American general's sympathy. The first of these was Scott's fatherly concern for the well-being of his son Merrill and his prospects at the mine in Chihuahua where he was employed as an engineer. Extending protection to the Alvarado mine in Parral allowed Villa not just to show solicitude for Scott's son, but also to demonstrate the extent of his regional power in being able to extend such protection. In the same letter in which he had written to Mary that he thought Villa was anxious to accommodate him, Scott also noted that "all this solicitude for Merrill" on Villa's part would "do him good with his employers who will reap the benefit of it in a measure for their mines."[22]

Beyond protecting his family's interests, Villa also seems to have identified Scott's passion for collecting authentic cultural artifacts, which he sought to cater to. In a letter to his mining son in Chihuahua, Scott discouraged Merrill from sending him a serape since Villa had already furnished him several superior (more authentic) specimens. "The only kind of serape I want is the kind which is not made new . . . like the one you sent Blanchard [Scott's daughter], which is very nice; black or terracotta, with a diamond in the center, but don't have one made."[23] Later, Scott wrote his wife that he was waiting for a hundred rugs that Villa had promised to send him. He joked that "possibly he thinks I am a rug merchant and want my store stocked but we will find a place for them if they appear."[24]

The anticipated carload of rugs turned out to be just two, which were delivered to Scott by one of Villa's main advisers and the man Villa had hoped to see become president, Felipe Ángeles. The blankets Villa had sent him were not of the traditional pattern for which Scott had expressed his preference to his son. They had been specially made for Scott and seem to have pleased him (since he described them in some detail in his memoirs). One bore the coat of arms of Mexico interwoven with the name of General Francisco Villa; the other bore the coat of arms of the United States and the legend "General Hugo L. Scott." The recipient of this gift stated that "the colors clashed so that they could be heard at a greater distance than the creaking of the old Red River carts in Minnesota, which," he added, "is saying a good deal." This final comment by Scott confirms the reader's sense of his delight in the gift.[25]

In another overture of friendship based on mutual interests, Villa extended an invitation for the American general to join him for a month of hunting in the Sierra Madre mountains of Chihuahua when the war was over "if he [Villa] should be still alive."[26] Once again, the manly sport of hunting was proposed as a way of fostering trust and intimacy. Ironically, of course, Scott ended up not hunting *with* Villa, but directing the hunt *for* him.

In April 1914, Scott became assistant chief of staff for the army. In November of that year, he replaced William Wotherspoon as chief of staff. For Villa, the capture of the state capital of Chihuahua City at the end of 1913 had represented the peak of his power and promise.

In October 1915, the United States formally recognized Carranza. "I never understood why," Scott wrote in his memoirs. He also claimed he had asked people in the State Department why it had been done and they could not account for the president's decision "for they had all advised against it, a month previous to the recognition. That information has always made the President's step even more of a mystery to me."[27]

In fact, Scott was a self-described *Villista*. When Villa's fortunes turned in 1915, Scott spoke of him in the same tragic tones he had used to lament the fate of other heroic but doomed wild men or primitive leaders he admired, like Chief Joseph, whom Scott had accompanied from Montana to Bismarck in 1877, and even Panglima Hassan, who had caused severe injuries to his hands in the 1903 ambush in the Philippines.[28] To Scott, both were heroic figures outmatched by the modernizing forces arrayed against them and their outmoded ways of life. Although no match for the army of which he was a part, nor the modern weaponry that Carranza was able to secure once he had the formal recognition of the United States, Scott deeply respected and mourned the passing of their noble way of fighting and the honor of the resistance they put up.

In his memoirs, Scott gave his official appraisal of the man he admired, who had provoked the invasion he had directed: "A hunted man during a large part of his life, he was as unmoral as a wolf; nevertheless he had some fine qualities if you could reach them, and with all his faults I considered him to have a far better character than Carranza." This assessment mirrors Scott's more general formulation on the "children of the world," quoted in the first epigraph of Part III of this book.[29]

Wilson's recognition of Carranza was a bitter blow to Villa. Some have attributed his raid on Columbus six months later to the rage and sense of betrayal Villa felt at this action by the United States. Others have analyzed this provocative act as a calculated strategy on Villa's part aimed at provoking a U.S. invasion, which would in turn rouse Mexicans to once again support Villa to drive out the Americans and provide a way for him to regain his standing. As with so much else, Villa's motives in mounting the attack are unknown. Villa would neither confirm nor deny that he had taken part in the raid.[30]

If Villa's intention was to provoke a U.S. invasion, he was certainly successful in doing that. By the spring of 1916, Scott had left the border behind him—at least in a physical sense. Besides serving as chief of staff, Scott also carried out the duties of interim secretary of war during the first few months of Wilson's second term. As it happened, the new secretary of war, Newton Baker, was sworn in only days before the cross-border raid. In his first meeting with the newly appointed Baker, Scott had offered to resign as chief of staff, as was customary. Baker indicated that he wished Scott to continue in his position, telling him, "I am going to look up to you as my father," and adding, "I am going to do as you advise me, and if either of us have to leave this building, I am going first."[31] On the new secretary's first official day in office, the following news reached Washington from the border: "Early this morning Villa attacked American garrison at Columbus, setting fire to several buildings and killing several American soldiers. Twenty-three Villistas were killed. It is believed Villa led attack in person."[32] Although incorrect in some of its details, subsequent reports confirmed that an attack on the border town in New Mexico had been carried out by followers of Pancho Villa. Shouting "Viva Villa" and "Viva México," the raiders set fire to buildings, sacked stores and shot civilians in their homes. Part of the force attacked nearby Camp Furlong where troops of the Thirteenth Cavalry were stationed. In all, eighteen Americans were killed in the raid: ten civilians and eight soldiers.[33] So it was that this unusual conversation, as recorded in Scott's memoirs, took place the following day: "I want you to start an expedition into Mexico to catch

Villa," the new secretary of war told Scott. "This seemed very strange to me," Scott wrote later, so he asked:

> "Mr. Secretary, do you want the United States to make war on one man? Suppose he should get on the train and go to Guatemala, Yucatan, or South America; are you going to go after him?"
>
> He said, "Well, no, I am not,"
>
> "That is not what you want then. You want his *band* captured or destroyed," I suggested.
>
> "Yes," he said, "that is what I really want."

Accordingly, Scott sent a telegram to General Frederick Funston—architect of the raid that led to Emilio Aguinaldo's capture in 1901 and now the commanding general of the Southern Department at San Antonio—which directed an invasion force to be commanded by General John J. Pershing to proceed across the border "in pursuit of the Mexican band which attacked the town of Columbus, New Mexico, and the troops there on the morning of the ninth instant. . . . The work of these troops will be regarded as finished as soon as Villa's band or bands are known to be broken up."[34]

To lead the punitive expedition into Mexico, Scott had chosen Pershing, who was then commanding the Eighth Brigade on the border. Within a week, a punitive force of over 5,000 men and almost as many pack animals was headed deep into Villa's home territory. Over the next eleven months, the force would swell to 15,000 troops and lead the United States and Mexico to the brink of war.

Chapter 10

The Punitive Expedition: Brigadier General John J. Pershing, 1916

On March 12 1916, the day after he learned he had been named to lead the expedition to chase and punish Villa, General Pershing met with one of Venustiano Carranza's most influential advisers, Luis Cabrera. Cabrera, who had arrived in El Paso by train from Douglas, Arizona, on the morning of the Columbus raid, sought Pershing out in the midst of wildly circulating rumors about what retaliatory actions the Americans would take. The men met at the Hotel Paso del Norte. In a later account of the meeting, Alberto Salinas Carranza, a nephew of the first chief, wrote that Cabrera believed Pershing had the ability to prevent forces being sent into Mexico. This was beyond Pershing's power, of course. Nonetheless, Pershing shared Cabrera's sense of the absurdity of sending a force after Villa, according to Salinas. Hunting for Villa in his own country was like searching for the proverbial needle in a haystack, or to use the Mexican idiom, like looking for a cat in the garbanzo patch. Pershing, in the Mexican account of this interview, felt constrained from discussing the situation with his highly placed Mexican interlocutor, but the American general did ask for Cabrera's opinion about how the border might best be protected from Villa's raids in the future. Cabrera responded that he thought American troops should reinforce their garrisons along the Chihuahua border. Mexico should have the exclusive responsibility for hunting Villa.

Pershing agreed that this would be the best approach but, he added, "the problem is that you Mexicans are always thinking things and never doing them." To which Cabrera replied that the Americans were always doing things without thinking, which was no better![1]

This reported exchange between Cabrera and Pershing is likely apocryphal, yet it nicely captures the stereotypes and assumptions that informed each side's assessment of the other over an episode which led the two nations to the brink of war as Pershing's Punitive Expedition, which crossed into Mexico the day following this interview, stretched into an eleven-month occupation of parts of Chihuahua. Carranza's government never wavered in its rejection of the premise for the expedition, which Cabrera had questioned in his meeting with Pershing. For its part, the Wilson administration faulted Mexico for failing to secure the border and protect American interests in Mexico. As the head of the Mexican delegation appointed by Carranza to negotiate with the United States later that year, Cabrera remained steadfast in upholding Mexican resistance in the face of a concerted American effort to extract Platt Amendment–like concessions as a condition for ending the occupation.

Villa's raid on Columbus occurred just seventy miles south of Fort Bayard, the frontier post where the twenty-six-year-old Pershing had reported for duty in 1886, just a few months after his graduation from West Point. While his quarry in the Mexican war was different, and the cavalry's pursuit of the bandit general was augmented by motorized transport and even a small squadron of airplanes, the methods of asymmetrical punitive warfare used in 1916 drew on those Pershing had practiced on horseback in the borderlands against the dwindling resistance of the Apaches three decades earlier. Just like the earlier American expeditions into the Sierra Madre in pursuit of Geronimo, Pershing's expedition into Mexico included a complement of Apache scouts.[2] Over the weeks and months to come, Pershing made a priority of recruiting other scouts and agents to serve as guides, interpreters, and spies for the American occupying force. These included Mormons from some of the colonies established in northwestern Chihuahua in the 1880s and 1890s by members of the Church of Jesus Christ of Latter-Day Saints, who welcomed the American presence, as well as more reluctant Mexican citizens who were impressed into service by the Americans.[3] The techniques Pershing relied on drew on the army's long history of policing the frontier as well as measures adopted from the repertoire of counterinsurgency techniques he had helped institute in the Philippines.

The hamlet of Columbus, still reeling from the attack the previous week, was designated as the headquarters for the Punitive Expedition. A second crossing point for troops was established at Culberson's ranch further to the west. Starting from these two points on the New Mexico–Chihuahua border, some 5,000 troops crossed the border into Mexico on March 15. It was the largest American force to enter Mexican territory since the Mexican-American War.[4] In spite of disavowals of imperialistic intent from Washington, the earlier war, which had led to the deaths of 13,000 Americans and upward of 25,000 Mexicans, as well as to Mexico's loss of half its territory, seemed much on the minds of the American commanders as they prepared to cross the border. Thus, in a symbolic nod to the start of the conflict seventy years earlier, the eastern column marching from Columbus halted at the border where the Sixth Infantry was allowed to take the lead. This ritual was observed in recognition of that unit's history as the first regiment to cross the Rio Grande in 1846.[5]

The Americans viewed speed in launching the expedition as critical if they were to have a chance of catching Villa. Out of expediency—but also out of a misplaced expectation of cooperation from Carranza's government—Pershing got his orders to enter Mexico *before* the Wilson administration had received Mexico's blessing for the enterprise. Such a blessing would prove elusive. In its eagerness to give chase to Villa, the United States had counted on at least tacit support from Mexico for the cross-border mission. A message from Secretary of State Robert Lansing to Carranza sent the day following the attack clearly made this assumption. A week later, the State Department followed up with a matter-of-fact request to the first chief to allow American forces to make use of the Northwest Railway from Juárez to Casas Grandes to transport the supplies needed for men and horses as the Punitive Expedition moved south into Chihuahua. By this time, American troops were already over 125 miles inside Mexican territory. The Wilson administration had made a miscalculation. The Americans had assumed that Carranza would cooperate and render assistance in catching their common adversary. The Mexican government, however, proved anything but accommodating.[6]

To the growing frustration of the U.S. State Department, which had to deal with communiqués from the first chief and his staff in which vociferous denunciations of U.S. policy were immediately forthcoming, Carranza rejected the premise of the Punitive Expedition. And he was not about to permit the use of Chihuahua's railway either. Calling Villa a "bandit" and a "traitor" and his followers "a band of brigands," Carranza made the case that a punitive expedition to catch Villa was not only unwarranted, since "the Government and people of Mexico" could not reasonably be held responsible for the acts of an outlaw, but that it was also counterproductive. There could be "no justification for any invasion of Mexican territory by an armed force of the United States, even under the pretext of pursuing and capturing Villa." The "only result" of such an ill-advised

American action, Carranza asserted, "would be to facilitate [Villa's] impunity to leave the country and bring about a war between two countries, with the numberless loss of life and property, *without such loss serving to avenge the crimes which the American Government is endeavoring to punish.*" Carranza went on to say that U.S. action further satisfied Villa's "deliberate purpose," which was to "provoke armed intervention by the United States in Mexico."[7]

The State Department's response to Carranza's objections to the Punitive Expedition was quick in coming and very revealing—perhaps more revealing than Secretary of State Lansing had intended. Besides condescension toward Mexico and scathing criticism of what the secretary baldly stated was the de facto government's incapacity "to suppress this state of lawlessness," of which the attack on Columbus, New Mexico, served as "a deplorable example," the telegram laid the groundwork for a new, more expansive argument for an American right of intervention in Mexico. Lansing's reworked rationale for sending troops to pursue Villa was similar to the one President William McKinley had put forward in 1898 when he urged Congress to approve a neutral intervention in Cuba's independence war. It also had a borderlands precedent in the protectorate President James Buchanan had proposed for portions of northern Chihuahua and Sonora to deal with "injuries alleged to have been inflicted by Mexican Indians and desperadoes upon citizens of the United States residing in northwestern Texas, New Mexico, and Arizona."[8] In terms that could not fail to be insulting—although they were couched in the most diplomatic language—Lansing laid out the American view that Mexico's government—just like the Spanish colonial government in insurgent Cuba—was incapable of ensuring peace and protection for American interests. As a result of the incapacity of the Mexican de facto government, American citizens were suffering. It was therefore incumbent on the U.S. Government to send troops across the border so that it might secure the protections for its citizens that its southern neighbor had proven itself incapable of providing.[9]

Needless to say, this expansive view of U.S. sovereignty was unacceptable to Carranza. It is likely that such a position would have been anathema to any Mexican president in the seventy years since trumped-up claims that Mexican soldiers had violated U.S. sovereignty to "shed American blood upon the American soil" had provided President James Polk with a timely justification for launching the Mexican-American War.[10] That was a precedent no Mexican leader could afford to ignore. But Venustiano Carranza was less amenable to accommodating American designs than most. The former governor of the border state of Coahuila had consistently opposed U.S. intervention even when it would have furthered his own political ambitions.[11] If there was one thing in which the first chief of the Constitutionalist Army was constant, it was in his uncompromising defense of Mexican sovereignty. He was still trying to consolidate his control over a nationalist revolution, informed in part by widespread grievances against the regime of Porfirio Díaz for supposedly privileging American interests over those of his own countrymen.[12]

As the diplomats wrangled, Carranza sent orders to his generals in Sonora and Veracruz to prepare to oppose an American attack should it come.[13] Within days of crossing the border, Pershing received secret orders which belied his government's official position that American troops had entered Mexican territory with Mexico's permission.[14] Once again, Pershing found himself operating in Indian Country, a place of heightened tensions over sovereignty where no one exercised effective control on the ground.

The army was in for a frustrating few months. The landscape through which Pershing's troops marched in March and April of 1916 had "a long history of breaking European ambitions," as Brian DeLay put it. In the Sierra Madre, where "mobile Athapascans" had long dominated and disrupted the settlement schemes of successive state-level powers, a common experience of defending their communities against Apache raids had helped forge the identities of the communities of the Sierra Madre where the American forces established their forward operating bases.[15] Some of the Serrano communities had their origins as military colonies established in the late eighteenth century as a buffer against the power and menace of nomadic tribes of the north. Such military colonies had received land grants, first from the Spanish colonial state and later from the Mexican national government, in return for their efforts to police the frontier. "By fighting the Apache and advancing the state's project of territorial conquest and colonization, these militarized peasants gained access to personal prestige and social honor, as well as to state-conferred honors including land grants and tax exemptions," wrote the anthropologist Ana María Alonso, who spent several months in the 1980s conducting research among the residents of Namiquipa, including some whose older family members had experienced firsthand their community's occupation by Pershing's forces seventy years earlier.[16] The Namiquipenses saw themselves as "defenders of civilization against the barbarians," as some inhabitants had described themselves in a letter to President Porfirio Díaz in 1908.[17] Ironically, as Friedrich Katz has pointed out in his analysis of the transformation of northern Mexico from frontier to border during the Porfiriato, the triumph of these free villagers over their enemies, the Apaches, led to an erosion of control over their lands. With the Apache threat gone, the terrain policed by the peasant freeholders gained market value as a result of regional railway construction, foreign investment, and an economic boom. Military colonists began losing their land in the 1880s as the Mexican government implemented new land policies whose cumulative effect was the dispossession and marginalization of the communities originally founded to secure the frontier for settlement. It was from the former Indian-fighting communities that Pancho Villa recruited many of the men who joined his Division del Norte. Indian fighting was an indelible part of their makeup, just as it was for the U.S. Army.[18]

In an adroit twist of nationalist rhetoric, Pancho Villa invoked that history of Indian fighting to define invading Americans as the newest "barbarian" threat from the north. With the Apaches defeated by the late 1880s, the Mormon colonists who settled in Chihuahua and Sonora represented the latest threat of "invasion [by] foreigners."[19] Even as he himself was being pursued like an Indian by Pershing's forces, Villa appealed to the descendants of the military colonists to turn their attention to the new threat by the American invaders, "our eternal enemies, the barbarians of the North," as he put it in a speech given in San Andrés, Chihuahua, in October 1916.[20]

As Pershing attempted to organize his unwieldy force to accomplish its stated mission of catching Villa and destroying his bands, his analysis of the military situation he faced was that destruction of Villa (and his base of support) would require the same kind of counterinsurgency techniques that the army had instituted in southern Luzon. In a message to General Frederick Funston, he outlined the approach he thought necessary: "It is very probably that the real object of our mission to Mexico can only be attained after an arduous campaign of considerable length. . . . Villa is entirely familiar with every foot of Chihuahua, and the Mexican people through friendship or fear have always kept him advised about every movement. He carries little food, lives off the country, rides his mounts hard and replaces them with fresh stock taken wherever found. Thus he has had the advantage since the end of the first twenty-four hours after the Columbus raid occurred."[21] If the U.S. troops were to stay and achieve their mission, Pershing informed Funston, they would need to work to implement a prolonged and intensive campaign of isolating the Villistas and controlling their sources of support:

Success then will depend upon a) our continuing occupation of as many distinct localities as possible in the territory to be covered, b) the establishment of intimate relations with a sufficient number of reliable inhabitants in each locality to assure their assistance in obtaining trustworthy information ... d) the maintenance of ample and regular lines of supply, especially to the large extent of unproductive or mountainous territory; and a sufficient number of men and animals to occupy localities and keep fresh columns constantly at work. . . . The execution of the general plan has already been begun and will be pushed to completion as fast as possible.[22]

From his earliest days as a district commander in the Lake Lanao region, Pershing had based his efforts to extend U.S. authority over Mindanao's inhabitants—American and Filipino alike—on methodical intelligence gathering and alliance building, and on intimidation and the demonstrative use of violence. He also employed tactics more dependent on persuasion, diplomacy, and the politics of attraction, which Friedrich Katz has characterized as a strategy of winning "hearts and minds" during the U.S. occupation of Chihuahua.[23]

Soon after their entry into Chihuahua, Pershing's troops had been successful in obtaining produce from residents of Guerrero District, an area that had been generally loyal to Villa. Paying in gold for labor and goods went some way to creating good will and an incentive for local people to cooperate with the Americans. In Namiquipa, a village from which a number of the Columbus raiders had come, the Americans were able to operate without open resistance to their presence and even with the active cooperation of some of the villagers. At Pershing's suggestion, a number of the residents formed a militia or *defensa social*. The function of such militias was to help Americans find weapons, gather intelligence, and promote anti-Villa ideology. Other municipios in the district organized their own *defensas sociales*, which, even after the Americans left the area in June, continued to supply them with intelligence.[24]

Having observed the role of Indian scouts in the frontier army, and also commanded a troop of Oglala scouts on the Pine Ridge Reservation himself in the aftermath of the Wounded Knee massacre, Pershing had been an early and enthusiastic advocate of the use of native auxiliaries in the Philippines.[25] As governor of Moro Province he had favored the use of scouts organized along ethnic lines, especially in punitive actions. In an example of the dissemination and adoption of counterinsurgency techniques along what the historian Alfred McCoy has called "the capillaries of empire," in late 1916 a number of influential army veterans of the war in the Philippines—most of them also veterans of the Indian Wars—recommended new policies to encourage the transfer of (white) officers from the Philippine Scouts to the regular army. They noted in particular the potential usefulness of such men in the ongoing occupation of Mexico, "where such scout officers would be especially valuable on account of their Philippine experience and knowledge of the Spanish language."[26] This initiative ultimately foundered, but its promotion by high-ranking officers with experience on the frontiers of empire demonstrates both a continuing support for the use of scouts as well as a more general transference of racial categories from the domestic frontier and the Philippines onto fighting "Indians" in Mexico.

Although the Punitive Expedition did not avail itself of scout officers from the Philippines, it continued the army's practice in areas of unfamiliar terrain, language, and culture, of relying on native auxiliaries for reconnaissance and intelligence. Pershing's expedition was joined by twenty Apache scouts from Fort Apache. In a new wrinkle on ethnic or communally based recruitment, he also recruited Mormons to scout for him. These men were drawn from some of the nine colonies that had been founded with the support of President Porfirio Díaz in the 1880s and 1890s by the Church of Jesus Christ of Latter-Day Saints. At the beginning of the Mexican Revolution, these colonies had been home to some four thousand Americans who had migrated from the United States. They had weathered the early years of the conflict fairly well by maintaining neutrality and arming themselves against the depredations of revolutionists.

When Pascual Orozco rebelled against Madero's government in 1912, however, things became difficult for the Mormons in Chihuahua and Sonora, and many returned to the United States. The impetus for this exodus was the attempt by Orozco's local commander in Casas Grandes, General José Ines Salazar, to force the surrender of all the colonies' weapons. After a defiant show by their leaders, the colonists complied with the letter of the command, although, like the Hunkpapa at Wounded Knee, the Mormons also retained their best weapons and relinquished only their old and obsolete hunting guns, hiding better weapons and ammunition for their future self-defense. At the same time, the renewed war in their area convinced the leaders of the colonies that evacuation of their women and children was prudent. After 1912 the Mormon colonies were populated primarily by young men who returned to harvest crops and look after their property as best they could. Although the colonies had been mostly spared by Villa himself, with whom many of the colonists felt a mutual respect—at least before the raid on Columbus—they were vulnerable to opportunistic raiding and suffered the violence of the period. The arrival of the American troops in their midst thus represented both security and also economic benefit. On the other hand, the Mormons wanted to remain in Mexico and had to be concerned with how their aid to the American soldiers would be viewed by their neighbors and other Mexicans following the war. For this reason, Bishop Anton Call of Colonia Dublán was initially hesitant to comply with Pershing's request for scouts. He later changed his mind and provided names of men who could fill the role.[27] Mexican citizens, for similar reasons, were reluctant to act as scouts. Even if they were not opposed to the American presence, they were afraid of reprisals for aiding the invaders. In several instances, officers of the Punitive Expedition resorted to intimidation to secure wanted scouts, implying that the Mexicans would be killed if they did not cooperate with American requests to act as guides and interpreters.[28]

After the battle at Carrizal and as the international negotiations dragged on throughout the summer and fall, Pershing's initial focus on searching for Villa and punishing Villistas had been replaced by the necessity to defend themselves from the possibility of attack by Carranza's forces. Even so, from his base at the Mormon colony of Dublán and throughout the five military districts he had set up a month into the occupation, Pershing continued a counterinsurgency campaign against the Villistas. He also seems to have explored some less conventional (and unlawful) means of eliminating Villa.

Since 1910 the Military Intelligence Division (MID) had been gathering intelligence and planning for possible intervention in Mexico. Robert Lee Bullard's spy mission to investigate rumors of collaboration between the Japanese and Mexican governments was just one aspect of MID intelligence-gathering activities. They also compiled field reports on Mexican bridges and roads and the capacity of various locations to provide forage for horses. During the Mexican Revolution, the Bureau of Investigation also expanded its intelligence work on the border and coordination with military authorities.[29] In addition, Pershing, whose counterinsurgency techniques in the southern Philippines privileged the collection of intelligence, made setting up his own intelligence division within the expedition a priority.[30]

Among the intelligence operatives recruited by the Americans in Mexico were several Japanese agents referred to in the records of the expedition as Suzuki, Sato, and Dyo. The complete range of activities carried out by these men remains unclear, but there is reason to believe they were employed as spies for the Americans and that they actually managed to penetrate Villa's camp.

In July Agent Edward Stone, who was in charge of the bureau's operations in El Paso, entered into discussions with two Japanese men who had previously worked as personal servants for Pancho Villa as well as for his brother Hipolito. Stone sounded them out on their ability to capture Villa and deliver him to agents on the border, either alive or dead. Stone never gave the men any specific orders; his superiors in the bureau did not approve Stone's plans for assassinating Villa. However, Stone also referred two Japanese agents, "Dyo" and "Fusita," to the Pershing Expedition. A month after the bureau had nixed the idea of employing the Japanese in an assassination plot, Dyo and Fusita reported back to the Pershing Expedition on their unsuccessful attempt to poison Villa. In the words of Friedrich Katz, "they proved to be excellent scouts but bad poisoners." According to their report, they had been sent by Pershing's head of intelligence, Captain William O. Reed, to infiltrate Villa's camp and slip poison into his coffee. The poison had been supplied by an army surgeon who was part of the expedition. In preparation for the mission, Dyo had tried out the poison on a dog to check its efficacy. Dyo and Fusita had been successful in entering Villa's camp and claimed in their report that they had put a dose of the poison into a cup of coffee set before Villa. The fugitive general, who had long been fearful that he might be poisoned, "poured half of this cup of coffee which contained the poison into another cup and handed it to a Mexican who sat on his right, and waited until this Mexican drank his portion of the coffee before he drank his own." For whatever reason, the poison (if it were ever in fact administered as Dyo and Fusita claimed), did not have the fatal effect on Villa that it had had on the dog. However, neither man waited around to see the effects of their actions. After witnessing Villa drink his half-cup of coffee, both men left the camp.[31]

Assassination of an enemy is, of course, prohibited by the laws of war, as Pershing and the rest of the army hierarchy well knew. When a report on the poisoning mission by Agent Stone reached the attention of Attorney General Thomas Watt Gregory, he sent a note to Secretary of War Newton Baker suggesting that the incident be investigated.[32] This Baker instructed the Southern Command to do "with as little publicity as possible." Pershing meanwhile upbraided his military intelligence officers for "writing too many reports on the Japanese agents." In short, according to Charles Harris, Louis Sadler, and Friedrich Katz, "the whole matter was quashed."[33] Playing a crucial role in shutting down the inquiry was Major Ralph H. Van Deman, who dismissed the poison plot as "absurd" even before the evidence had been reviewed.[34] Often called "the father of Military intelligence," Van Deman had been influential in developing a formidable field intelligence operation in the Philippines. Coordinating intelligence gathering and analysis among several clandestine services, MID in the Philippines played a crucial role, according to Alfred McCoy, in the Americans' ability to track and contain Filipino resistance to the American occupation. McCoy also details how clandestine techniques developed for undermining anticolonial resistance abroad were incorporated into the repertoire of domestic surveillance and espionage following the war, and especially on the home front during World War I. One of the tactics the MID had employed to great effect in the Philippines was the strategic use of scandal to embarrass and manipulate political opponents of the United States and its local allies. Van Deman's prominent decisive action to quell a rumor about the poisoning, which would have proved damaging both to the U.S. military and to Pershing personally, is consistent with his agency's earlier strategic husbanding of scandal.

In fact, Pershing's honor and job prospects had been threatened in the Philippines, too. When he was serving in Mindanao, Pershing was widely rumored to have had a *querida*, or mistress, by whom it was said he had fathered two children. In 1906, a year after Pershing's marriage to Frances Warren—daughter of Senator Francis Warren, who chaired the Senate Military Affairs Committee—stories about the affair in the Philippine press threatened to derail Pershing's promotion to brigadier general. Only his father-in-law's deft management of the confirmation process saved Pershing's promotion and reputation.[35] Now, once again, Pershing seems to have been shielded from the taint of scandal by powerful friends. On September 25, just three days after Dyo and Fusita submitted their report in which they detailed their attempt to poison Villa, Pershing was promoted to the rank of major general. Villa, meanwhile, launched a new offensive on September 16 (Mexican Independence Day). For the rest of September and October, he led attacks on Carrancista garrisons throughout the state and even made a daring attack on the state capital, where he liberated political prisoners from the penitentiary, briefly occupied the governor's palace, and made off with some booty.[36]

As the weeks passed and the main target, Villa, remained elusive, the Punitive Expedition began to look less like a cumbersome bandit-chasing operation and more like an occupation. Continued U.S. presence of a large number of troops, especially when some of them were involved in carrying out counter-insurgency measures, increased the risk of escalating an already tense situation into a full-scale war with Mexico. In private correspondence, the operation's U.S. commanders questioned the wisdom and necessity of maintaining such a large force deep inside Chihuahua in the face of unwavering Mexican opposition.

Three weeks into the American invasion, key figures in the Wilson administration were growing concerned about the risks of keeping their forces in Mexico and began to consider whether it was time to bring the soldiers home even though Villa remained at large. Secretary of War Baker told the president's confidant Colonel Edward House that he was in favor of "giving up on the Villa chase and bringing the troops back." It was foolish, said Baker, "to chase a single bandit all over Mexico."[37] General Scott, although he had set the whole operation in motion as army chief of staff, also expressed his doubts in a letter to a friend written in early April: "I do not know how long this thing is going to continue. It seems to me that Pershing has accomplished all he was sent for. . . . It does not seem dignified for all the United States to be hunting for one man in a foreign country." Scott also reflected that "if the thing were reversed, we would not allow any foreign army to be sloshing around in our country, 300 miles from the border, no matter who they were."[38] Others among the president's advisers, however, felt that it would be damaging to U.S. prestige to withdraw troops from Mexico without accomplishing the goal of capturing Villa. It was their arguments to remain that prevailed.[39]

One of the eventualities Scott worried about was that a skirmish between U.S. troops and Mexicans could lead to an escalation of the conflict. In fact, such an incident in the southern Chihuahua town of Parral raised tensions to a new high only a few days after troop withdrawal had been taken up in a cabinet meeting and the president had made the decision against it.

Major Frank Tompkins, who had led the first punitive expedition after the "Indians" (his word for the Villistas) who had raided Columbus, was detailed by Pershing to lead a mission to search for Villa. "It was a hot little campaign of less than two weeks typical of our cavalry campaigns against the Indians immediately following the Civil War," Tompkins wrote. In spite of his claim that the mission was "well planned and gallantly executed," in fact Tompkins was guided only by a hunch and led his men into the far southern reaches of Chihuahua, more than five hundred miles from the U.S. border, without a map and lacking adequate supplies.[40] It was actually an attempt to obtain food and fodder that brought Major Tompkins and a squadron of men into Parral on

April 12. There, they found themselves the focus of a hostile crowd. Shouting "Viva México" and "Viva Villa," citizens of the town, some of them brandishing weapons, demanded that the Americans leave. The town's garrison was under the command of the Carrancista General Lozano, who had been cooperating to provide the Americans with the supplies they required, but after the crowd drove the American soldiers out of town, Lozano cautioned Tompkins that his troops could not guarantee their safety. Tompkins requested that Lozano show them where they should camp before continuing their search for Pancho Villa further to the south. Tompkins later accused Lozano of trying to lure him into a trap. Lozano claimed he was merely unable to control his troops, who began firing on the American troops as they waited outside the town for delivery of supplies. Two Americans were killed by the Mexican forces at this point and several others wounded, including Tompkins, who was shot in the shoulder. The Carrancistas gave chase to Tompkin's men, who numbered only about a hundred. Forty-two Mexicans were killed when the Americans returned fire. Tompkins sought shelter in an adobe ranch, where they were reinforced the next day by troops of the Tenth Cavalry, commanded by Colonel Charles Young.[41]

The situation for the U.S. forces in Mexico a month into their occupation was tense. The deaths of Mexican soldiers added to nationalist resentment and galvanized opposition to their presence. Five days after the incident at Parral, Pershing made the following assessment: "At first people exhibited only passive disapproval [of] American entry into country. Lately sentiment has changed to hostile position." He expressed his opinion that the "recent outbreak in Parral against troops [was] undoubtedly premeditated." Finally, he had no faith in Carranza's forces, which were being moved into Chihuahua to counter the American presence. He wrote that he saw "little difference" between them and Villa's forces.[42]

Alarmed at the prospect of further hostilities between American and Mexican forces, President Wilson sent General Scott to San Antonio on April 22 to confer with the commanding general of the Southern Department, Frederick Funston. Based on their discussions, Scott advised the president of three possible courses of action. The first was to continue aggressive operations including seizing railways and committing additional troops to the search for Villa. The second option was to restrict Pershing's command to an area around Colonia Dublán where ration supply and forage for animals was less of a problem; U.S. forces would be maintained in this relatively secure location in order to pressure Carranza to kill or capture Villa. The final option was to withdraw the expedition from Mexico. Scott and Funston recommended the second option, which the president promptly adopted, although he rejected the idea of seizing railroads, at least for the time being.[43]

President Wilson also made an overture to Carranza while Scott was still in Texas to bring high-level military leaders on both sides together to discuss the situation in the interest of diminishing the prospect of war. Accordingly, Scott and Funston proceeded to Ciudad Juárez, where Carranza, who was also anxious to avoid war and intent on securing U.S. withdrawal, sent his newly appointed secretary of war and navy—and Villa's bitter enemy—General Álvaro Obregón for talks with the Americans.

Privately, Scott did not welcome the commission; he expressed his displeasure and implicit criticism of U.S. policy in a letter to his wife: "I had made up my mind after the recognition of Carranza to let the State Dept skin their own skunks but was given no opportunity this time to decline to come here as I might have done had I been in Washington at the time—no more State Dept skunks to be skinned by me."[44] Skunk-skinning or no, less than three weeks after he had counseled withdrawal from Mexico, Scott found the predicament of the U.S. occupation completely changed. Withdrawal with honor was no longer an option, as Scott wrote to his wife from El Paso the day following his initial meeting with General Álvaro Obregón.

> We believe it is imminent now that the ultimatum [from Mexico] cannot be put off any more & so reported in language that is grave & serious putting it squarely to the President to withdraw from Mexico leaving the Mexicans triumphant over the U.S. who are already too arrogant and making further aggressions probably, or get ready to fight. . . . The time has passed to withdraw without loss of prestige in our estimation—now get ready with large force to resist attack not only on Pershing but on the whole border—for the Mexicans are foolish and ignorant enough to believe they can cope with us successfully and mean to make the attempt and the only way to prevent attack on us if it can now be prevented at all is by a show of competent force to convince them that we are able and willing to punish aggression—this is a very serious moment while peace and war are hanging in the balance.[45]

In this letter to his wife, Scott's rationale for punitive war is clear. The Mexicans were "foolish and ignorant." Like the other primitive people he had dealt with, they could be disciplined only by demonstrable violence. It was the same argument Pershing had made two weeks earlier when he called for an attack on Chihuahua City.[46]

Generals Funston, Scott, and Obregón met in high-level talks on the border from April 30 to May 9. Acting on strict instructions from Carranza, Obregón insisted that withdrawal of U.S. troops was a prerequisite for discussing any other matters. Scott and Funston tried repeatedly to exact commitments from the Mexicans to go after Villa more forcefully. In their report on an all-night session with the Mexican secretary of war, Scott and Funston characterized their negotiations as "a continuous struggle of twelve hours duration which was not equaled by any similar struggle with the *wildest and most exasperated Indian heretofore encountered.*"[47] Elsewhere, the Americans reported that the conference had been "usually amicable throughout." In addition to the implicit comparison between the Mexican secretary of war and a wild and "exasperated" Indian, the American generals implied that theirs were the cool heads. Funston was not known for possessing either tact or diplomatic skill—which the historian J. D. Eisenhower has suggested explains why he was passed over to command the Punitive Expedition.[48] Of the two, Scott had a reputation for steadiness and reliability. He prided himself, as we have seen, on his patience and courtesy, especially in negotiations with Latin Americans. In the reports he furnished Carranza on their conferences, Obregón left a record of his meeting with the Indian negotiator that is at odds with Scott's self-reported courteous and unflappable demeanor. With the agreement the two sides had reached in their all-night session in disarray, since Carranza would not approve it without a clear date for the withdrawal of American troops, Scott became "nervous and impatient," according to Obregón. The Mexican secretary of war claimed that Scott had made a threat. "He went so far as telling me, rather excitedly, that instead of withdrawing the troops actually in our territory, his Government would order at once the mobilization of many more forces to the border if we did not accept his conditions." When Obregón replied that Mexico would not tolerate such an act, General Scott became even more "excited" and said: "'My Government shall immediately order the mobilization of one hundred and fifty thousand or two hundred thousand men upon Mexico.'" At this point, General Funston, who had remained silent throughout this outburst, seems to have intervened to try to calm the conversation, clarifying that those troops would only be sent to "keep the border" and would not be sent into Mexico.[49] In fact, Scott had recommended that 150,000 troops be sent to the border when the Punitive Expedition was first launched.[50]

When the conference of the generals disbanded without agreement, the U.S. military situation remained precarious. Funston and Scott summarized their bleak assessment of the U.S. position in a joint statement sent the day following the disappointing conclusion of talks. "Our line is thin and weak everywhere and inadequate to protect the border anywhere if it is attacked in force," they wrote. As Scott had threatened in the meeting, he again called for an additional 150,000 militia to be sent to the border. This time Wilson delivered.[51]

At the same time Scott and Funston were invoking comparisons with Indians in reports on their dealings with Obregón, the Indian War dimensions of the Mexican border threat were finding expression through that venerable institution of popular cultural interpretation, Buffalo Bill's Wild West show. In fact, the day after Scott concluded his negotiations with his wild and exasperated interlocutor on the border, his old friend William Cody (aka Buffalo Bill) sent him a description of a new pageant the show was putting on. "We are doing *Villa's Last Raid on Columbus*," wrote Cody. "With scenery. Mexicans etc." In his note, Cody expressed his approval that Scott had not "let Obregón get his way." In the symbolically powerful performance of the Wild West shows, created to tell the epic story of Indians raiding settlers and cowboys chasing Indians, Indians had been replaced by Mexicans, not just metaphorically, but literally, under the direction of "Buffalo Bill, himself" as his stationery identified the larger-than-life folk hero of the Indian Wars.

Following the attack on Tompkins's troops at Parral, Pershing's forces had withdrawn to Namiquipa in Guerrero District. Meanwhile, tens of thousands of Carrancista troops were being brought into the city of Chihuahua as well as deployed further north. The official word was that the troops were being brought to pursue Villa, but Pershing believed they were readying to fight the Americans. In his memoirs, he recalled the shift in attitude among Mexicans in the area: "The population began to hold themselves aloof from us and people who had been friendly became decidedly otherwise. Those whom we had employed as secret agents withdrew their assistance, and it became necessary to depend for information entirely upon the resources within the command. Constant reconnaissance in all directions became imperative to preclude surprise."[52] On June 16 the Mexican commander at Chihuahua, J. B. Treviño, sent Pershing

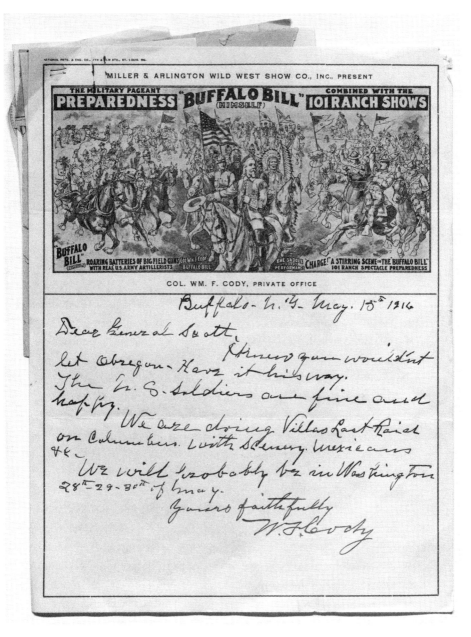

Figure 14. William F. "Buffalo Bill" Cody, letter to General Scott, May 10, 1916: "We are doing Villa's Last Raid on Columbus. With scenery. Mexicans etc." Hugh Lenox Scott Collection, Manuscript Division, Library of Congress.

a letter informing him that he had orders "to prevent the American forces that are in this state from moving to the south, east or west of the places they now occupy."[53]

Pershing replied that, since his own government had placed no restrictions on the movement of the forces under his command, he would "therefore use [his] own judgment as to when and in what direction I shall move my forces in pursuit of bandits or in seeking information regarding bandits."[54]

Pershing continued to send out reconnoitering detachments to search for Villistas and information about their elusive chief. On June 21 one of these detachments attempted to pass through the town of Carrizal in order to obtain information about a large force of Carrancista troops reported to be at the railway town of Ahumara some seven miles beyond. On that day, Captain Charles Boyd attempted to lead two troops of the Tenth Cavalry through Carrizal. They were met in the field outside the settlement where Félix U. Gómez, who was in command of the Carrancista garrison at Carrizal, made plain his intention to oppose the American intention to pass through the town. Captain Boyd was not to be dissuaded from this course of action and, when his men dismounted to advance toward Carrizal on foot, the Mexican troops opened fire on them. In the ensuing fight, casualties on the U.S. side were ten killed and ten wounded. The Mexicans also took nineteen troopers prisoner. On the Mexican side, they had lost twelve officers, including General Gómez. The Americans had also killed thirty-three Mexican enlisted men; fifty-three more had been wounded.[55]

Since early June, Pershing had been drawing up plans to take aggressive action, including destroying railways and telegraphs and carrying out smashing assaults on the Carrancista forces.[56] After the Carrizal attack, Pershing again proposed an assault on the capital, Chihuahua City. Funston told him to wait.[57] Following the Carrizal fight, both sides took steps to de-escalate tensions. The United States acknowledged that Captain Boyd's aggressive actions had contributed to the confrontation. Carranza ordered the release of the troopers of the Tenth Cavalry who had been taken prisoner. On June 29 they marched home across the international bridge to El Paso.[58] In his account of this most disastrous encounter of the occupation to date, Salinas snidely asserted that if so many of the Americans who were killed and captured at Carrizal had not been black, the United States would have reacted with more concern to the incident. It seems clear, however, that both sides acted with deliberation following the battle to avoid further escalation of the conflict.

In July Carranza and Wilson agreed to enter into talks to resolve the situation. The resulting Joint High Commission was led on the Mexican side by Luis Cabrera, who had made the visit to Pershing the previous March at the Hotel Paso del Norte in a vain effort to avert the occupation. Secretary of the Interior Franklin Lane headed the U.S. side. Secretary of War Baker had sounded Scott out about serving on the commission, but Scott, anxious to avoid more "skunk-skinning," demurred, saying "You will do me a very great kindness, Mr. Secretary, if you will leave me off the list." Baker inquired why Scott was loath to serve on the commission, noting that his participation was desired because of his knowledge of Spanish and "experience with Spanish speaking-peoples." Scott replied that it was precisely because of that experience that he knew already what would be the outcome of the commission. He went on to explain to the secretary in greater detail:

> Secretary Lane is entirely without experience with Latin American peoples—their peculiar psychology and how to deal with them— and I will be at variance with him all the time. I have known in the past how to treat such questions successfully when I have had them to myself, but I know now the futility of this Commission. Those Mexicans have been trained in a school our people know nothing about. The Mexicans are past masters in drawing red herrings across the trail if you allow them to do it. . . . Those Mexicans are going to play horse with Secretary Lane all summer, and after it is all over no one will be proud of having been on the commission.[59]

The commission was formed in July and began meeting in September 1916. They met fifty-five times in four months. The negotiating sessions began in New London, Connecticut, and continued in Atlantic City, New Jersey.[60] Although Carranza steadfastly insisted on the removal of U.S. forces from Mexico, the United States not only kept them there, but attempted to use their presence to extract concessions that would have allowed for more American control over its interests in Mexico. In late 1916, the U.S. commissioners wanted Mexico to accept a clause that stated: "The Government of Mexico solemnly agrees to afford full and adequate protection to the lives and property of citizens of the United States, or other foreigners, and this protection shall be adequate to enable such citizens of the United States . . . [to operate] industries in which they might be interested. The United States reserves the right to re-enter Mexico and to afford such protection by its military forces, in the event of the

Mexican Government failing to do so."[61] The provision, as Friedrich Katz put it, would have "Cubanized" Mexico, and created a protectorate "by imposing something very close to a Platt Amendment," which would have allowed U.S. troops to enter Mexico at will.[62] In the midst of wrangling over such proposals, Carranza made a series of exploratory overtures to Germany. These involved Mexico's attempt to obtain weapons, and possibly even submarines, and a transmitter and other equipment from Germany. In November, Carranza's attaché in Berlin invited German military instructors to be integrated into the Mexican army.[63]

Although the commission never reached a formal agreement, at the end of January, President Wilson decided it was time to end the occupation. On February 5, 1917, the last men sent into Mexico to punish Pancho Villa as part of Pershing's Punitive Expedition re-crossed the border south of Columbus, where the whole affair had begun almost a year earlier. For Carranza, the unilateral withdrawal of the occupying forces was something of a triumph. He had stood firm and (eventually) the United States had blinked. For the Wilson administration, the whole episode had been an expensive and fruitless test of its ability to impose order over the restless southern edge of its continental empire. Thus, the last of America's frontier Indian Wars—launched in an effort to discipline and circumscribe the sovereignty of a neighbor—came to an end.

For most of the troops, there would be little respite at home. While they had been in Mexico, Wilson—and the country—had become more preoccupied with the war in Europe. A couple of weeks after the return of the expedition, the British shared the shocking contents of the "Zimmerman Telegram" with the American president. It reflected an attempt by Germany to form an alliance with Mexico against the United States in return for the promise of the return to Mexico of some of the territory she had lost in the Mexican-American War. It also represented one more step on the path toward an American declaration of war against Germany. That came on April 4, 1917.

Pershing, Scott, and Bullard all played prominent roles in the war that followed. After his return from Mexico, Pershing was chosen by President Wilson to command the American Expeditionary Force in Europe. Scott continued the work he had been doing as chief of staff of the army to prepare for possible entry into the war; he was retired for age in September but returned to active duty, commanding the Seventy-Eighth Division at Camp Dix, New Jersey. At the beginning of the war, Pershing appointed Bullard to command one of six national camps set up to train thousands of volunteer soldiers to become company grade officers ready to lead men into battle. In May of 1918, he was sent to France as a brigade commander. He finished the war as commanding general of the First Division.[64]

For Pershing, Bullard, Scott, and the Indian-fighting army in which they served, American commitment to the European war marked a departure from the Indian Wars that were central to the nation's development and its maturation as a hemispheric power. World War I began a new phase of America's emergence as a world industrial power, poised to project unparalleled global military might and economic influence for the rest of the twentieth century. The Indian Country origins of American empire continued to resonate, however, even into the second millennium. Mythologized images of the frontier West are still conjured up to convey the sense of a continuous destiny between westward expansion and the nation's exercise of global power. Indian Country continues to provide a lexicon for the expression of twenty-first-century fears and frustrations over the empire's lack of control over new realms of chaos, anarchy, and threats to American global influence.

President George W. Bush famously invoked such mythic imagery the day following the 9-11 terrorist attacks. "I want justice. There's an old poster out West that said 'wanted, dead or alive.' . . . All I'm doing is remembering when I was a kid. I remember they used to put out there in the Old West wanted posters that said 'wanted dead or alive.' All I want and America wants him brought to justice. That's what I want."[65] The triumphant message that such justice had been served was received in the Situation Room of the White House by Bush's successor a decade later. "Geronimo—EKIA" (Enemy Killed in Action) were the words used by Navy SEALs to confirm Osama bin Laden's death in a raid on his Abbottabad compound. The use of the Chiricahua Apache leader's name to refer to America's primary foe in the Global War on Terror sparked dismay and anger across contemporary Indian Country. Harlyn Geronimo, great grandson of the historical Goyathlay, a hero of native resistance to many, called the code name a "grievous insult" and asked for an apology from the Pentagon.[66] His protests were echoed by Native American organizations across the country. To others, the metaphor made perfect sense. When information about the code name came to light, the British newspaper the *Telegraph* juxtaposed an iconic photo of Geronimo taken following his capture, kneeling among cactus, scowling and holding a rifle, against one of the Al Qaeda leader, wearing a turban and sitting in a relaxed fashion on a sofa, his own weapon laid prominently to one side. A caption below the images from two different conflicts (and centuries) explained, "The code name Geronimo had apparently been chosen for bin Laden because, like the Native American chief, he had managed to evade capture for years."[67] Robert Kaplan, chronicler of the American military stationed on the remote frontiers of global empire, defended the use of such imagery. Army and marine field commanders had "embraced the red Indian metaphor because it captures perfectly the combat challenge of the 21st century," he explained. "The American military is back to the days of fighting the Indians," Kaplan wrote. "Indian country has been expanding in recent years because of the security vacuum created by the collapse of traditional dictatorships and the emergence of new democracies."[68]

Others have suggested that the U.S. military has never *stopped* fighting Indians. In his book *Facing West: The Metaphysics of Indian-Hating*, Richard Drinnon traced America's "wars of subjugation shaped by attitudes toward native peoples ('goo-goos' and 'gooks')," which, he argued, linked "massacres in Vietnam's 'Indian Country' in the 1960s . . . with those of Filipinos in Batangas at the turn of the century and with those of Indians on the continent earlier."[69] More recently, the anthropologist Stephen Silliman has explored how nineteenth-century Indian Wars serve as a source of "heritage metaphors" for the U.S. military in Iraq and Afghanistan. He quotes a retired army officer's comment from 2004 that "Ramadi is Indian Country—'the wild, wild West,' as the region is called." A soldier explains that his unit "refer[s] to our base as 'Fort Apache' because it's right in the middle of Indian country."[70] Generally unremarked in the 2011 Abbotabad raid was the name for the helicopters that penetrated 120 miles inside Pakistani territory. Two Black Hawks carried the Navy SEALs, with two Chinook helicopters providing support for the operation. Since 1957 the army has applied the names of Native American tribes and warriors to its whirlybirds and light planes: Mohawk, Shawnee, Seminole, Iroquois. The Korean-era helicopter made famous by the television series *M*A*S*H* was the H-13 Sioux. Naming the army's helicopters for Indian tribes and mythic warriors was the brainchild of Major General Hamilton Howze, who introduced this policy as a way to burnish the image of the helicopter "as a fast, mobile, stealthy machine on the field of battle using terrain and vegetation to an advantage similar to the Warrior Tribes," according to the U.S. Army Aviation Museum curator, Bob Mitchell.[71] Helicopters were airborne scouts; it made sense that they should have names like the quintessential scouts, who were Indians.

Notes

Introduction

1   Nelson Appleton Miles, "The Work of the Army as a Whole," in *The American-Spanish War: A History by the War Leaders, Illustrated with Numerous Original Engravings, Maps and Diagrams* (Norwich, Conn: Chas C. Haskell & Son, 1899), 531.

2   Félix Matos Bernier and Nelson A. Miles, "The War with Spain: III," *North American Review* 169, no. 512 (July 1, 1899), 129, http://www.jstor.org/stable/25104853.

3   On the invasion of Puerto Rico, with an emphasis on the prevalence of disease among the troops, see Fernando Picó, Sylvia Korwek, and Psique Arana Guzmán, trans., *Puerto Rico, 1898: The War After the War* (Princeton, N.J.: Markus Wiener, 2004), 33–37.

4   The Teller Amendment was proposed by Senator Henry Teller of Colorado; it disclaimed an American interest in controlling Cuba and instead committed the United States to leaving control of the island and its government to the Cubans. The description of American treatment of Cuban allies draws from Louis A. Pérez Jr., *The War of 1898: The United States and Cuba in History and Historiography* (Chapel Hill: University of North Carolina Press, 1998), and "Between Meanings and Memories of 1898," *Orbis* 42, no. 4 (Fall 1998): 501, accessed May 6, 2016, *EBSCO MegaFILE*, EBSCO*host*.

5   Henry H. Whitney, "Miles's Campaign in Puerto Rico, in *The American-Spanish War: A History by the War Leaders, Illustrated with Numerous Original Engravings, Maps and Diagrams* (Norwich, Conn.: Chas. C. Haskell & Son, 1899), 200.

6   Miles, "Work of the Army," 531.

7   Virginia Weisel Johnson, *The Unregimented General: A Biography of Nelson A. Miles* (Boston, Mass.: Houghton Mifflin, 1962), 128–29 (quoted in Beth LaDow, *The Medicine Line: Life and Death on a North American Borderland* [London: Taylor and Francis, 2013], 52–53).

8   Robert M. Utley, *The Lance and the Shield: The Life and Times of Sitting Bull* (London: Pimlico, 1998), 179–80; on Miles's winter clothing, see also LaDow, *Medicine Line*, 53.

9   Matos Bernier and Miles, "War with Spain," 129.

10   The total forces landed in Puerto Rico were 15,199, according to Secretary of War Russell A. Alger, *The Spanish-American War* (New York: Harper & Brothers, 1901), 308.

11   Whitney, "Miles's Campaign in Puerto Rico," 204.

12   Instructions from President William McKinley for Maj. Gen Wesley Merritt,

U.S. Army, Commanding Army of Occupation to the Philippines, Washington, May 28, 1898, published in United States Adjutant-General's Office, *Correspondence Relating to the War with Spain and Conditions Growing Out of the Same: Including the Insurrection in the Philippine Islands and the China Relief Expedition, between the Adjutant-General of the Army and Military Commanders in the United States, Cuba, Porto Rico, China, and the Philippine Islands, from April 15, 1898, to July 30, 1902* (Washington, D.C.: Government Printing Office, 1902), 2:676. Merritt's August proclamation hewed closely to the principles outlined for him two months earlier by the president. McKinley wished to reassure the Filipinos that the war would be "free from severity" and said they had nothing to fear as long as they cooperated with the military authorities.

13   See, for example, the proclamations to the inhabitants of New Mexico made by Gen. Philip Kearny on July 31 and August 22, 1846. James R. Arnold and Roberta Wiener, eds., *Understanding U.S. Military Conflicts Through Primary Sources* (Santa Barbara: ABC-CLIO, 2016), 1:320–21. I am grateful to Brian DeLay for pointing out the similarities between the way representatives of the U.S. military talked to Indians and the way they addressed Mexican citizens in the Southwest during the Mexican-American War.

14   Transcript of conversation between General Miles and Sioux Indian Chiefs "Red Cloud" and "Little Wound," at Pine Ridge Agency, S.Dak., October 27, 1890, regarding "Ghost Dance," box 4, "Sioux War 1890–91," Nelson A. Miles Papers, Military History Institute, Carlisle, Pa.

15   Ibid. For a thorough analysis of the Ghost Dance, which argues against those who interpreted it—then and subsequently—as a millenarian movement, see Louis S. Warren, *God's Red Son: The Ghost Dance Religion and the Making of Modern America* (New York: Basic Books, 2017).

16   John Marshall, in *Worcester v. Georgia* (1832), discussed in Paul Francis Prucha, *American Indian Treaties: The History of a Political Anomaly* (Berkeley: University of California Press, 1984), 5.

17   In his book *The Blood of Government*, Paul Kramer analyzes how American racial ideologies informed colonial practice in the Philippines. He details, in particular, the importance of American racism in providing the justification for limiting Filipino sovereignty. The book also explores how empire affected ideas about race and citizenship on the domestic front; Paul Kramer, *The Blood of Government: Race, Empire, the United States, and the Philippines* (Chapel Hill: University of North Carolina Press, 2006). Another important book that explores how racial ideas have operated between the spheres of domestic and overseas empire is Amy Kaplan's *The Anarchy of Empire in the Making of U.S. Culture* (Cambridge, Mass.: Harvard University Press, 2002).

18   Robert M. Utley, *The Last Days of the Sioux Nation* (New Haven, Conn.: Yale University Press, 2004), 227–28. The number of casualties at Wounded Knee remains a matter of debate until today. In his 1891 Report to the War Department on the "affair at Wounded Knee Creek," Major General Miles, who had visited the field where the bodies of many of those killed lay, reported "30 officers and soldiers and 200 Indians (men, women, and children) were killed or mortally wounded." *Annual Report of the Secretary of War* (Washington, D.C.: Government Printing Office, 1891), 150.

19   Significant contributions to examining the history of imperial continuities in American expansion include Walter LaFeber's classic work, first published in 1963, *The New Empire: An Interpretation of American Expansion, 1860–1898* (Ithaca, N.Y.: Cornell University Press, 1998); Richard Drinnon, *Facing West: The Metaphysics of Indian-Hating*

and Empire-Building (Norman: University of Oklahoma Press, 1997); and Jeffrey Ostler, *The Plains Sioux and U.S. Colonialism from Lewis and Clark to Wounded Knee* (Cambridge: Cambridge University Press, 2004). Richard Slotkin's exploration of the cultural power of myths about the frontier and the way such thinking has informed the U.S. role on the world stage in the twentieth century remains relevant to understanding the enduring resonance of Indian Country in the twenty-first; Richard Slotkin, *Gunfighter Nation: The Myth of the Frontier in Twentieth-Century America* (Norman: University of Oklahoma Press, 1998).

20   Walter L. Williams, "United States Indian Policy and the Debate over Philippine Annexation: Implications for the Origins of American Imperialism," *Journal of American History* 66, no. 4 (1980): 810–31.

21   One of the most frequently quoted observations in Williams's article is his calculation that twenty-six of the thirty generals in service in the Philippines between 1898 and 1902 had had "experience with Indians in the West." Ibid., 828n105.

22   "Indian Wars and their Cost, and Civil Expenditures for Indians," in United States Department of the Interior, Census Office, *Report on Indians Taxed and Indians Not Taxed in the United States (except Alaska)* (Washington, D.C.: Government Printing Office, 1894), 636–44 (quoted in Brian DeLay, "Indian Polities, Empire, and the History of American Foreign Relations," *Diplomatic History* 39, no. 5 [2015]: 934).

23   David J. Silbey, *A War of Frontier and Empire: The Philippine-American War, 1899–1902* (New York: Farrar, Straus and Giroux, 2007). For two military histories that put the U.S. occupation of the Philippines in broader context, see Brian McAllister Linn, *The Philippine War, 1899–1902* (Lawrence: University Press of Kansas, 2000); and Linn, *The U.S. Army and Counterinsurgency in the Philippine War, 1899–1902* (Chapel Hill: University of North Carolina Press, 2008).

24   Robert A. Fulton, "The Battle of Bud Bagsak," *Uncle Sam, the Moros, and the Moro Campaigns: A Pictorial History from 1899 to 1920*, http//:www.morolandhistory.com. Almost as soon as he arrived in the Southern Philippines, Pershing advocated for the creation of native auxiliary forces. He received permission from General J. Franklin Bell to form two companies of Moro Scouts, the Fifty-First, made up of Maguindanaos from Cotabato, and the Fifty-Second, made up of Maranaos from Lanao.

25   As at Wounded Knee, the total number of Tausugs killed in the Bud Bagsak attack remains unknown. Pershing estimated deaths at between two and three hundred; one American officer and fourteen of the "native" scouts were also killed. J. J. Pershing, *My Life Before the War, 1860–1917: A Memoir*, ed. John T. Greenwood (Lexington: University Press of Kentucky), 295–302.

26   Juliana Barr and Edward Countryman, eds., *Contested Spaces of Early America* (Philadelphia: University of Pennsylvania Press, 2014), 18–20.

27   "Proclamation of 1763," *The American Revolution*, Primary Source Media, 1999, American Journey, *Student Resources Context*, link.galegroup.com/apps/doc/EJ2153000004/SUIC?u=clic_hamline&xid=4d0f29e6.

28   William E. Unrau, *The Rise and Fall of Indian Country, 1825–1855* (Lawrence: University Press of Kansas, 2007), 97. Section 1 of the 1834 act redefined Indian Country (neither for the first nor last time) as "that part of the United States west of the Mississippi, and not within the states of Missouri and Louisiana, or the territory of Arkansas, and, also, that part of the United States east of the Mississippi River, and not within any state to which the Indian title as not been extinguished." Ibid., 2. On the definition of "Indian Country" in federal law, see also Felix S. Cohen, *Handbook of Federal Indian Law* (Charlottsville, Va:

Michie Bobbs-Merrill, 1982), 7–46. I am grateful to Stephen Dow Beckham for steering me toward this valuable source and also for sharing his knowledge of the legal history of "Indian Country" with me.

29   Unrau, *Rise and Fall of Indian Country*, 147.

30   DeLay, "Indian Polities," 935. On the history of the Bureau of Insular Affairs, see Katharine Bjork, "Prairie Imperialists: The Bureau of Insular Affairs and Continuities in Colonial Expansion from Nebraska to Cuba and the Philippines," *Nebraska History* 95, no. 4 (2014): 216–29.

31   Prucha, *American Indian Treaties*, 4. Daniel Richter notes that the boundary drawn by the Proclamation of October 1763 "conformed to the principles negotiated at the Treaty of Easton and to longstanding aims of Ottawa, Iroquois, Delaware, Shawnee, Cherokee, and countless other Native American leaders seeking recognition of territorial integrity." Daniel K. Richter, *Facing East from Indian Country: A Native History of Early America* (Cambridge: Harvard University Press, 2001), 208.

32   Supreme Court decision in *Cherokee Nation v. the State of Georgia*, reprinted in Edward H. Spicer, *A Short History of the Indians of the United States* (New York: D. Van Nostrand, 1969), 186–87. For a discussion of the "protected nation" idea of the status of Indian nations as developed in the three early Marshall decisions, see Vine Deloria Jr. and David Wilkins, *The Legal Universe: Observations on the Foundations of American Law* (Golden, Colo.: Fulcrum Pub., 2011), 144–46.

33   James Edward Kerr, *The Insular Cases: The Role of the Judiciary in American Expansionism* (Port Washington, N.Y.: Kennikat Press, 1982), 53. This and other aspects of the Insular Cases are discussed in my dissertation; see Katharine Bjork, "Incorporating an Empire: From Deregulating Labor to Regulating Leisure in Cuba, Puerto Rico, Hawaii, and the Philippines, 1898–1909" (PhD diss., University of Chicago, 1998), chap. 1.

34   Kerr, *Insular Cases*, 66.

35   Pérez, *War of 1898*, 33.

36   U.S. Supreme Court, Downes v. Bidwell, 182 U.S. at 287, cited in José A. Cabranes, *Citizenship and the American Empire: Notes on the Legislative History of the United States Citizenship of Puerto Ricans* (New Haven, Conn.: Yale University Press, 1979), 46.

37   Kerr, *Insular Cases*, 52.

38   Stephen W. Silliman, "The 'Old West' in the Middle East: U.S. Military Metaphors in Real and Imagined Indian Country," *American Anthropologist* 110, no. 2 (2008): 237.

39   Phillip H. Stevens, *Search Out the Land: A History of American Military Scouts* (New York: Rand McNally, 1969).

40   Robert Lee Bullard, "The Scout," unpublished manuscript, box 9, Robert Lee Bullard Collection, Manuscript Division, Library of Congress.

41   On the history and cultural meaning of scouting, see Michael Rosenthal, *The Character Factory: Baden-Powell and the Origins of the Boy Scout Movement* (New York: Pantheon Books, 1986); Shari M. Huhndorf, *Going Native: Indians in the American Cultural Imagination* (Ithaca, N.Y.: Cornell University Press, 2001); Philip Joseph Deloria, *Playing Indian* (New Haven, Conn.: Yale University Press, 1998); and J. McIver Weatherford, *Native Roots: How the Indians Enriched America* (New York: Fawcett Columbine, 1992).

42   Gonzalo de Quesada y Aróstegui to Elizabeth Sherman Cameron, September 1898, box 3, family correspondence file, Nelson A. Miles Family Collection, Manuscript Di-

vision, Library of Congress. Quesada's letter roundly criticizes General Shafter for saying he didn't want Cubans to fight but to be scouts, a comment for which Quesada claimed he had nineteen witnesses.

Chapter 1

1   Scott recorded the information he collected in four clothbound ledger books. Anthropologist William C. Meadows has published Scott's ledgers in an edited volume in which he has provided extensive ethnographic and historical context for them. William C. Meadows, ed., *Through Indian Sign Language: The Fort Sill Ledgers of Hugh Lenox Scott and Iseeo, 1889–1897* (Norman: University of Oklahoma Press, 2015).

2   Woodrow Wilson to Hugh Lenox Scott, December 11, 1903, Princeton, N.J., box 7, general correspondence file, Hugh Lenox Scott Papers, Manuscript Division, Library of Congress (hereafter cited as Scott Papers). The stocks are discussed in chapter 5.

3   William Berryman Scott, *Some Memories of a Paleontologist* (Princeton, N.J.: Princeton University Press, 1939), 3.

4   Ibid., 6.

5   Hugh Lenox Scott, *Some Memories of a Soldier* (New York: Century, 1928), 1–7; W. B. Scott, *Some Memories of a Paleontologist*, 21. In 1866 ties between the Hodge and Stockton families were further strengthened when Dr. Hodge's youngest daughter Sarah married Mary Hunter Hodge's son Samuel Stockton, a captain in the Fourth U.S. Cavalry who had fought with that regiment during the whole of the Civil War. On the death of Commodore Richard Stockton a week after the wedding, Samuel inherited the house, known as Morven, which was built in 1702 on land whose title had been conveyed directly by William Penn.

6   H. L. Scott, *Some Memories of a Soldier*, 14.

7   Henry Ossian Flipper, *The Colored Cadet at West Point* (Lincoln: University of Nebraska Press, 1878), 73–74.

8   H. L. Scott, *Some Memories of a Soldier*, 15. On the life-saving incident on the Hudson, see 18–21.

9   Ibid., 17.

10   Hugh Lenox Scott to his mother, January 23, 1876, West Point, microfilm 16,787, roll 1 of 4, Scott Papers. General Order 100, "Instructions for the Government of Armies of the United States in the Field," was issued by President Lincoln in April 1863. The instructions were drafted by historian and legal scholar Francis Lieber. They were intended to clarify a number of issues relating to the conduct of war under martial law. Some parts of the Lieber Code dealt with the treatment of *guerilla* combatants, over whom it accorded battlefield commanders considerable discretion. Four decades after it was written, American commanders in the Philippines invoked the Lieber Code to justify harsh measures against the civilian population who they believed to be harboring ununiformed soldiers of the Philippine Liberation Army.

11   Hugh Lenox Scott to his mother, May 24, 1876, West Point, microfilm 16,787, roll 1 of 4, Scott Papers.

12   Ibid.

13   Hugh Lenox Scott to his mother, January 23, 1876, Scott Papers.

14   W. B. Scott, *Some Memories of a Paleontologist*, 21. W. B. Scott noted that for a

"considerable family" such as his grandfather's, three maids, a cook, waitress, and chambermaid "were regarded as the minimum." Additionally, their family retained a coachman-gardener. He recalled that "Negro servants were then few in the North . . . though it was permissible to have a black butler."

15   William H. Leckie and Shirley A. Leckie, *The Buffalo Soldiers: A Narrative of the Black Cavalry in the West* (Norman: University of Oklahoma Press, 2003), 4.

16   Bruce Catton, *This Hallowed Ground: The Story of the Union Side of the Civil War* (Garden City, N.Y.: Doubleday, 1956), 222 (quoted in Leckie and Leckie, *Buffalo Soldiers*, 4). Commanding federal troops in South Carolina in 1862, Scott's uncle, David Hunter, organized the Union Army's first African American regiment. *Britannica Academic*, s.v. "David Hunter," accessed July 15, 2016, http://ezproxy.hamline.edu:6118/levels/collegiate/article/41563.

17   L. D. Reddick, "The Negro Policy of the United States Army, 1775–1945," *Journal of Negro History* 34, no. 1 (January 1949): 9–29. Almost all their officers were white. Until June of 1864, the Union paid white soldiers thirteen dollars a month, but black soldiers only ten dollars per month, according to Catton, *This Hallowed Ground*, 222 (cited in Leckie and Leckie, *Buffalo Soldiers*, 4). Of the 4,200 officers of the United States Colored Troops, only about one hundred were black; see Marvin Fletcher, "The Negro Soldier and the United States Army, 1891–1917" (PhD diss., University of Wisconsin, 1968), 9. By the end of the war, almost 180,000 African Americans had fought for the Union; 33,380 of them had given their lives for it. Leckie and Leckie, *Buffalo Soldiers*, 5.

18   Reddick, "Negro Policy of the United States Army," 18.

19   Charles L. Kenner, *Buffalo Soldiers and Officers of the Ninth Cavalry, 1867–1898: Black and White Together* (Norman: University of Oklahoma Press, 1999) 306.

20   Ibid., 19.

21   James Parker, *The Old Army: Memories 1872–1918* (Philadelphia: Dorrance, 1929), 92–93. For more on the attitudes of white army officers toward black officers and enlisted soldiers, see also Willard B. Gatewood Jr., "Black Americans and the Quest for Empire, 1898–1903," *Journal of Southern History* 38, no. 4 (November 1972): 545–66; and Marvin Fletcher, "The Black Volunteers in the Spanish-American War," *Military Affairs* 38, no. 2 (1974): 48–53.

22   Frances Marie Antoinette Roe, *Army Letters from an Officer's Wife, 1871–1888* (New York: Appleton, 1909); reprinted with introduction by Sandra L. Myres (Lincoln: University of New Mexico Press, 1981), 77–78, 103–4 (quoted in Leckie and Leckie, *Buffalo Soldiers*, 65).

23   Reddick, "Negro Policy of the United States Army," 19.

24   Fletcher, "Black Volunteers in the Spanish-American War," 48.

25   Excerpt from a report on West Point by Major General John Schofield written when he was superintendent of West Point in 1870. The report appears in Jack D. Foner, *Blacks and the Military in American History* (New York: Praeger, 1971), 65; it is quoted by Quintard Taylor, Jr., in his introduction to Henry Ossian Flipper, *The Colored Cadet at West Point: Autobiography of Henry Ossian Flipper* (Lincoln: University of Nebraska Press, 1998), xv.

26   William C. Meadows characterizes such views as "social evolutionism." Meadows, *Through Indian Sign Language*, 79.

27   Hugh Lenox Scott to his mother, January 23, 1876, Scott Papers.

28   John J. Pershing to George D. Meiklejohn, July 16, 1898, box 28, folder 176,

Record Group 3500, George D. Meiklejohn Collection, Nebraska State Historical Society. This episode is examined in more detail in Chapter 4.

29   Hugh Lenox Scott to his mother, May 24, 1876, Scott Papers.

30   H. L. Scott, *Some Memories of a Soldier*, 7.

31   Hugh Lenox Scott to his mother, May 24, 1876, Scott Papers.

32   Hugh Lenox Scott to his mother, May 28, 1876, West Point, microfilm 16,787, roll 1 of 4, Scott Papers.

33   H. L. Scott, *Some Memories of a Soldier*, 24.

34   Robert W. Rydell, *All the World's a Fair: Visions of Empire at American International Expositions, 1876–1916* (Chicago: University of Chicago Press, 1987), 15.

35   John T. Dale, *What Ben Beverly Saw at the Great Exposition* (Chicago: Warren, 1877), 10.

36   James D. McCabe, *The Illustrated History of the Centennial Exhibition: Held in Commemoration of the One Hundredth Anniversary of American Independence* (Philadelphia: National Pub. Co., 1876), 582–84.

37   Edward Henry Knight, *A Study of the Savage Weapons at the Centennial Exhibition, Philadelphia, 1876* (Washington, D.C.: Government Printing Office, 1880), 213.

38   Rydell, *All the World's a Fair*, 23–25.

39   Robert A. Trennert, "The Indian Role in the 1876 Centennial Celebration," *American Indian Culture and Research Journal* 1, no. 4 (1976): 9.

40   Joanna C. Scherer, "Artifact Identification Using Historical Photographs: The Case of Red Cloud's Manikin," *Visual Anthropology* 27, no. 3 (May 2014): 230, accessed July 8, 2016, available from Academic Search Premier, Ipswich, Mass., http://search.ebscohost.com.ezproxy.hamline.edu:2048/login.aspx?direct=true&db=aph&AN=95284850&site=ehost-live. The contemporary description of the Red Cloud manikin is quoted from Craig H. Miner, "The United States Government Building at the Centennial Exhibition, 1874–77," *Prologue: The Journal of the National Archives* 4 (4): 1972, 211.

41   McCabe, *Illustrated History of the Centennial Exhibition*, 666–71.

42   Robert M. Utley, *Custer and the Great Controversy: The Origin and Development of a Legend* (Lincoln: University of Nebraska Press, 1998), 45. Sturgis was the son of Samuel D. Sturgis, who was colonel of the regiment, although the command was more associated with Custer, who was lieutenant colonel; both men held the brevet rank of general.

43   Samuel Stockton was both the husband of H. L. Scott's aunt Sarah and the son of his step-grandmother Mary Stockton Hodge.

44   H. L. Scott, *Some Memories of a Soldier*, 24–26.

45   Utley, *Custer and the Great Controversy*, 42–44. General Terry also wrote a second, confidential report from the mouth of the Little Big Horn, which he sent with a staff officer to Bismarck where he had it wired to Chicago. Whereas the first report merely stated the facts of the battle and implicitly accepted the blame for the defeat, Terry's second confidential report was critical of Custer. Through a misunderstanding and the misrepresentation of a reporter for the *Philadelphia Enquirer* as a messenger to whom General Sherman entrusted a copy of the report to take to the secretary of war, the second (confidential) account ended up being published on July 7 before the official account, to the embarrassment of General Terry, who was then accused of making "unbecoming haste to throw the fault on the gallant man whose life was sacrificed in the attempt to carry out his impracticable and stupidly planned campaign," as the *Indianapolis Sentinel* put it in an editorial comment on July 12, 1876.

46   Utley, *Custer and the Great Controversy*, 32–33.

47   Frederick Whittacker, *A Complete Life of Gen. George A. Custer: Major General of Volunteers, Brevet Major-General U.S. Army, and Lieutenant-Colonel Seventh U.S. Cavalry* (New York: Sheldon, 1876).

48   Richard White, *The Middle Ground: Indians, Empires, and Republics in the Great Lakes Region, 1650–1815* (Cambridge: Cambridge University Press, 1992), 1. The British turned Fort Pitt over to the colonists in 1772. At this time whether Pittsburgh fell under the jurisdiction of Pennsylvania or Virginia was in dispute. While under the control of Virginians, the fort was renamed for their governor, Lord Dunmore.

49   William Cronon, *Nature's Metropolis: Chicago and the Great West* (New York: W. W. Norton, 1991), 25–26.

50   Robert M. Utley, *The Lance and the Shield: The Life and Times of Sitting Bull* (London: Pimlico, 1998), 167.

51   H. L. Scott, *Some Memories of a Soldier*, 6; William C. Davis, *Jefferson Davis: The Man and His Hour* (Baton Rouge: Louisiana State University Press, 1996), 43. The 1870 U.S. Census of Population for Chicago (Cook County: 349,966) is discussed in Cronon, *Nature's Metropolis*, 301.

52   H. L. Scott, *Some Memories of a Soldier*, 27.

53   Ibid., 6. Although Scott says the distance his uncle walked on the Mississippi from Prairie du Chien to Fort Snelling was three hundred miles, in fact the distance is closer to two hundred miles. For David Hunter's military service record, see George Washington Cullum and Wirt Robinson, *Biographical Register of the Officers and Graduates of the U. S. Military Academy at West Point, N. Y., from its establishment, in 1802, to 1890; with the Early History of the United States Military Academy* (Boston: Houghton, Mifflin, 1891), 290.

54   Mary Lethert Wingerd and Kirsten Delegard, *North Country: The Making of Minnesota* (Minneapolis: University of Minnesota Press, 2010), 82.

55   Ibid., 89.

56   Ibid., 174. Wingerd writes: "Federal troops stationed at Fort Snelling created at least a feeble presence, but for the most part the fur traders had free rein and British influence exerted more persuasive power than American law, especially in the border region."

57   Ibid., 124.

58   Ibid., 219–20.

59   Anton Treuer, *The Assassination of Hole in the Day* (Minnesota Historical Society, 2011), 25. Treuer says that the desire to create a buffer from Dakota attacks "explains the Pillager Ojibwe's willingness to cede an 890,000-acre parcel of land in exchange for only two hundred beaver traps, seventy-five guns, and an annuity of blankets with no financial compensation" stipulated in the Long Island Prairie Land Cession Treaty of 1847.

60   Wingerd and Delegard, *North Country*, 219–23.

61   Ibid., 340.

62   *An Act for the Relief of Persons for Damages sustained by Reason of Depredations and Injuries by certain Bands of Sioux Indians and the Rules Adopted by the Commissioners under said Act*, 37th Cong., 3rd sess. (1863).

63   Colette A. Hyman, "Survivial at Crow Creek, 1863–1866," *Minnesota History* 61, no. 4 (Winter 2008–9): 151. Hyman puts the deaths at the Fort Snelling internment camp at 293. Of the 1,601 Dakota recorded on the military census of the camp in December 1862, 133 were Whpekute; 295 were Sissetunwan and Wahpetunwan; and 122 were "'half-breeds' without tribal affiliation." The remaining 1,051 were Mdwakantunwan.

64   The Minnesota legislature approved the payment of bounties for Indian scalps. When the Mdewakantunwan leader Little Crow (Taoyateduta) returned the next summer to Minnesota with his son and was shot to death in a raspberry patch, the farmer who assassinated him claimed a bounty of five hundred dollars and received the commendation of a grateful state for his heroism. The state then had the Dakota chief's scalp tanned and put on exhibit, along with his skull and forearm bones, first at the state capitol and later at the state historical society, where they remained on display until 1915. "The decision to exhibit such grisly trophies was representative of the genocidal rage faced by the Dakota in Minnesota after 1862," according to Kirsten Delegard. It also reflected the "new racial order" that prevailed in the state. "The exhibit declared the unequivocal ascendance of American power in the region, providing reassurance to white residents, who saw it as evidence that the savagery of 1862 was safely in the past." Kirsten Delegard, interpretive essay on reproduced postcard image bearing the legend "Scalp of 'Little Crow,' Leader of Minnesota Indian Massacre 1862." The "Little Crow" postcard is plate 129, Wingerd and Delegard, *North Country*.

65   Wingerd and Delegard, *North Country*, 1.

66   Brandon D. Newton, *Punishment, Revenge, and Retribution: A Historical Analysis of Punitive Operations* (Ft. Belvoir, Va.: Defense Technical Information Center), 6–7, http://handle.dtic.mil/100.2/ADA436111http://oai.dtic.mil/oai/oai?&verb=getRecord&metadataPrefix=html&identifier=ADA436111.

67   Louis Pfaller, *The Sully Expedition of 1864: Featuring the Killdeer Mountain and Badlands Battles* (Bismarck: State Historical Society of North Dakota, 1964), 64.

68   Michael Clodfelter, *The Dakota War: The United States Army Versus the Sioux, 1862–1865* (Jefferson, N.C.: McFarland, 2006), 90.

69   Ibid., chaps. 9 and 10.

70   The wagon master, Captain R. B. Mason, is quoted in ibid., 141.

71   Oscar Garrot Wall, *Recollections of the Sioux Massacre: An Authentic History of the Yellow Medicine Incident, of the Fate of Marsh and His Men, of the Siege and Battles of Fort Ridgely, and of Other Important Battles and Experiences; Together with a Historical Sketch of the Sibley Expedition of 1863* (Lake City, Minn.: printed at "Home Printery," 1909), 275.

72   Clodfelter, *Dakota War*, 174–75. The quotation from Alfred Sully is from *Minnesota in the Civil and Indian Wars*, 1:673.

73   Utley, *Lance and the Shield*, 58–59.

74   Ibid., 71.

Chapter 2

1   Hugh Lenox Scott, *Some Memories of a Soldier* (New York: Century, 1928), 26.

2   Ibid., 28.

3   Francis Parkman, *Conspiracy of Pontiac* (New York: Collier Books, 1962).

4   H. L. Scott, *Some Memories of a Soldier*, 30–31.

5   Ibid.

6   Parkman, Conspiracy of Pontiac, 17.

7   For the biography of Iseeo (Plenty of Round Fireplaces) and a sensitive portrait of his relationship with Hugh L. Scott, see William C. Meadows, ed., *Through Indian Sign Language: The Fort Sill Ledgers of Hugh Lenox Scott and Iseeo, 1889–1897* (Norman: University of Oklahoma Press, 2015), chap 3.

8   William Meadows characterizes Scott's views on the stages of development of

human civilization as "social evolutionism," which he defines as "a Eurocentric approach that views human societies as evolving from simple to more complex (often presented in stages: savagery to barbarism, to civilization)." See ibid., 79.

9   H. L. Scott, *Some Memories of a Soldier*, 29, 40.

10   Louis S. Warren, *Buffalo Bill's America: William Cody and the Wild West Show* (New York: Alfred A. Knopf, 2005), 85.

11   "Squaw men" was also a term used by American soldiers in the Philippines to refer to men who had "shacked up" with native women.

12   Hugh L. Scott, "Notes on Sign Language, Part I," 4, box 4, folder 1 of 3, Hugh L. Scott Papers, series 2932, National Anthropological Archives, Smithsonian Institution (hereafter cited as Scott Papers, National Anthropological Archives).

13   Warren, *Buffalo Bill's America*, 100–101.

14   Ibid., 105.

15   Ibid., 103. Although he is remembered as their commander, Warren points out that North's primary role was that of "translator and liaison between the Pawnee scouts and the military command."

16   Thomas W. Dunlay, *Wolves for the Blue Soldiers: Indian Scouts and Auxiliaries with the United States Army, 1860–90* (Lincoln: University of Nebraska Press, 1982), 24.

17   Joyce E. Mason, *The Use of Indian Scouts in the Apache Wars, 1870–1886* (PhD diss., Indiana University, 1970), 25–26.

18   James D. Campbell, *"Making Riflemen from Mud": Restoring the Army's Culture of Irregular Warfare* (Carlisle, Pa.: Strategic Studies Institute, U.S. Army War College, 2007), 7.

19   H. L. Scott, *Some Memories of a Soldier*, 32.

20   Ibid., 35.

21   Scott regarded Ben Clark, who was an interpreter and scout, as the "best white sign talker" he had ever known. Clark also wrote a Cheyenne grammar. After Ben Clark, Scott considered Captain William Philo Clark as the second-best white sign talker. Captain Clark had begun work on a book on the sign language and Scott spent ten days in 1881 going over his notes with him. The work was not published before Clark died, however. Some of Scott's notes on the history of sign language were included in a talk he delivered to "Princeton Ladies," on October 28, 1932. The notes for the talk are in Hugh L. Scott, "Notes on Sign Language, General," box 4, Scott Papers, National Anthropological Archives. Other information is contained in a manuscript titled "History" in the same box.

22   H. L. Scott, *Some Memories of a Soldier*, 35.

23   Ibid., 36.

24   Nelson Appleton Miles, *Serving the Republic: Memoirs of the Civil and Military Life of Nelson A. Miles, Lieutenant-General, United States Army* (New York: Harper & Brothers, 1911), 146.

25   Robert M. Utley, *The Lance and the Shield: The Life and Times of Sitting Bull* (London: Pimlico, 1998), 165, 167.

26   After the Custer battle, the Cheyenne and Lakota villages moved to the head of the Rosebud River, traveled down to Greenleaf Creek, and then went east to the Tongue River. There they split up to search up and down the river for game. On August 1, 1876, they reunited about twenty miles above the mouth of the Powder River. Since provisioning such a large village was difficult, the bands broke up to hunt. Sitting Bull took most of the Hunkpapas, as well as some Miniconjous and Sans Arcs down the Little Missouri, while

Crazy Horse led another group upstream toward the Black Hills. Utley, *Lance and the Shield*, 165–66.

27   Ibid., 169–71. The wagon train carried materials for constructing a cantonment at the mouth of the Tongue River. Their first attempt to move supplies into the territory was harassed by Indians as it moved up the Yellowstone River from Glendive Creek. An initial train of ninety-four wagons, escorted by four infantry companies, was turned back after several attacks. For the second attempt to carry the supplies the demoralized teamsters were replaced by soldiers and the escort was increased to five companies of infantry with eleven officers and 185 men under the command of Lieutenant Colonel E. S. Otis of the Twenty-Second Infantry. Brian C. Pohanka and John M. Carroll, eds., *Nelson Miles: A Documentary History of His Military Career, 1861–1903* (Glendale, Calif.: Arthur H. Clark, 1985), 93.

28   Colonel Miles, October 25, *Annual Report 1876 of the Secretary of War* (quoted in Robert Wooster, *Nelson A. Miles and the Twilight of the Frontier Army* [Lincoln: University of Nebraska Press, 1996], 84).

29   Miles, *Serving the Republic*, 164.

30   Ibid., 147; on Miles's winter clothing, see also Beth LaDow, *Medicine Line: Life and Death on a North American Borderland* (London: Taylor and Francis, 2013), 53.

31   Utley, *Lance and the Shield*, 179–80. As colonel in command of the Twenty-Seventh Infantry in Mindanao, Frank D. Baldwin led some of the first U.S. forces into the Lake Lanao region and directed the assault on Bayan in May 1900. He later commanded the Department of Visayas in the Philippines (1902–3). "Biographical Index," in *My Life Before the World War, 1860–1917: A Memoir by General of the Armies John J. Pershing*, ed. John T. Greenwood (Lexington: University Press of Kentucky, 2013), 471; see also chap. 7.

32   Utley, *Lance and the Shield*, 175.

33   Colonel W. H. Wood to AAG, Department of Dakota, Cheyenne River Agency, February 27, 1877 (quoted in Utley, *Lance and the Shield*, 181).

34   H. L. Scott, *Some Memories of a Soldier*, 51.

35   Ibid., 52.

36   Ibid., 50.

37   Ibid., 56–57.

38   Wooster, *Nelson A. Miles and the Twilight of the Frontier Army*, 105–10.

39   H. L. Scott, *Some Memories of a Soldier*, 79.

40   Ibid., 83–84.

41   Letter from E. A. Garlington to Adjutant General, June 19, 1902, reproduced in H. L. Scott, *Some Memories of a Soldier*, 88.

42   Ibid., 97.

43   The pioneering work of Lewis Henry Morgan, often called "the father of American Anthropology," laid the foundations for the study of kinship. "Morgan conceptualized a set of stages through which human groups moved: savagery to barbarism to civilization." Steven Conn, *History's Shadow: Native Americans and Historical Consciousness in the Nineteenth Century* (Chicago: University of Chicago Press, 2006), 179. Conn also discusses the early prominence of anthropometry—the measurement of the human skeleton, which was part of a scientific study of racial difference and diffusion, as well as the basis for claims about the inferiority and superiority of different races, specimens of whose skulls were filled with mustard seed and lead shot to measure cranial capacity.

44   H. L. Scott, *Some Memories of a Soldier*, 96.

45   Ibid., 33.

46   The account of Scott's method for finding out what made a good buffalo horse is drawn from two sources. The first quotation about the debate he sparked on the subject among Crow chiefs is detailed in an unpublished manuscript titled "Tales of the Kiowa," box 2, "Kiowa," Scott Papers, National Anthropological Archives; the contrast Scott drew between a cavalry horse and Crow buffalo horse is from Scott's published memoirs, *Some Memories of a Soldier*, 71.

47   H. L. Scott, *Some Memories of a Soldier*, 102–4.

48   Meadows, *Through Indian Sign Language*, 58–60.

49   Letters from Ernest Thompson Seton to Col. Hugh Lenox Scott, February 15 and June 14, 1912, box 14, General Correspondence, Hugh Lenox Scott Papers, Manuscript Division, Library of Congress.

50   Hugh Lenox Scott's ideas on the Plains Indian Sign language are laid out in the talk he delivered to "Princeton Ladies," on October 28, 1932. The notes for the talk are in Hugh L. Scott, "Notes on Sign Language, General," box 4, Scott Papers, National Anthropological Archives.

51   Meadows, *Through Indian Sign Language*, 51–52.

52   Ibid., 52.

53   Hugh Lenox Scott, "The 'Messiah Dance' in the Indian Territory," essay for the Fort Sill Lyceum, March 1892, 8, 14. Scott's language and punctuation are given as in the original. I am grateful to Patrick Kerwin in the Manuscript Division of the Library of Congress for locating this document and sending me a copy.

54   Ibid.

55   Ibid., 1.

56   Ibid., 3–4.

57   Ibid., 5.

58   Hugh Lenox Scott to his mother, November 23, 1877, Fort Abraham Lincoln, Dakota Territory, microfilm 16787, roll 1 of 4, Hugh Lenox Scott Papers, Manuscript Division, Library of Congress.

59   H. L. Scott, *Some Memories of a Soldier*, 55.

60   Shepard Krech III and Barbara A. Hail, *Collecting Native America, 1870–1960* (Washington, D.C.: Smithsonian Institution Press, 1999), 155.

61   H. L. Scott, *Some Memories of a Soldier*; Hugh L. Scott, "Notes on Sign Language," box 4, various folders, Scott Papers, National Anthropological Archives; MS 4525, "Apache Ethnography," box 1, Scott Papers, National Anthropological Archives; see also Meadows, *Through Indian Sign Language*.

62   "History," handwritten draft manuscript, 5, 7, Hugh L. Scott, "Notes on Sign Language," box 4, Scott Papers, National Anthropological Archives.

63   Hugh L. Scott, lecture notes, "Notes on Sign Language, Part I," box 4, folder 2 of 3, Scott Papers, National Anthropological Archives.

64   Notes for lecture "The Sign Language of the Plains Indians," delivered before the graduate college Princeton University, December 6, 1933, and at the dinner of Society of Indian Wars, Army & Navy Club, Washington, February 16, 1934. In his speech, Scott further quoted from Whitney: "The Indo-European roots are the elements of speech which existed prior to the whole development of the means of grammatical distinction; before the growth of inflection, before the separation of the parts of speech [p. 201]." Scott thought this exactly described the condition of sign language. William Dwight Whitney, *Language, and*

the Study of Language (New York: Charles Scribner, 1867). *Author's note: I do not mean to suggest that this is the particular edition of the book Scott consulted. In fact, it looks doubtful that it was, since the page numbers he cites do not align with the text in this edition.*

65 Hugh L. Scott, Notes for lecture "The Sign Language of the Plains Indians," 11.

66 H. L. Scott to Mary Scott, December 21, 1905, Joló, microfilm 17249, roll 2 of 4, Hugh Lenox Scott Papers, Manuscript Division, Library of Congress.

67 Letters of response from librarians at the Texas State Library and at the University of Texas at Austin suggest that Scott had made inquiries about sources held by those institutions concerning "the early Spanish occupation of Texas and the early exploration with special reference to the Indians and the sign language of the plains." These letters became part of the Bureau of Ethnology collection of the National Anthropological Archives after Scott's death in 1934. Scott also published an article on aspects of Arapaho and Cheyenne history and interactions with other people on the plains over the previous two centuries. Scott published this article during the time he was superintendent of West Point. Hugh Lenox Scott, "The Early History and the Names of the Arapaho," *American Anthropologist* 9 (1907): 545–60.

Chapter 3

1 Robert Lee Bullard, unpublished autobiography, chap. 3, "Geronimo and Garrison Years," 14, box 9, Robert Lee Bullard Collection, Manuscript Division, Library of Congress (hereafter cited as Bullard, unpublished autobiography). Former Apache Scout John Rope described the customary apparel of scouts in the 1880s as "moccasins, white drawers, gee string, shirt and vest." Grenville Goodwin, "Excerpts from the Life of John Rope, an 'Old-Timer' of the White Mountain Apaches," *Arizona Historical Review* 7, no. 1 (1936): 48. Bullard seems to have eschewed the gee-string and the vest.

2 W. H. Hutchinson, introduction to *A Report to the Citizens, Concerning Certain Late Disturbances on the Western Frontier: Involving Sitting Bull, Crazy Horse, Chief Joseph and Geronimo, Opposed in the Field by Forces Under the Command of General Nelson A. (Bear-Coat) Miles,* by George W. Baird and Frederic Remington (Ashland, Calif.: L. Osborne, 1972), 19.

3 Bullard, unpublished autobiography, 15. Bullard refers to the Mexicans who confronted him in the crater as "revenue guards." However, in his account of the expedition he commanded in which Bullard served as quartermaster and commissary, James Parker says that the Mexican Guardia Rural was keeping them under surveillance as they moved into Sonora. James Parker, *The Old Army: Memories, 1872–1918* (Philadelphia: Dorrance, 1929), 173–74.

4 Colin M. MacLachlan and William H. Beezley, *El Gran Pueblo: A History of Greater Mexico* (Upper Saddle River, N.J.: Prentice Hall, 2004, 29. As the authors point out, Texas was not technically included in the territories ceded to the United States by the provisions of the Treaty of Guadalupe Hidalgo in 1848 since Texas had gained its independence from Mexico separately in 1836. Taken together, Mexico lost about half its national territory to the United States.

5 J. P. Dunn, Jr., *Massacre of the Mountains: A History of the Indian Wars of the Far West* (New York: Harper & Brothers, 1886), 617 (quoted in Donald E. Worcester: "The Apaches in the History of the Southwest," *New Mexico Historical Review* 50, no. 1 [January 1975]: 41).

6   Allan Reed Millett, *The General: Robert L. Bullard and Officership in the United States Army, 1881–1925* (Westport, Conn.: Greenwood Press, 1975), 57–60. Robert Lee Bullard was commissioned as a second lieutenant in the Tenth Infantry, stationed at Fort Union, New Mexico, in August of 1885. He was assigned to act as temporary quartermaster and commissary for Lieutenant James Parker's expedition of his Fourth Cavalry Troop H to pursue Geronimo in Mexico in August 1886.

7   Although the Mexicans did not kill Bullard in this instance, racial tensions between Mexicans and Americans did result in killings of one side by the other. Bullard notes at least one case of deliberate misreading of Mexicans as "Indians" by American troops. Bullard reports with approval that, "when Mexican troops that had beset other American commands in Mexico were reported to be coming toward us, [Lieutenant James] Parker issued a written order of attack against Indians and then orally had it understood all round that he meant Mexicans!" Bullard, unpublished autobiography, chap. 3, "Geronimo and Garrison Years," 18.

8   Theodore Roosevelt, *The Strenuous Life: Essays and Addresses* (New York: Century Company, 1902). Vice President Roosevelt exalted the benefits of an active outdoor life for both the individual and the nation in a speech he gave to an all-male audience at the Hamilton Club in Chicago on April 10, 1899. See Thomas Winter, "Strenuous Life," in *American Masculinities: An Historical Encyclopedia*, ed. Bret E. Carroll (Thousand Oaks, Calif.: Sage, 2004): 439–40, https://doi.org/10.4135/9781412956369.n223. The concept originated with Francis Parkman, who saw the kind of rugged experience he had had in the West as a corrective to elite culture that had grown soft, according to Winter. In Roosevelt's day, the expression "the strenuous life" became associated with a more muscular and masculine national identity that embraced imperialism and Anglo-Saxon racial superiority.

9   Bullard, unpublished autobiography, chaps. 1 and 3.

10   Bullard, unpublished autobiography, chap. 3, "Geronimo and Garrison Years," note following p. 20.

11   Robert L. Bullard to Mrs. Marie Bankhead Owen, Department of Archives, Montgomery, Alabama, September 10, 1946, box 5, Correspondence, 1945–46, Robert Lee Bullard Collection, Manuscript Division, Library of Congress. Bullard sent a version of this story to the Alabama State Archives in 1946 to accompany some decorations and medals he had earlier donated to his home state. It is not clear when the visit to Lee County took place—possibly in 1912, when Bullard made a visit to his family, according to Allan Millett, *General*, 250.

12   Bullard, unpublished autobiography, chap. 3, "Geronimo and Garrison Years," 3–4.

13   Robert Lee Bullard, "Military Pacification," *Journal of the Military Service Institution of the United States* 46, no. 163 (January–February 1910): 1–24.

14   Robert Lee Bullard, "Lecture notes," n.d., 1–2, box 9, autobiographical writings file, Robert Lee Bullard Collection, Manuscript Division, Library of Congress. In the 1870 Census for Lee County, the family of P. Christian, "B[lack]," is listed immediately following six members of the Bullard family "W[hite]." Peter Christian was nineteen years older than Robert Bullard; his wife, Sally (Bullard's nurse), was fourteen years Bullard's senior. The Christians had two sons in 1870: a boy named Robert, who was four years younger than the (white) Robert Bullard, and another son Frank, who was three in 1870. Lee County Census, taken on August 3, 1870, 94, accessed through Ancestry.com.

15   Bullard, unpublished autobiography, chaps. 1 and 3.

16   Ibid.

17   Millett, *General*, 23.

18   Bullard, unpublished autobiography, 5.

19   Millett, *General*, 23. Millett describes Pete's wife (and Bullard's nurse), Sally, as a "mulatto." He also added a detail he apparently learned from descendants of the Bullard family that Sally had irritated her employers by "addressing them as equals."

20   Bullard's racism against blacks increased over time as did the influence of his prejudice in the army. During the Spanish-Cuban-American War, he leveraged his supposed "understanding of the Negro" along with his Alabama political connections to get command of a colored volunteer regiment (the Third Alabama). At the end of World War I, he again invoked his privileged knowledge of black men to persuade General Foch to send home the Ninety-Second Division before the Armistice on the grounds that they posed a danger to the honor of French Women, whom Bullard feared they would "ravish" in the war's aftermath. "I told the American Headquarters to say to Marshal Foch that no man could be responsible for the acts of these Negroes [troops of the 92nd Division] toward Frenchwomen, and that he had better send this division home at once." Robert Lee Bullard, *Personalities and Reminiscences of the War* (Garden City, N.Y.: Doubleday, 1925), 297.

21   David Murray, *Matter, Magic, and Spirit: Representing Indian and African American Belief* (Philadelphia: University of Pennsylvania Press, 2007), 50.

22   Edward A. Pollard, *Black Diamonds Gathered in the Darkey Homes of the South* (quoted in Murray, *Matter, Magic, and Spirit*, 50–51).

23   Robert Lee Bullard, "The Scout," unpublished manuscript, box 9, Robert Lee Bullard Collection, Manuscript Division, Library of Congress.

24   Hugh Lenox Scott, *Some Memories of a Soldier* (New York: Century, 1928), 26.

25   Ibid.

26   Robert Lee Bullard, Diary Book 1–3, 54–55, box 1, Robert Lee Bullard Collection, Manuscript Division, Library of Congress (hereafter cited as Bullard, Diary Book).

27   Bullard, Diary Book 1–3, 49–50.

28   Bullard, Diary Book 1–4, 58.

29   Ibid., 54.

30   Bullard, Diary Book 1–3, 49–50.

31   Bullard, unpublished autobiography, chap. 3, "Geronimo and Garrison Years," 15–16.

32   Friedrich Katz, *The Life and Times of Pancho Villa* (Stanford, Calif.: Stanford University Press, 1998), 11.

33   Friedrich Katz. *The Ancient American Civilizations* (New York: Praeger, 1972).

34   On Indian enslavement in the Americas, see Andrés Reséndez, *The Other Slavery: The Uncovered Story of Indian Enslavement in America* (Boston: Houghton Mifflin Harcourt), 2016.

35   John Francis Bannon, *The Spanish Borderlands Frontier, 1513–1821* (Albuquerque: University of New Mexico Press, 1974), 30; Gregory Rodriguez, *Mongrels, Bastards, Orphans, and Vagabonds: Mexican Immigration and the Future of Race in America* (New York: Pantheon Books, 2007), 55.

36   On military colonies in the late colonial and early republican period, see Ana María Alonso, *Thread of Blood: Colonialism, Revolution, and Gender on Mexico's Northern Frontier* (Tucson: University of Arizona Press, 1995); and Daniel Nugent, *Spent Cartridges of Revolution: An Anthropological History of Namiquipa, Chihuahua* (Chicago: University of

Chicago Press, 1993). See also Andrés Reséndez, *Changing National Identities at the Frontier: Texas and New Mexico, 1800–1850* (Cambridge: Cambridge University Press, 2005).

37   R. Douglas Hurt, *The Indian Frontier, 1763–1846* (Albuquerque: University of New Mexico Press, 2002), 28. See also Brian Delay, *War of a Thousand Deserts: Indian Raids and the U.S.-Mexican War* (New Haven, Conn: Yale University Press, 2010). Delay argues that Indian politics and war-making played an influential role in how Mexico and the United States developed as nation-states in the nineteenth century and also shaped their relations with one another. Comanche domination of the north—and American perceptions of it—were major factors that led the United States to make war on Mexico, he argues. "Throughout the late 1830s and early 1840s, [American] editors, diplomats, congressmen, and administration officials invoked Mexicans' manifest inability to control Indians in order to denigrate Mexico's claims to its northern territories, first in Texas and, later, across the whole of the Mexican north. These fateful attitudes reached their logical conclusion in 1846 and 1847, when the United States invaded Mexico and exploited the tensions and tragedies of the ongoing war with Comanches, Kiowas, Apaches, and Navajos to conquer the north and frame the dismemberment of Mexico as an act of salvation" (p. xvii).

38   DeLay, *War of a Thousand Deserts*, 145.

39   Hurt, *Indian Frontier*, 28.

40   DeLay, *War of a Thousand Deserts*, xv.

41   Juan Bautista Pino, "Manifesto," November 24, 1829, in *American Indian Policy in the Jacksonian Era*, by Ronald N. Satz (Lincoln: University of Nebraska Press, 1975) (quoted in David J. Weber, *The Mexican Frontier, 1821–1846* [Albuquerque: University of New Mexico Press, 1982], 100–101).

42   Weber, *Mexican Frontier*, 102.

43   Worcester, "Apaches in the History of the Southwest," 30.

44   In 1849 Chihuahua paid out 7,896 pesos in bounties for scalps. Between 1871 and 1873 Sonora budgeted 4,000 for scalp bounties. In 1874 the state paid out 9,620 pesos for scalps. Hatfield, *Chasing Shadows*, 10–12.

45   José Fuentes Mares, *Y México se refugió en el desierto* (México, D.F.: Editorial Jus, S.A., 1954), 148 (quoted in Ralph A. Smith, "Indians in American Mexican Relations Before the War of 1846," *Hispanic American Historical Review* 43, no. 1 [February 1963]: 62).

46   J. Fred Rippy, "The Indians of the Southwest in the Diplomacy of the United States and Mexico, 1848–1853," *Hispanic American Historical Review* 2, no. 3 (August 1919): 363–96. See also Delay, *War of a Thousand Deserts*, xiii.

47   Bullard, unpublished autobiography, chap. 3, "Geronimo and Garrison Years," 14.

48   Joyce E. Mason, "The Use of Indian Scouts in the Apache Wars, 1870–1886" (PhD diss., Indiana University, Bloomington, 1970), 26.

49   Ibid., 29.

50   Sherry Robinson and Eve Ball, *Apache Voices: Their Stories of Survival as Told to Eve Ball* (Albuquerque: University of New Mexico Press, 2000), 102.

51   Reséndez, *Other Slavery*, 7. Reséndez notes that, in the nineteenth century, Apaches also entered the regional slave trade, raiding Mexican villages and selling captives.

52   George Crook, "The Apache Problem," *Journal of the Military Service Institution of the United States* 7 (October 1886): 263.

53   Ibid., 269.

54   Ibid.

55   John Bourke, "General Crook in the Indian Country," *Century Magazine* 41 (March 1891): 654 (quoted in J. E. Mason, "Use of Indian Scouts," 49).

56   *Tombstone Daily Epigraph*, January 17, 1883 (quoted in Hatfield, *Chasing Shadows*, 57).

57   Crook, "Apache Problem," 261.

58   Ibid., 262, 269.

59   James Kaywaykla and Eve Ball, *In the Days of Victorio: Recollections of a Warm Springs Apache* (Tucson: University of Arizona Press, 1970), 147–48. Kaywaykla notes that the appellation of Tzoe, or coyote, connotes contempt. To compare someone to a coyote is an insult.

60   Robinson and Ball, *Apache Voices,* 104.

61   Britton Davis, *The Truth About Geronimo* (Lincoln: University of Nebraska Press, 1976), ix.

62   Hermann Hagedorn, *Leonard Wood: A Biography* (New York: Harper & Brothers, 1931), 68.

63   Jack C. Lane, ed., *Chasing Geronimo: The Journal of Leonard Wood, May–September, 1886* (Albuquerque: University of New Mexico Press, 1970), 25.

64   Hagedorn, *Leonard Wood* (cited in J. E. Mason, "Use of Indian Scouts," 335).

65   Leonard Wood, "Geronimo Campaign of 1886," Gatewood Collection, Arizona Pioneer History Association (quoted in J. E. Mason, "Use of Indian Scouts," 351).

66   J. E. Mason, "Use of Indian Scouts," 184.

67   Parker, *Old Army*, 172–73.

68   Ibid., 17. Bullard exaggerated the speed and distance Apaches were capable of covering, but only slightly. George Crook reported that they could cover from forty to sixty miles a day in the rough mountainous country. Crook, "Apache Problem," 264. It should be noted that General Crook, along with many other officers who took part in wars against the Apaches, often echoed Bullard's tones of admiration for the Indians' physical prowess and feats of endurance, which they helped to turn into the stuff of legend.

69   Ibid.

70   Jack McCallum, *Leonard Wood: Rough Rider, Surgeon, Architect of American Imperialism* (New York: New York University Press, 2006), 43–44.

Chapter 4

1   The account of the origin of Pershing's nickname, Black Jack, is in Donald Smythe, *Guerrilla Warrior: The Early Life of John J. Pershing* (New York: Scribner, 1973), 44–45.

2   Military historians and biographers of John J. Pershing have understandably focused on his command of the American Expeditionary Forces in World War I. Among those who deal in some depth with his experience in the frontier West and in the Philippines are Smythe, *Guerilla Warrior*, and Frank Everson Vandiver, *Black Jack: The Life and Times of John J. Pershing* (College Station: Texas A&M University Press, 1977). Pershing's experience and unpopularity as a tactical officer at West Point are detailed in Vandiver, *Black Jack*, 1:169–72. See also Avery De Lano Andrews, *My Friend and Classmate John J. Pershing; with Notes from My War Diary* (Harrisburg, Pa.: Military Service Pub. Co., 1939).

3   According to War Department figures, the number of troops under Pershing's command in Mexico fluctuated between 8,000 and 12,000, with a monthly average of 10,000; Charles H. Harris and Louis R. Sadler, *The Great Call-Up: The Guard, the Border,*

and the Mexican Revolution (Norman: University of Oklahoma Press, 2015), 4.

4   In his message to Congress urging reform of the system of army promotion, President Roosevelt mentioned Pershing in particular at the opening of the second session of the Fifty-Eighth Congress on December 7, 1903. President Roosevelt referred to Pershing's punitive actions against the Moros: "When a man renders such service as Captain Pershing rendered last spring in the Moro campaign, it ought to be possible to reward him without at once jumping him to the grade of brigadier general." It took another three years for Pershing's promotion to come through. Andrews, *My Friend and Classmate John J. Pershing*, 61–62. See also Richard Goldhurst, *Pipe Clay and Drill: John J. Pershing, the Classic American Soldier* (New York: Reader's Digest Press, 1977), 132.

5   Vandiver, *Black Jack*, 1:22.

6   Frederick Palmer, *John J. Pershing, General of the Armies: A Biography* (Harrisburg, Pa.: Military Service Pub. Co., 1948), 13. Pershing biographer Frank Vandiver suggests that, in addition to his mother's concerns for his safety, the Civil War had been a source of tension between Pershing's parents. His mother, Anne Elizabeth Thompson, was from Tennessee and supported the Confederacy; John's father, John Frederick Pershing, opposed slavery and showed his support for the Union by flying the Stars and Stripes over their house. The senior Pershing also served as sutler to the Eighteenth Missouri Volunteer Infantry and later to the First Missouri state militia regiment when they were stationed in LaClede. This support for the Union led to a raid on the Pershings' store in 1864. On Pershing's age at the time of his application to West Point, see Smythe, *Guerrilla Warrior*, "Appendix: Pershing's Falsified Birthday," 283–84.

7   Robert Lee Bullard, *Personalities and Reminiscences of the War* (Garden City, N.Y.: Doubleday, Page, 1925), 42.

8   Vandiver, *Black Jack*, 1:51.

9   Ibid., 55.

10   George MacAdam, "The Life of General Pershing," *The World's Work* (New York: Doubleday, Page, 1918–19), 37:289–90; Angie Debo, *Geronimo: The Man, His Time, His Place* (Norman: University of Oklahoma Press, 1976), 310–11.

11   Smythe, *Guerrilla Warrior*.

12   Vandiver, *Black Jack*, 1:70–71.

13   Hugh L. Scott, "The 'Messiah Dance' in the Indian Territory," essay for the Fort Sill Lyceum, (March 1892), 14, Hugh Lenox Scott Papers, Manuscript Division, Library of Congress.

14   Richard E. Jensen, R. Eli Paul, and John E. Carter, *Eyewitness at Wounded Knee* (Lincoln: University of Nebraska Press, 1991), 27.

15   Ibid., 29.

16   American Horse's words about the railroad were recorded by Charles A. Eastman in his autobiography *From the Deep Woods to Civilization* (Mineola, N.Y.: Dover, 2003) (quoted in Jensen, Paul, and Carter, *Eyewitness at Wounded Knee*, 27).

17   Herbert T. Hoover, "The Sioux Agreement of 1889 and Its Aftermath," *South Dakota History* 19, no. 1 (1989): 58. The Sioux Agreement of March 2, 1889, reduced reservation lands in the Dakotas by 9,274,668.7 acres and left the Teton and Yanktonai tribes only 9,274,911 acres (of their original 60 million acres) split up into six smaller reservations: Cheyenne River, Crow Creek, Lower Brule, Pine Ridge, Rosebud, and Standing Rock.

18   The account of the military response to the Ghost Dance is informed by the fol-

lowing books: Richard E Jensen., R. Eli Paul, and John E. Carter, *Eyewitness at Wounded Knee* (Lincoln: University of Nebraska Press, 1991), 17–20; Robert M. Utley, *The Last Days of the Sioux Nation* (New Haven, Conn.: Yale University Press, 1963), 200–230; Jeffrey Ostler, *The Plains Sioux and U.S. Colonialism from Lewis and Clark to Wounded Knee* (Cambridge: Cambridge University Press, 2006); and Eli Seavey Ricker and Richard E. Jensen, *Voices of the American West* (Lincoln: University of Nebraska Press, 2005), 1:208–26.

19   Jim Lacey, *Pershing* (New York: Palgrave Macmillan, 2008), 73.

20   John J. Pershing *My Life Before the World War, 1860–1917: A Memoir by General of the Armies John J. Pershing*, ed. John T. Greenwood (Lexington: University Press of Kentucky, 2013), 80.

21   Pershing wrote to his friend Assistant Secretary of War George D. Meiklejohn on February 12, 1900, to recommend the organization of irregular troops made up of different ethnic groups from Mindanao in the Philippines; Pershing to Meiklejohn, box 28, folder 179, Record Group 3500, George D. Meiklejohn Collection, Nebraska State Historical Society. This initiative is discussed in more detail in Chapter 6.

22   Willa Cather Sibert and James R. Shively, *Writings from Willa Cather's Campus Years* (Lincoln: University of Nebraska Press, 1950), 16.

23   Palmer, *John J. Pershing, General of the Armies*, 32.

24   Vandiver, *Black Jack*, 1:107–8.

25   Ibid., 123; Palmer, *John J. Pershing, General of the Armies*, 32.

26   *Lincoln (Neb.) Daily Star*, February 17, 1903; I am grateful to James E. Potter, senior research historian at the Nebraska Historical Society for searching University and Nebraska newspapers for information about the "Pershing cannon" on my behalf.

27   John J. Pershing to the Board of Regents, University of Nebraska, October 2, 1891, reproduced in Vandiver, *Black Jack*, 1:112.

28   For an insightful account of the educational deficiencies of outstate Nebraska students matriculating at the university, see Alvin Saunders Johnson, *Pioneer's Progress: An Autobiography* (Lincoln: University of Nebraska Press, 1962). This autobiography also includes a sensitively rendered account of the author's education, a bout of typhoid he suffered as a volunteer in the Spanish-American War, and his subsequent academic career.

29   Cather and Shively, *Writings from Willa Cather's Campus Years*, 124, 128. The quotations are drawn from letters solicited from classmates Jesse B. Becker and Jasper Hunt in 1948. Jesse Becker also recollected that Cather was "the first girl that I ever saw in 'suspenders'" and speculated that they were "merely pieces of cloth crossed over her waist and attached to her belt . . . the effect is what I remember," 124.

30   Many years later, Cather told one of her sisters that she had a recurring dream in which she was seated outside the office of her mathematics professor (not Pershing) waiting for him to make a decision on a provisional exam she had taken to satisfy the math requirement. "In her dream, he always came out and told her that she had failed and could not graduate." Cather and Shively, *Writings from Willa Cather's Campus Years*, 19. In fact, Willa Cather graduated from the University of Nebraska in 1895, the same year Pershing left for Fort Assinniboine in Montana.

31   Louise Pound and Willa Cather were both members of the women's cadet corps, known variously as Company D' (Company D prime) or Company E. The female cadet unit had been disbanded under Pershing's predecessor Lieutenant Thomas W. Griffith, Eighteenth Infantry. Vandiver, *Black Jack*, 1:108.

32   Dorothy Canfield Fisher to Henry Castor, July 30, 1953 (quoted in Vandiver, *Black Jack*, 1:117). Dorothy Canfield was the daughter of the chancellor. She remained in contact with Pershing for the rest of his life.

33   Alvin Saunders Johnson, *Pioneer's Progress*, 78.

34   Vandiver, *Black Jack*, 1:119.

35   For more on the relationship between Pershing, Magoon, and Meiklejohn and their role in creating the Bureau of Insular Affairs, see Katharine Bjork, "Prairie Imperialists: The Bureau of Insular Affairs and Continuities in Colonial Expansion from Nebraska to Cuba and the Philippines," *Nebraska History* 95, no. 4 (Winter 2014): 216–29.

36   Vandiver, *Black Jack*, 1:38, 125.

37   Ibid., 125.

38   William H. Leckie and Shirley A. Leckie, *The Buffalo Soldiers: A Narrative of the Black Cavalry in the West* (Norman: University of Oklahoma Press, 2003), 8.

39   Matthew F. Steele, "The 'Color Line' in the Army," *North American Review* 183 (December 21, 1906): 1287.

40   Vandiver, *Black Jack*, 1:125.

41   The fort was originally given the name Assinniboine. This was later changed to reflect the more common spelling, Assiniboine.

42   Beth LaDow, *The Medicine Line: Life and Death on a North American Borderland* (New York: Routledge, 2001), 24.

43   Ibid., xviii.

44   Paul L. Hedren, *After Custer: Loss and Transformation in Sioux Country* (Norman: University of Oklahoma Press, 2011), 12, 60.

45   LaDow, *Medicine Line*, 22.

46   Ibid., 42. LaDow's wonderful metaphor for the border of the buoy at sea is on p. 7.

47   Hedren, *After Custer*, 153.

48   David G. McCrady, *Living with Strangers: The Nineteenth-Century Sioux and the Canadian-American Borderlands* (Lincoln: University of Nebraska Press, 2006), 4–6. As McCrady astutely observes, the historiography of Indian Wars often stops at the border. Thus, neither Canadian nor U.S. history has adequately dealt with the continuity of interactions between native peoples and European settlers or their governments. He goes on to argue that the Sioux in particular were a quintessential "borderlands people," who were skilled in making use of the border for their own political ends. "They made tremendous tactical use of their proximity to different groups of Europeans," he writes. "They were pragmatic, switching their support from one group to another, always with Sioux needs uppermost in their minds," 113.

49   *Encyclopedia of North American Indians*, ed. Frederick E. Hoxie (Boston: Houghton Mifflin, 1996), s.v. "Riel, Louis (1844–85)," by Olive Patricia Dickason, accessed August 18, 2016, *Credo Reference*, http://ezproxy.hamline.edu:2048/login?qurl=http%3A%2F%2Fsearch.credoreference.com%2Fcontent%2Fentry%2Fhmenai%2Friel_louis_1844_85%2F0. See also LaDow, *Medicine Line*, 66–69.

50   Hedren, *After Custer*, 60.

51   McCrady, *Living with Strangers*, 111–12.

52   Verne Dusenberry, "The Rocky Boy Indians," *Montana Magazine of History* 4, no. 1 (1954): 1–15.

53   Pershing, *My Life Before the World War*, 124.

54   Ibid., 88.

55   Nicholas P. Hardeman, "Brick Strong Hold of the Border: Fort Assinniboine, 1879–1911," *Montana: The Magazine of Western History* 29, no. 2 (1979): 54–67. Major General Nelson A. Miles assumed command of the Army of the United States on October 5, 1895. General Order No. 54, reprinted in Nelson Appleton Miles, *Serving the Republic: Memoirs of the Civil and Military Life of Nelson A. Miles, Lieutenant-General, United States Army* (New York: Harper & Brothers, 1911), 260.

56   Robert Wooster, *Nelson A. Miles and the Twilight of the Frontier Army* (Lincoln: University of Nebraska Press, 1996), 105–10; George William Baird and Frederic Remington, *A Report to the Citizens, Concerning Certain Late Disturbances on the Western Frontier: Involving Sitting Bull, Crazy Horse, Chief Joseph and Geronimo, Opposed in the Field by Forces Under the Command of General Nelson A. (Bear-Coat) Miles* (Ashland, Calif.: L. Osborne, 1972), 50–51.

57   Baird and Remington, *Report to the Citizens*, 53. On February 9, General Sherman (whose niece Mary was Miles's wife) wrote to warn him not to campaign north of the border. Sherman to Miles, February 9, 1878, quoted in Brian C. Pohanka and John M. Carroll, eds., *Nelson Miles: A Documentary History of His Military Career, 1861–1901* (Glendale, Calif.: Arthur H. Clark, 1985), 116.

58   Robert M. Utley, *The Lance and the Shield: The Life and Times of Sitting Bull* (London: Pimlico, 1998), 207–9.

59   Hedren, *After Custer*, 57.

60   LaDow, *Medicine Line*, 59.

61   Ibid., xviii–xv.

62   Pershing, *My Life Before the World War*, 94.

63   Ibid.; Andrews, *My Friend and Classmate John J. Pershing*, 54.

64   Goldhurst, *Pipe Clay and Drill*, 56. On Theodore Roosevelt's actions in Cuba, Pershing later wrote: "Without disparagement of Mr. Roosevelt's brief few weeks of military experience, it must be said it was the extensive publicity it received rather than the actual service that brought him such exceptional political preferment" (quoted in Goldhurst, *Pipe Clay and Drill*, 80).

65   Bjork, "Prairie Imperialists: The Bureau of Insular Affairs," 228n2. In his memoirs, Pershing relates how he was "guilty of play[ing] politics" in the matter of Meiklejohn's appointment as assistant secretary of war. Pershing, *My Life Before the World War*, 95.

66   Pershing, *My Life Before the World War*, 102. See also Andrews, *My Friend and Classmate John J. Pershing*, 53. The order prohibiting officers on the West Point faculty from transferring to active duty was intended to prevent loss of personnel from the academy.

Chapter 5

1   Jimmy M. Skaggs, *The Great Guano Rush: Entrepreneurs and American Overseas Expansion* (New York: St. Martin's Press, 1994), 66. Sixty-six of the rocks, islands, and keys claimed by individuals were recognized by the U.S. Department of State as appurtenances of the United States. Fewer than two dozen were ever mined for guano. Nine of the islands continue as U.S. possessions.

2   Paul T. Burlin, *Imperial Maine and Hawai'i: Interpretive Essays in the History of Nineteenth-Century Expansion* (New York: Lexington, 2006), 172–74.

3   Walter LaFeber, *The New Empire: An Interpretation of American Expansion, 1860–1898* (Ithaca, N.Y.: Cornell University Press, 1998), 28.

4   William Seward, quoted in Louis A Pérez Jr., *The War of 1898: The United States and Cuba in History and Historiography* (Chapel Hill: University of North Carolina Press, 1998), 1.

5   John Quincy Adams to Hugh Nelson, April 28, 1823, U.S. Congress, House of Representatives, 32nd Cong., 1st sess., H.R. Doc. No. 121, Ser. 648: 7, cited in Louis Pérez Jr., *Cuba and the United States: Ties of Singular Intimacy* (Athens: University of Georgia Press, 2003), 38.

6   William Seward, quoted in Pérez, *War of 1898*, 1.

7   Paul Lawrence Farber, *Discovering Birds: The Emergence of Ornithology as a Scientific Discipline, 1760–1850* (Baltimore, Md.: Johns Hopkins University Press, 1997), 33. See also Stephen Jay Gould, *The Mismeasure of Man* (New York: W. W. Norton, 1981).

8   Darrin P. Lunde, *The Naturalist: Theodore Roosevelt and the Rise of American Natural History* (New York: Crown, 2016), 16.

9   Mark V. Barrow, Jr., *A Passion for Birds: American Ornithology After Audubon* (Princeton, N.J.: Princeton University Press, 1998), 9.

10   Lunde, *Naturalist*, 70, 78.

11   Asa Briggs, *Victorian Things* (Stroud: Sutton, 2003), 353 (quoted in Mark V. Barrow Jr., *Passion for Birds*, 12).

12   Pérez, *War of 1898*, 5.

13   "The Ostend Manifesto," October 18, 1854, House Executive Document 93, 33rd Cong., 2nd sess. (Washington, D.C.,1855), 127–32 (quoted in Pérez, *War of 1898*, 19).

14   Pérez, *War of 1898*, 13.

15   Pérez, *Cuba and the United States*, 92–93.

16   Louis A. Pérez, Jr., *Cuba Between Empires: 1878–1902* (Pittsburgh: University of Pittsburgh Press, 1983), 182.

17   Pérez, *Cuba and the United States*, 18–19, 59–65.

18   Ibid., 69.

19   Pérez, *War of 1898*, 58. In 1974 Admiral Hyman G. Rickover coordinated a reappraisal of the causes of the destruction of the USS *Maine*. The judgment reached in this inquiry was that the ship had been destroyed by an internal explosion. Hyman George Rickover, *How the Battleship Maine Was Destroyed* (Annapolis, Md.: Naval Institute Press, 1995).

20   Amy Kaplan, "Black and Blue on San Juan Hill," in *The Anarchy of Empire in the Making of U.S. Culture* (Cambridge, Mass.: Harvard University Press, 2002), 141. On the symbolic reunification of North and South through the Spanish-American War, see also Kristin Hoganson, *Fighting for American Manhood: How Gender Politics Provoked the Spanish-American and Philippine-American Wars* (New Haven, Conn.: Yale University Press, 1998).

21   Booker T. Washington,"The Spanish-American War, Causes of It; Vivid Descriptions of Fierce Battles; Superb Heroism and Daring Deeds of the Negro Soldier," in *A New Negro for a New Century* (New York: Arno Press, 1969), 26.

22   George P. Marks III, *The Black Press Views American Imperialism* (New York: Arno Press, 1971).

23   Ada Ferrer, *Insurgent Cuba: Race, Nation, and Revolution, 1868–1898* (Chapel Hill: University of North Carolina Press, 1999), 3

24   "Bishop Turner Against Negro's Enlistment," *Cleveland (Ohio) Gazette*, October 8, 1898, reprinted in Marks, *Black Press*, 89.

25   Richard Goldhurst, *Pipe Clay and Drill: John J. Pershing, the Classic American Soldier* (New York: Reader's Digest Press, 1977), 58; Donald Smythe, *Guerrilla Warrior: The Early Life of John J. Pershing* (New York: Scribner, 1973), 60.

26   Jim Lacey, *Pershing: A Biography* (New York: Palgrave Macmillan, 2008), 22. George D. Meiklejohn approved Pershing's transfer from his teaching duty at West Point, whose staff were supposedly "frozen" in place, to the Tenth Cavalry on a day when Secretary of War Russell Alger was absent from Washington. Goldhurst, *Pipe Clay and Drill*, 66.

27   John J. Pershing to George D. Meiklejohn, July 16, 1898, box 28, folder 176, Record Group 3500, George D. Meiklejohn Collection, Nebraska State Historical Society (hereafter cited as Meiklejohn Collection).

28   Ibid. Emphasis in the original.

29   Marvin Fletcher, "The Negro Soldier and the United States Army, 1891–1917" (PhD diss., University of Wisconsin, 1968), 184–85.

30   Ibid., 231–32.

31   Pershing to George D. Meiklejohn, July 16, 1898, Meiklejohn Collection.

32   Russell K. Brown, "A Flag for the Tenth Immunes," in *Brothers to the Buffalo Soldiers: Perspectives on the African American Militia and Volunteers, 1865–1917*, ed. Bruce A. Glasrud (Columbia: University of Missouri Press, 2013), 215–16.

33   Ibid., 209.

34   Pershing to George D. Meiklejohn, July 16, 1898, Meiklejohn Collection.

35   Ibid.

36   Richard Gott, *Cuba: A New History* (New Haven, Conn.: Yale University Press, 2005), 115.

37   Pérez, *Cuba and the United States*, 119–21.

38   Patricio N. Abinales, *Making Mindanao: Cotabato and Davao in the Formation of the Philippine Nation-State* (Quezon City: Ateneo de Manila University Press, 2000), 71; for more on the Nebraska ties of Pershing and Meiklejohn, see Katharine Bjork, "Prairie Imperialists: The Bureau of Insular Affairs and Continuities in Colonial Expansion from Nebraska to Cuba and the Philippines," *Nebraska History* 95, no. 4 (Winter 2014): 216–29.

39   Irene Aloha Wright, *Cuba* (New York: Macmillan, 1910), 322 (quoted in Pérez, *Cuba and the United States*, 127).

40   Goldhurst, *Pipe Clay and Drill*, 56.

41   Hugh Lenox Scott, *Some Memories of a Soldier* (New York: Century, 1928), 221.

42   H. L. Scott to Mary Scott, August 19, 1899, microfilm 17,249, Hugh Lenox Scott Papers, Manuscript Division, Library of Congress (hereafter cited as Scott Papers).

43   H. L. Scott to Mary Scott, December 8, 1899, microfilm 17,249, Scott Papers.

44   Ibid.

45   H. L. Scott, *Some Memories of a Soldier*, 230.

46   Shephard Krech III and Barbara A. Hail, *Collecting Native America, 1870–1960* (Washington, D.C.: Smithsonian Institution Press, 1999), 155.

47   H. L. Scott to Mary Scott, July 1, 1899, microfilm 17,249, Scott Papers. On the practice and significance of American soldiers taking symbols of Spanish rule as souvenirs, see Mariel Iglesias Utset, *A Cultural History of Cuba During the U.S. Occupation, 1898–1902*, trans. Russ Davidson (Chapel Hill: University of North Carolina Press, 2011), 13–14.

48   Woodrow Wilson to Hugh Lenox Scott, December 11, 1903, Princeton, N.J., box 7, general correspondence file, Scott Papers. In his letter acknowledging the gift of the stocks, Wilson refers to their purpose as the punishment of criminals. Whether Scott or Wilson

knew it or not, stocks were used in Cuba to discipline slaves.

49   H. L. Scott to his wife, February 28, 1899, microfilm 16,787, Scott Papers.

50   *La aurora de Yurumí:* "Por la tangente," July 26, 1881 (quoted in John Charles Chasteen, *National Rhythms, African Roots: A Deep History of Latin American Popular Dance* [Albuquerque: University of New Mexico Press, 2004], 81).

51   Mariel Iglesias Utset, *Las metáforas del cambio en la vida cotidiana: Cuba, 1898–1902* (Havana: Ediciones Unión, 2003), 96.

52   H. L. Scott to Mary Scott, July 21, 1899, microfilm 17,249, Scott Papers.

53   Chasteen, *National Rhythms, African Roots,* 81.

54   H. L. Scott, *Some Memories of a Soldier,* 253.

55   Ibid.

56   Ibid., 253. Scott also wrote in his memoirs about the success of such courtesy in winning him friendship and influence with Mexicans during his border service. See in particular Scott's account of treating the "grafting lawyer" Pedro Morales to breakfast on the train from El Paso to Naco, 511.

57   Louis A. Pérez, Jr., *Cuba: Between Reform and Revolution* (Oxford: Oxford University Press, 2015), 144.

58   Pérez, *Cuba,* 147–48; Jack Edward McCallum, *Leonard Wood: Rough Rider, Surgeon, Architect of American Imperialism* (New York: New York University Press, 2006), 182–85.

59   H. L. Scott, *Some Memories of a Soldier,* 263.

60   Ibid., 264.

61   The reference to "mopping up Havana affairs," is in H. L. Scott, *Some Memories of a Soldier,* 273. For Scott's report on destroying the records of the Military Occupation of Cuba by the United States from 1898 to 1902, see Memorandum for the Chief of Staff, War Department, Bureau of Insular Affairs, October 27, 1911, from Col. Scott, 3rd Cavalry, U.S. Army, box 54, file 4, general correspondence, 1911, Leonard Wood Collection, Manuscript Division, Library of Congress. Incoming President Estrada Palma attempted to convince the outgoing American military government to turn over its thirty tons of records to the new government, but this request was strenuously rejected by Wood. McCallum, *Leonard Wood,* 195, 322n212.

62   Robert Lee Bullard, Diary Book 1 (December 1, 1899 to June 13, 1901), account of April 1898, 82, Robert Lee Bullard Manuscript Collection, Manuscript Division, Library of Congress (hereafter cited as Diary Book).

63   The quotation is from Bullard, Diary Book 1 (December 1, 1899 to June 13, 1901), account of April 1898, 93; see also Allan Reed Millett, *The General: Robert L. Bullard and Officership in the United States Army, 1881–1925* (Westport, Conn.: Greenwood Press, 1975), 104–5.

64   Bullard, Diary Book 1 (December 1, 1899 to June 13, 1901), account of September–November 1898, 88–94; Millett, *General,* 106.

65   Bullard, unpublished autobiography, chap. 6, p. 27, Robert Lee Bullard Collection, Manuscript Division, Library of Congress.

66   Ibid., 24.

67   Ibid.

68   Robert Lee Bullard, "The Negro Volunteer: Some Characteristics," *Journal of the Military Service Institution of the United States* 29 (July 1901): 29.

69   Ibid., 38–39.

70   Robert Lee Bullard, *Personalities and Reminiscences of the War* (Garden City, N.Y.; Doubleday, Page, 1925), 295.

71   J. (James) Franklin Bell, biographical entry, in *My Life Before the War, 1860–1917: A Memoir by General of the Armies John J. Pershing*, by John J. Pershing, ed. John T. Greenwood (Lexington: University Press of Kentucky, 2013), 477–78. Bell served with the Seventh Cavalry in the Dakotas. He was on leave during the Wounded Knee massacre, but later became aide-de-camp to James W. Forsyth, who had been in command at Wounded Knee when the latter was made commanding general of the Department of California (1894–1897). Bell's command of the Third Separate Brigade against Filipino insurgents in Luzon is treated in more detail in Chapter 6.

72   U.S. War Department, "Report Army of Cuban Pacification," in *Annual Reports of the War Department, 1906–1907*, vols. 3–4 (Washington, D.C.: Government Printing Office, 1907); Bullard's diary accounts of his intelligence work on behalf of the provisional governor are fairly vague, but do provide a sense of his travels throughout the island to look into rumors of unrest as well as to investigate alleged corruption and minor disputes.

73   Bjork, "Prairie Imperialists," 227.

74   Bullard, Diary Book 3, December 22, 1906, 143–45, and May 10, 1907, 164, Havana, box 1.

75   Robert Lee Bullard, "The Cuban Negro," *North American Review* 184, no. 611 (1907): 623–30 (quotation on 623).

76   Robert Lee Bullard, Notebook 15, pp. 28–29, box 4, folder 3, Robert Lee Bullard Collection, Manuscript Division, Library of Congress; and Robert Lee Bullard, "Military Pacification," *Journal of the Military Service Institution of the United States* 46, no. 163 (January–February 1910): 1–24.

77   Bullard, Diary Book 4, entries for October and November 1907, and February 9, 1908; see also Millett, *General*, 196–97.

78   Rebecca Scott, *Degrees of Freedom: Louisiana and Cuba After Slavery* (Cambridge, Mass.: Harvard University Press, 2008), 214.

79   Bullard, Diary Book 4, [January 8, 1909].

80   Bullard, Diary Book 4, February 9, 1908, p. 30, Washington, D.C.; Robert Lee Bullard, "The Teddy Buck: His Getting in Cuba and Journey to the White House," *Sports Afield*, June 1910, 513–14.

81   Bullard, Diary Book 4, January 8, [1909]; Bullard's diary entry gives the year as 1908, but the entry seems to have been written at the beginning of 1909.

Chapter 6

1   Brian McCallister Linn, *The Philippine War, 1899–1902* (Lawrence: University Press of Kansas, 2000), 8.

2   The figures on deaths from war and disease are from Patricio N. Abinales and Donna J. Amoroso, *State and Society in the Philippines* (Lanham, Md.: Rowman & Littlefield, 2005), 117; Abinales and Amoroso in turn cite John Morgan Gates, "War-Related Deaths in the Philippines, 1898–1902," *Pacific Historical Review* 53, no. 3 (1984): 367; and Ken De Bevoise, *Agents of Apocalyse: Epidemic Disease in the Colonial Philippines* (Princeton, N.J.: Princeton University Press), 1995.

3   "Treaty of Peace between the United States of America and the Kingdom of Spain (Treaty of Paris)" (1898), reproduced in *The Philippine National Territory: A Collec-*

tion of Related Documents, ed. Raphael Perpetuo M. Lotilla (Quezon City: University of the Philippines Law Center, 1995), 32–39.

4   Instructions from President William McKinley for Maj. Gen. Wesley Merritt, U.S. Army, Commanding Army of Occupation to the Philippines, Washington, May 19, 1898, published in United States Adjutant-General's Office, *Correspondence Relating to the War with Spain and Conditions Growing Out of the Same: Including the Insurrection in the Philippine Islands and the China Relief Expedition, between the Adjutant-General of the Army and Military Commanders in the United States, Cuba, Porto Rico, China, and the Philippine Islands, from April 15, 1898, to July 30, 1902* (Washington: Government Printing Office, 1902), 2:676.

5   Linn, *Philippine War,* 198.

6   Ibid., 100–101.

7   Most of the companies of the Thirty-Ninth were organized at Fort Crook, Nebraska. They entrained for the Pacific coast in October. Augmented by several more companies organized at Vancouver Barracks, Bullard's regiment of some 1,300 men and fifty officers embarked on two transport ships that left Portland on November 2. Robert Lee Bullard, unpublished autobiography, chap. 6, "A New Volunteer Regiment and Its Start in the War in the Philippines," 31, box 1, Robert Lee Bullard Collection, Library of Congress (hereafter cited as Bullard Collection); Arthur W. Orton, Fred D. Shadell, and C. Duffy Lewis, *History of the Thirty-Ninth U.S. Volunteer Infantry, "Bullard's Indians"* (s.l.: 39th U.S. Volunteer Infantry Association, 1949).

8   Instructions from President William McKinley for Maj. Gen. Wesley Merritt, U.S. Army, Commanding Army of Occupation to the Philippines, Washington, May 19, 1898, published in United States Adjutant-General's Office, *Correspondence Relating to the War with Spain,* 1:676.

9   Robert Lee Bullard, "Military Pacification," *Journal of the Military Service Institution of the United States* 46, no. 163 (January–February 1910): 22.

10   Bullard, "Military Pacification," 8.

11   John J. Pershing to George Meiklejohn, April 5, 1900, Zamboanga, box 319, John J. Pershing Collection, Manuscript Division, Library of Congress.

12   In addition to the four commanding generals who had served in the Indian Wars, William A. Williams points out that twenty-six out of thirty generals who served there were also veterans of the Indian Wars. Walter L. Williams, "United States Indian Policy and the Debate over Philippine Annexation: Implications for the Origins of American Imperialism," *Journal of American History* 66, no. 4 (1980): 810–31. On the continuities between the frontier army and U.S. imperial expansion, see also Frank Schumacher, "The American Way of Empire: National Tradition and Transatlantic Adaptation in America's Search for Imperial Identity, 1898–1910," *German Historical Institute Bulletin,* no. 31 (Fall 2002): 35–50.

13   Elwell S. Otis, *The Indian Question* (New York: Sheldon, 1878), 260–61.

14   David J. Silbey, *A War of Frontier and Empire: The Philippine-American War, 1899–1902* (New York: Farrar, Straus and Giroux, 2007), 121. This reinforced an earlier decree that all males throughout the archipelago between the ages of sixteen and fifty-nine must equip themselves with bolos and join a militia directed by municipal officials loyal to the revolution throughout the Philippines; see Linn, *Philippine War,* 58.

15   John J. Pershing, *My Life Before the World War, 1860–1917: A Memoir by General of the Armies John J. Pershing,* ed. John T. Greenwood (Lexington: University Press of Kentucky, 2013), 140–42; Allan Reed Millett, *The General: Robert L. Bullard and Officership in*

the United States Army, 1881–1925 (Westport, Conn.: Greenwood Press, 1975), 124–25.

16   Bullard, autobiography, 33–34.

17   Orton, Shadell, and Lewis, *History of the Thirty-Ninth U.S. Volunteer Infantry*, 4. For an account of the Luzon campaigns, see also Linn, *Philippine War*, chap. 8.

18   Bullard, autobiography, 34.

19   Ibid., 38.

20   Orton, Shadell, and Lewis, *History of the Thirty-Ninth U.S. Volunteer Infantry*, 5–6.

21   Bullard, autobiography, 34.

22   Thomas J. Breen, stanza 13 of "Song, respectfully dedicated to Colonel L. R. Bullard [*sic*] of the 39th Infantry U.S.V.," following entry for March 7, 1901, San Tomás, P.I., Diary Book 1, box 1, Bullard Collection.

23   Robert Lee Bullard, "The Scout," unpublished manuscript, box 9, Bullard Collection.

24   "39th U.S. Vol. Infty. Assn.: Bullard's American Indians," *Bulletin* 126 (October 1968): 1; Spanish-American War Veterans Survey, 39th Regiment, box 71, Military History Institute, U.S. Army War College.

25   Handwritten note by Robert L. Bullard on a copy of his military service record, box 5, Correspondence, 1945–46, Bullard Collection.

26   Millett, *General*, 138.

27   Bullard, "Military Pacification," 19.

28   Millett, *General*, 149.

29   Ibid., 142.

30   Bullard, "Military Pacification," 15.

31   Linn, *Philippine War*, 170.

32   Millet, *General*, 139.

33   Ibid., 141.

34   Silbey, *War of Frontier and Empire*, 132.

35   Bullard, "Military Pacification," 9. Bullard's notes on the subject of pacification are to be found in Notebook 15, box 4, folder 3, Bullard Collection.

36   "Annual Report of Maj. Gen. Arthur MacArthur, U.S.A., Commanding the Division of the Philippines and Military Governor in the Philippine Islands," in *Annual Reports of the War Department, 1901*, vol. 1, pt. 4, 88–114, quoted in Millett, *General*, 141.

37   Millett, *General*, 142.

38   Bullard, "The Tricksters Tricked," unpublished short story, box 9, autobiographical writings file, Bullard Collection.

39   Italics added. Bullard, "Deafness Cured; Spanish Taught," unpublished short story, box 9, autobiographical writings file, Bullard Collection.

40   Ibid.

41   Bullard, September 9, 1903, Diary Book 2, p. 165, box 1, Bullard Collection.

42   Bullard, "Military Pacification," 22.

43   Col. R. L. Bullard to Adj. Gen. Second District, Department of Southern Luzon, September 2, 1900, cited in Millett, *General*, 144.

44   Historian Alfred W. McCoy has written extensively on the history and contemporary uses of torture. He notes that "Waterboarding, though scientifically refined by CIA scientists after 9/11, dates back to the sixteenth century and was described in graphic detail in a 1541 French judicial handbook." Alfred W. McCoy, *Torture and Impunity: The U.S. Doc-*

trine of Coercive Interrogation (Madison: University of Wisconsin Press, 2012), 19.

45   Private Hines, quoted in "Returned Soldiers tell of Brutal Deeds Committed in the Philippines," *San Francisco (Calif.) Call*, April 29, 1902, "Chronicling America: Historic American Newspapers," Library of Congress, http://chroniclingamerica.loc.gov/lccn/sn85066387/1902-04-29/ed-1/seq-1/.

46   Paul Kramer, "The Water Cure," *New Yorker*, February 28, 2008.

47   Silbey, *War of Frontier and Empire*, 175–76.

48   Linn, *Philippine War*, 299.

49   Ibid., 310.

50   Bullard, "Military Pacification," 8.

51   Linn, *Philippine War*, 311.

52   Ibid.

53   Paul L. Hedren, *After Custer: Loss and Transformation in Sioux Country* (Norman: University of Oklahomoa Press, 2011), 51.

54   Stuart Creighton Miller, *"Benevolent Assimilation": The American Conquest of the Philippines, 1899–1903* (New Haven, Conn.: Yale University Press, 1982), 220.

55   Linn, *Philippine War*, 303.

56   The quotations are from John Morgan Gates, *Schoolbooks and Krags: The United States Army in the Philippines, 1898–1902* (Westport, Conn.: Greenwood Press, 1973), 263, and Linn, *Philippine War*, 301; they are both included in a laudatory paper by Robert D. Ramsey III, *A Masterpiece of Counterguerrilla Warfare: BG J. Franklin Bell in the Philippines, 1901–1902*, Long War Series Occasional Paper 25 (Fort Leavenworth, Kans.: Combat Studies Institute Press, 2007), 1.

57   See James D. Campbell, *"Making Riflemen from Mud": Restoring the Army's Culture of Irregular Warfare* (Carlisle, Pa.: Strategic Studies Institute, U.S. Army War College), 2007; also see Timothy K. Deady, "Lessons from a Successful Counterinsurgency: The Philippines, 1899–1902," U.S. Army War College, *Parameters* 35, no. 1 (Spring 2005): 53–68.

58   Ramsey, *Masterpiece of Counterguerilla Warfare*, 6.

59   Italics added. Neville Chamberlain, commandant of the Punjab Frontier Force in the 1850s (not the prime minister) (quoted in Byron Farwell, *Queen Victoria's Little Wars* [New York: Harper & Row, 1972], 325).

60   Remarks of Brig. Gen. J. Franklin Bell to officers stationed at Batangas, December 1, 1901, reprinted in Ramsey, *Masterpiece of Counterguerilla Warfare*, 32–33.

J. Franklin Bell to Gen. Wheaton, Batangas, December 26, 1901 (quoted in Ramsey, *Masterpiece of Counterguerilla Warfare*, 10).

61   Ibid., 32–33.

62   Remarks of Brig. Gen. J. Franklin Bell (quoted in Ramsey, *Masterpiece of Counterguerilla Warfare*, 34).

63   Ibid., 37.

64   J. Franklin Bell to Loyd Wheaton, December 26, 1901, Batangas, reproduced in Ramsey, *Masterpiece of Counterguerrilla Warfare*, 10.

65   Glenn Anthony May, *A Past Updated: Further Essays on Philippine History and Historiography* (Quezon City: New Day, 2013), 99–100.

66   Telegraphic Circular No. 2, December 8, 1901, reproduced in Campbell, "Making Riflemen from Mud," 45.

67   Glenn Anthony May, *Battle for Batangas: A Philippine Province at War* (New Haven, Conn.: Yale University Press, 1991), 255–56. The figures on the crowding of

Balaguenos into the "zones" is from another article by May, "The 'Zones' of Batangas," *Philippine Studies* 29, no. 1 (1981): 99.

68   Two authors who have reviewed the claims of historians about the number of deaths in the war include Gates, "War-Related Deaths in the Philippines, 1898–1902," and Bruce Gordon, "Mass Deaths in the Philippine-American War," *Bulletin of the American Historical Collection* 32, no. 2 (April 2004): 63–66.

69   May, "'Zones' of Batangas," 95.

70   Ibid.

71   Linn, *Philippine War*, 304.

Chapter 7

Source for first epigraph: The quotation attributed to the Sultan of Sulu was reportedly made during the visit of Captain E. B. Pratt with two battalions of the Twenty-Third Infantry, consisting of about eight hundred men and officers, in May 1899. Entry 5, "The Sulu Islands, General Conditions," 6, box 152, file 980: Summary of Army Relations with Sultan of Sulu, May 1899 through March 1900, Records of the Bureau of Insular Affairs, Record Group 350, National Archives and Records Administration.

1   George Ade, *The Sultan of Sulu: An Original Satire in Two Acts* (New York: R. H. Russell, 1903). A "Note" introducing the play says, in part: "Sulu, or Jolo, is the largest of the southerly islands in the Philippine group. The chief ruler of the island is Hadji Mohammed Jamlul Ki-Ram, Sultan of Sulu and Brother of the Sun. His rule has been disputed by certain dattos or chiefs, with whom he has kept up a running warfare. One of the characteristic features of this warfare has been the abduction of women. The natives of Sulu are Mohammedans, polygamists, and slave-holders."

2   Ibid., 17.

3   Patricio N. Abinales and Donna J. Amoroso, *State and Society in the Philippines* (Lanham, Md.: Rowman & Littlefield, 2005), 70. The italicized text is as it appears in the original.

4   Ade, *Sultan of Sulu*, 13.

5   Proclamation to Lake Lanao Moros by General Chaffee, April 13, 1902, box 370, file 1: Philippines, 1901–1903, John J. Pershing Collection, Manuscript Division, Library of Congress (hereafter cited as Pershing Collection).

6   Copy of U.S. Consul General at Singapore to Secretary of State John Hay, September 22, 1903, 3, entry 5, box 152, file 980-27, Records of the Bureau of Insular Affairs, Record Group 350, National Archives and Records Administration (hereafter cited as NARA). The treaty became known as the Bates Agreement.

7   "The Sulu Islands, General Conditions," 2, entry 5, box 152, file 980, Records of the Bureau of Insular Affairs, Record Group 350, NARA.

8   See note on Annex 3 to Protocol 16, "Treaty," 221, entry 5, file 980-17, Records of the Bureau of Insular Affairs, Record Group 350, NARA.

9   *Treaty with the Sultan of Sulu*, 56th Cong., 1st sess., S. Doc. 136, February 1, 1900, 1.

10   Robert Lee Bullard, Diary Book 1–4, p. 58, box 1, Robert Lee Bullard Collection, Manuscript Division, Library of Congress (hereafter cited as Bullard Collection).

11   English translation of Report [in Spanish] by Rufino Deloso on an expedition

ordered by the Filipino Junta at Hong Kong with the objective of making an alliance with the Moros in order to "advise them to assume a hostile attitude towards the United States troops," June–July 1901, box 317, file 4: Camp Vicars, Pershing Collection; see also Brian McAllister Linn, *The Philippine War, 1899–1902* (Chapel Hill: University of North Carolina Press, 2008), 227–28; and George William Jornacion, *The Time of the Eagles: United States Army Officers and the Pacification of the Philippines Moros, 1899–1913* (Ann Arbor, Mich.: University Microfilms International, 1978), 50–52.

12   Peter G. Gowing, "Mandate in Moroland: The American Government of Muslim Filipinos, 1899–1920" (PhD diss., Syracuse University, 1968), 26. Robert A. Fulton notes that the Americans did not find out that the Sultan had never responded to Aguinaldo's overture until after the war; Robert A. Fulton, *Moroland: The History of Uncle Sam and the Moros, 1899–1920* (Bend, Ore.: Tumalo Creek Press, 2009), 377.

13   H. L. Scott to daughter Blanchard, August 23, 1903, Joló, microfilm 17249, roll 2, Hugh Lenox Scott Papers, Manuscript Division, Library of Congress (hereafter cited as Scott Papers).

14   H. L. Scott to Mary Scott, August 15, 1903, Joló, microfilm 17249, roll 2, Scott Papers.

Scott wrote: "We saw a great many *dattos* of various sultans also the sultans themselves not so near so much of a sultan as Quanah Parker—and we have concluded that the military situation has been immensely exaggerated."

15   William A. Kobbe, Commanding Department of Mindanao and Joló, Extract from Annual Report, September 10, 1900, box 370, Pershing Collection.

16   John J. Pershing, "Field Notes Among the Moros," n.d., box 279, Pershing Collection.

17   John J. Pershing to Assistant Secretary of War George Meiklejohn, April 2, 1900, box 28, folder 179, Record Group 3500, George D. Meiklejohn Collection, Nebraska State Historical Society.

18   Pershing to Meiklejohn, February 12, 1900, box 28, folder 179, Record Group 3500, George D. Meiklejohn Collection. Pershing goes on to suggest that such native troops could be commanded by regular officers and projects that their clothing, pay, and rations would cost about a third of what American troops cost.

19   Ibid.

20   Alfred W. McCoy, *Policing America's Empire: The United States, the Philippines, and the Rise of the Surveillance State* (Madison: University of Wisconsin Press, 2009), 83.

21   James Richard Wollard, "The Philippine Scouts: The Development of America's Colonial Army" (PhD diss., Ohio State University, 1975), 1.

22   Memo from John J. Pershing to General Bell, 1–2, April 5, 1913, box 371, file 3: Governor of Moro Province, Pershing Collection.

23   John J. Pershing, *My Life Before the World War, 1860–1917: A Memoir by General of the Armies John J. Pershing,* ed. John T. Greenwood (Lexington: University Press of Kentucky, 2013), 300–301.

24   John J. Pershing to Albert J. Beveridge, May 3, 1902, box 7, file: 1902 January–March, Henry T. Allen Collection, Manuscript Division, Library of Congress (quoted in McCoy, *Policing America's Empire*, 89).

25   Pershing to Assistant Secretary of War George Meiklejohn, April 5, 1900, box 319, Pershing Collection. The population estimate comes from another letter from Pershing

to Judge C. E. Magoon, January 28, 1903, Camp Vicars, Mindanao, box 370, file 2: Memoirs, Pershing Collection.

26   Pershing to Assistant Secretary of War George Meiklejohn, April 5, 1900, 4–5, box 319, Pershing Collection. For the edited version of this incident, as told in Pershing's memoirs, see Pershing, *My Life Before the World War*, 148. This incident is described in detail in Sydney A. Cloman, *Myself and a Few Moros* (Garden City, N.Y.: Doubleday, Page, 1923), 119–37.

27   Sydney A. Cloman graduated from the United States Military Academy in 1889. He served as a lieutenant with the First Infantry in the Pine Ridge campaign, 1890–91. John T. Greenwood, "Biographical Appendix," in Pershing, *My Life Before the World War*, 494.

28   In notes he took on his "Study of Mexico," Bullard condemned the practice of *ley fuga.* "Civilized men condemn the habit which Mexicans have in war of putting prisoners to death under the pretense that prisoners were trying to escape." Robert Lee Bullard, Notebook 28, p. 197, box 14, Robert Lee Bullard Collection, Manuscript Division, Library of Congress. In the Battle of Bayan, the first engagement in which Pershing participated on Lake Lanao, eighty-three prisoners were taken; about half were shot attempting to escape, according to Fulton, *Moroland*, 111.

29   Fulton, *Moroland*, 87; Fulton also points out that Cloman's execution of the ten men on Tawi Tawi contributed a full third to the number of Moros killed by Americans in the first two years of the occupation.

30   Pershing seems to have derived the population figure of 600,000 Moros from a report by George W. Davis that relied on the account of General *Julián González Parrado*, the Spanish commander in Mindanao before the Americans took over. George W. Davis, "Report on Moro Affairs," October 14, 1901, box 317, file 3: Camp Vicars, Pershing Collection.

31   Pershing to Assistant Secretary of War George Meiklejohn, April 5, 1900, Zamboanga, box 319, Pershing Collection.

32   Gowing, "Mandate in Moroland," 47.

33   Maj. Gen. Chaffee to Adj. Gen., U.S.A., April 24, 1902, in United States Adjutant-General's Office, *Correspondence Relating to the War with Spain and Conditions Growing Out of the Same: Including the Insurrection in the Philippine Islands and the China Relief Expedition, between the Adjutant-General of the Army and Military Commanders in the United States, Cuba, Porto Rico, China, and the Philippine Islands, from April 15, 1898, to July 30, 1902* (Washington: Government Printing Office, 1902), 2:1332 (quoted in Jornacion, *Time of the Eagles,* 77).

34   Bullard, December 31, 1903, Marahui, Diary Book 2, p. 185, box 1, Bullard Collection.

35   Ibid.; Pershing to Judge C. E. Magoon, January 28, 1903, Camp Vicars, Mindanao, 2, box 370, file 2: Memoirs, Pershing Collection. Pershing included Davis's complimentary judgment on his expertise with Moros in one of his regular letters to Judge Magoon at the War Department, confident that his friend Charley would repeat and amplify this aspect of his expertise, which Magoon did, thus burnishing Pershing's reputation for "understanding Moros."

36   Maj. Gen. George Davis to Adj. Gen., U.S. Army, February 19, 1903, Manila, box 370, file 3: Philippines, 1901–1903, Pershing Collection.

37   John J. Pershing, Report to Adjutant General, May 15, 1903, Zamboanga, 17, box 370, file 1, Pershing Collection.

38   Bullard, Notebook 28, p. 28, box 14, Robert Lee Bullard Collection.

39   Ibid., 50.

40   Bullard, May 18, 1903, Pantar, Dairy Book 2, box 1, Bullard Collection.

41   Robert Lee Bullard, "Military Pacification," *Journal of the Military Service Institution of the United States* 46, no. 163 (January–February 1910): 12, 13.

42   H. L. Scott to Mary Scott, October 28, 1903, Joló, microfilm 17249, roll 2, Scott Papers.

43   Hugh Lenox Scott, *Some Memories of a Soldier* (New York: Century, 1928), 320.

44   Jornacion, *Time of the Eagles*, 125–26.

45   Bullard, November 12, 1903, Dairy Book 2, box 1, Bullard Collection.

46   Fulton, *Moroland*, 204. The quotation about the wedding party being "killed like a flock of birds" cited by Fulton is from a poem by the Tausug poet Jawadil, writing about the American campaign against Panglima Hassan.

47   H. L. Scott to Mary Scott, February 25, 1904, "In Camp near Cotta Punai," microfilm 17249, roll 2, Scott Papers.

48   Ibid. I am grateful to Professor William C. Meadows for his help in deciphering Scott's scrawled handwriting in this message, made less than three months after Scott had sustained injuries to both his hands, and hard to read.

49   Oscar J. Charles to Mary Scott, March 7, 1904, Joló, Sulu Island, microfilm 17249, roll 2, Scott Papers. Charles was secretary of the Sulu District.

50   Bullard, July 26, 1903, Marahui, Diary Book 2, p. 159, box 1, Bullard Collection.

51   Fulton, *Moroland*, 196–97.

52   H. L. Scott to Mary Scott, August 23, 1903, Zamboanga, microfilm 17249, roll 2, Scott Papers.

53   Leonard Wood to Gen. Dodge, December 26, 1903 (cited in McCallum, *Leonard Wood*, 218).

54   Italics added. Report of Brig. General S. S. Sumner, Division Commander for Mindanao, Zamboanga to Adjutant General, Division of the Philippines, June 13, 1903, box 30, file: Philippines (1901–1903), Pershing Collection; Bullard, September 9, 1903, Diary Book 2, p. 165, box 1, Bullard Collection.

55   McCallam, *Leonard Wood*, 217; McCoy is quoted in Fulton, *Moroland*, 197.

56   Robert A. Fulton, *Honor for the Flag: The Battle of Bud Dajo—1906 and the Moro Massacre* (Bend, Ore.: Tumalo Creek Press, 2011), 179–83. See also Pershing, *My Life Before the World War*, 664–65.

57   The 1911 siege of Bud Dajo led to twelve Tausug deaths and some injuries; on the American side, three scouts were wounded. Fulton, *Honor for the Flag*, 182; see also Pershing, *My Life Before the World War*, 295.

58   The comment about the "wholesome" fear inspired by the sight of a "soldier mounted on a large American horse," is from a report by Captain Charles B. Hagadorn to the Adj. Gen., Dept. of Mindanao and Joló, August 1, 1901, box 317, file 6: Camp Vicars, Pershing Collection.

59   Pershing to Sultan of Maciu, May 23, 1902, box 318, letters file: May '02 to March '03, Pershing Collection.

60   Fulton, *Moroland*, 101–6.

61   Maj. Gen. Chaffee to Adj. Gen. U.S.A., April 15, 1902, in *Correspondence Relating to the War with Spain*, 1327 (quoted in Jornacion, *Time of the Eagles*, 73).

62   Fulton, *Moroland*, 108–10; and Jornacion, *Time of the Eagles*, 71–80.

63   Pershing, *My Life Before the World War*, 151.

64   "Conversation with the Sultan of Pualas, June 4, 1902," box 317, file: Camp Vicars, Pershing Collection.

65   List of Sultans and Dattos, May 15, 1903, box 317, file: Camp Vicars, Pershing Collection.

66   Pershing, *My Life Before the War*, 402.

67   C. C. Bateman, "Military Taming of the Moro," *Journal of the Military Service Institution* 34 (1904): 259.

68   Pershing to General George W. Davis, March 4, 1903, box 379, file 2: Memoirs, Pershing Collection.

69   List of Sultans and Dattos, May 15, 1903, box 317, file: Camp Vicars, Pershing Collection.

70   C. C. Bateman, "Military Taming of the Moro," 259.

71   H. L. Scott, *Some Memories of a Soldier*, 279–80.

72   Ibid., 280.

73   John J. Pershing, "Report," May 15, 1903, 11, box 317, file: Camp Vicars, Pershing Collection.

74   John J. Pershing, "Conquest of the Moros," n.d. [1908], box 278, Pershing Collection.

75   Bullard, July 15, 1903, Marahui, Diary Book 2, 156, box 1, Bullard Collection (hereafter cited as Diary Book 2).

76   Bullard, August 26, 1903, Diary Book 2, 164.

77   Bullard, September 6, 9, 1903, Marahui, Diary Book 2, 165.

78   Bullard, October 8, 1903, Marahui, Diary Book 2, 171.

79   Bullard, July 8, 1903, Diary Book 2, 154.

80   Bullard, September 1, 1903, Marahui, Diary Book 2, 165.

81   Bullard, July 15 and September 27, 1903, Marahui, Diary Book 2, 155, 169.

Part III

1   United States Department of State, *Papers Relating to the Foreign Relations of the United States with the Address of the President to Congress, December 5, 1916* (Washington, D.C.: Government Printing Office, 1925). Analogies between the raid by Villa's forces on Columbus and the raids by Apaches into Mexico in the 1880s were made almost immediately, first by the Mexican secretary for foreign affairs, Jesús Acuña, who cited the cooperation between the two governments as a precedent for possible *future* cooperation to deal with Villa. This model was affirmed by a later communication from Secretary of State Lansing to Special Agent John Belt to be communicated to First Chief Carranza. See telegrams of March 10, 1916, 485; and March 13, 1916, 487.

2   Friedrich Katz has suggested that Villa was motivated by the conviction that Venustiano Carranza had compromised Mexico's sovereignty in a secret agreement with the United States entered into to secure official U.S. recognition of his government; Friedrich Katz, "Pancho Villa and the Attack on Columbus, New Mexico," *American Historical Review* 83, no. 1 (1978): 101–30. For other treatments of the motives behind Villa's raid on Columbus, see Joseph Allen Stout, *Border Conflict: Villistas, Carrancistas and the Punitive Expedition, 1915–1920* (Fort Worth: Texas Christian University Press, 1999); Clarence C. Clendenen, *Blood on the Border: The United States Army and the Mexican Irregulars* (New York: Macmil-

lan, 1969); and Alberto Salinas Carranza, *La expedición punitiva* (México: Ediciones Botas, 1936).

3   Hugh Lenox Scott, *Some Memories of a Soldier* (New York: Century, 1928), 331, 516. "Had I been able with former Secretary Garfield to establish peace in Mexico while Villa was still in Mexico City, I had intended to put the latter in school at Fort Leavenworth where he might learn the rudiments of morals."

Chapter 8

1   Robert Lee Bullard, Supplemental Diaries #1–4, Re Mission to Mexico, entry for May 20, 1911, Camp Loma, San Diego, Robert Lee Bullard Collection, Manuscript Division, Library of Congress (hereafter cited as Supplemental Diaries #1–4).

2   Ibid.

3   Revolutionaries attacked government positions in Morelos, Puebla, Sonora, and Yucatán. While there were many areas of the country not affected by fighting, the "impression of general upheaval" was widespread in the first half of 1911. Colin M. MacLachlan and William H. Beezley, *El Gran Pueblo: A History of Greater Mexico* (Upper Saddle River, N.J.: Prentice Hall, 2004), 224. In response to events in Mexico and predictions of more unrest to come by the U.S. ambassador Lane Wilson, in March 1911 President Taft directed the organization of thirty thousand troops as a "Maneuver Division" to be stationed at three points near the border: San Diego, Galveston, and San Antonio.

4   Bullard, Supplemental Diaries #1–4, Re Mission to Mexico, entry for April 22, 1911, Way Camp, Dulzura, Calif.; entry for May 20, 1911, Camp Loma, San Diego.

5   Bullard, Supplemental Diaries #1–4, Re Mission to Mexico, entry for April 19, 1911, San Diego. I am grateful to the historian James Newland, whose generosity in sharing his knowledge of the history and geography of San Diego's backcountry helped me to better orient myself (and the text) to the terrain through which Bullard rode in April 1911.

6   MacLachlan and Beezley, *El Gran Pueblo*, 212.

7   H. L. Scott, *Some Memories of a Soldier*, 495–96. Scott further commented on Díaz: "He had a tremendous task to keep order over that enormous territory with an ignorant people, 80 per cent of whom were unable to read or write and were mainly of Indian blood."

8   MacLachlan and Beezley, *El Gran Pueblo*, 218–19.

9   For a detailed account of intrigue, espionage, and gunrunning in a key city on the border during the Mexican Revolution, see Charles H. Harris and Louis R. Sadler, *The Secret War in El Paso: Mexican Revolutionary Intrigue, 1906–1920* (Albuquerque: University of New Mexico Press, 2009).

10   President William Howard Taft to Army Chief of Staff Leonard Wood, March 12, 1911, box 54, General Correspondence, Leonard Wood Collection, Manuscript Division, Library of Congress.

11   Friedrich Katz, *The Secret War in Mexico: Europe, the United States and the Mexican Revolution* (Chicago: University of Chicago Press, 1981), 94, 106.

12   Bullard, Supplemental Diaries #1–4, Re Mission to Mexico, entry for April 19, 1911, San Diego. The "neutrality-enforcing" camps Bullard set out to visit were established in an attempt to police the cross-border activities of opponents of the Díaz regime who were running men and guns from Matamoros on the Gulf to Tijuana on the Pacific. Allan Reed

Millett, *The General: Robert L. Bullard and Officership in the United States Army, 1881–1925* (Westport, Conn.: Greenwood Press, 1975), 213–14.

13   Bullard, Supplemental Diaries #1–4, Re Mission to Mexico, entry for April 22, 1911, Dulzura, Calif. William H. Prescott was the author of the book *History of the Conquest of Mexico*, published in 1843.

14   Ibid.

15   Ibid.

16   Friedrich E. Schuler, *Secret Wars and Secret Policies in the Americas, 1842–1929* (Albuquerque: University of New Mexico Press, 2010), 61.

17   Bullard, Supplemental Diaries #1–4, Re Mission to Mexico, entry for April 24, 1911, San Diego.

18   Ibid.

19   Bullard, Supplemental Diaries #1–4, Re Mission to Mexico, entry for April 28, 1911, San Francisco.

20   Ibid.

21   Katz, *Secret War in Mexico*, 76–77. For a more recent and multifaceted analysis of relations between Mexico, Japan, and Germany during this time, see Schuler, *Secret Wars and Secret Policies*.

22   Entry A, MID, box 6274, various files, 1910–1911, Records of the War Department General and Specific Divisions, War College Division, Record Group 165, National Archives and Records Administration. The invasion plans and projected troop strengths are referred to, for example, in a memorandum on "Local military supplies in Mexico," November 14, 1910, from Major D. H. Boughton to Hunter Liggett, Secretary, War College Division. The files of the War College Division were screened in 1920 and partially destroyed. Some information survives on index cards for some of the destroyed files, which are in the National Archives. John A. Hixson, "The United States Army General Staff Corps, 1910–1917: Its Relationship to the Field Forces" (master's thesis, Rice University, 1971), 5–6, http://hdl.handle.net/1911/89095.

23   Schuler, *Secret Wars and Secret Policies*.

24   MacLachlan and Beezley, *El Gran Pueblo*, 224–28.

25   Bullard, Supplemental Diaries #1–4, Re Mission to Mexico, entry for May 9, 1911, Guaymas.

26   Ibid.

27   Friedrich Katz, *The Life and Times of Pancho Villa* (Stanford, Calif.: Stanford University Press, 1998), 114.

28   Bullard, Supplemental Diaries #1–4, Re Mission to Mexico, entry for May 17, 1911, Manzanillo.

29   Ibid. Friedrich Schuler gives a detailed account of the naval delegation that Japan sent to take part in the centenary events. The delegation was led by Admiral Moriyama and hosted by the Mexican secretary of war at a banquet held at a Chapultepec cafe. In an exchange of toasts, the admiral declared that "Japan will feel honored to endeavor to give full support" to Mexico in the event of a war with a "neighboring" country (understood to be the United States). Schuler, *Secret Wars and Secret Policies*, 68.

30   Bullard, Supplemental Diaries #1–4, Re Mission to Mexico, entry for May 25, 1911, Vera Cruz.

31   Bullard, Supplemental Diaries #1–4, Re Mission to Mexico, entry for May 26, 1911, Puebla.

32   Ibid.

33   Ibid.

34   Ibid.

35   Ibid.

36   Bullard, Supplemental Diaries #1–4, Re Mission to Mexico, entry for May 27, 1911, Mexico City.

37   William H. Beezley and Colin M. MacLachlan, *Mexicans in Revolution, 1910–1946: An Introduction* (Lincoln: University of Nebraska Press, 2009), 22.

38   Katz, *Life and Times of Pancho Villa*, 197.

39   Bullard, Supplemental Diaries #1–4, Re Mission to Mexico, entry for June 16, 1911, Presidio, Monterey.

Chapter 9

1   Scott's assignment to sort through the records of the American government in Cuba during its period of occupation from 1906 to 1909 is detailed in Chapter 5. Scott submitted the report on this work to Congress on May 24, 1911, the same day Bullard reached Salina Cruz and began his rail journey across the Isthmus of Tehuantepec from Salina Cruz to Veracruz. Scott's Report on Cuban Records, May 24, 1911, H. Doc. 9, at 68, 92, 62nd Cong., 1st sess. (1911); H. R. Rep. 2, at 333, 62nd Cong., 2nd sess. (1911–12) (cited in James William Harper, "Hugh Lenox Scott: Soldier-Diplomat, 1876–1917" [PhD diss., University of Virginia, 1968]).

2   For insightful discussions of distinctive racial formations and identities in northern Mexico, see Friedrich Katz, *The Life and Times of Pancho Villa* (Stanford, Calif.: Stanford University Press, 1998), chap. 1, "From the Frontier to the Border," 11–48; see also Ana María Alonso, "U.S. Military Intervention, Revolutionary Mobilization, and Popular Ideology in the Chihuahuan Sierra, 1916–1917," in *Rural Revolt in Mexico: U.S. Intervention and the Domain of Subaltern Politics*, 207–38 (Durham, N.C.: Duke University Press, 1998).

3   In detailing the actions of the provisional squadron he commanded as part of the Punitive Expedition, Major Frank Tompkins, Thirteenth Cavalry, wrote: "We had the usual cavalry equipment except the sabers and the curb bits. I knew we didn't need sabers in chasing Indians." Frank Tompkins, *Chasing Villa: The Last Campaign of the U.S. Cavalry* (Silver City, N.Mex.: High-Lonesome Books, 1996), 110.

4   For an example of the Indian Wars metaphor of "coming in," applied to Villa, see Scott's letter to Mary, January 7, 1915, microfilm 17249, roll 3, Scott Family Collection, Manuscript Division, Library of Congress (hereafter cited as Scott Family Collection).

5   Mark Cronlund Anderson, *Pancho Villa's Revolution by Headlines* (Norman: University of Oklahoma Press, 2000), 119–20. Based on his analysis of depictions of Villa in the American press and U.S. diplomatic records, Anderson argues that Villa was a shrewd manipulator of U.S. stereotypes about Mexicans and used them to disparage his rivals, such as Huerta and Carranza. Ironically, Anderson claims that Villa "achieved for a time a framing draped in the language of heartfelt Americana, an imagery that reached all the way to the White House. In short, Villa as Mexican hero for a time became "Villa the Americanized hero," 12–13. On racial stereotypes of Indians in U.S. culture, see also Robert F. Berkhofer, *The White Man's Indian: Images of the American Indian, from Columbus to the Present* (New York: Vintage Books, 1979; and Raymond William Stedman, *Shadows of the Indian:*

Stereotypes in American Culture (Norman: University of Oklahoma Press, 1982).

6   While he notes that Woodrow Wilson was personally opposed to intervening in Mexico to protect U.S. investments, property, and business interests, Katz details several moments of Wilson's presidency in which he argues that such interests tipped the administration's actions in favor of occupation and threats of war. Katz, *Life and Times of Pancho Villa*, 315–16, 578–79. For a detailed account of the history of American investment in and influence on Mexican economic and social development, as well as politics, see John Mason Hart, *Empire and Revolution: The Americans in Mexico Since the Civil War* (Berkeley: University of California Press, 2005).

7   Hugh Lenox Scott, *Some Memories of a Soldier* (New York: Century, 1928), 517.

8   Hugh Lenox Scott to George Carothers, March 17, 1916, box 22, Hugh Lenox Scott Papers, Manuscript Division, Library of Congress (hereafter cited as Scott Papers).

9   H. L. Scott, *Some Memories of a Soldier*, 499. For a description of Villa's surprise attack on Ciudad Juárez, see also Katz, *Life and Times of Pancho Villa*, 224–25.

10   Hugh Lenox Scott to Mary, September 26, 1914, microfilm 17249, roll 3, Scott Family Collection.

11   Hugh Lenox Scott to Mary, April 24, 1914, microfilm 17249, roll 3, Scott Family Collection

12   Hugh Lenox Scott to Mary, June 24, 1914, microfilm 17249, roll 3, Scott Family Collection.

13   Hugh Lenox Scott to Mary, September 26, 1914, microfilm 17249, roll 3, Scott Family Collection.

14   H. L. Scott, *Some Memories of a Soldier*, 507–8. Scott wrote that Villa had always disclaimed any ambition to be president, "and he thought Ángeles the best man in Mexico for the position. Had this triumph been possible, Mexico would long ago have entered into her own." Felipe Ángeles was captured in 1919, put on trial by Carranza's government, and executed.

15   Katz, *Life and Times of Pancho Villa*, 526.

16   H. L. Scott, *Some Memories of a Soldier*, 491–94; 294. It also bears noting that Scott attributes the same declaration, "I am going to do what you advise me," to Secretary of War Newton Baker in the matter of Pancho Villa's raid on Columbus. Ibid., 519.

17   Hugh Lenox Scott to Mary, June 28, 1914, microfilm 17249, roll 3, Scott Family Collection. Interestingly, the other reason Scott was not keen on being sent to keep an eye on Villa and exert influence over him, as he wrote to Mary, was that General Funston had told him he was to be given command of U.S. forces in Veracruz (which never happened).

18   Hugh Lenox Scott to Mary, January 9, 1915, El Paso, microfilm 17249, roll 3, Scott Family Collection.

19   Scott, *Some Memories of a Soldier*, 501.

20   Katz, *Life and Times of Pancho Villa*, 319.

21   H. L. Scott, *Some Memories of a Soldier*, 492.

22   Hugh Lenox Scott to Mary, June 24, 1914, microfilm 17249, roll 3, Scott Family Collection.

23   Hugh Lenox Scott to "Pudd," September 28, 1915, microfilm 17249, roll 3, Scott Family Collection.

24   Hugh Lenox Scott to Mary, April 24, 1914, microfilm 17249, roll 3, Scott Family Collection.

25   H. L. Scott, *Some Memories of a Soldier*, 507.

26   Hugh Lenox Scott to Mary, July 14, 1914, microfilm 17249, roll 3, Scott Family Collection.

27   H. L. Scott, *Some Memories of a Soldier*, 517.

28   Ibid., 82. Following his surrender to Miles after the Bears Paw battle, Chief Joseph and other Nez Percé prisoners were sent to Bismarck, and from there by train to prison at Fort Leavenworth. This history is related in Chapter 2.

29   H. L. Scott, *Some Memories of a Soldier*, 516.

30   Katz, *Life and Times of Pancho Villa*, 604.

31   Ibid., 519.

32   Special Agent Carothers to the Secretary of State, March 9, 1916, El Paso, United States Department of State, *Papers Relating to the Foreign Relations of the United States with the Address of the President to Congress, December 5, 1916* (Washington, D.C.: Government Printing Office, 1925), 480.

33   Friedrich Katz, "Pancho Villa and the Attack on Columbus, New Mexico," *American Historical Review* 83, no. 1 (1978): 115. After driving one group of attackers away from the military camp, soldiers of the Thirteenth advanced to the nearby town center where the main force was concentrated. After about two hours of fighting, the troopers repulsed the raid and chased the attackers back across the border, killing about a hundred Villistas and capturing others whom they brought back to New Mexico for trial.

34   H. L. Scott, *Some Memories of a Soldier*, 520.

Chapter 10

1   Alberto Salinas Carranza, *La expedición punitiva* (México: Ediciones Botas, 1936), 127–28. The meeting between Pershing and Cabrera took place on March 12, three days after the raid on Columbus, at the Hotel Paso del Norte in El Paso. It was unofficial, arranged by Cabrera without prior authorization from his government. The Mexican aphorism included in Salinas's account of the interview is "buscar el gato en el garbanzal" (to search for the cat in the garbanzo patch).

2   H. L. Scott to General Pershing, April 4, 1916, box 22, General Correspondence, April 1916, Henry Lenox Scott Papers, Manuscript Division, Library of Congress (hereafter cited as Scott Papers). Scott notifies Pershing that he is being sent twenty Apache scouts from Fort Apache.

3   Information on the Punitive Expedition is drawn from a number of sources: Robert S. Thomas and Inez V. Allen, *The Mexican Punitive Expedition Under Brigadier General John J. Pershing, United States Army, 1916–1917* (Washington: University Microfilms, 1967); Friedrich Katz, *The Life and Times of Pancho Villa* (Stanford, Calif.: Stanford University Press, 1998); Frank Tompkins, *Chasing Villa: The Last Campaign of the U.S. Cavalry* (Silver City, N.Mex.: High-Lonesome Books, 1996); John M. Cyrulik, *Strategic Examination of the Punitive Expedition into Mexico, 1916–1917* (Fort Leavenworth, Kans.: U.S. Army Command and General Staff College, [2003]), http://cgsc.contentdm.oclc.org/u?/p4013coll2; and Pershing's memoirs, among others.

4   Tompkins, *Chasing Villa*, 72–74. In his edited volume of Pershing's memoirs, John Greenwood gives the number of troops that crossed the border into Mexico as 4,800 men: 192 officers; and 4,175 animals. John J. Pershing, *My Life Before the World War, 1860–1917: A Memoir*, ed. John T. Greenwood (Lexington: University Press of Kentucky, 2013), 673n3.

5   Clarence C. Clendenen, *Blood on the Border: The United States Army and the Mexican Irregulars* (New York: Macmillan, 1969), 220, 228n13. Clendenen received the information about the ritual of allowing the Sixth Infantry to cross the border at the head of the column from Colonel Carrol A. Bagby. In 1916 Bagby had taken part as a lieutenant in the Sixteenth Infantry. The casualty figures for the Mexican-American War are from Peter Guardino, *The Dead March: A History of the Mexican-American War* (Cambridge, Mass.: Harvard University Press, 1917), 1.

6   Telegram from Office of the Special Agent of the State Department to Hon. Jesús Acuña, Secretary in Charge of the Foreign Office, March 11, 1916, Querétaro, in Mexico, Secretaría de Relaciones Exteriores, *Diplomatic Dealings of the Constitutionalist Revolution of Mexico* (México: Impr. Nacional, 1918), doc. no. 13, 142–43; for the request to use Chihuahua's railways, see Acting Secretary of State Polk to Special Representative Rodgers, March 18, 1916, Washington, file no. 812.00/17528a, in United States Department of State, *Papers Relating to the Foreign Relations of the United States with the Address of the President to Congress, December 5, 1916* (Washington, D.C.: Government Printing Office, 1925) (hereafter cited as *Papers Relating to the Foreign Relations of the United States*), 492. Information on troop movements is from Tompkins, *Chasing Villa*, 72–77.

7   Italics added. This line of argument against the Punitive Expedition by Venustiano Carranza is contained in a telegram the first chief sent to the Mexican ambassador in Washington, Eliseo Arredondo. The telegram was read to U.S. Secretary of State Robert Lansing on March 12, 1916. First Chief Carranza to Mr. Arredondo, March 11, 1916, Querétaro, in United States Department of State, *Papers Relating to the Foreign Relations of the United States*, 486. The exchange of telegrams between the governments is extensive and complex. For a more complete sense of the internal discussions informing Mexican communiqués, see Mexico, Secretaría de Relaciones Exteriores, *Diplomatic Dealings of the Constitutionalist Revolution of Mexico*.

8   J. Fred Rippy, "Some Precedents of the Pershing Expedition into Mexico," *Southwestern Historical Quarterly* 24, no. 4 (April 1921): 297.

9   Secretary of State Lansing to Special Agent Silliman, March 13, 1916, Washington, United States Department of State, *Papers Relating to the Foreign Relations of the United States*, 487.

10   James K. Polk, President of the United States at Washington, D.C., to the Congress of the United States, "A special message calling for a declaration of war against Mexico," May 11, 1846, Washington; Steven R. Butler, *A Documentary of the Mexican War* (Richardson, Tex.: Descendants of Mexican War Veterans, 1995), 71.

11   In November of 1913, the Wilson administration offered to support Carranza in a bid to force Victoriano Huerta from power. According to the plan proposed by the Americans, their troops would occupy the largest cities in northern Mexico, as well as some on the Gulf in support of Carranza moving his troops to take Mexico City. Five months later, in April 1914, Carranza strongly criticized the U.S. occupation of Veracruz, even though this action on the part of the United States was aimed at toppling Huerta and was intended to benefit Carranza. Katz calls nationalism Carranza's "most deeply held conviction"; Katz, *Life and Times of Pancho Villa*, 310–11, 337.

12   For a vigorous argument in support of Carranza's unwavering defense of Mexican sovereignty, see Luis Cabrera, "Carta Prologo," in *La expedición punitiva*, by Alberto Salinas Carranza (México: Ediciones Botas, 1936), 14–22.

13   Cyrulik, *Strategic Examination of the Punitive Expedition*, 30.

14   Pershing received a confidential telegram, dated March 16, that laid out the actions he should be prepared to take if his force was met by armed resistance, according to Tompkins, *Chasing Villa*, 71. The following day, the U.S. Senate adopted a resolution in support of sending troops into Mexico on the understanding, as the second *Whereas* clause put it, "the President has obtained the consent of the de facto government of Mexico for this punitive expedition," Congressional Record, March 17, 1916, vol. 53, p. 4274 (quoted in George A. Finch, "Mexico and the United States," *American Journal of International Law* 11, no. 2 [April 1917]: 400). In spite of Scott's later efforts to emphasize that the objective of the mission was to break up Villa's band and was not solely focused on capturing Villa (and thus not to be judged a failure when Villa evaded their grasp), in fact the first intimations of plans for retaliatory action to reach the Southern Department put the emphasis squarely on punishing Villa. On March 10, 1916, Adjutant General McCain sent a telegram to General Funston, who was in command of the Southern Department. "President has directed that an armed force be sent into Mexico with the sole object of capturing Villa and preventing any further raids by his band," file no. 812.00/17398, United States Department of State, *Papers Relating to the Foreign Relations of the United States*, 483. Later the same day, Secretary of State Lansing had the following telegram sent to all consular agents in Mexico: March 10, 1916, 6 p.m., Washington, "The following statement has just been given to the press by the President: 'An adequate force will be sent at once in pursuit of Villa with the single object of capturing him and putting a stop to his forays. This can and will be done in entirely friendly aid of the constituted authorities in Mexico and with scrupulous respect for the sovereignty of that Republic,'" file no. 812.00/17426a, United States Department of State, *Papers Relating to the Foreign Relations of the United States*, 483. By July 20, 1916, Carranza had begun to allow the use of Mexican railroads to bring supplies such as forage to the American troops. Charles H. Harris and Louis R. Sadler, *The Great Call-Up: The Guard, the Border, and the Mexican Revolution* (Norman: University of Oklahoma Press, 1915), 4.

15   Brian DeLay, *War of A Thousand Deserts: Indian Raids and the U.S.-Mexican War* (New Haven, Conn.: Yale University Press, 2010), 10.

16   Ana María Alonso, "U.S. Military Intervention, Revolutionary Mobilization, and Popular Ideology in the Chihuahuan Sierra, 1916–1917," in *Rural Revolt in Mexico: U.S. Intervention and the Domain of Subaltern Politics*, ed. Daniel Nugent (Durham, N.C.: Duke University Press, 1988), 207.

17   Katz, *Life and Times of Pancho Villa*, 17, 841n11.

18   Ibid., 17–21.

19   The reference to the presence of the Mormon colonies as an "invasion of foreigners" appears in a contract Villa signed with the inhabitants of the community of Morelos in Sonora. The contract commits Villa to providing arms and ammunition to Morelos to enable them to fight the North American Mormons. The contract, signed October 26, 1915, was located by the scholar Ana María Alonso in the United States National Archives. Alonso gives the citation as MR RG 94 DF 2384662. Alonso, "U.S. Military Intervention, Revolutionary Mobilization, and Popular Ideology in the Chihuahuan Sierra, 1916–1917," 211n17.

20   Speech given in San Andrés, Chihuahua, in October 1916, cited in Alonso, "U.S. Military Intervention, Revolutionary Mobilization, and Popular Ideology in the Chihuahuan Sierra, 1916–1917," 211n18.

21   Arthur Link, ed., *Woodrow Wilson Papers* (Princeton, N.J.: Princeton University Press, 1947–65), 4:280 (quoted in Katz, *Life and Times of Pancho Villa*, 577, 887n95).

22   Katz, *Life and Times of Pancho Villa*, 577; Katz cites Link, *Woodrow Wilson Papers*, 4:280–81.

23   Katz, *Life and Times of Pancho Villa*, 606.

24   Alonso, "U.S. Military Intervention, Revolutionary Mobilization, and Popular Ideology in the Chihuahuan Sierra, 1916–1917," 218–19. Alonso says she does not know whether the *defensas sociales* of the other Guerrero District pueblos were also created at Pershing's behest. The other municipios that formed *defensas sociales* during the U.S. occupation were Bachiniva, Guerrero, Madera, Temosachic, Yepomera, Tejolacachic, Santo Tomás, Matachic, San Isidro, Tosanachic, and Bocoyna.

25   Pershing's advocacy of native troops in the Philippines is discussed in Chapter 6.

26   Colonel C. W. Kennedy, "Memorandum for the Chief, War College Division," March 31, 1916, M1024, roll 253, Records of the War Department General and Specific Divisions, War College Division, Record Group 165, National Archives and Records Administration. Colonel Kennedy's memorandum expresses a dissenting opinion apparently on an earlier veto of this proposal. In support of the transfer of officers in the Philippine Scouts, he excerpts statements of approval for the work of the scouts by Brigadier General Frank D. Baldwin, Major General Davis, Major General Wood, Brigadier General Miles, Major General Duvall, Major General Bell, Brigadier General Pershing, and Major General T. H. Barry. Just as interesting, in a document dated December 1, 1916, the chief of the War College Division is informed that the proposed legislation to allow for the transfer of Philippine Scouts officers is "not favorably considered at this time" by the chief of staff (Hugh Lenox Scott).

27   Elizabeth H. Mills, "The Mormon Colonies in Chihuahua After the 1912 Exodus" (master's thesis, University of Arizona, 1950), 22–23. Before leaving El Paso, Pershing had consulted the Mormon bishop there, who had recommended seven Mormon scouts who were selected for their knowledge of northern Mexico and the Spanish language and their familiarity with Mexican culture. See also Clarence F. Turley et al., *History of the Mormon Colonies in Mexico: (The Juárez Stake), 1885–1980, Consisting of Colonia Díaz, Colonia Juárez, Colonia Dublán, Colonia Pacheco, Colonies Surrounding Colonia Pacheco, Colonia Garcia, Colonia Chuichupa, Colonia Oaxaca (Sonora), Colonia Morelos (Sonora), Colonia San José (Sonora)* ([Mexico?]: printed by Publishers Press for L. B. Lee and M. T. Lee, 1996), 217.

28   Clendenen, *Blood on the Border*, 237. Elizabeth Mills also notes that Lemuel Spillsbury, who served as a scout for Lieutenant Charles T. Boyd in what turned into a deadly fight with Carrancista forces in Carrizal on June 21, 1916, said he had wanted to serve with the forces because he wanted to help catch Villa; he later criticized the Americans for causing trouble with the Mexicans, among whom he had many friends. He tried to abandon scouting at that point, but Pershing refused to release him. Mills, "Mormon Colonies in Chihuahua" (1950), 28. Mills uses the name *Spillsbury*, but in the volume edited by Clarence Turley et al., the surname is given as *Spilsbury*.

29   Charles H. Harris and Louis R. Sadler, *The Secret War in El Paso: Mexican Revolutionary Intrigue, 1906–1920* (Albuquerque: University of New Mexico Press, 2009), 13–14. Although the army's Military Intelligence Division had been disbanded in 1908, Van Deman was working at the Army War College on implementing and adapting techniques he had developed in the Philippines within an unauthorized alternative division called the Military Information Section of the General Staff. When Hugh Lenox Scott found out about it, he gave Van Deman "strict orders" to abandon his efforts. Van Deman went around the army chief of staff to get authorization from Secretary of War Newton

Baker who ordered the reestablishment of a Military Intelligence Section under Van Deman's command on May 11, 1917. Alfred W. McCoy, *Policing America's Empire: The United States, the Philippines, and the Rise of the Surveillance State* (Madison: University of Wisconsin Press, 2009), 297. According to McCoy—who locates the origins of the American "surveillance state" in the migration of intelligence techniques developed for colonial rule from the periphery to the metropole—the American colonial state in the Philippines had made ample use of the intelligence gathered by Van Deman's office not only to inform its counterinsurgency efforts but also to gather information that could be used to exploit (or silence) scandal, and for political blackmail.

    30   Clendenen discusses the intelligence activities of the Pershing Expedition in *Blood on the Border*, 331–32. Friedrich Katz also discusses Pershing's interest in intelligence gathering, which he discusses in relation to Pershing's experience with counterinsurgency. He also discusses the plot to poison Villa in some detail. Katz, *Life and Times of Pancho Villa*, 567, 608–10.

    31   Katz, *Life and Times of Pancho Villa*, 608–10. Katz gives the names of the Japanese agents as Dyo, Jah (Hawakawa), and Fusita, which seem to be their code names. In their exhaustive study of the records of the Bureau of Investigations in El Paso during the Mexican Revolution, which Katz cites as one of his sources for his account of the poisoning incident, the authors Harris and Sadler give the names of the agents as Gemichi "Gustavo" Tatematsu and Lucas G. Hayakawa, whom they describe as "Japanese residing in El Paso who had been personal servants of Pancho and Hipolito Villa." Hayakawa had recently been employed as an informant for military intelligence at Fort Bliss. Tatematsu was given the code designation "Jat" and Hayakawa was referred to as "Jah." Agent Stone also recruited a third Japanese informant, Hidekichi Tuschiya, code-named "Frank" and later "Jaf." Tuschiya, however, was handled out of San Antonio by Stone's superior in the service, Agent Robert Barnes. Tuschiya later admitted to working simultaneously for the Japanese embassy in Washington. Harris and Sadler, *Secret War in El Paso*, 13–14.

    32   Lieber Code, section 9, article 148. "Civilized nations look with horror upon the offer of rewards for the assassination of enemies as relapses into barbarism." Richard Shelly Hartigan, *Lieber's Code and the Law of War* (Chicago: Precedent, 1983), 69.

    33   Katz, *Life and Times of Pancho Villa*, 610. See also Harris and Sadler, *Secret War in El Paso*, 16–22.

    34   Katz, *Life and Times of Pancho Villa*, 610.

    35   Wayne Wray Thompson, "Governors of the Moro Province: Wood, Bliss, and Pershing in the Southern Philippines, 1903–1913" (PhD diss., University of California, San Diego, 1975), 176–79. Thompson quotes correspondence between Leonard Wood and General Henry Corbin discussing Pershing's affair and illegitimate child. Wood wrote that the affair was "one of very general knowledge" in the Philippines. Corbin noted that the army was "talking of it in no uncertain way" and predicted that the scandal might derail Pershing's promotion. The woman's name was Joaquina B. Ignacio. Joaquina, along with her three sisters and their father, operated a beer cantina on the edge of Zamboanga. In 1907 Pershing returned to Zamboanga, where he obtained an affidavit from Joaquina, which said that she had been "merely an acquaintance" of his.

    36   Katz, *Life and Times of Pancho Villa*, 589.

    37   The views of Secretary of War Newton Baker are given in the *Woodrow Wilson Papers*, edited by Arthur Link, and are quoted in Katz, *Life and Times of Pancho Villa*, 577.

    38   H. L. Scott to J. T. Dickman, April 8, 1916, Scott Papers (quoted in Arthur Link,

Wilson: Confusion and Crises 1915–1916 [Princeton, N.J.,: Princeton University Press, 1947–65], 282.

39   Katz, *Life and Times of Pancho Villa*, 578. In the debate over leaving or withdrawing troops in early April, Katz argues that men with business interests in Mexico were influential in persuading Secretary of the Interior Lane and also Colonel House that the troops should remain.

40   Salinas Carranza, *La expedición punitiva*, 110–11; see also Tompkins, *Chasing Villa*, 118.

41   According to some reports, the aggressive verbal taunting of the U.S. troops was led by an Alsatian woman who lived there. Friedrich Katz identifies her as Elsa Griensen de Alvarado; Alberto Salinas Carranza calls her Elisa Griensa and notes that she was still living in Parral after the Revolution, married to an American. Forty-two Mexicans were killed in the engagement. Tompkins, *Chasing Villa*, 142. Two Americans were killed and six wounded, including Tompkins. The incident at Parral is treated by Salinas Carranza, Tompkins, Clendenen, and Katz.

42   John J. Pershing to War Department, April 17, 1916, in *Woodrow Wilson Papers*, ed. Arthur Link, 36:502–3 (quoted in Cyrulik, *Strategic Examination of the Punitive Expedition into Mexico*, 49). Colonel Charles Young was one of three black commissioned officers in the army; he served with the Tenth Cavalry.

43   Ibid., 50–51.

44   H. L. Scott to Mary, May 5, 1916, Scott Papers.

45   H. L. Scott to Mary, May 1, 1916, El Paso, Scott Papers.

46   J. J. Pershing to War Department, April 17, 1916, in *Woodrow Wilson Papers*, ed. Arthur Link, 36:502–3 (quoted in Cyrulik, *Strategic Examination of the Punitive Expedition into Mexico*, 49).

47   Italics added. Funston and Scott Telegram, May 8, 1916, El Paso, to Secretary of War, in United States Department of State, *Papers Relating to the Foreign Relations of the United States*, 538.

48   J. D. Eisenhower, *Intervention! The United States and the Mexican Revolution, 1913–1917* (New York: W.W. Norton, 1993), 235. Funston's temperament, as it influenced selection for command of the Punitive Expedition, is discussed in Cyrulik, *Strategic Examination of the Punitive Expedition into Mexico*, 28.

49   Álvaro Obregón to Carranza, "Eleventh Day" of negotiations (May 8, 1916), in Mexico, Secretaría de Relaciones Exteriores, *Diplomatic Dealings of the Constitutionalist Revolution of Mexico*, doc. no. 61, 197–205.

50   Hugh L. Scott to Mary Scott, May 9, 1916, El Paso, Scott Papers. "We had an interview last evening [May 8] with Obregón and Juan Amador sub Secy State Dept—in which Obregón told me Carranza would not ratify agreement he had signed with me because no definite date was mentioned for withdrawal of our troops from Mexico." Scott notes that he had struggled for twelve hours to keep stipulation of a date out of the agreement. He further writes to his wife that he has "renewed my request made when Pershing first crossed the border to put 150,000 troops on the border at once."

51   Funston and Scott Telegram, May 8, 1916, El Paso, to Secretary of War, in United States Department of State, *Papers Relating to the Foreign Relations of the United States*, 544. The Organized Militia was "federalized" by the National Defense Act of 1916, approved on June 3. Henry J. Reilly, "The National Guard on the Mexican Border," in *Chasing Villa: The Last Campaign of the U.S. Cavalry*, by Frank Tompkins (Silver City, N.Mex.: High-Lone-

some Books, 1996), 228–29. By July 31, 1916, there were 110,957 officers and enlisted men of the National Guard on the border; there were an additional 40,139 in state mobilization camps. The maximum number on the border was 111,096. Between May 8 and December, 1916, a total of 158,664 men had been called into service on the border.

52   Pershing, *My Life Before the World War*, 356.

53   General Treviño to General Pershing, June 16, 1916, included in Pershing, *My Life Before the World War*, 357.

54   Pershing to Treviño, in Pershing, *My Life Before the World War*, 357.

55   Pershing, *My Life Before the World War*, 358; Clendenen, *Blood on the Border*, 305–8, gives the number of dead and wounded Mexicans at more than seventy-five.

56   Clendenen, *Blood on the Border*, 302.

57   Ibid. See also Pershing, *My Life Before the World War*, 359.

58   Joseph Allen Stout, *Border Conflict: Villistas, Carrancistas and the Punitive Expedition, 1915–1920* (Fort Worth: Texas Christian University Press, 1999), 90.

59   Hugh Lenox Scott, *Some Memories of a Soldier* (New York: Century, 1928), 529. Secretary Baker honored Scott's request and left him off the commission.

60   Cyrulik, *Strategic Examination of the Punitive Expedition into Mexico*, 41.

61   Friedrich Katz, *The Secret War in Mexico: Europe, the United States and the Mexican Revolution* (Chicago: University of Chicago Press, 1981), 312.

62   Ibid.

63   Friedrich E. Schuler, *Secret Wars and Secret Policies in the Americas, 1842–1929* (Albuquerque: University of New Mexico Press, 2010), 180–84. Carranza's attaché and propagandist in Europe was Major Arnoldo Krumm-Heller, a forty-two-year-old inspector of military and public schools in Mexico who had also served as Carranza's doctor.

64   Allan Reed Millett, *The General: Robert L. Bullard and Officership in the United States Army, 1881–1925* (Westport, Conn.: Greenwood Press, 1975), chap. 16.

65   President George W. Bush, quoted in the *London Times*, September 18, 2001; see interpretation in Tom Engelhardt, "Injun Country: Western Double Standards in the 'War Against Terror,'" *Le Monde diplomatique*, February 2006, accessed May 14, 2016, http://mondediplo.com/2006/02/07brown. This kind of attention to the resonances of frontier and Indian War imagery in contemporary foreign policy discourse follows in the tradition of the classic work of Richard Slotkin, *Gunfighter Nation: the Myth of the Frontier in Twentieth-Century America* (Norman: University of Oklahoma Press, 1998).

66   Winona LaDuke and Sean Aaron Cruz, *The Militarization of Indian Country* (East Lansing, Mich.: Makwa Enewed, 2012), xvi.

67   Nick Allen, "Osama bin Laden Dead: Code Name Geronimo," *Telegraph*, May 3, 2011, online edition, http://www.telegraph.co.uk/news/worldnews/asia/pakistan/8489354/Osama-bin-Laden-dead-code-name-Geronimo.html. Geronimo was not a chief.

68   Robert D. Kaplan, "Indian Country," *Wall Street Journal*, September 21, 2004, A22, retrieved from http://search.proquest.com/docview/398893186?accountid=28109.

69   Richard Drinnon, *Facing West: The Metaphysics of Indian-Hating and Empire-Building* (Norman: University of Oklahoma Press, 1997), xiv.

70   Stephen W. Silliman, "The 'Old West' in the Middle East: U.S. Military Metaphors in Real and Imagined Indian Country," *American Anthropologist* 110, no. 2 (June 2008): 240. The first quotation is from Lieutenant Colonel Ralph Peters, U.S. Army (Ret.), reported by John Gibson, Mike Tobin, and Mike Emmanuel, in "US Soldier Kidnapped by

Terrorists in Iraq," *The Big Story with John Gibson*, Fox News Network, April 16, 2004; the second statement was attributed to a self-identified and unnamed "member of the Special Operations Community" (quoted in Michal Peirce, "A View from the Frontline in Iraq," April 13, 2003, LewRockwell.com, http://www.lewrockwell.com/peirce/peirce73.html).

71   Crispin Burke, "Everyone Relax—The Army's Native American Helicopter Names Are Not Racist," *War Is Boring* (blog), June 29, 2014, https://warisboring.com/everyone-relax-the-armys-native-american-helicopter-names-are-not-racist-d21beb55d782#.yjofo4tmy; Nicholas Schmidle, "Getting Bin Laden: What Happened That Night in Abbotabad," *New Yorker*, August 8, 2011; "Army Helicopters Get Names of Indian Tribes," *New York Times*, July 7, 1957, 53, ProQuest Historical Newspapers (1923–Current file).

Bibliography

Abinales, Patricio N. *Images of State Power: Essays on Philippine Politics from the Margins.* Quezon City: University of the Philippines Press, 1998.

———. *Making Mindanao: Cotabato and Davao in the Formation of the Philippine Nation-State.* Quezon City: Ateneo de Manila University Press, 2000.

Abinales, Patricio N., and Donna J. Amoroso. *State and Society in the Philippines.* Lanham, Md.: Rowman & Littlefield, 2005.

Acosta de Arriba, Rafael. *Debates Historiográficos.* Havana: Editorial de Ciencias Sociales, 1999.

Ade, George. *The Sultan of Sulu: An Original Satire in Two Acts.* New York: R. H. Russell, 1903.

Aleshire, Peter. *The Fox and the Whirlwind: General George Crook and Geronimo: A Paired Biography.* New York: Wiley, 2001.

Alger, R. A. *The Spanish-American War.* New York: Harper & Brothers, 1901.

Allen, David E. *The Naturalist in Britain: A Social History.* Princeton, N.J.: Princeton University Press, 1976.

Alonso, Ana María. *Thread of Blood: Colonialism, Revolution, and Gender on Mexico's Northern Frontier.* Tucson: University of Arizona Press, 1995.

———. "U.S. Military Intervention, Revolutionary Mobilization, and Popular Ideology in the Chihuahuan Sierra, 1916–1917." In *Rural Revolt in Mexico: U.S. Intervention and the Domain of Subaltern Politics*, edited by Daniel Nugent, 207–38. Durham, N.C.: Duke University Press, 1998.

Anderson, Gary Clayton. *The Conquest of Texas: Ethnic Cleansing in the Promised Land, 1820–1875.* Norman: University of Oklahoma Press, 2005.

Anderson, Mark Cronlund. *Pancho Villa's Revolution by Headlines.* Norman: University of Oklahoma Press, 2000.

Andersson, Rani-Henrik. *The Lakota Ghost Dance of 1890.* Lincoln: University of Nebraska Press, 2008.

Andrews, Avery De Lano. *My Friend and Classmate John J. Pershing; with Notes from My War Diary.* Harrisburg, Pa.: Military Service Pub. Co., 1939.

Arnold, James R., and Lawrence Freedman. *The Moro War: How America Battled a Muslim*

Insurgency in the Philippine Jungle, 1902–1913. New York: Bloomsbury Press, 2011.

Arnold, James R., and Roberta Wiener, eds. *Understanding U.S. Military Conflicts Through Primary Sources*. Santa Barbara: ABC-CLIO, 2016.

Bacevich, A. J. *American Empire: The Realities and Consequences of U.S. Diplomacy*. Cambridge, Mass.: Harvard University Press, 2002.

———. *Diplomat in Khaki: Major General Frank Ross McCoy and American Foreign Policy, 1898–1949*. Lawrence: University Press of Kansas, 1990.

———. *The Limits of Power: The End of American Exceptionalism*. New York: Metropolitan Books, 2008.

Baden-Powell, Robert Stephenson Smyth. *Aids to Scouting for N.-C. Os. & Men*. London: Gale & Polden, 1915.

Baird, George William, and Frederic Remington. *A Report to the Citizens, Concerning Certain Late Disturbances on the Western Frontier: Involving Sitting Bull, Crazy Horse, Chief Joseph and Geronimo, Opposed in the Field by Forces Under the Command of General Nelson A. (Bear-Coat) Miles*. Ashland, Calif.: L. Osborne, 1972.

Baker, Kevin. "Black Jack Pershing: From the Old West to the Western Front, from a Troop of Buffalo Soldiers to a Million Doughboys, Pershing's Globe-Circling Career Is a Virtual History of the U.S. Army." *Military History* 24, no. 7 (2007): 44–53.

Bannon, John Francis. *The Spanish Borderlands Frontier, 1513–1821*. Albuquerque: University of New Mexico Press, 1974.

Barr, Juliana, and Edward Countryman, eds. *Contested Spaces of Early America*. Philadelphia: University of Pennsylvania Press, 2014.

Barrantes, Vicente. *Guerras Piráticas de Filipinas (1570–1806)*. Málaga: Algazara, 2004.

Barrow, Mark V., Jr. *A Passion for Birds: American Ornithology After Audubon*. Princeton, N.J.: Princeton University Press, 1998.

Bateman, C. C. "Military Taming of the Moro." *Journal of the Military Service Institution* 34 (1904): 259–66.

Bates, John C. *Treaty with the Sultan of Sulu: Message from the President of the United States: Transmitting, in Response to Resolution of the Senate of January 24, 1900, Copy of the Report and all Accompanying Papers of Brig. Gen. John C. Bates in Relation to the Negotiation of a Treaty Or Agreement made by Him with the Sultan of Sulu on the 20th Day of August, 1899*. Washington, D.C.: Government Printing Office, 1900.

Beezley, William H., and Colin M. MacLachlan. *Mexicans in Revolution, 1910–1946: An Introduction*. Lincoln: University of Nebraska Press, 2009.

Bell, J. Franklin, and M. R. Davis. *Telegraphic Circulars and General Orders Regulating Campaign Against Insurgents and Proclamations and Circular Letters Relating to Reconstruction After Close of War in the Provinces of Batangas, Laguna and Mindoro, Philippine Islands*. Batangas Province, P.I.: Headquarters, Third Separate Brigade, 1902.

Benteen, Frederick William, and John M. Carroll. *Camp Talk: The Very Private Letters of Frederick W. Benteen of the 7th U.S. Cavalry to His Wife, 1871 to 1888*. Mattituck, N.Y.: J. M. Carroll, 1983.

Berbusse, Edward J. *The United States in Puerto Rico, 1898–1900*. Chapel Hill: University of North Carolina Press, 2012.

Berg, Manfred, and Simon Wendt. *Racism in the Modern World: Historical Perspectives on Cultural Transfer and Adaptation.* New York: Berghahn, 2014.

Berkhofer, Robert F. *The White Man's Indian: Images of the American Indian, from Columbus to the Present.* New York: Vintage Books, 1979.

Bernier, Felix Matos and Nelson A. Miles. "The War with Spain: III." *North American Review* 169, no. 512 (1899): 125–137. http://www.jstor.org/stable/25104853.

Bigelow, Donald N. *William Conant Church & the Army and Navy Journal.* New York: AMS Press, 1968.

Billington, Monroe Lee. *New Mexico's Buffalo Soldiers, 1866–1900.* Niwot: University Press of Colorado, 1991.

Bird, S. Elizabeth. *Dressing in Feathers: The Construction of the Indian in American Popular Culture.* Boulder, Colo.: Westview Press, 1996.

Birtle, A. J. *U.S. Army Counterinsurgency and Contingency Operations Doctrine, 1860–1941.* Washington, D.C.: Center of Military History, U.S. Army, 1999.

Bjork, Katharine. "Incorporating an Empire: From Deregulating Labor to Regulating Leisure in Cuba, Puerto Rico, Hawaii, and the Philippines, 1898–1909." PhD diss., University of Chicago, 1998.

———. "Prairie Imperialists: The Bureau of Insular Affairs and Continuities in Colonial Expansion from Nebraska to Cuba and the Philippines." *Nebraska History* 95, no. 4 (Winter 2014): 216–29.

Blackhawk, Ned. *Violence over the Land: Indians and Empires in the Early American West.* Cambridge, Mass.: Harvard University Press, 2008.

Bland, T. A. *A Brief History of the Late Military Invasion of the Home of the Sioux . . .* Washington, D.C.: National Indian Defence Association, 1891.

Bonsal, Stephen. "The Negro Soldier in War and Peace." *North American Review* 185, no. 616 (1907): 321–27.

Boot, Max. *The Savage Wars of Peace: Small Wars and the Rise of American Power.* New York: Basic Books, 2002.

Bourke, John Gregory. *An Apache Campaign in the Sierra Madre: An Account of the Expedition in Pursuit of the Hostile Chiricahua Apaches in the Spring of 1883.* New York: Scribner, 1958.

———. *The Diaries of John Gregory Bourke.* Edited by Charles M. Robinson. Denton: University of North Texas, 2005.

———. "General Crook in the Indian Country." *Century Magazine* 41 (March 1891): 643–60.

Brasch, Walter M. *Brer Rabbit, Uncle Remus, and the «Cornfield Journalist»: The Tale of Joel Chandler Harris.* Macon, Ga.: Mercer University Press, 2000.

Briggs, Asa. *Victorian Things.* Stroud, Gloucestershire: Sutton, 2003.

Bristow, Katie S. *Moro Magic in Mindanao.* Fresno, Calif.: Academy Library Guild, 1958.

Britten, Thomas A. *American Indians in World War I: At Home and at War.* Albuquerque: University of New Mexico Press, 1997.

Brown, Russell K. "A Flag for the Tenth Immunes." In *Brothers to the Buffalo Soldiers: Perspectives on the African American Militia and Volunteers, 1865–1917,* edited by Bruce A.

Glasrud, 208–22. Columbia: University of Missouri Press, 2013.

Buck, Beaumont B. *Memories of Peace and War*. San Antonio, Tex.: Naylor, 1935.

Bullard, Robert Lee. "The Cuban Negro." *North American Review* 184, no. 611 (1907): 623–30.

———. "Military Pacification." *Journal of the Military Service Institution of the United States* 46, no. 163 (January–February 1910): 1–24.

———. *Personalities and Reminiscences of the War*. Garden City, N.Y.: Doubleday, Page, 1925.

———. "Some Characteristics of the Negro Volunteer." *Journal of the Military Service Institution of the United States* 29 (July 1901): 29–39.

———. "The Teddy Buck: His Getting in Cuba and Journey to the White House." *Sports Afield* (June 1910): 513–14.

Burlin, Paul T. *Imperial Maine and Hawai'i: Interpretive Essays in the History of Nineteenth-Century American Expansion*. New York: Lexington, 2006.

Cabranes, José A. *Citizenship and the American Empire: Notes on the Legislative History of the United States Citizenship of Puerto Ricans*. New Haven, Conn.: Yale University Press, 1979.

Cabrera, Luis. "Carta Prologo." In *La expedición punitiva*, by Alberto Salinas Carranza. México: Ediciones Botas, 1936.

Calhoun, Craig J., Frederick Cooper, and Kevin W. Moore, eds. *Lessons of Empire: Imperial Histories and American Power*. New York: New Press, 2006.

Camagay, Maria Luisa T. *French Consular Dispatches on the Philippine Revolution*. Diliman, Quezon City: University of the Philippines Press in cooperation with the Office of the Chancellor, University of the Philippines, 1997.

Campbell, James D. *"Making Riflemen from Mud": Restoring the Army's Culture of Irregular Warfare*. Carlisle, Pa.: Strategic Studies Institute, U.S. Army War College, 2007.

Carroll, Bret E. *American Masculinities: An Historical Encyclopedia*. Thousand Oaks, Calif.: Sage, 2004.

Carson, Kevin. *The Long Journey of the Nez Perce: A Battle History from Cottonwood to the Bear Paw*. Yardley, Pa.: Westholme, 2011.

Cashin, Herschel V. *Under Fire with the 10th Cavalry*. New York: Bellwether, 1970.

Cather, Willa Sibert, and James R. Shively. *Writings from Willa Cather's Campus Years*. Lincoln: University of Nebraska Press, 1950.

Catton, Bruce. *This Hallowed Ground: The Story of the Union Side of the Civil War*. Garden City, N.Y.: Doubleday, 1956.

Cave, Alfred A. *The Pequot War*. Amherst: University of Massachusetts Press, 1996.

Cayton, Andrew R. L., and Fredrika J. Teute. *Contact Points: American Frontiers from the Mohawk Valley to the Mississippi, 1750–1830*. Chapel Hill: published for the Omohundro Institute of Early American History and Culture by the University of North Carolina Press, 1998.

Chanda, Nayan. *Bound Together: How Traders, Preachers, Adventurers, and Warriors Shaped Globalization*. New Haven, Conn.: Yale University Press, 2007.

Chasteen, John Charles. *National Rhythms, African Roots: The Deep History of Latin Ameri-*

can Popular Dance. Albuquerque: University of New Mexico Press, 2004.

Chipman, Donald E. *Spanish Texas, 1519–1821*. Austin: University of Texas Press, 1992.

Christian, Garna L., and Marvin E. Fletcher. "Black Soldiers in Jim Crow Texas, 1899–1917." *American Historical Review* 102, no. 5 (1997): 1630–87.

Clark, W. P. *The Indian Sign Language*. Lincoln: University of Nebraska Press, 1982.

Clendenen, Clarence C. *Blood on the Border: The United States Army and the Mexican Irregulars*. New York: Macmillan, 1969.

———. *The United States and Pancho Villa: A Study in Unconventional Diplomacy*. Ithaca, N.Y.: published for the American Historical Association by Cornell University Press, 1961.

Clodfelter, Michael. *The Dakota War: The United States Army Versus the Sioux, 1862–1865*. Jefferson, N.C.: McFarland, 2006.

Cloman, Sydney A. *Myself and a Few Moros*. Garden City, N.Y.: Doubleday, Page, 1923.

Coats, George Yarrington. *The Philippine Constabulary, 1901–1917*. Ann Arbor, Mich.: University Microfilms International, 1982.

Coffman, Edward. *Batson of the Philippine Scouts*. Carlisle Barracks, Pa.: Army War College, 1977.

Cohen, Felix S. *Handbook of Federal Indian Law*. Charlottsville, Va.: Michie Bobbs-Merrill, 1982.

Cojuangco, Margarita R. *Konstable: The Story of the Philippine Constabulary, 1901–1991*. Manila: AboCan, 1991.

Coleman, William S. E. *Voices of Wounded Knee*. Lincoln: University of Nebraska Press, 2002.

Collins, Charles. *An Apache Nightmare: The Battle at Cibecue Creek*. Norman: University of Oklahoma Press, 1999.

Conn, Steven. *History's Shadow: Native Americans and Historical Consciousness in the Nineteenth Century*. Chicago: University of Chicago Press, 2006.

Connell, Evan S. *Son of the Morning Star General Custer and the Battle of the Little Bighorn*. London: Pimlico, 2005.

Cowan, William Tynes. *The Slave in the Swamp: Disrupting the Plantation Narrative*. New York: Routledge, 2005.

Crane, Charles Judson. *The Experiences of a Colonel of Infantry*. New York: Knickerbocker Press, 1923.

Crane, Leo. *Indians of the Enchanted Desert*. Glorieta, N.M.: Rio Grande Press, 1973.

Crapol, E. P. "Coming to Terms with Empire: The Historiography of Late-Nineteenth-Century American Foreign Relations." *Diplomatic History* 16, no. 4 (1992): 573– 97.

Cronon, William. *Nature's Metropolis: Chicago and the Great West*. New York: W. W. Norton, 1991.

Crook, George. "The Apache Problem." *Journal of the Military Service Institution of the United States* 7 (October 1886): 257–69.

Crook, George, and Martin F. Schmitt. *General George Crook: His Autobiography*. Norman: University of Oklahoma Press, 1986.

Cruz, Romeo V. *America's Colonial Desk and the Philippines, 1898–1934.* Quezon City: University of the Philippines Press, 1974.

Cuba Advisory Commission. *Project of Organic Provincial Law.* Havana: Rambla and Bouza Printers, 1908.

Cullum, George Washington, and Wirt Robinson. *Biographical Register of the Officers and Graduates of the U. S. Military Academy at West Point, N. Y., from its Establishment, in 1802, to 1890; with the Early History of the United States Military Academy.* Boston: Houghton, Mifflin, 1891.

Cunningham, Roger D. *Black Citizen-Soldiers of Kansas, 1864–1901.* Columbia: University of Missouri Press, 2007.

Curry, Margaret. *The History of Platte County, Nebraska.* Culver City, Calif.: Murray & Gee, 1950.

Cutright, Paul Russell. *Theodore Roosevelt: The Making of a Conservationist.* Urbana: University of Illinois Press, 1985.

Cyrulik, John M. *Strategic Examination of the Punitive Expedition into Mexico, 1916–1917.* Fort Leavenworth, Kans.: U.S. Army Command and General Staff College, [2003]. http://cgsc.contentdm.oclc.org/u?/p4013coll2.

Dale, John T. *What Ben Beverly Saw at the Great Exposition.* Chicago: Warren, 1877.

Dale, Raymond E. *History of the state of Nebraska: Containing a Full Account of its Growth from an Uninhabited Territory to a Wealthy and Important State; of its Early Settlements; its Rapid Increase in Population, and the Marvellous Development of its Great Natural Resources; also an Extended Description of its Counties, Cities, Towns and Villages . . . Biographical Sketches . . .* Evansille, Ind.: Unigraphics, 1975.

Davis, Britton. *The Truth About Geronimo.* Lincoln: University of Nebraska Press, 1976.

Davis, Kenneth C. *The Hidden History of America at War: Untold Tales from Yorktown to Fallujah.* New York: Hachette Books, 2015.

Davis, William C. *Jefferson Davis: The Man and His Hour.* Baton Rouge: Louisiana State University Press, 1996.

Deady, Timothy K. "Lessons from a Successful Counterinsurgency: The Philippines, 1899–1902." U.S. Army War College, *Parameters* 35, no. 1 (Spring 2005): 53–68.

Dean, Christopher Thomas. "Atrocity on Trial: The Court-Martial of Littleton Waller." Master's thesis, Arizona State University, 2009.

De Barthe, Joseph, and Frank Grouard. *The Life and Adventures of Frank Grouard: Chief of Scouts.* New York: Skyhorse, 2014.

De Bevoise, Ken. *Agents of Apocalypse: Epidemic Disease in the Colonial Philippines.* Princeton, N.J.: Princeton University Press, 1995.

Debo, Angie. *Geronimo: The Man, His Time, His Place.* Norman: University of Oklahoma Press, 1976.

DeLay, Brian. "Indian Polities, Empire, and the History of American Foreign Relations." *Diplomatic History* 39, no. 5 (2015): 927–42.

———. *War of a Thousand Deserts: Indian Raids and the U.S.-Mexican War.* New Haven, Conn.: Yale University Press, 2010.

Deloria, Philip Joseph. *Playing Indian.* Yale Historical Publications. New Haven, Conn.: Yale University Press, 1998.

Deloria, Vine. *Custer Died for Your Sins: An Indian Manifesto.* New York: Macmillan, 1969.

Deloria, Vine, Jr., and David Wilkins. *The Legal Universe: Observations on the Foundations of American Law.* Golden, Colo.: Fulcrum Pub., 2011.

Dobak, William A., and Thomas D. Phillips. *The Black Regulars, 1866–1898.* Norman: University of Oklahoma Press, 2001.

Dowling, Michael J., and Barry Prichard. *Bolos, Bandits, and Bamboo Schools: Michael Dowling's Letters from the Philippines During President McKinley's War with Aguinaldo; His Plan to Transform Manila and His Bizarre Interview with the "Sultan of Sulu."* Gonvick, Minn.: Richards Pub. Co., 2009.

Drinnon, Richard. *Facing West: The Metaphysics of Indian-Hating and Empire-Building.* Norman: University of Oklahoma Press, 1997.

DuBois, Cora. *The 1870 Ghost Dance.* Millwood, N.Y.: Kraus Reprint, 1976.

Dunlay, Thomas W. *General George Crook and the "Indian Problem."* Kearney, Neb.: Kearney State College, 1972.

———. *Kit Carson and the Indians.* Lincoln: University of Nebraska Press, 2005.

———. *Wolves for the Blue Soldiers: Indian Scouts and Auxiliaries with the United States Army, 1860–90.* Lincoln: University of Nebraska Press, 1982.

Dunn, J. P., Jr. *Massacre of the Mountains: A History of the Indian Wars of the Far West.* New York: Harper & Brothers, 1886.

Dusenberry, Verne. "The Rocky Boy Indians." *Montana Magazine of History* 4, no. 1 (1954): 1–15.

———. *The Rocky Boy Indians: Montana's Displaced Persons.* Helena: Montana Historical Society Press, 1954.

Early, Gerald H. "The Negro Soldier in the Spanish-American War." Master's thesis, Shippensburg State College, 1970.

Eastman, Charles A. *From the Deep Woods to Civilization.* Mineola, N.Y.: Dover, 2003.

Eisenhower, John S. D. *Intervention! The United States and the Mexican Revolution, 1913–1917.* New York: W. W. Norton, 1993.

———. *Teddy Roosevelt and Leonard Wood: Partners in Command.* Columbia: University of Missouri Press, 2014.

Elliott, Charles B. *The Philippines to the End of the Military Régime.* Indianapolis, Ind.: Bobbs-Merrill, 1917.

Escalante, Rene R. *The American Friar Lands Policy: Its Framers, Contexts, and Beneficiaries, 1898–1916.* Manila: De La Salle University Press, 2002.

Farber, Paul Lawrence. *Discovering Birds: The Emergence of Ornithology as a Scientific Discipline, 1760–1850.* Baltimore, Md.: Johns Hopkins University Press, 1997.

Farrell, Cullom Holmes. *Incidents in the Life of General John J. Pershing.* Chicago: Rand, McNally, 1918.

Farrell, John T. "Background of the 1902 Taft Mission to Rome. I." *Catholic Historical Review* 36, no. 1 (1950): 1–32. http://www.jstor.org/stable/25015111.

Farrow, Edward S. *Mountain Scouting: A Hand-Book for Officers and Soldiers on the Frontiers.* Norman: University of Oklahoma Press, 2000.

Farwell, Byron. *Queen Victoria's Little Wars.* New York: Harper & Row, 1972.

Ferrer, Ada. *Insurgent Cuba: Race, Nation, and Revolution, 1868–1898.* Chapel Hill: University of North Carolina Press, 1999.

Feuer, A. B. *America at War: The Philippines, 1898–1913.* Westport, Conn.: Greenwood Press, 2002. http://site.ebrary.com/lib/hamline/docDetail.action?docID= 10023328&ppg=1.

Filiberti, Edward J. "The Roots of US Counterinsurgency Doctrine." *Military Review* 68, no. 1 (1988): 50–61.

Finch, George A. "Mexico and the United States." *American Journal of International Law* 11, no. 2 (April 1917): 399–406.

Flamming, Douglas. *African Americans in the West.* Santa Barbara, Calif.: ABC-CLIO, 2009.

Fleming, Thomas. *West Point in Review.* New York: American Heritage, 1988.

Fletcher, Marvin. *The Black Soldier and Officer in the United States Army, 1891–1917.* Columbia: University of Missouri Press, 1974.

———. "The Black Volunteers in the Spanish-American War." *Military Affairs* 38, no. 2 (1974): 48–53.

———. "The Negro Soldier and the United States Army, 1891–1917." PhD diss., University of Wisconsin, 1968.

Flipper, Henry Ossian. *The Colored Cadet at West Point.* Lincoln: University of Nebraska Press, 1998.

Foner, Eric, and Joshua Brown. *Forever Free: The Story of Emancipation and Reconstruction.* New York: Vintage Books, 2005.

Foner, Philip Sheldon. *The Spanish-Cuban-American War and the Birth of American Imperialism, 1895–1902.* New York: Monthly Review Press, 1972.

Fonte, Luisa. *La nación cubana y Estados Unidos: Un estudio del discurso periodístico (1906–1921).* México, D.F.: El Colegio de México, Universidad Autónoma Metropolitana-Iztapalapa, 2002.

Forbes, W. Cameron, Dean C. Worcester, and Frank W. Carpenter. *The Friar-Land Inquiry, Philippine Government: Reports.* Department of the Interior, Philippines Executive Bureau. Manila: Bureau of Printing, 1910.

Fowler, Arlen L. *The Black Infantry in the West, 1869–1891.* Norman: University of Oklahoma Press, 1996.

Frank, Ross. *From Settler to Citizen: New Mexican Economic Development and the Creation of Vecino Society, 1750–1820.* Berkeley: University of California Press, 2007.

Frazer, Chris. *Competing Voices from the Mexican Revolution: Fighting Words.* Santa Barbara, Calif.: Greenwood Press/ABC-CLIO, 2010.

Frazer, Robert Walter. *Forts of the West: Military Forts and Presidios, and Posts Commonly Called Forts, West of the Mississippi River to 1898.* Norman: University of Oklahoma Press, 1965.

Freeman, Needom N., James Edgar Allen, and John J. Reidy. *Philippine-American War: Two*

Personal Accounts of the Conflict Against Philippine and Moro Forces. S.l.: Leonaur, 2009.

Fuentes Mares, José. *Y México se refugió en el desierto: Luis Terrazas, historia y destino.* México, D.F.: Editorial Jus S.A., 1954.

Fulton, Robert A. *Honor for the Flag: The Battle of Bud Dajo—1906 and the Moro Massacre.* Bend, Ore.: Tumalo Creek Press, 2011.

———. *Moroland: The History of Uncle Sam and the Moros, 1899–1920.* Bend, Ore.: Tumalo Creek Press, 2009.

———. "The Battle of Bud Bagsak." *Uncle Sam, the Moros, and the Moro Campaigns: A Pictorial History from 1899 to 1920.* http://www.morolandhistory.com/13.PG-Battle%20 of%20Bud%20Bagsak/battle_of_Bud_Bagsak_account.htm.

Funston, Frederick. *Memories of Two Wars: Cuban and Philippine Experiences.* New York: C. Scribner's Sons, 1911.

Gaddis, John Lewis. *Surprise, Security, and the American Experience.* Cambridge, Mass.: Harvard University Press, 2005.

García, Gervasio Luis. "I Am the Other: Puerto Rico in the Eyes of North Americans, 1898." *Journal of American History* 87, no. 1 (2000): 39–64.

García, Margarita. *Antes de Cuba libre: El surgimiento del primer presidente de Cuba Tomás Estrada Palma.* Madrid: Betania, 2016.

García de la Torre, Armando. *José Martí and the Global Origins of Cuban Independence.* Kingston: University of the West Indies Press, 2015.

Garnett, William, Hugh Lenox Scott, and James McLaughlin. *Report of William Garnett, Interpreter, to General H. L. Scott and Major James McLaughlin. Big Foot Massacre enumeration, 1890.* Chicago: [Fred B. Hackett?], 1890.

Gates, John Morgan. *Schoolbooks and Krags: The United States Army in the Philippines, 1898–1902.* Contributions in Military History, vol. 3. Westport, Conn.: Greenwood Press, 1973.

———. "War-Related Deaths in the Philippines, 1898–1902." *Pacific Historical Review* 53, no. 3 (1984): 367–78.

Gatewood, Charles B., and Louis Kraft. *Black Americans and the White Man's Burden, 1898–1903.* Blacks in the New World. Urbana: University of Illinois Press, 1975.

———. *Lt. Charles Gatewood and His Apache Wars Memoir.* Lincoln: University of Nebraska Press. 2005.

———. *"Smoked Yankees" and the Struggle for Empire: Letters from Negro Soldiers, 1898–1902.* Urbana: University of Illinois Press, 1971.

Gatewood, Willard B., Jr. "Black Americans and the Quest for Empire, 1898–1903." *Journal of Southern History* 38, no. 4 (November 1972): 545–66.

Gibbon, John. *Gibbon on the Sioux Campaign of 1876.* Bellevue, Neb.: Old Army Press, 1970.

Glasrud, Bruce A., ed. *Brothers to the Buffalo Soldiers: Perspectives on the African American Militia and Volunteers, 1865–1917.* Columbia: University of Missouri Press, 2010.

Glass, Edward L. N. *History of the Tenth Cavalry, 1866–1921.* S.l.: Nabu Press, 2010.

Go, Julian, and Anne L. Foster. *The American Colonial State in the Philippines: Global Perspectives.* Durham, N.C.: Duke University Press, 2003.

Goetzmann, William H. *Army Exploration in the American West, 1803–1863.* Ann Arbor, Mich.: University Microfilms International, 1993.

Golay, Frank H. *Face of Empire: United States–Philippine Relations, 1898–1946.* Madison: University of Wisconsin–Madison, Center for Southeast Asian Studies, in cooperation with Ateneo de Manila University Press, 1998.

Goldhurst, Richard. *Pipe Clay and Drill: John J. Pershing, the Classic American Soldier.* New York: Reader's Digest Press, 1977.

Gómez, Juan Gualberto, Enrique José Varona, Salvador Cisneros y Betancourt, and Manuel Sanguily. *Antimperialismo y república.* La Habana: Editorial de Ciencias Sociales, 1975.

Goodwin, Doris Kearns. *The Bully Pulpit: Theodore Roosevelt, William Howard Taft, and the Golden Age of Journalism.* New York: Simon and Schuster, 2013.

Goodwin, Grenville. "Excerpts from the Life of John Rope, an 'Old-Timer' of the White Mountain Apaches." *Arizona Historical Review* 7, no. 1 (1936): 31–68.

Gordon, Bruce. "Mass Deaths in the Philippine-American War." *Bulletin of the American Historical Collection* 32, no. 2 (April 2004): 63–66.

Gott, Richard. *Cuba: A New History.* New Haven, Conn.: Yale University Press, 2005.

Gould, Lyman Jay. *La Ley Foraker: Raíces de la política colonial de los Estados Unidos.* Río Piedras: Editorial Universitaria Universidad de Puerto Rico, 1975.

Gould, Stephen Jay. *The Mismeasure of Man.* New York: W. W. Norton, 1981.

Gowing, Peter G. "Mandate in Moroland: The American Government of Muslim Filipinos, 1899–1920." PhD diss., Syracuse University, 1968.

———. *Mandate in Moroland: The American Government of Muslim Filipinos, 1899–1920.* Quezon City: New Day, 1983.

———. "Moros and Indians: Commonalities of Purpose, Policy and Practice in American Government of Two Hostile Subject Peoples." *Philippine Quarterly of Culture and Society* 8, no. 2/3 (1980): 125–49.

Graham, W. A. *Custer Myth, a Source Book of Custeriana; to which is Added Important Items of Custeriana and a Complete and Comprehensive Bibliography by Fred Dustin.* New York: Bonanza Books, 1953.

Grand Manifestation of the Cuban People to the Honorable Charles E. Magoon, Provisional Governor of Cuba, on the Occasion of His Trip to Matanzas and Washington. Havana: Lib. é Imp. "La Moderna Poesia," 1908.

Green, Rayna. "The Tribe Called Wannabee: Playing Indian in America and Europe." *Folklore* 99, no. 1 (1988): 30–55.

Greene, Jerome A. *Nez Perce Summer, 1877: The U.S. Army and the Nee-Me-Poo Crisis.* Helena, Mont.: Montana Historical Society Press, 2000.

———. "Out with a Whimper: The Little Missouri Expedition and the Close of the Great Sioux War." *South Dakota History* 35, no. 1 (2005): 1–39.

———. *Yellowstone Command: Colonel Nelson A. Miles and the Great Sioux War, 1876–1877.* Norman: University of Oklahoma Press, 2006.

Greenwood, John T. "Biographical Appendix." In *My Life Before the World War, 1860–1917: A Memoir by General of the Armies John J. Pershing,* edited by John T. Greenwood, 465–608. Lexington: University Press of Kentucky, 2013.

Grinnell, George Bird. *Two Great Scouts and their Pawnee Battalion: the Experiences of Frank J. North and Luther H. North, Pioneers in the Great West, 1856–1882, and Their Defence of the Building of the Union Pacific Railroad.* Lincoln: University of Nebraska Press, 1928.

Guardino, Peter. *The Dead March: A History of the Mexican-American War.* Cambridge, Mass.: Harvard University Press, 2017.

Guerra, Ramiro. *La expansión territorial de los Estados Unidos a expensas de España y de los países hispanoamericanos.* La Habana: Editorial de Ciencias Sociales, 2008.

Gwynne, S. C. *Empire of the Summer Moon: Quanah Parker and the Rise and Fall of the Comanches, the most Powerful Indian Tribe in American History.* New York: Scribner, 2010.

Hagedorn, Hermann. *Leonard Wood: A Biography.* New York: Harper & Brothers, 1931.

Haley, P. E. *Revolution and Intervention: The Diplomacy of Taft and Wilson with Mexico, 1910–1917.* Cambridge, Mass.: Massachusetts Institute of Technology Press, 1971.

Haller, John S. *Outcasts from Evolution: Scientific Attitudes of Racial Inferiority, 1859–1900.* Urbana: University of Illinois Press, 1971.

Hardeman, Nicholas P. "Brick Strong Hold of the Border: Fort Assinniboine, 1879–1911." *Montana: The Magazine of Western History* 29, no. 2 (1979): 54–67.

Hargrave, John. *Lonecraft: The Handbook for Lone Scouts.* London: Constable, 1918.

Harlow, Alvin F., and Joel Chandler Harris. *Joel Chandler Harris, Plantation Storyteller.* New York: J. Messner, 1963.

Harper, James William. "Hugh Lenox Scott: Soldier-Diplomat, 1876–1917." PhD diss., University of Virginia, 1968.

Harrington, Dale B. "Hugh Lenox Scott: The Forgotten Influence." History seminar paper, University of Texas at El Paso, 1996.

Harris, Charles H., and Louis R. Sadler. *The Great Call-Up: The Guard, the Border, and the Mexican Revolution.* Norman: University of Oklahoma Press, 2015.

———. *The Secret War in El Paso: Mexican Revolutionary Intrigue, 1906–1920.* Albuquerque: University of New Mexico Press, 2009.

Harris, Joel Chandler. *On the Plantation: A Story of a Georgia Boy's Adventures During the War.* Illustrated by E. W. Kemble. Foreword by Erskine Caldwell. Athens: University of Georgia Press, 1989.

Harris, Joel Chandler, and A. B. Frost. *Uncle Remus: His Songs and His Sayings.* New and rev. ed. New York: Appleton, 1896.

Hart, John Mason. *Empire and Revolution: The Americans in Mexico Since the Civil War.* Berkeley: University of California Press, 2005.

Hartigan, Richard Shelly. *Lieber's Code and the Law of War.* Chicago: Precedent, 1983.

Hatfield, Shelley Ann Bowen. *Chasing Shadows: Indians Along the United States–Mexico Border, 1876–1911.* Albuquerque: University of New Mexico Press, 1999.

Haverstock, Nathan A. *Fifty Years at the Front: The Life of War Correspondent Frederick Palmer.* Washington, D.C.: Brassey's, 1996.

Hawkins, Michael C. *Making Moros: Imperial Historicism and American Military Rule in the Philippines' Muslim South.* DeKalb: Northern Illinois University Press, 2013.

Healy, David. *The United States in Cuba, 1898–1902: Generals, Politicians, and the Search for Policy.* Madison: University of Wisconsin Press, 1963.

Hector-Schneider, Dietmar. "The Apache Scouts, 1871–1886: Nemesis of the Netdahe." Master's thesis, Austin Peay State University, 1980.

Hedren, Paul L. *After Custer: Loss and Transformation in Sioux Country.* Norman: University of Oklahoma Press, 2011.

———. *We Trailed the Sioux: Enlisted Men Speak on Custer, Crook, and the Great Sioux War.* Mechanicsburg, Pa.: Stackpole Books, 2003.

Hibben, Paxton. "The Story of a Soldier's Life: A Half-Century of Army Service." *Mentor* 16, no. 8, serial no. 308 (September 1928): 1–10.

Hinsley, Curtis M. *The Smithsonian and the American Indian: Making a Moral Anthropology in Victorian America.* Washington, D.C.: Smithsonian Institution Press, 1994.

Hitchman, James H. *Leonard Wood and Cuban Independence, 1898–1902.* The Hague: Nijhoff, 1971.

Hixson, John A. "The United States Army General Staff Corps, 1910–1917: Its Relationship to the Field Forces." Master's thesis, Rice University, 1971. http://hdl.handle.net/1911/89095.

Hobusch, Erich. *Fair Game: A History of Hunting, Shooting, and Animal Conservation.* New York: Arco, 1981.

Hodge, Hiram C. *Arizona as It Was, 1877.* Chicago: Rio Grande Press, 1965.

Hoganson, Kristin. *Fighting for American Manhood: How Gender Politics Provoked the Spanish-American and Philippine-American Wars.* New Haven, Conn.: Yale University Press, 1998.

Holbrook, Franklin F. *Minnesota in the Spanish-American War and the Philippine Insurrection.* Saint Paul: Minnesota War Records Commission, 1923.

Holli, Melvin G., and Cornelius Gardner. "A View of the American Campaign Against 'Filipino Insurgents': 1900." *Philippine Studies* 17, no. 1 (1969): 97–111.

Holm, Tom. "Stereotypes, State Elites, and the Military Use of American Indian Troops." *Plural Societies* 15, no. 3 (1984): 265–82.

Hooker, Forrestine C., and Steve Wilson. *Child of the Fighting Tenth: On the Frontier with the Buffalo Soldiers.* Norman: University of Oklahoma Press, 2011.

Hoover, Herbert T. "The Sioux Agreement of 1889 and Its Aftermath." *South Dakota History* 19, no. 1 (1989): 56–94.

Horsman, Reginald. *Race and Manifest Destiny: The Origins of American Racial Anglo-Saxonism.* Cambridge, Mass.: Harvard University Press, 1981.

Hoxie, Frederick E., ed. *Encyclopedia of North American Indians.* Boston: Houghton Mifflin, 1996.

Huhndorf, Shari M. *Going Native: Indians in the American Cultural Imagination.* Ithaca, N.Y.: Cornell University Press, 2001.

Hurley, Vic. *Swish of the Kris: The Story of the Moros.* New York: E. P. Dutton, 1936.

Hurst, James W. *Pancho Villa and Black Jack Pershing: The Punitive Expedition in Mexico.* Westport, Conn.: Praeger, 2008.

Hurt, R. Douglas. *The Indian Frontier, 1763–1846*. Albuquerque: University of New Mexico Press, 2002.

Hyde, George E. *Red Cloud's Folk: A History of the Oglala Sioux Indians*. Norman: University of Oklahoma Press, 1937.

Hyman, Colette A. "Survival at Crow Creek, 1863–1866." *Minnesota History* 61, no. 4 (Winter 2008-9): 148–61.

Hyman, George. *How the Battleship Maine Was Destroyed*. Annapolis, Md.: Naval Institute Press, 1995.

Iglesias Utset, Mariel. *A Cultural History of Cuba During the U.S. Occupation, 1898–1902*. Translated by Russ Davidson. Chapel Hill: University of North Carolina Press, 2011.

———. *Las metáforas del cambio en la vida cotidiana: Cuba, 1898–1902*. Havana: Ediciones Unión, 2003.

Ignacio, Abe. *The Forbidden Book: The Philippine-American War in Political Cartoons*. San Francisco, Calif.: T'Boli, 2004.

Jackson, Bruce, ed. *The Negro and His Folklore in Nineteenth-Century Periodicals*. Austin: published for the American Folklore Society by the University of Texas Press, 1967.

Jacobson, Matthew Frye. *Barbarian Virtues: The United States Encounters Foreign Peoples at Home and Abroad, 1876–1917*. New York: Hill and Wang, 2001.

James, Edmund J. *Military Training in Our Land Grant Colleges . . .* Urbana, Ill.: University, 1916.

———. *The Origin of the Land Grant Act of 1862 (the So-Called Morrill Act) and Some Account of Its Author Jonathan B. Turner*. Urbana-Champaign: University of Illinois Press, 1984.

Jenks, Maud Huntley. *Death Stalks the Philippine Wilds: Letters of Maud Huntley Jenks*. Minneapolis, Minn.: Lund Press, 1951.

Jensen, Richard E., R. Eli Paul, and John E. Carter. *Eyewitness at Wounded Knee*. Lincoln: University of Nebraska Press, 2011.

Johnson, Alvin Saunders. *Pioneer's Progress: An Autobiography*. Lincoln: University of Nebraska Press, 1962.

Johnson, Robert David. *On Cultural Ground: Essays in International History*. Chicago: Imprint Publications, 1994.

Johnson, Virginia Weisel. *The Unregimented General: A Biography of Nelson A. Miles*. Boston: Houghton Mifflin, 1962.

Jones, Gregg R. *Honor in the Dust: Theodore Roosevelt, War in the Philippines, and the Rise and Fall of America's Imperial Dream*. New York: New American Library, 2012.

Jornacion, George William. *The Time of the Eagles: United States Army Officers and the Pacification of the Philippine Moros, 1899–1913*. Ann Arbor, Mich.: University Microfilms International, 1978.

Kagan, Robert. *Dangerous Nation*. New York: Alfred A. Knopf, 2006.

Kalaw, Teodoro M. *The Philippine Revolution*. Kawilihan: Jorge B. Vargas Filipiniana Foundation, 1969.

Kaplan, Amy. *The Anarchy of Empire in the Making of U.S. Culture*. Cambridge, Mass.: Harvard University Press, 2002. .

———. "Black and Blue on San Juan Hill." In *The Anarchy of Empire in the Making of U.S. Culture*, 121–45. Cambridge, Mass.: Harvard University Press, 2002.

———. "Where Is Guantánamo?" *American Quarterly* 57, no. 3 (2005): 831–58.

Kaplan, Robert D. *Imperial Grunts: On the Ground with the American Military, from Mongolia to the Philippines to Iraq and Beyond*. New York: Vintage Books, 2005.

Kappler, Kathryn J. *My Own Pioneers, 1830–1918*. Vol. 3, *The Last Pioneers: Refuge in Mexico, 1876–1918*. Parker, Colo.: Outskirts Press, 2015.

Karnow, Stanley. *In Our Image: America's Empire in the Philippines*. New York: Ballantine Books, 1990.

Katakis, Michael. *Excavating Voices: Listening to Photographs of Native Americans*. Philadelphia: University of Pennsylvania Museum of Archaeology and Anthropology, 1998.

Katz, Friedrich. *The Ancient American Civilizations*. New York: Praeger, 1972.

———. *The Life and Times of Pancho Villa*. Stanford, Calif.: Stanford University Press, 1998.

———. "Pancho Villa and the Attack on Columbus, New Mexico." *American Historical Review* 83, no. 1 (1978): 101–30.

———. *The Secret War in Mexico: Europe, the United States and the Mexican Revolution*. Chicago: University of Chicago Press, 1981.

Kaywaykla, James, and Eve Ball. *In the Days of Victorio: Recollections of a Warm Springs Apache*. Tucson: University of Arizona Press, 1970.

Kennan, George. *Campaigning in Cuba*. New York: Century, 1899.

Kenner, Charles L. *Buffalo Soldiers and Officers of the Ninth Cavalry, 1867–1898: Black and White Together*. Norman: University of Oklahoma Press, 1999.

Kerr, James Edward. *The Insular Cases: The Role of the Judiciary in American Expansionism*. Port Washington, N.Y.: Kennikat Press, 1982.

Kessler, Richard J. *Rebellion and Repression in the Philippines*. New Haven, Conn.: Yale University Press, 1991.

Kilroy, David P. *For Race and Country: The Life and Career of Colonel Charles Young*. Westport, Conn.: Praeger, 2003.

King, Charles. *Campaigning with Crook: And Stories of Army Life*. Vol. 4. S.l.: Nabu Press, 2011.

King, James T. *War Eagle: A Life of General Eugene A. Carr*. Lincoln: University of Nebraska Press, 1963.

Knight, Edward Henry. *A Study of the Savage Weapons at the Centennial Exhibition, Philadelphia, 1876*. Washington, D.C.: Government Printing Office, 1880.

Knoll, Robert E. *Prairie University: A History of the University of Nebraska*. Lincoln: published by the University of Nebraska Press for the Alumni Association of the University of Nebraska, 1995.

Kramer, Paul A. *The Blood of Government: Race, Empire, the United States, and the Philippines*. Chapel Hill: University of North Carolina Press, 2006.

———. "The Water Cure—the First Torture Debate." *New Yorker*, February 25, 2008, 38–43.

Krech, Shepard, III, and Barbara A. Hail. *Collecting Native America, 1870–1960*. Washington, D.C.: Smithsonian Institution Press, 1999.

Krenn, Michael L. *Race and U.S. Foreign Policy in the Ages of Territorial and Market Expansion.* New York: Garland, 1998.

Lacey, Jim. *Pershing.* New York: Palgrave Macmillan, 2008.

LaDow, Beth. *The Medicine Line: Life and Death on a North American Borderland.* New York: Routledge, 2001.

LaDuke, Winona, and Sean Aaron Cruz. *The Militarization of Indian Country.* East Lansing, Mich.: Makwa Enewed, 2012.

LaFeber, Walter. *The New Empire: An Interpretation of American Expansion, 1860–1898.* Ithaca, N.Y.: Cornell University Press, 1998.

Lamar, Howard Roberts. *The Far Southwest, 1846–1912: A Territorial History.* Albuquerque: University of New Mexico Press, 2000.

Lamm, Alan K. "Buffalo Soldiers Chaplains: A Case Study of the Five Black United States Army Chaplains, 1884–1901." PhD diss., University of South Carolina, 1995.

Landor, Arnold Henry Savage. *The Gems of the East: Sixteen Thousand Miles of Research Travel Among Wild and Tame Tribes of Enchanting Islands.* Whitefish, Mont.: Kessinger, 2004.

Lane, Jack C., ed. *Chasing Geronimo: The Journal of Leonard Wood, May–September, 1886.* Albuquerque: University of New Mexico Press, 1970.

Lane, Jill. *Blackface Cuba, 1840–1895.* Philadelphia: University of Pennsylvania Press, 2005.

Lazarus, Edward. *Black Hills/White Justice: The Sioux Nation Versus the United States, 1775 to the Present.* New York: HarperCollins, 1991.

Leckie, William H., and Shirley A. Leckie. *The Buffalo Soldiers: A Narrative of the Black Cavalry in the West.* Norman: University of Oklahoma Press, 2003.

Lee, Fitzhugh, Joseph Wheeler, Theodore Roosevelt, and Richard Wainwright. *Cuba's Struggle Against Spain with the Causes of American Intervention and a Full Account of the Spanish-American War, Including Final Peace Negotiations.* New York: American Historical Press, 1899.

Lee, Ivy L., Joel Chandler Harris, James Wideman Lee, and Frank Lebby Stanton. *"Uncle Remus," Joel Chandler Harris as seen and Remembered by a Few of His Friends: Including a Memorial Sermon by the Rev. James W. Lee, D.D., and a Poem by Frank Stanton.* [New York?]: s.n., 1908.

León García, Ricardo, and Carlos González Herrera. *Civilizar o exterminar: Tarahumaras y apaches en Chihuahua, siglo XIX.* Tlalpan, México, D.F.: CIESA, 2000.

Leonard, Elizabeth D. *Men of Color to Arms! Black Soldiers, Indian Wars, and the Quest for Equality.* Lincoln: University of Nebraska Press, 2012.

LeRoy, James A. *Americans in the Philippines: A History of the Conquest, and First Years of Occupation . . . with an Introductory Account of the Spanish Rule.* S.l.: Forgotten Books, 2016.

Lhamon, W. T. *Raising Cain: Blackface Performance from Jim Crow to Hip Hop.* Cambridge, Mass.: Harvard University Press, 1998.

———. *The U.S. Army and Counterinsurgency in the Philippine War, 1899–1902.* Chapel Hill: University of North Carolina Press, 1989.

Lieber, Francis, and Richard Shelly Hartigan, eds. *Lieber's Code and the Law of War.* Chicago: Precedent, 1983.

Link, Arthur, ed. *Woodrow Wilson Papers*. 69 vols. Princeton, N.J.: Princeton University Press, 1947–65.

Linn, Brian McAllister. *Guerrilla Fighter: Frederick Funston in the Philippines, 1900–1901*. Topeka: Kansas State Historical Society, 1987.

———. *The Philippine War, 1899–1902*. Lawrence: University Press of Kansas, 2000.

———. *The U.S. Army and Counterinsurgency in the Philippine War, 1899–1902*. Chapel Hill: University of North Carolina Press, 2008.

Lockmiller, David A. *Enoch H. Crowder: Soldier, Lawyer, and Statesman*. University of Missouri Studies, vol. 27. Columbia: University of Missouri, 1955.

———. *Magoon in Cuba: A History of the Second Intervention, 1906–1909*. New York: Greenwood Press, 1969.

———. *This, That, and the Other: Writings of David A. Lockmiller, President, University of Chattanooga, 1942–1959*. Hermitage, Tenn.: Serendipity Press, 2002.

Logan, Enid Lynette. "The 1899 Cuban Marriage Law Controversy: Church, State and Empire in the Crucible of Nation." *Journal of Social History* 42, no. 2 (2008): 469–94.

Logan, Herschel C. *Buckskin and Satin: The Life of Texas Jack (J. B. Omohundro) Buckskin Clad Scout, Indian Fighter, Plainsman, Cowboy, Hunter, Guide, and Actor, and His Wife, Mlle. Morlacchi, Premiere Danseuse in Satin Slippers*. Harrisburg, Pa.: Stackpole, 1954.

Lorini, Alessandra. *An Intimate and Contested Relation: The United States and Cuba in the Late Nineteenth and Early Twentieth Centuries = Una relación íntima y controvertida: Estados Unidos y Cuba entre los siglos XIX y XX*. Florence: Firenze University Press, 2005.

Lotilla, Raphael Perpetuo M., ed. *The Philippine National Territory: A Collection of Related Documents*. Quezon City: Institute of International Legal Studies, University of the Philippines Law Center; Foreign Service Institute, Department of Foreign Affairs, 1995.

Lowe, Percival G., and Don Russell, eds. *Five Years a Dragoon ('49 to '54) and Other Adventures on the Great Plains with an Introduction and Notes*. Norman: University of Oklahoma Press, 1965.

Lowell, A. Lawrence. "The Government of Dependencies." *Annals of the American Academy of Political and Social Science* 13, no. 12 (1899): 46–59.

Luce, Edward S. *Keogh, Comanche, and Custer*. St. Louis, Mo.: John S. Swift, 1939.

Lunde, Darrin P. *The Naturalist: Theodore Roosevelt and the Rise of American Natural History*. New York: Crown, 2016.

Lynk, Miles V. *The Black Troopers; Or, the Daring Heroism of the Negro Soldiers in the Spanish-American War*. New York: AMS Press, 1971.

MacAdam, George. "The Life of General Pershing." *World's Work* 37 (1918–1919): 45–681.

MacArthur, Arthur. *Report of Major General Arthur MacArthur, U.S. Army, Commanding, Division of the Philippines. Military Governor in the Philippine Islands . . .* United States, Army Division of the Philippines. Manila: s.n., 1900.

MacDonald, Robert H. *Sons of the Empire: The Frontier and the Boy Scout Movement, 1890–1918*. Toronto: University of Toronto Press, 1993.

MacKenzie, John M. *The Empire of Nature: Hunting, Conservation, and British Imperialism*. Manchester: Manchester University Press, 1988.

MacLachlan, Colin M., and William H. Beezley. *El Gran Pueblo: A History of Greater Mexico.* Upper Saddle River, N.J.: Prentice Hall, 2004.

Magoon, Charles E. *The Organic Law of the Executive Power and the General Regulations for the Department of the Government of Cuba of January 26, 1909.* Havana: Rambla and Bouza, 1909.

———. *Report on the Right of the Government of the Philippine Islands, Instituted by the President of the United States, to Regulate Commercial Intercourse with the Archipelago, and, as an Incident to such Regulation, to Impose Import and Export Duties.* Washington, D.C.: Government Printing Office, 1901.

———. *Reports on Law of Civil Government in Territory Subject to Military Occupation by Military Forces of the United States.* Division of Insular Affairs. Washington, D.C.: Government Printing Office, 1902.

———. *What Followed the Flag in the Philippines.* New York: Freitag, 1904.

Majul, Cesar Adib. *Mabini and the Philippine Revolution.* Quezon City: University of the Philippines Press, 1996.

———. "Political and Historical Notes on the Old Sulu Sultanate." *Journal of the Malaysian Branch of the Royal Asiatic Society* 38, no. 1 (207) (1965): 23–42. http://www.jstor.org/stable/41491838.

Malmros, Oscar. *Perspective on the Sioux War: Oscar Malmros, Minnesota's Adjutant General; Reports of the Adjutant General to the Governor of Minnesota, September 1862 & January 1863.* Edited by Mary Hawker Bakeman. Roseville, Minn.: Prairie Echoes, 2007.

Marcy, Randolph Barnes. *The Prairie Traveler: A Hand-Book for Overland Expeditions.* Williamstown, Mass.: Corner House, 1859.

Marks, George P., III. *The Black Press Views American Imperialism.* New York: Arno Press, 1971.

Marshall, Joseph. *The Day the World Ended at Little Bighorn: A Lakota History.* New York: Penguin Books, 2008.

Martinez, J. Michael. *Carpetbaggers, Cavalry, and the Ku Klux Klan: Exposing the Invisible Empire during Reconstruction.* Lanham, Md.: Rowman & Littlefield, 2007.

Mason, Herbert Molloy. *The Great Pursuit.* New York: Smithmark, 1995.

Mason, Joyce Evelyn. "The Use of Indian Scouts in the Apache Wars, 1870–1886." PhD diss., Indiana University, Bloomington, 1970.

Matos Bernier, Félix, and Nelson A. Miles. "The War with Spain: III." *North American Review* 169, no. 512 (July 1, 1899): 125–37. http://www.jstor.org/stable/25104853.

May, Glenn Anthony. *Battle for Batangas: A Philippine Province at War.* New Haven, Conn.: Yale University Press, 1991

———. *A Past Updated: Further Essays on Philippine History and Historiography.* Quezon City: New Day, 2013.

———. *Social Engineering in the Philippines: The Aims, Execution, and Impact of American Colonial Policy, 1900–1913.* Quezon City: New Day, 1984.

———. "The 'Zones' of Batangas." *Philippine Studies* 29, no. 1 (1981): 89–103.

McCabe, James D. *The Illustrated History of the Centennial Exhibition: Held in Commemoration of the One Hundredth Anniversary of American Independence, with a Full De-*

scription of the Great Buildings . . . Philadelphia: National Pub. Co., 1876.

McCallum, Jack Edward. *Leonard Wood: Rough Rider, Surgeon, Architect of American Imperialism.* New York: New York University Press, 2006.

McCoy, Alfred W. *Policing America's Empire: The United States, the Philippines, and the Rise of the Surveillance State.* Madison: University of Wisconsin Press, 2009.

———. *Torture and Impunity: The U.S. Doctrine of Coercive Interrogation.* Madison: University of Wisconsin Press, 2012.

McCrady, David G. *Living with Strangers: The Nineteenth-Century Sioux and the Canadian-American Borderlands.* Lincoln: University of Nebraska Press, 2006.

McGinnis, Anthony. *Counting Coup and Cutting Horses: Intertribal Warfare on the Northern Plains, 1738–1889.* Evergreen, Colo.: Cordillera Press, 1990.

McIntyre, Frank. "American Territorial Administration." *Foreign Affairs* 10, no. 2 (1932): 293–303.

McKenna, Thomas M. *Muslim Rulers and Rebels: Everyday Politics and Armed Separatism in the Southern Philippines.* Manila: Anvil, 2002.

Meadows, William C. *Through Indian Sign Language: The Fort Sill Ledgers of Hugh Lenox Scott and Iseeo, 1889–1897.* Norman: University of Oklahoma Press, 2015.

Mellander, Gustavo A., and Nelly Mellander. *Charles Edward Magoon: The Panama Years.* San Juan: Editorial Plaza Mayor, 1999.

Merry, Sally Engle. "Law and Colonialism." *Law & Society Review* 25, no. 4 (1991): 889–922.

México, Secretaría de Relaciones Exteriores. *Diplomatic Dealings of the Constitutionalist Revolution of Mexico.* México: Impr. Nacional, 1918.

Michno, Gregory. *Lakota Noon: The Indian Narrative of Custer's Defeat.* Missoula, Mont.: Mountain Press, 1997.

Miles, Nelson Appleton. *Annual Report of Major General Nelson A. Miles, U.S. Army: Commanding the Department of the Missouri.* Chicago: Assistant Adjutant General's Office, Dept. of the Missouri, 1891.

———. *The Future of the Indian Question.* S.l.: s.n., 1891.

———. *Rounding Up the Redmen: Personal Narrative of the Stirring Encounters with the Indians Who Killed Custer and of the Events Leading Up to the Defeat of the Great Chiefs, Sitting Bull and Crazy Horse.* New York: Hearst, 1911.

———. *Serving the Republic: Memoirs of the Civil and Military Life of Nelson A. Miles, Lieutenant-General, United States Army.* New York: Harper & Brothers, 1911.

———. "The Work of the Army as a Whole." In *The American-Spanish War: A History by the War Leaders, Illustrated with Numerous Original Engravings, Maps and Diagrams,* 509–40. Norwich, Conn.: Chas. C. Haskell & Son, 1899.

Miles, Nelson Appleton. *Personal Recollections and Observations of General Nelson A. Miles Embracing a Brief View of the Civil War, Or, from New England to the Golden Gate: And the Story of His Indian Campaigns, with Comments on the Exploration, Development and Progress of our Great Western Empire.* Edited by Frederic Remington. Chicago: Werner, 1897.

Miles, Nelson Appleton. *Personal Recollections and Observations of General Nelson A. Miles.* Edited by Robert M. Utley. New York: Da Cape Press, 1969.

Military Order of Moro Campaigns [Philip Reade, Wassell Hildreth, W. H. McCain, et al.]. *Constitution and By-Laws of the Military Order of Moro Campaigns: Organized at Malabang, Mindanao, P.I., April 22, 1905.* Malabang, Philippines: s.n., 1905.

Miller, David Humphreys. *Ghost Dance.* Lincoln: University of Nebraska Press, 1985.

Miller, Edward A. *Lincoln's Abolitionist General: The Biography of David Hunter.* Columbia: University of South Carolina Press, 1997.

Miller, Stuart Creighton. *"Benevolent Assimilation": The American Conquest of the Philippines, 1899–1903.* New Haven, Conn.: Yale University Press, 1982.

Millett, Allan Reed. *The General: Robert L. Bullard and Officership in the United States Army, 1881–1925.* Westport, Conn.: Greenwood Press, 1975.

———. *The Politics of Intervention: The Military Occupation of Cuba, 1906–1909.* Columbus: Ohio State University Press, 1968.

Millett, Allan Reed, and Peter Maslowski. *For the Common Defense: A Military History of the United States of America.* New York: Collier Macmillan, 1984.

Mills, Elizabeth H. "The Mormon Colonies in Chihuahua After the 1912 Exodus." Master's thesis, University of Arizona, 1950.

Miner, Craig H. "The United States Government Building at the Centennial Exhibition, 1874–77." *Prologue: The Journal of the National Archives* 4 (Winter 1972): 202–18.

Minger, Ralph Eldin. "William H. Taft and the United States Intervention in Cuba in 1906." *Hispanic American Historical Review* 41, no. 1 (1961): 75–89.

Minnesota. Board of Commissioners on Publication of History of Minnesota in Civil and Indian Wars. *Minnesota in the Civil and Indian Wars, 1861–1865.* 2nd ed. St. Paul, Minn.: printed for the State by the Pioneer Press Company, 1899.

Mooney, James. *The Ghost-Dance Religion, and the Sioux Outbreak of 1890.* Classics in Anthropology. Chicago: University of Chicago Press, 1965.

Morgan, H. Wayne. *America's Road to Empire: The War with Spain and Overseas Expansion.* New York: McGraw-Hill, 1993.

Murray, David. *Matter, Magic, and Spirit: Representing Indian and African American Belief.* Philadelphia: University of Pennsylvania Press, 2007.

Nash, Willard Lee. *A Study of the Stated Aims and Purposes of the Departments of Military Science and Tactics, and of Physical Education in the Land-Grant Colleges of the United States.* New York: Teachers College, Bureau of Publications, 1934.

Newton, Brandon D. *Punishment, Revenge, and Retribution: A Historical Analysis of Punitive Operations.* Ft. Belvoir, Va.: Defense Technical Information Center. http://handle.dtic.mil/100.2/ADA436111.

Nugent, Daniel. *Rural Revolt in Mexico: U.S. Intervention and the Domain of Subaltern Politics.* Durham, N.C.: Duke University Press, 1998.

———. *Spent Cartridges of Revolution: Anthropological History of Namiquipa, Chihuahua.* Chicago: University of Chicago Press, 1993

Nugent, Walter. *Habits of Empire.* New York: Vintage Books, 2009.

Nye, Wilbur Sturtevant. *Carbine and Lance: The Story of Old Fort Sill.* Norman: University of Oklahoma Press, 1943.

O'Connor, Richard. *Black Jack Pershing.* Garden City, N.Y.: Doubleday, 1961.

Order of the Indian Wars, and James T. Kerr. "Proceedings of the Annual Meeting and

Dinner of the Order of Indian Wars of the United States: Held at the Army and Navy Club, Washington D.C.," January 24, 1931. S.l.: s.n., 1931.

Orton, Arthur W., Fred D. Shadell, and C. Duffy Lewis. *History of the 39th U.S. Volunteer Infantry, "Bullard's Indians."* S.l.: 39th U.S. Volunteer Infantry Association, 1949.

Osterreich, Shelley Anne. *The American Indian Ghost Dance, 1870 and 1890: An Annotated Bibliography.* New York: Greenwood Press, 1991.

Ostler, Jeffrey. *The Plains Sioux and U.S. Colonialism from Lewis and Clark to Wounded Knee.* Cambridge: Cambridge University Press, 2006.

Oswald, Mark G. *The "Howling Wilderness" Courts-Martial of 1902.* Carlisle Barracks, Pa.: U.S. Army War College, 2001.

Otis, Elwell S. *The Indian Question.* New York: Sheldon, 1878.

Owen, Norman G. *Compadre Colonialism.* Ann Arbor: Center for South and Southeast Asian Studies, University of Michigan, 1971.

Palmer, Frederick. *Bliss, Peacemaker: The Life and Letters of General Tasker Howard Bliss.* Freeport, N.Y.: Books for Libraries Press, 1970.

———. *John J. Pershing, General of the Armies: A Biography.* Harrisburg, Pa.: Military Service Pub. Co., 1948.

———. *Newton D. Baker: America at War; Based on the Personal Papers of the Secretary of War in the World War, His Correspondence with the President and Important Leaders at Home and Abroad, the Confidential Cablegrams Between the War Department and Headquarters in France, the Minutes of the War Industries Board, and Other First-Hand Material.* New York: Dodd, Mead, 1931.

———. *With My Own Eyes: A Personal Story of Battle Years.* London: Jarrolds, 1934.

Palmer, Steven Paul, José A. Piqueras Arenas, and Amparo Sánchez Cobos, eds. *State of Ambiguity: Civic Life and Culture in Cuba's First Republic.* Durham, N.C.: Duke University Press, 2014.

Paredes, Ruby R. *Philippine Colonial Democracy.* Quezon City: Ateneo de Manila University Press, 1989.

Parker, James. *The Old Army: Memories, 1872–1918.* Philadelphia, Pa.: Dorrance, 1929.

Parkman, Francis, and Samuel Eliot Morison. *The Conspiracy of Pontiac.* New introduction by Samuel Eliot Morison. New York: Collier, 1962.

———. *Francis Parkman: Representative Selections.* Edited by Wilbur Schramm. New York: American Book, 1938.

Paul, R. Eli. *The Nebraska Indian Wars Reader, 1865–1877.* Lincoln: University of Nebraska Press, 1998.

Pérez, Louis A., Jr. "Between Meanings and Memories of 1898." *Orbis* 42, no. 4 (Fall 1998): 501–16. Accessed May 6, 2016, *EBSCO MegaFILE,* EBSCO*host.*

———. *Cuba between Empires: 1878-1902.* Pittsburgh: University of Pittsburgh Press, 1983.

———. *Cuba: Between Reform and Revolution.* Oxford: Oxford University Press, 2015.

———. *Cuba and the United States: Ties of Singular Intimacy.* Athens: University of Georgia Press, 2003.

———. *Cuba Under the Platt Amendment, 1902–1934.* Pittsburgh, Pa.: University of Pittsburgh Press, 1991.

———. *Essays on Cuban History: Historiography and Research.* Gainesville: University Press of Florida, 1995.

———. *The War of 1898: The United States and Cuba in History and Historiography.* Chapel Hill: University of North Carolina Press, 1998.

Pershing, John J. *My Life Before the World War, 1860–1917: A Memoir by General of the Armies John J. Pershing.* Edited by John T. Greenwood. Lexington: University Press of Kentucky, 2013.

Pfaller, Louis. *The Sully Expedition of 1864: Featuring the Killdeer Mountain and Badlands Battles.* Bismarck, N.Dak.: State Historical Society of North Dakota, 1964.

Picó, Fernando, Sylvia Korwek, and Psique Arana Guzmán, trans. *Puerto Rico, 1898: The War After the War.* Princeton, N.J.: Markus Wiener, 2004.

Pier, Arthur Stanwood. *American Apostles to the Philippines.* Freeport, N.Y.: Books for Libraries Press, 1971.

Pogue, Forrest C. *George C. Marshall.* New York: Viking Press, 1963.

Pohanka, Brian C., and John M. Carroll, eds. *Nelson A. Miles: A Documentary Biography of His Military Career, 1861–1903.* Glendale, Calif.: Arthur H. Clark, 1985.

Pollard, Edward Alfred. *Black Diamonds Gathered in the Darkey Homes of the South.* New York: Pudney & Russell, 1859.

Polzer, Charles W. *Military History of the Spanish-American Southwest: A Seminar.* Fort Huachuca, Ariz.: s.n., 1976.

Porter, Joseph C. *Paper Medicine Man: John Gregory Bourke and His American West.* Norman: University of Oklahoma Press, 1989.

Powers, Thomas. *The Killing of Crazy Horse.* New York: Alfred A. Knopf, 2010.

Preston, Douglas J. *Dinosaurs in the Attic: An Excursion into the American Museum of Natural History.* New York: St. Martin's Press, 1986.

"Proclamation of 1763." *The American Revolution*, Primary Source Media, 1999, American Journey, *Student Resources Context.* Accessed August 14, 2017. link.galegroup.com/apps/doc/EJ2153000004/SUIC?u=clic_hamline&xid=4d0f29e6.

Prucha, Paul Francis. *American Indian Treaties: The History of a Political Anomaly.* Berkeley: University of California Press, 1984.

Quesada, Gonzalo de, and Henry Davenport Northrop. *The War in Cuba.* New York: Arno Press, 1970.

Raat, W. Dirk, and George Janecek. *Mexico's Sierra Tarahumara: A Photohistory of the People of the Edge.* Norman: University of Oklahoma Press, 1996.

Ramsey, Robert D., III. *A Masterpiece of Counterguerrilla Warfare: BG J. Franklin Bell in the Philippines, 1901–1902.* Long War Series Occasional Paper 25. Fort Leavenworth, Kans.: Combat Studies Institute Press, 2007.

Ravage, John W. *Black Pioneers: Images of the Black Experience on the North American Frontier.* Salt Lake City: University of Utah Press, 2008.

Reber, Bruce, Louise A. Arnold-Friend, and Richard J. Sommers. *The United States Army and the Indian Wars in the Trans-Mississippi West, 1860–1898.* Carlisle Barracks, Pa.: U.S. Army Military History Institute, 1978.

Reddick, L. D. "The Negro Policy of the United States Army, 1775–1945." *Journal of Negro History* 34, no. 1 (January 1949): 9–29.

Reilly, Henry J. "The National Guard on the Mexican Border." In *Chasing Villa: The Last Campaign of the U.S. Cavalry*, by Frank Tompkins, 221–30. Silver City, N.Mex.: High-Lonesome Books, 1996.

Reilly, Hugh J. *The Frontier Newspapers and the Coverage of the Plains Indian Wars*. Santa Barbara, Calif.: Praeger, 2010.

Renda, Mary A. *Taking Haiti: Military Occupation and the Culture of U.S. Imperialism, 1915–1940*. Chapel Hill: University of North Carolina Press, 2001.

Resek, Carl. *Lewis Henry Morgan, American Scholar*. Chicago: University of Chicago Press, 1960.

Reséndez, Andrés. *Changing National Identities at the Frontier: Texas and New Mexico, 1800–1850*. Cambridge: Cambridge University Press, 2005.

———. *The Other Slavery: The Uncovered Story of Indian Enslavement in America*. Boston: Houghton Mifflin Harcourt, 2016.

Richards, Jeffrey. *Imperialism and Juvenile Literature*. Studies in Imperialism. Manchester: Manchester University Press, 1989.

Richter, Daniel K. *Facing East from Indian Country: A Native History of Early America*. Cambridge, Mass.: Harvard University Press, 2001.

Ricker, Eli Seavey, and Richard E. Jensen. *Voices of the American West: The Settler and Soldier Interviews of Eli S. Ricker, 1903–1919*. 2 vols. Lincoln: University of Nebraska Press, 2006.

Rickover, Hyman George. *How the Battleship Maine Was Destroyed*. Annapolis, Md.: Naval Institute Press, 1995.

Rippy, J. Fred. "The Indians of the Southwest in the Diplomacy of the United States and Mexico, 1848–1853." *Hispanic American Historical Review* 2, no. 3 (August 1919): 363–96.

———. "Some Precedents of the Pershing Expedition into Mexico." *Southwestern Historical Quarterly* 24, no. 4 (April 1921): 292–316

Riseman, Noah. "The Rise of Indigenous Military History." *History Compass* 12, no. 12 (2014): 901–11.

Robinson, Sherry, and Eve Ball. *Apache Voices: Their Stories of Survival as Told to Eve Ball*. Albuquerque: University of New Mexico Press, 2000.

Rodil, B. R. *The Lumad and Moro of Mindanao*. London: Minority Rights Group, 1993.

Rodriguez, Gregory. *Mongrels, Bastards, Orphans, and Vagabonds: Mexican Immigration and the Future of Race in America*. New York: Pantheon Books, 2007.

Rogers, Dorothy M. *A History of American Occupation and Administration of the Sulu Archipelago, 1899–1920*. Master's thesis. University of San Francisco, 1959.

Rogers, Robert, and William Smith. *Warfare on the Colonial American Frontier*. Bargersville, Ind.: Dresslar, 1997.

Ronda, James P. *Beyond Lewis and Clark: The Army Explores the West*. Tacoma: Washington State Historical Society, 2003.

Roosevelt, Theodore. *The Rough Riders.* New York: Modern Library, 1999.

———. *The Strenuous Life: Essays and Addresses.* New York: Century, 1902.

———. *The Winning of the West.* New York: Capricorn Books, 1962.

Root, Elihu. *Military and Colonial Policy of the United States: Addresses and Reports.* Classic Reprint. S.l.: Forgotten Books, 2015.

Root, Elihu, Robert Bacon, and James Brown Scott. *The Military and Colonial Policy of the United States: Addresses and Reports by Elihu Root.* Cambridge, Mass.: Harvard University Press, 1916.

Rooy, P. de, Ann Laura Stoler, W. F. Wertheim, and Jan Breman. *Imperial Monkey Business: Racial Supremacy in Social Darwinist Theory and Colonial Practice.* Amsterdam: VU University Press, 1990.

Rosenthal, Michael. *The Character Factory: Baden-Powell and the Origins of the Boy Scout Movement.* New York: Pantheon Books, 1986.

Roth, Dennis M. *The Friar Estates of the Philippines.* Ann Arbor, Mich.: University Microfilms International, 1984.

Roth, Russell. *Muddy Glory: America's "Indian Wars" in the Philippines, 1899–1935.* West Hanover, Mass.: Christopher Pub. House, 1981.

Rowe, L. S. *The United States and Porto Rico.* New York: Arno Press, 1975.

Rydell, Robert W. *All the World's a Fair: Visions of Empire at American International Expositions, 1876–1916.* Chicago: University of Chicago Press, 1987.

Salamanca, Bonifacio S. *The Filipino Reaction to American Rule, 1901–1913.* Hamden, Conn.: Shoe String Press, 1968.

Saleeby, Najeeb Mitry. *The History of Sulu.* Manila: Bureau of Printing, 1908.

———. *Studies in Moro History, Law, and Religion.* Manila: Bureau of Printing, 1905.

Salinas Carranza, Alberto. *La expedición punitiva.* México: Ediciones Botas, 1936.

Salman, Michael. *The Embarrassment of Slavery: Controversies over Bondage and Nationalism in the American Philippines, 1896–1916.* Berkeley: University of California Press, 2001.

Scherer, Joanna. C. "Artifact Identification Using Historical Photographs: The Case of Red Cloud's Manikin." *Visual Anthropology* 27, no. 3 (May 2014): 217–47. Accessed July 8, 2016. Available from Academic Search Premier, Ipswich, Mass. http://search.ebscohost.com.ezproxy.hamline.edu:2048/login.aspx?direct=true&db=aph&AN=95284850&site=ehost-live.

Schmidle, Nicholas. "Getting Bin Laden: What Happened That Night in Abbotabad." *New Yorker*, August 8, 2011.

Schott, Joseph L. *The Ordeal of Samar.* Indianapolis, Ind.: Bobbs-Merrill, 1964.

Schumacher, Frank. "The American Way of Empire: National Tradition and Transatlantic Adaptation in America's Search for Imperial Identity, 1898–1910. *German Historical Institute Bulletin*, no. 31 (Fall 2002): 35–50.

Schubert, Frank N. "The Black Regular Army Regiments in Wyoming, 1885–1912." Master's thesis, University of Wyoming, 1970.

———. "Black Soldiers on the White Frontier: Some Factors Influencing Race Relation." *Phylon (1960–)* 32, no. 4 (1971): 410–15.

———. *Black Valor: Buffalo Soldiers and the Medal of Honor, 1870–1898.* Lanham, Md.: Rowman & Littlefield, 2009.

———. *Buffalo Soldiers, Braves, and the Brass: The Story of Fort Robinson, Nebraska.* Shippensburg, Pa.: White Mane, 1993.

———. *Buffalo Soldiers and Officers of the Ninth Cavalry, 1867–1898: Black and White Together.* Norman: University of Oklahoma Press, 1999.

———. *On the Trail of the Buffalo Soldier: Biographies of African Americans in the U.S. Army, 1866–1917.* Wilmington, Del.: Scholarly Resources, 1995.

Schuler, Friedrich E. *Secret Wars and Secret Policies in the Americas, 1842–1929.* Albuquerque: University of New Mexico Press, 2010.

Schurman, Jacob Gould, George Dewey, Elwell Otis, Charles Denby, and Dean C. Worcester. *Report of the Philippine Commission to the President, January 31, 1900 [–December 20, 1900].* United States Philippine Commission (1899–1900). Washington, D.C.: Government Printing Office, 1900.

Scott, Hugh Lenox. "The Early History and the Names of the Arapaho." *American Anthropologist* 9 (1907): 545–60.

———. *Notes on the Sign Language of the Plains Indian.* S.l.: s.n., 1915.

———. *Some Memories of a Soldier.* New York: Century, 1928.

Scott, Rebecca J. *Degrees of Freedom: Louisiana and Cuba After Slavery.* Cambridge, Mass.: Harvard University Press, 2008.

Scott, William Berryman. *Some Memories of a Paleontologist.* Princeton, N.J., Princeton University Press, 1939.

Searles, Michael N., and Bruce A. Glasrud. *Buffalo Soldiers in the West: A Black Soldiers Anthology.* College Station: Texas A&M University Press, 2007.

Secunda, Eugene, and Terence P. Moran. *Selling War to America: From the Spanish American War to the Global War on Terror.* Westport, Conn.: Praeger Security International, 2007.

Segal, Daniel Alan, and Sylvia Junko Yanagisako. *Unwrapping the Sacred Bundle: Reflections on the Disciplining of Anthropology.* Durham, N.C.: Duke University Press, 2005.

Seton, Ernest Thompson. *The Gospel of the Redman: A Way of Life.* Santa Fe, N.Mex.: Seton Village, 1963.

———. *Two Little Savages; Being the Adventures of Two Boys Who Lived as Indians and What They Learned.* New York: Dover, 1903.

Seton, Ernest Thompson, Hugh Lenox Scott, and Lillian Delger Powers. *Sign Talk; a Universal Signal Code, without Apparatus, for Use in the Army, the Navy, Camping, Hunting, and Daily Life.* Garden City, N.Y.: Doubleday, Page, 1918.

Sexton, William Thaddeus. *Soldiers in the Philippines: A History of the Insurrection.* Freeport, N.Y.: Books for Libraries Press, 1971.

Seymour, Flora Warren. *Indian Agents of the Old Frontier.* New York: Octagon Books, 1975.

Shannon, James A. "With the Apache Scouts in Mexico." *Journal of the United States Cavalry Association* 27 (1917): 339–57.

Sheridan, Philip Henry. *Personal Memoirs of P. H. Sheridan.* New York: Charles L. Webster, 1888.

Silber, Nina. *The Romance of Reunion: Northerners and the South, 1865–1900*. Chapel Hill: University of North Carolina Press, 2002.

Silbey, David J. *A War of Frontier and Empire: The Philippine-American War, 1899–1902*. New York: Farrar, Straus and Giroux, 2007.

Silliman, Stephen W. "The 'Old West' in the Middle East: U.S. Military Metaphors in Real and Imagined Indian Country." *American Anthropologist* 110, no. 2 (2008): 237–47.

Silver, Peter Rhoads. *Our Savage Neighbors: How Indian War Transformed Early America*. New York: W. W. Norton, 2008.

Skaggs, Jimmy M. *The Great Guano Rush: Entrepreneurs and American Overseas Expansion*. New York: St. Martin's Press, 1994.

Slotkin, Richard. *Gunfighter Nation: The Myth of the Frontier in Twentieth-Century America*. Norman: University of Oklahoma Press, 1998.

Smallman-Raynor, M., and A. D. Cliff. "The Epidemiological Legacy of War: The Philippine- American War and the Diffusion of Cholera in Batangas and La Laguna, South-West Luzón, 1902–1904." *War in History* 7, no. 1 (2000): 29–64.

Smith, Clifford N. "A History of the Moros: A Study in Conquest and Colonial Government." PhD diss., University of Chicago, 1948.

Smith, Gene. *Until the Last Trumpet Sounds: The Life of General of the Armies John J. Pershing*. New York: Wiley, 1999.

Smith, Ralph A. "Indians in American-Mexican Relations Before the War of 1846." *Hispanic American Historical Review* 43, no. 1 (February 1963): 34–64.

Smith, Sherry L. *View from Officers' Row: Army Perceptions of Western Indians*. Tucson: University of Arizona Press, 1991.

Smythe, Donald. *Guerrilla Warrior: The Early Life of John J. Pershing*. New York: Scribner, 1973.

———. *Pershing, General of the Armies*. Bloomington: Indiana University Press, 1986.

———. "Pershing and the Mount Bagsak Campaign of 1913." *Philippine Studies* 12, no. 1 (1964): 3–31.

Spicer, Edward H. *The American Indians*. Cambridge, Mass.: Harvard University Press, 1982.

———. *Cycles of Conquest: The Impact of Spain, Mexico, and the United States on the Indians of the Southwest, 1533–1960*. Tucson: University of Arizona Press, 2006.

———. *Indian Wars of Mexico, Canada and the United States, 1812–1900*. London: Routledge, 2006.

———. *A Short History of the Indians of the United States*. New York: D. Van Nostrand, 1969.

———. *The Yaquis: A Cultural History*. Tucson: University of Arizona Press, 1980.

Stedman, Raymond William. *Shadows of the Indian: Stereotypes in American Culture*. Norman: University of Oklahoma Press, 1982.

Steele, Matthew F. "The 'Color Line' in the Army." *North American Review* 183, no. 605 (December 21, 1906): 1285–88.

Stevens, Phillip H. *Search Out the Land: A History of American Military Scouts*. New York: Rand McNally, 1969.

Steward, T. G. *The Colored Regulars in the United States Army.* New York: Arno Press, 1969.

Stigand, C. H. *Scouting and Reconnaissance in Savage Countries.* London: Hugh Rees, 1907.

Stout, Joseph Allen. *Border Conflict: Villistas, Carrancistas and the Punitive Expedition, 1915–1920.* Fort Worth: Texas Christian University Press, 1999.

Takaki, Ronald T. *Iron Cages: Race and Culture in Nineteenth-Century America.* New York: Oxford University Press, 2000.

Tan, Samuel K. *The Filipino Muslim Armed Struggle, 1900–1972.* Manila: Filipinas Foundation, 1977.

———. *Sulu Under American Military Rule, 1899–1913.* Quezon City: University of the Philippines, 1968.

Taylor, I. N. *History of Platte County, Nebraska.* Columbus, Neb.: Columbus Republican Print, 1876.

Taylor, Quintard. *In Search of the Racial Frontier: African Americans in the American West, 1528–1990.* New York: W. W. Norton, 1998.

Tenorio-Trillo, Mauricio. *Mexico at the World's Fairs: Crafting a Modern Nation.* Berkeley: University of California Press, 1996.

Terry, T. Philip. *Terry's Mexico: Handbook for Travellers.* Boston: Houghton Mifflin, 1911.

Thomas, Robert S., and Inez V. Allen. *The Mexican Punitive Expedition Under Brigadier General John J. Pershing, United States Army, 1916–1917.* Washington: University Microfilms, 1967.

Thompson, Wayne Wray. "Governors of the Moro Province: Wood, Bliss, and Pershing in the Southern Philippines, 1903–1913." PhD diss., University of California, San Diego, 1975.

Thompson, Winfred Lee. *The Introduction of American Law in the Philippines and Puerto Rico, 1898–1905.* Fayetteville: University of Arkansas Press, 1989.

Thrapp, Dan L. *Al Sieber: Chief of Scouts.* Norman: University of Oklahoma Press, 1995.

———. *The Conquest of Apacheria.* Norman: University of Oklahoma Press, 1988.

Thweatt, Hiram H. *What the Newspapers Say of the Negro Soldier in the Spanish-American War.* [Thomasville, Ga.?]: s.n., 1982.

Timmons, Bascom N. *Portrait of an American: Charles G. Dawes.* New York: H. Holt, 1953.

Tompkins, Frank. *Chasing Villa: The Last Campaign of the U.S. Cavalry.* Silver City, N.Mex.: High-Lonesome Books, 1996.

Trachtenberg, Alan. *Shades of Hiawatha: Staging Indians, Making Americans, 1880–1930.* New York: Hill and Wang, 2004.

Trennert, Robert A. *Alternative to Extinction: Federal Indian Policy and the Beginnings of the Reservation System, 1846–51.* Philadelphia: Temple University Press, 1975.

———. "The Indian Role in the 1876 Centennial Celebration." *American Indian Culture and Research Journal* 1, no. 4 (1976): 7–13.

Treuer, Anton. *The Assassination of Hole in the Day.* St. Paul: Minnesota Historical Society, 2011.

Tuason, Julie A. "The Ideology of Empire in *National Geographic Magazine*'s Coverage of the Philippines, 1898–1908." *Geographical Review* 89, no. 1 (1999): 34–53.

Turley, Clarence F., Anna Tenney Turley, Lawrence Benson Lee, and Marilyn Turley

Lee. *History of the Mormon Colonies in Mexico: (The Juárez Stake), 1885–1980, Consisting of Colonia Díaz, Colonia Juárez, Colonia Dublán, Colonia Pacheco, Colonies Surrounding Colonia Pacheco, Colonia Garcia, Colonia Chuichupa, Colonia Oaxaca (Sonora), Colonia Morelos (Sonora), Colonia San José (Sonora).* [Mexico?]: printed by Publishers Press for L. B. Lee and M. T. Lee, 1996.

United States Adjutant-General's Office. *Correspondence Relating to the War with Spain and Conditions Growing Out of the Same: Including the Insurrection in the Philippine Islands and the China Relief Expedition, between the Adjutant-General of the Army and Military Commanders in the United States, Cuba, Porto Rico, China, and the Philippine Islands, from April 15, 1898, to July 30, 1902.* 2 vols. Washington, D.C.: Government Printing Office, 1902.

United States Army, Department of Arizona. *Annual Report of Colonel August V. Kautz, Eighth U.S. Infantry, Brevet Major-General, (Assigned) Commanding Department of Arizona, for Year 1876–77.* Prescott, Ariz.: s.n., 1975.

United States Army, Department of California. *Report of the Part Taken by the Troops of the Department of Dakota in the Sioux Indian Campaign During the Latter Part of 1890 and the Early Part of the Present Year.* San Francisco, Calif.: s.n., 1891.

United States Army, Department of the Missouri. *Annual Report of Brigadier General W. Merritt, U.S. Army, Commanding Department of the Missouri, 1889.* Fort Leavenworth, Kans.: s.n., 1889.

United States Congress, House Committee on Insular Affairs. *Sale of Friar Lands in the Philippines Hearings Before the United States House Committee on Insular Affairs, Sixty-First Congress, Second Session, on June 7, 1910.* Washington, D.C.: Government Printing Office, 1971.

United States Department of the Interior, Census Office. "Indian Wars and their Cost, and Civil Expenditures for Indians." In *Report on Indians Taxed and Indians Not Taxed in the United States (except Alaska),* 636–44. Washington, D.C.: Government Printing Office, 1894.

United States Department of State. *Letters Concerning the Annexation of Cuba: Message from the President of the United States, Transmitting a Report from the Secretary of State, with Accompanying Papers, in Response to the Resolution of the Senate of March 2, 1901.* Washington, D.C.: Government Printing Office, 1901.

———. *Papers Relating to the Foreign Relations of the United States with the Address of the President to Congress, December 5, 1916.* Washington, D.C.: Government Printing Office, 1925.

United States Division of Insular Affairs. *Report on the Legal Status of the Territory and Inhabitants of the Islands Acquired by the United States During the War with Spain, Considered with Reference to the Territorial Boundaries, the Constitution, and Laws of the United States.* Washington, D.C.: Government Printing Office, 1900.

United States War Department. *Annual Reports of the War Department for the Fiscal Year Ended June, 30, 1901: Report of the Lieutenant-General Commanding the Army in Five Parts.* Washington, D.C.: Government Printing Office, 1901.

Unrau, William E. *The Rise and Fall of Indian Country, 1825–1855*. Lawrence: University Press of Kansas, 2007.

Urban, Andrew. "Asylum in the Midst of Chinese Exclusion: Pershing's Punitive Expedition and the Columbus Refugees from Mexico, 1916–1921." *Journal of Policy History* 23, no. 2 (2011): 204–29.

Utley, Robert M. *Custer and the Great Controversy: The Origin and Development of a Legend*. Lincoln: University of Nebraska Press, 1998.

———. *Frontier Regulars: The United States Army and the Indian, 1866–1891*. Lincoln: University of Nebraska Press, 1984.

———. *The Lance and the Shield: The Life and Times of Sitting Bull*. London: Pimlico, 1998.

———. *The Last Days of the Sioux Nation*. New Haven, Conn.: Yale University Press, 2004.

Utley, Robert M., and Wilcomb Washburn. *Indian Wars*. Boston: Houghton Mifflin, 2002.

Vandervort, Bruce. *Indian Wars of Mexico, Canada and the United States, 1812–1900*. New York: Routledge, 2006.

VanDevelder, Paul. *Savages and Scoundrels: The Untold Story of America's Road to Empire Through Indian Territory*. New Haven, Conn.: Yale University Press, 2012.

Vandiver, Frank Everson. *Black Jack: The Life and Times of John J. Pershing*. Vol. 1. College Station: Texas A&M University Press, 1977.

Waldrep, Christopher, and Michael A. Bellesiles. *Documenting American Violence: A Sourcebook*. Oxford: Oxford University Press, 2006.

Walker, Martin. *America Reborn: A Twentieth-Century Narrative in Twenty-Six Lives*. New York: Vintage, 2001.

Wall, Oscar Garrett. *Recollections of the Sioux Massacre: An Authentic History of the Yellow Medicine Incident, of the Fate of Marsh and His Men, of the Siege and Battles of Fort Ridgely, and of Other Important Battles and Experiences; Together with a Historical Sketch of the Sibley Expedition of 1863*. Lake City, Minn.: printed at "Home Printery," 1909.

Walton, Clifford Stevens. *The Civil Law in Spain and Spanish-America: Including Cuba, Puerto Rico, and Philippine Islands, and the Spanish Civil Code in Force, Annotated and with References to the Civil Codes of Mexico, Central and South America, with History of All Spanish Codes, and Summary of Canonical Laws* . . . Memphis, Tenn.: General Books LLC, 2012.

Warren, Louis S. *Buffalo Bill's America: William Cody and the Wild West Show*. New York: Alfred A. Knopf, 2005.

———. *God's Red Son: The Ghost Dance Religion and the Making of Modern America*. New York: Basic Books, 2017.

Washington, Booker T. "The Spanish-American War, Causes of It; Vivid Descriptions of Fierce Battles; Superb Heroism and Daring Deeds of the Negro Soldier." In *A New Negro for a New Century*. New York: Arno Press, 1969.

Weatherford, J. McIver. *Native Roots: How the Indians Enriched America*. New York: Fawcett Columbine, 1992.

Webb, Walter Prescott, and Lyndon B. Johnson. *The Texas Rangers: A Century of Frontier Defense*. Austin: University of Texas Press, 1989.

Weber, David J. *The Mexican Frontier, 1821–1846: The American Southwest Under Mexico.* Albuquerque: University of New Mexico Press, 1982.

Weeks, William Earl. *Building the Continental Empire: American Expansion from the Revolution to the Civil War.* Chicago: Ivan R. Dee, 1996.

Weigley, Russell Frank. *History of the United States Army.* Bloomington: Indiana University Press, 1984.

Weisenburger, Francis P. "The Middle Western Antecedents of Woodrow Wilson." *Mississippi Valley Historical Review* 23, no. 3 (1936): 375–90.

Welch, James, and Paul Jeffrey Stekler. *Killing Custer: The Battle of the Little Bighorn and the Fate of the Plains Indians.* New York: W. W. Norton, 2007.

Weldon, Florence. *History of Opelika from 1836 through 1900.* Opelika, Ala.: Opelika Daily News, 1939.

Welliver, Judson. C. *Dawes, Banker, Brigadier, Budgeteer: The Picturesque and Effective Business Man and Publicist Who Has Been Drafted to Put Business Methods into Government.* New York: Review of Reviews, 1921.

Welsome, Eileen. *The General and the Jaguar: Pershing's Hunt for Pancho Villa; A True Story of Revolution and Revenge.* Lincoln: University of Nebraska Press, 2007.

West, Elliott. *The Contested Plains: Indians, Goldseekers, and the Rush to Colorado.* Lawrence: University Press of Kansas, 1998.

Wharfield, H. B. *Alchesay: Scout with General Crook, Sierra Blanca Apache Chief, Friend of Fort Apache Whites, Counselor to Indian Agents.* El Cajon, Calif.: H. B. Wharfield, 1969.

———. *10th Cavalry and Border Fights.* El Cajon, Calif.: 1965.

———. *With Scouts and Cavalry at Fort Apache.* Tucson: Arizona Pioneers' Historical Society, 1965.

White, John Roberts. *Bullets and Bolos: Fifteen Years in the Philippine Islands.* New York: Century, 1928.

White, Richard. *"It's Your Misfortune and None of My Own": A New History of the American West.* Norman: University of Oklahoma Press, 1993.

———. *The Middle Ground: Indians, Empires, and Republics in the Great Lakes Region, 1650–1815.* Cambridge: Cambridge University Press, 1992.

Whitney, Henry H. "Miles's Campaign in Puerto Rico." In *The American-Spanish War: A History by the War Leaders, Illustrated with Numerous Original Engravings, Maps and Diagrams,* 199–218. Norwich, Conn.: Chas. C. Haskell & Son, 1899.

Whitney, William Dwight. *Language, and the Study of Language.* New York: Charles Scribner, 1867.

Whittaker, Frederick. *A Complete Life of Gen. G. A. Custer: Major-General of Volunteers, Brevet Major-General U.S. Army, and Lieutenant-Colonel Seventh U.S. Cavalry.* New York: Sheldon, 1876.

Williams, Walter L. "United States Indian Policy and the Debate over Philippine Annexation: Implications for the Origins of American Imperialism." *Journal of American History* 66, no. 4 (1980): 810–31.

Williams, William Appleman. *Empire as a Way of Life.* New York: Ig, 2007.

———. *The Tragedy of American Diplomacy.* New York: W. W. Norton, 2009.

Wingerd, Mary Lethert, and Kirsten Delegard. *North Country: The Making of Minnesota*. Minneapolis: University of Minnesota Press, 2010.

Winter, Thomas. "Strenuous Life." In *American Masculinities: An Historical Encyclopedia*, edited by Bret E. Carroll, 439–40. Thousand Oaks, Calif.: SAGE, 2004. https://doi.org/10.4135/9781412956369.n223.

Wishart, David J. *Unspeakable Sadness: The Dispossession of the Nebraska Indians*. Lincoln: University of Nebraska Press, 1994.

Wollard, James Richard. "The Philippine Scouts: The Development of America's Colonial Army." PhD diss., Ohio State University, 1975.

Wood, Leonard. "The Military Government of Cuba." *Annals of the American Academy of Political and Social Science* 21 (1903): 1–30.

———. *Report of the Military Governor of Cuba on Civil Affairs*. Washington, D.C.: Government Printing Office, 1901.

Woodward, C. Vann. *The Strange Career of Jim Crow*. Oxford: Oxford University Press, 2002.

Wooster, Robert. *The American Military Frontiers: The United States Army in the West, 1783–1900*. Albuquerque: University of New Mexico Press, 2013.

———. *Nelson A. Miles and the Twilight of the Frontier Army*. Lincoln: University of Nebraska Press, 1996.

Worcester, Donald E. "The Apaches in the History of the Southwest." *New Mexico Historical Review* 50, no. 1 (January 1975): 25–44.

Wright, Irene Aloha. *Cuba*. New York: Macmillan, 1910.

Ziff, Bruce H., and Pratima V. Rao. *Borrowed Power: Essays on Cultural Appropriation*. New Brunswick, N.J.: Rutgers University Press, 1997.

Zimmer, William Frederick, and Jerome A. Greene. *Frontier Soldier: An Enlisted Man's Journal of the Sioux and Nez Perce Campaigns, 1877*. Helena: Montana Historical Society Press, 1998.

Zion, James W., and Robert Yazzie. "Indigenous Law in North America in the Wake of Conquest." *Boston College International and Comparative Law Review* 20, no. 1 (1997): 55–84.

Zogbaum, Rufus Fairchild. *Horse, Foot, and Dragoons: Sketches of Army Life at Home and Abroad*. New York: Harper & Brothers, 1888.

Index

Acknowledgments

Drafting these words of acknowledgment has been a humbling experience, as it has reminded me how many people have helped and supported me in the long process of bringing this book into being. First among those I wish to thank is my editor Peter Agree. From the very inception of the project, Peter has provided effective advice and unstinting encouragement. His engagement has made this a better book; it certainly made the process of writing it more rewarding. I also acknowledge with gratitude the valuable comments of Brian DeLay as well as those of an anonymous reader who reviewed the manuscript for the University of Pennsylvania Press.

Among the many friends and family members who have served as patient sounding boards for the ideas explored here, I am particularly grateful to Peter Guardino for the many conversations we have had about U.S. and Mexican historiography, about doing transnational history, and about how two self-respecting social historians like us could have found ourselves so taken up with military history. I am also grateful to Peter for the excellent comments he provided me on the multiple drafts I was shameless in sending him to read.

Closer to home, two other friends—both talented writers and historians—helped nurture this book when it was only a jumble of promising observations. During many walks along some of Minnesota's beautiful waterways, Nora Murphy, Kirsten Delegard, and I have exchanged ideas and updates on our respective projects. Besides getting blood flowing to brains and limbs, these walking conversations helped sustain wonderful friendships that have greatly enriched my life. Nora also came to the rescue with a dry and quiet place for me to write when the roof over my study started to leak and was being repaired (which took a lot longer than this sentence suggests. Thanks, Nora!) Another dear friend who provided generous comments on an early draft is Rosalind

James. Katherine Bowie has been an active interlocutor in this as well as so many other undertakings. This book owes much to the late Friedrich Katz, generous teacher and humane scholar. In addition to these significant influences on the book, a number of other friends and colleagues read drafts related to the project at various points in its long gestation or engaged with me on it in other substantive (or just supportive) ways: Stephen Dow Beckham, Andrea Bell, Colleen Bell, Dain Borges, Julie Bunn, Christopher Capozzola, Sarah Chambers, John Coatsworth, Liz Coville, Veena Deo, Robin Derby, Cheryl Duncan, Van Dusenbery, George Frakes, Juan Giusti-Cordero, Michel Gobat, Olga González, Laura Gotkowitz, Kathryn Guerts, Marlon and Lauren Gunderson, Maya Hanna, Brian Horrigan, Danny Kaplan, Adeeb Khalid, Aldo Lauria-Santiago, Kristin Mapel-Bloomberg, Al McCoy, Andrea Moerer, Mark Olson, Gaines Post, Tamara Root, Peter Rosen, Susie Steinbach, Alex Stern, Jane Walter, and Jack Weatherford. Although I have not always heeded the good advice some have tried to give me, I am deeply grateful for their efforts. The resulting book, of course, is my responsibility alone.

William Meadows assisted me in deciphering a puzzling piece of Hugh Lenox Scott's handwriting. He also lent his expertise in identifying subjects in the photo of the hunting party that appears in Chapter 2. Most important, I appreciate Bill's reading of an early draft of the manuscript and his work on Scott's use of sign language in ethnography. James Newland generously shared his knowledge of the history and geography of San Diego County in response to a query I sent to him about the army camps established in the area to enforce neutrality at the start of the Mexican Revolution.

Robert A. Fulton, who has written several well-researched and highly readable books on the history of the U.S. military occupation of the southern Philippines from 1899 to 1913, has also made available on the web a number of valuable historical photographs that he found in the course of his research. ("Moroland History," http://www.morolandhistory.com/.) He has been generous in sharing a digital copy of one of the photos he scanned in the National Archives with me for this book. It appears on the cover.

My parents, Gordon and Susan Bjork, supported this undertaking of mine as they have all the others: with love and just the right degree of constructive involvement. Both read the manuscript in its entirety, more than once, and my mother improved the book's readability through skillful and much-appreciated editing. My husband, Arjun Guneratne, has read and helped me think about this project from the beginning. He has been constant in his love and care for me. More than anyone, he has provided the encouragement, in all the possible ways, which has enabled me to finish it. Our children, Sara and Ananda, have been an abiding source of joy and, in contrast to all the other people I have acknowledged here, they have provided a salutary dose of disinterest in my work. When I exulted to Sara recently that I was "almost done" with the book, she reminded me just how much of a constant my never-ending preoccupation with writing it has been in their growing up. "Are you sure?" she asked with warranted skepticism. Yes, I'm sure, Sara, and I hope it will mean more time for us all to spend together. Also in the category of people to whom I am grateful for getting me *away* from the book is my friend and tennis partner, Susan Bernstein.

Like most historians, I owe much to the knowledge and good will of archivists. I appreciate the work of all those who made my research possible in the various archives and libraries I visited in the course of my research. In particular, I want to thank Patrick Kerwin in the Manuscript Division of the Library of Congress for his assistance and the interest he expressed in my research at an early stage, which meant a lot to me. At the Nebraska State Historical Society, both James Potter and David Bristow were generous with their time and knowledge of the society's collections. The entire reading room staff of the U.S. Army Military History Institute in Carlisle, Pennsylvania, were extremely helpful and gracious. In particular, I would like to thank MHI's senior historian Richard Sommers, and also archivists Richard Baker and Jessica Sheets for their help and solicitude during my research there. Dwayne Cox and Joyce Hicks at the Special Collections and Archives department of the Auburn University Library were very helpful; my research in Auburn was also enriched by the welcome provided by David Carter. Local historian J. Newell Floyd was also generous in sharing his knowledge about Opelika and the surrounding county where Robert Lee Bullard spent his early years. Jim Spangelo, curator of the Clack Museum in Havre, Montana, took time on a cold Veterans' Day to show Nora and me around Fort Assinniboine and share his knowledge of the fort and the surrounding area. In the rare books collection of the University of Havana, I appreciated the assistance of archivists Indiana Rosa Leyva Fernández and Abel Tioche Méndez.

During several of my research trips, I enjoyed the hospitality of friends who put me up, fed me, and drove me around. I especially want to thank Chris Rodrigo and Milan Lin Rodrigo for taking such good care of me on several such visits to the Washington, D.C. area. Dwight and Rosalind James also hosted me during a week of work in the Library of Congress. Soraya Castro Mariño and her wonderful family made me feel completely at home in Havana. Soraya also offered me valuable research advice, which, alas, I have not yet been able to take up. At the Universidad de Cienfuegos, Haens Beltrán Alonso and Vero Edilio Rodríguez Orrego gave my work the benefit of their deep knowledge of Cuban history; I am also grateful to them both for their technical support during the presentation of my research in the workshop on sociocultural studies that they both encouraged me to attend. Rebecca Scott was generous, as always, in responding to requests for help.

My research (as well as my teaching) has always been ably supported by an outstanding library staff at Hamline University. In particular, I want to thank Kimberly Feilmeyer, not just for the research and bibliographic assistance she provided on this project but for all she does to support history at Hamline. Gail Peloquin, now retired, filled literally hundreds of interlibrary loan requests over the years I have worked on this project, always promptly and cheerfully. Other members of the library staff whose help facilitated the completion of this book are Siobhan DiZio, Kristopher Scheid, Amy Sheehan, Luanne Terveer, Kate Borowske, and former director of the library (now retired) Diane Clayton. Beyond the library, I have been blessed by wonderful colleagues at Hamline too numerous to mention. Besides the intellectual community they provide, I am grateful for the support my colleagues and the college have shown for my research in the form of several faculty development research grants. Allocation of Hanna Grant funds also helped underwrite the indexing of the book. In the context of scarce resources that is our professional reality, this demonstration of support for my work has meant a lot to me. Wendy Werdin, the talented faculty assistant in the Division of Social Sciences has devoted more hours to this project than anyone else on campus. Her help in compiling the bibliography has been invaluable. I also appreciate all the transcriptions she has performed over the years on the often less-than-legible handwriting of Hugh Lenox Scott as well as the slightly more decipherable fist of Robert Lee Bullard. I had able research assistance from Nathan Walker during the time he was a student at Hamline. Nathan helped transcribe a number of original documents and also carried out bibliographic research that contributed to the book.

I gratefully acknowledge the National Endowment for the Humanities fellowship that supported a sabbatical-year leave from teaching during which I was able to move the book toward completion.